AF570702

GEORGE A. KENDALL

WITNESS FOR THE TRUTH

THE WANDERER'S 130 YEAR ADVENTURE IN CATHOLIC JOURNALISM

Published jointly by

THE WANDERER PRESS

THE ST. GEORGE PRESS

Dust jacket designed by Anna Mycek-Wodecki

St. George Press logo designed by Jeanne M. Schrauben

Published jointly by

The Wanderer Press
201 Ohio St.
St. Paul, Minnesota 55107

The St. George Press
P.O. Box 460
Grand Marais, MI 49839

ISBN 0-915245-03-5

TABLE OF CONTENTS

FOREWORD 5
A NOTE FROM THE PUBLISHER 7
INTRODUCTION 13

PART ONE: DISASTER IN DETROIT 23

1. THE DARK FOREST 25
2. THE NPC DEBATE — THE FIRST COUP ATTEMPT 33
3. MANIPULATION —THE NAME OF THE GAME 44
4. A TRIUMPH OF LIBERAL AUTHORITARIANISM 50

PART TWO: *HUMANAE VITAE* — THE CHURCH STANDS FIRM 61

1. A DECISIVE BATTLE BEGINS 63
2. *HUMANAE VITAE*'S HUMANISM 78
3. *HUMANAE VITAE*'S DEFENSE OF THE SOCIAL ORDER 88
4. THE MAGISTERIUM UNDER ATTACK 98

PART THREE: ABORTION — THE GODLESS STATE AND THE GUTLESS CHRISTIANS 107

1. THE OPENING SKIRMISHES 109
2. A DAY THAT WILL LIVE IN INFAMY 121
3. THE GREAT WIMPOUT 131
4. THE ANTI-LIFE STATE AND THE CIVIL DISOBEDIENCE QUESTION 152
5. ABORTION AND SPIRITUAL WARFARE 168

PART FOUR: THE MASS — A GIFT REJECTED 189

1. WHERE GOD AND MAN MEET 191
2.LITURGICAL REFORM OR LITURGICAL REVOLUTION? 195
3. TRANSUBSTANTIATION OR TRANSIGNIFICATION? 216
4. SACRIFICE OR COMMUNAL MEAL? 221
5. COUNTERREVOLUTION IN THE CHURCH: ORTHODOXY VS. RIGHT-WING SECTARIANISM 229

PART FIVE: SPIRITUAL DISEASE, SECTION I — THE CORRUPTION OF THE INTELLECT 267

1. THE ATTACK ON CHRISTIAN WHOLENESS 269

2. THE DISEASE — ORIGINS IN THE INTELLECT 272
3. FATHER BROWN'S ASSAULT ON THE BIBLE AND THE INCARNATION 280
4. THE TRIUMPH OF SUBJECTIVISM 294
5. THE NEW CATECHETICS — THE CANCER METASTASIZES 299
6. THE EVALUATION INSTRUMENT 307
7. THE NATIONAL CATECHETICAL DIRECTORY 316
8. METHODOLOGY AND FAITH 322
9. A LIGHT IN THE DARKNESS 325

PART FIVE: SPIRITUAL DISEASE, SECTION II — THE CORRUPTION OF THE WILL 335

1. LOSS OF THE GOOD 337
2. THE POPE SAYS NO TO SEXUAL CHAOS 339
3. THE *HUMAN SEXUALITY* DISASTER 342
4. THE HOMOSEXUAL MOVEMENT 350
5. THE CHURCH'S RESPONSE TO MILITANT SODOMY 357
6. FATHER CURRAN — THE LITTLE POPE 362
7. *VERITATIS SPLENDOR*: THE POPE STRIKES BACK 369
8. ANOTHER METASTASIS — THE SEX EDUCATION DISASTER 380

EPILOGUE 409

EXTREMISM OR PROPHETIC WITNESS? A FINAL REFLECTION 411

INDEX 417

FOREWORD

In the second half of this century a virulent effort was mounted to modernize and Americanize the Catholic Church in the United States, similar to the Anglicanizing and Protestantizing of that Church in England, Scotland, and Wales in the 16th and 17th centuries. The details of the present struggle have been entered into history's record in this book by George Kendall.

The only national weekly publication to enter the lists on the side of tradition and Rome is *The Wanderer*, published out of St. Paul, Minnesota. That journal offers the fullest and most indispensable source for finding the major issues, the clashes of opposite analyses, the contending concepts and positions that make up this conflict between faith, loyalty, and religious submission of will to Catholic doctrine on the one hand, versus novelty, desertions, and rebellion on the other. Mr. Kendall, eye witness and participant, here becomes recorder and takes full advantage of his source.

Thus his book is exciting reading for all who recognize and care for what is at stake, namely, the genuine Catholic heritage, and at the same time is a case history of apologetics that could be used to train a growing cadre able and willing to defend the faith. Week to week for now more than a generation, *The Wanderer* has flung into the fray the thoughts and words of a corps of strongly competent and knowledgeable commentators, drafted by grace, aroused by determined fidelity, and eager to bring their talents to serve that journal's generous availability. As this book shows, those contributions were significant, effective, and often brilliant. As readers of *The Wanderer* often testify, that newspaper is a solitary light in a dark night that has often been their only solace.

As we near the third millennium of the era of our Lord, at a time nearly four decades since the Second Vatican Council provided a catalyst for movements both Catholic and counter-Catholic, it is none too soon to chronicle this still ongoing struggle between what Catholics are called to believe and what they may not believe. The anticipations on both sides for a quick and complete resolution have been disappointed. But I believe we can find here, by comparing details of the adventures in prophetic witness which Kendall chronicles here with what is already evident of that adventure's outcome, that the battle has turned in favor of the knights and ladies of the Pope.

It would be a joyless and disappointing witness were that not so. Every similar struggle in history has shown that the only Catholic position was with the Pope. Mr. Kendall's chronicle shows the same thing is happening in the Church now. Defenders of Rome have never been put to shame.

Of all the many books published about this, it can be truly said that this one had to be done. If it is not Scripture, nevertheless there is certainly considerable inspiration to it. Where this number of talented intellectual and devotedly loyal Catholics write, surely the Lord they serve is present. That gives assurance of the outcome.

Frank Morriss
Wheat Ridge, Colorado
Solemnity of Christ's Resurrection, 1997

A NOTE FROM THE PUBLISHER

Over five years ago, George Kendall and I outlined a plan to publish a book about *The Wanderer* which has come to fruition with the publication of *Witness for the Truth.* With 130 years of this journal's history to consider, a major challenge was whether or not to present a general overview of *The Wanderer*'s entire work or to focus in some detail on a particularly crucial period that might typify its character and purpose. We chose the latter course, and thus the last 35 years or so — the most critical years in the life of the Church in the United States — are those that Mr. Kendall researched and now chronicles in these pages.

As Kendall suggests in his introduction, the first hundred years in *The Wanderer's* journalistic participation in the life of the Catholic Church in America and its unwavering loyalty to the Papacy and its teaching, "vaccinated" this journal from the virus of dissent, disloyalty, and revolution which has so infected millions of Catholics in the post-Vatican II era.

Witness for the Truth will provide its readers with unique insights and understandings of the key contested issues and events which have divided and confused Catholics for more than a generation. Historians will find this volume invaluable in assessing how loyalist Catholics responded to, and coped with, the challenges to their faith, to their Church, and to her authority during a period of great turmoil and rebellion.

On a personal note, I would like publicly to thank and to express my profound gratitude to those hundreds of Catholic laymen and women, scores of nuns, priests, bishops, and even a few Cardinals whose essays, commentaries, reports, and observations filled the pages of *The Wanderer* and made it what it has been during my tenure as editor. When you read *Witness for the Truth* you will find quoted the words of many among this distinguished company of loyal and courageous Catholics.

Alphonse J. Matt, Jr.
Editor-Publisher
The Wanderer

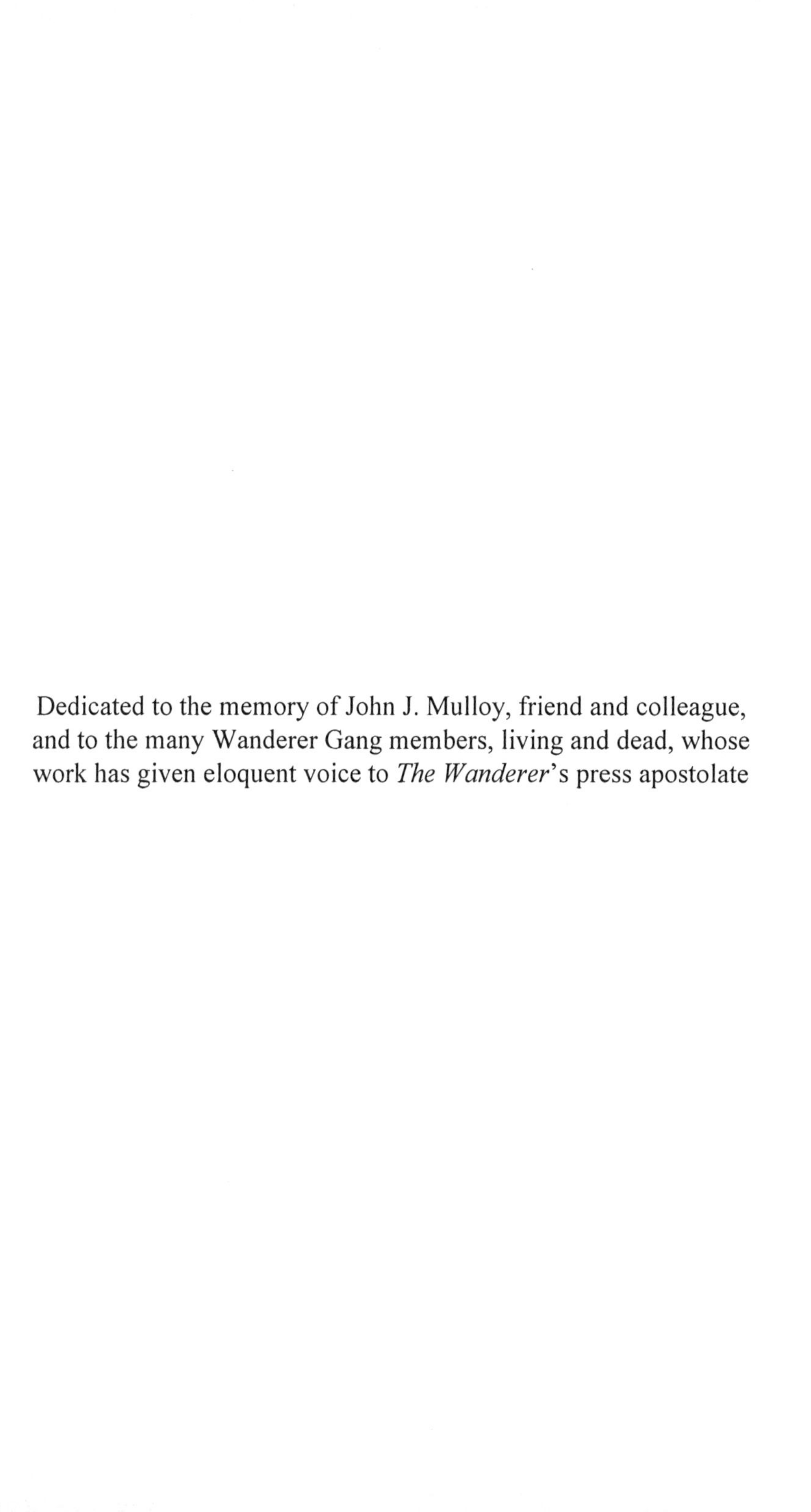

Dedicated to the memory of John J. Mulloy, friend and colleague, and to the many Wanderer Gang members, living and dead, whose work has given eloquent voice to *The Wanderer*'s press apostolate

WITNESS FOR THE TRUTH

INTRODUCTION

By the rivers of Babylon, there we sat down, yea, we wept, when we remembered Zion. We hanged our harps upon the willows in the midst thereof. For there they that carried us away captive required of us a song; and they that wasted us required of us mirth, saying, Sing us one of the songs of Zion. How shall we sing the LORD'S *song in a strange land? If I forget thee, O Jerusalem, let my right hand forget her cunning. If I do not remember thee, let my tongue cleave to the roof of my mouth; if I prefer not Jerusalem above my chief joy.*

— Psalm 137

The (in some opinions) eccentric Catholic weekly newspaper that we today know as *The Wanderer* began its earthly existence in 1867 as *Der Wanderer*, a German-language paper printed in St. Paul, Minnesota for the benefit of German Catholics living in the Midwest. The German word *wanderer* had a slightly different range of meanings than the cognate English word, the closest English translation being "emigrant," a word conveying the idea of someone who goes from one place to another and then stays there, either permanently or at least for a long time. In contrast, the English *wanderer* carries with it the connotation of someone who continually travels from one place to another but never really settles down. Yet this divergence of meaning contributes something of value to our reflections, when we consider that the Christian living in time and history is really and truly homeless throughout this earthly existence — his home, his true Fatherland, is always in heaven. Liberal Catholics today love to talk about the "pilgrim Church," but they hardly have a monopoly on the idea. Christians throughout the ages have been wanderers and strangers in a strange land, an experience conveyed with powerful poetic feeling by Psalm 137, quoted above.

German Catholic immigrants of the late nineteenth century, settled (more or less) in places like St. Paul, Milwaukee, Chicago, Detroit, Saginaw, Michigan (in my own ancestors' case), found themselves homeless in a double sense. They were foreigners, speaking a foreign language, in American society, and they were Catholics in a predominantly Protestant society which, even then, was beginning to be a secularized society. Most of us, whatever nationality our ancestors, can relate to this situation of being somehow members of two different and conflicting cultural and spiritual worlds. Where the two worlds have come into close contact, as in marriages crossing the lines between those worlds, the sense of conflict has been more acute. In my own family, I have Anglo-Saxon Protestant relatives on my father's side, and devout German Catholics on my mother's. As far back as I can remember, I recall having at least an obscure sense that these were not just different people but different worlds. The Kendalls (the Protestants) were always the more secularized, the more "modern," the more "sophisticated." They were the first ones to drive cars. They were the first ones to go to college. They were the ones who were likely to call their parents and grandparents by their first names. They were the first to get around to deciding that practices like divorce and contraception and abortion were all right (alas, most of their Catholic relatives have now "caught up"). Because of their advanced views on such things, they were always the less numerous side of the family. I have quite literally hundreds of cousins now among the Hammises (my mother's family), and maybe a dozen or so among the Kendalls. That is what "reproductive freedom" does for you. When you grow up with such a background, you have to work your way through a lot of moral and spiritual confusion, as you find yourself drawn alternately toward one group or the other. You find yourself straddling two cultures, and I think this was very much the story of the German Catholic's life in the nineteenth century.

Today, of course, the Catholic of German descent has been assimilated to the point where he no longer has the acute sense of his Germanness that his ancestors two or three generations back had. Generally, he does not speak German unless he studied it as an adult.

So he no longer has the sense of tension between his native German culture and his adopted Anglo-Saxon American culture. But if he is not just a Catholic, but a *traditional*, an *orthodox* Catholic, then, in escaping from one form of homelessness, he has fallen into another, because he now finds himself trying to live out his Catholicism in the midst of a modernist Catholic culture which has largely assimilated itself to an American culture which is now no longer even Protestant, but radically secularist. So homelessness is still the story of his life, as it is for all orthodox Catholics in America today, whether their ancestors were Irish, Polish, Italian, or anything else.

The Wanderer started out in the first place as a way to deal with the Catholic emigrant's homelessness, and today has expanded into a project to deal with the orthodox Catholic's spiritual homelessness. In doing so, it has expanded from a focus primarily on German Catholics to one on all Catholics of the true faith, German and otherwise. There were good reasons in the beginning for calling it *The Wanderer*, and there still are.

Its beginnings, like the beginnings of most great undertakings, were obscure. According to an account by Alphonse J. Matt, Sr.,[1] father of the current *Wanderer* editor, it began in October, 1867, with a small meeting in the back room (that almost sounds a little conspiratorial) of Nick Bures' book and stationery store in St. Paul, Minnesota. The people there included Father Clemens Staub, O.S.B., the Benedictine Pastor of the Church of the Assumption in St. Paul; Nick Bures; Eugene Eckhardt, a native of the Rhineland and first editor of *The Wanderer*; Franz Schlick, Sr.; and Adam Willerscheid. The immediate problem this group was trying to grapple with was that the

---

[1] Alphonse J. Matt, Sr., "'All His People Are Wanderers,'" *The Wanderer*, 10-6-77. *The Wanderer* will hereafter be cited simply as "W." In direct quotes from *The Wanderer*, I have taken the liberty of correcting obvious printing errors, misspellings, etc., as well as bringing such things as punctuation, use of quotes and italics, and capitalization into accord with current *Wanderer* editorial practice.

faith of German Catholic immigrants was beginning to be shaken by the ideas of the new German "enlightenment," ideas which had burst onto the political scene with the various revolutions and attempted revolutions in Germany in 1848. In addition to this, the Masons were beginning to be influential among German immigrants, many of whom were joining to buy insurance, and, one suspects, simply to feel more at home in their adopted land. The paper was started, then, in the effort to do something to keep German immigrants in touch with their Catholic faith and thus to head off some of these anti-Catholic influences. The first issue came out November 14, 1867.

In 1878, the paper went under the editorship of Hugo Klaproth, a German Lutheran who had converted to Catholicism. According to Farley Clinton,[2] Klaproth, while still a Lutheran studying Church history, had made the error of trying to refute the Catholic version of the Reformation, and had instead refuted himself. Klaproth died in 1897, and his son-in-law, Joseph Matt, took over as editor, thus beginning the long association of the Matt family with *The Wanderer*. Joseph Matt was 18 at the time, and continued editing *The Wanderer* until 1966, when he died at the age of 87. This has to be one of the longest journalistic careers ever. Following his death in 1966, his son, Alphonse, Sr., took over as business manager, and his younger son, Walter, as editor. Walter stepped down as Editor in 1967, leaving Alphonse, Sr., as executive editor until his death in 1973, and his son, Alphonse, Jr., as Associate Editor. Alphonse, Jr., took over as Editor in 1973, and remains in that position today.

From the very beginning, the atmosphere which characterized *The Wanderer* was one of uncompromising witness to that which its editors and contributors saw as the permanent truth in a world where error was becoming more and more rampant (that is something both its friends and enemies would agree to be true, though they would certainly differ in the "spin" they would put on it — as always, *my* prophetic witness is likely to be *your* obstinacy, and vice versa). This is the way Farley Clinton, in a 1967 article, summed it up:

---

[2] Farley Clinton, "The Happy 'Wanderer'", *Triumph*, June, 1967.

> A certain grimness does pervade *The Wanderer*, but it seems to be the grimness of prophecy. A resolute devotion to the Catholic faith has inspired it from its earliest days, and it has set itself the goal of identifying, and fighting, the enemies of God. Religion pure and undefiled is the supreme value; but in *The Wanderer* religion is fortified, as it must be, by the most uncompromising morality, and by an almost violent combative spirit that inspires a dissatisfaction with nearly every aspect of public life. Leading parts of the world, and even in the Church, have fallen to men of whom *The Wanderer* does not approve — and with no fear of persons, it says so, loudly and repeatedly. All this seems to catch the remembered spirit of Jeremiah more than other modern "prophets" do; and besides, *The Wanderer* has been far more accurate than almost anybody else in predicting the real character of public men and popular movements.[3]

The Wanderer, for instance, spoke out against Hitler before he came to power, and at a time when many western intellectuals, to their lasting shame, seemed drawn to him and his ideas (a fact which it is now considered taboo to mention). That criticism continued after Der Fuehrer's rise to dictatorial power, and led him to prohibit distribution of *The Wanderer* in Germany, where many Germans with connections in America read it. That is an important fact in light of the recurrent accusation made by liberals over the years that *The Wanderer* is some kind of neo-Nazi or neo-Fascist rag. The real Nazis didn't agree, obviously.

Quite consistently with the above, *The Wanderer*, throughout its history, has condemned all totalitarian movements, including socialism, whether of the Bolshevik or Menshevik variety. It bore a powerful witness throughout the Cold War era against Soviet imperialism and the threat of world Communism to all human freedom. Yet it did so without committing itself to classical economic liberalism or laissez-faire capitalism, an ideology which, in its own way, is equally

[3] Ibid., p. 12.

destructive of human dignity. Instead, *The Wanderer* took its stand by the social teachings of the Church, found in especially clear form in the social encyclicals of Leo XIII and Pius XI. These teachings condemned both the radical individualism of modern capitalism and the totalitarian collectivism of socialism, while affirming property rights and the principle of subsidiarity, with its effort to protect the community from the excesses of statism. That is a balancing act that only those solidly grounded in the Church's social teaching could possibly get away with — many "conservative" publications have not been so successful.

By 1931, the German-speaking population of *Wanderer* readers had decreased considerably, and the numbers of their English-speaking children and grandchildren had grown correspondingly. To meet this challenge, an English-language edition was added. By the 1950s, the German speakers had grown so few and far between that *The Wanderer* became an exclusively English publication, as it is today.[4]

There was a long period, from the end of World War II to the early 1960s, when *The Wanderer* appeared destined to go under at almost any time, as its readership continually decreased. Then suddenly it experienced an unlooked-for rejuvenation when the Catholic Church in America entered into a state which can only be accurately described as chaos. The revolution in the Church during and following the Council, bad as it was for the Catholic people, was good for *The Wanderer*, because it called into being a counterrevolutionary movement, a movement for which *The Wanderer* became a principal spokesman. Suddenly, subscriptions reached all-time highs. This is the role *The Wanderer* continues to play to this day.

---

[4] The complete German edition from 1867 on is available on microfiche at the Minnesota Historical Society, 345 W. Kellogg Blvd., St. Paul, Minnesota 55102-1906. The English language edition from its beginning in 1931 to the present is also available from this source. The English edition from 1981 on is available on 35 mm. microfilm (each year on one spool) at University Microfilms, Inc., 300 N. Zeeb Rd., P.O. Box 1346, Ann Arbor, MI 48106-1346.

The Wanderer had trained for this role for many years by playing the role of spokesman against the heresy known as "Americanism." The "Americanist" controversy seemed to peak during the 1890s, but continued to be a source of conflict for years afterward. Basically, the "Americanists" were Catholics who saw no real conflict between Catholic teaching and culture, on the one hand, and American Protestant-secularist culture on the other. Thus they sought assimilation of Catholic immigrants to American values which were in many ways anti-Christian. According to Farley Clinton,

> The essential points at issue in the controversy were whether, in the American Church, there was not a tendency to narrow and warp the Catholic faith to conform with the national prejudices; to exalt the active life over the contemplative — Martha rather than Mary — in direct contradiction of Christ's words; to prefer natural virtues to supernatural ones; to dislike and disapprove of religious orders and the religious life; to rely far too much on individual inspirations from the Holy Ghost; and to use questionable new methods in making converts. In a word, was not the faith of Jesus Christ being Protestantized, betrayed, denied? It was difficult to speak of heresy in dealing with a group of persons whose outstanding quality was a busy contempt for anything so impractical as theology.[5]

Of course, the issue here was not, for the most part, one of out-and-out, formal heresy, but rather of a mood, a practical outlook on life, which was not truly Catholic but largely Protestant and even secularist in its spirit.

St. Paul, Minnesota was a major center for this conflict. German immigrants tended to take the radically anti-Americanist position, holding out for such things as German ethnic neighborhoods and exclusively German parishes where German Catholic culture could be

---

[5] Ibid., p. 13.

preserved and assimilation avoided. Americanists, in contrast, tended to think in terms of assimilation and were greatly concerned that Catholics would be thought "un-American." Ultimately, neither side got all it wanted when Rome decided the issue. The demands of anti-assimilationists for ethnic churches and dioceses were not granted, but at the same time, the extreme assimilationists, of whom James Cardinal Gibbons was typical, were soundly, but gently, rebuked. *The Wanderer*, needless to say, was in the forefront of the anti-Americanist position.

By the turn of the century, the matter seemed more or less resolved, but events since then certainly have shown that Americanism, as a general mood tending to accommodate Catholicism, with its insistence on embodying absolute and permanent truths, with American pragmatism and secularism, did not so much disappear as become an undercurrent, as did modernism in general. When the revolution in the Church broke out in the 1960s, it returned with a vengeance in the form of the liberal Catholic's determination to bring his Catholicism into full conformity with American secularist views on such things as abortion, divorce, and contraception, not to mention his desire to remove from the religious sphere itself anything hinting at a realm of the sacred or belief in the supernatural. *The Wanderer*'s brush with Americanism in its earlier, less virulent, incarnation, left it well prepared to do battle with the new Americanists. It had been vaccinated.

One of Church history's great ironies is that *The Wanderer*, now regarded by almost everyone as hopelessly reactionary, was one of the earliest Catholic periodicals to support the movement for liturgical reform. Farley Clinton notes that

> The Matts were inclined to be grateful to Pius XII because of his strong support for the liturgical movement, a pet project of theirs for many years. The Matts and their newspaper were among those who first introduced the liturgical movement to the United States. For a long time they had very close and warm relations with St. John's Abbey in Collegeville, Minnesota, and especially with the brilliant Dom Vergil Michel

> (1890-1938) who was, more than anyone else, the inspiration of liturgical enthusiasm.[6]

Clinton goes on to quote Alphonse J. Matt, Sr., to the effect that

> Nothing is more ironic in our position than that we were sponsors of the liturgical movement from the first....But we were very attached to the Holy See, and we loved the liturgy for expressing the Catholic faith. Nobody thought then that the liturgical movement would become the haven for all those who hated Rome and were cold or lukewarm in their faith, as is the case today.[7]

Here, again, we see *The Wanderer*'s rejection of the anti-contemplative, anti-supernatural, outlook of the American secularist and his liberal Catholic groupies. The chapters which follow will try to trace *The Wanderer*'s history of prophetic witness on those issues where the battle between orthodox Catholicism and Americanist modernism came to a head in the revolutionary era that began in the 1960s. Catholic teaching on social justice and the sanctity of human life (reflected in the controversies over birth control and abortion) played a central role here, as did the widespread rejection, by modernists, of central doctrines of the faith such as the Incarnation, as well as almost the whole of Catholic moral teaching. The prophetic role of *The Wanderer* in contemporary America has come to mean a standing out against everything that is worst in America, things like secularism, materialism, and a pragmatic utilitarianism which seeks to reform the social order by denying the dignity and sanctity of the human person as a child of God. At the same time, its witness has been a resounding affirmation of America's true integrities — her Christian origins, and her respect for the rights and dignity of the person, a respect still enshrined in her constitution even if frequently violated. Above all, we have tried to bear witness against the American Church's capitulation to the worst in America while it neglects

[6] Ibid., p. 15.
[7] Ibid., p. 15.

the best. As Alphonse J. Matt, Sr., put it in his account of *The Wanderer*'s origins,

> The very name of *The Wanderer* — no less than its career — has become a symbol in these 100 years. If, as the Second Vatican Council points out, in God's Design, all His people are wanderers until the end of time, then *The Wanderer*, taken from the midst of the people to help guide a segment of God's people in their wanderings through the world of their time, may well have been an instrument of Providence, even if the little group of founders in Nick Bures' back room had not the slightest awareness of the role designed for them.[8]

Like those devout German Catholics who have now long since passed from the scene, we too continue to be wanderers and strangers in a strange land. Let us try to accept that role with joy, along with the witness to which it calls us, and, who knows, perhaps we may occasionally sing a few of the songs of Zion to cheer us on our way.

[8] Matt, op. cit., W, 10-6-77.

PART ONE: DISASTER IN DETROIT

1. THE DARK FOREST

Midway this way of life we're bound upon,
I woke to find myself in a dark wood,
Where the right road was wholly lost and gone.

Ay me! how hard to speak of it — that rude
And rough and stubborn forest! the mere breath
Of memory stirs the old fear in the blood;

It is so bitter, it goes nigh to death;
Yet there I gained such good, that, to convey
The tale, I'll write what else I found therewith.

How I got into it, I cannot say,
Because I was so heavy and full of sleep
When first I stumbled from the narrow way.

— Dante, *Inferno, Canto I, verses 10-12*

Some stories need to be told from the inside out, starting, not at the beginning, but in the middle, as Dante well knew when he sought to tell the story of the soul's descent into hell. The story of the collapse of the Catholic Church in the United States during the second half of the twentieth century is that kind of story. In the strictly chronological order, it can be said to start approximately in the early 1960s. But in the order of the meaningful interrelation of events, the order in which we think, not so much in terms of beginning, middle, and end, but in terms of centers and peripheries, the story can be considered to begin in 1976, the year of the infamous Detroit convocation known as the Call to Action. At that incongruous congress, held at Detroit's Cobo Hall October 21 to October 23, 1976, people able to get themselves recognized as spokesmen for the Catholic Church in America managed, in the course of three days, to issue a series of proclamations which denied virtually every Catholic teaching on matters of right order in the Church, in society, and in the soul, replacing historical Catholicism, at least in the vision of the participants, with a totalitarian religion which sought, by revolutionary methods and by social engineering, to force a distorted and bizarre Utopia on both Church and civil society. The evils did not, of course, begin with that unspeakable convocation, but it was only with its occurrence that they became part of the institutional structure of the American Church. The analogy with the French Revolution is irresistible, as so many of *The Wanderer*'s commentators noted at the time. The convoking of the Call to Action by the Bishops' Bicentennial Committee on Liberty and Justice for All bears an all too obvious resemblance to Louis XVI's convoking of the Estates General. Certainly, the breakdown of French political institutions and the proliferation of the deeply anti-Christian and anti-Western ideas of the so-called Enlightenment preceded by many years the explosion of disorder that began in 1789 — nevertheless, it is only in the light of that culminating event that we can really understand the meaning of the events that led up to it. And for those of us who have suffered through the revolution in the late twentieth- century Church, it is only in the light of a watershed event like the Call to Action that we can really begin to comprehend the meaning of the things we have done and suffered during these years of shaken faith and, for many, spiritual homelessness. For so many of us, the experience of those years has been one of waking to find ourselves lost in a dark and tangled forest, with a confused memory of seemingly endless and pointless wandering in the desert, a confused recollection and feeling that somehow or other we had wandered away from the right path, but with little or no understanding of how it happened. Only an analysis of that middle time of our lives in which we then woke to find ourselves will help us to reconstruct and understand what happened earlier, as well as the later events which flowed from that middle time. The reader had better beware. What follows will be in many ways a journey through Hell, yet it will be, I think, also a journey into hope, a journey of purgation which may lead us to a partial glimpse at least of the light at the top of Mount Purgatory and beyond. Getting back to Dante, we tell our story, not to frighten people or lead them to despair, but to tell of the good which we found on the journey. The Call to Action is the beginning of the story, but hardly the end.

In February, 1975, the consultation process for the national Call to Action was begun under the auspices of the United States Catholic Conference (USCC) then chaired by John Cardinal Dearden. From the very beginning of this process, involving parish and diocesan meetings where current issues were debated, people complained about the heavy bias toward the left in the whole procedure. Interestingly enough, one of its severest critics in this regard was none other than Father Andrew Greeley, not exactly a member of the extreme right. Eventually, out of these consultations, a booklet was issued as a discussion guide, one which called for the final convocation in Detroit to issue recommendations under the following heads: 1) The Church; 2) Personhood; 3) Family; 4) Neighborhood; 5) Humankind; 6) Nationhood; 7) Ethnicity and Race; 8) Work. While space does not permit a detailed presentation of the convocation's final recommendations on these areas, a brief sketch is in order, because the reader needs to have some idea what was at stake in the battle which is the principal subject of this chapter.[9] Here is a synopsis:

1) The Church: The convocation advocated such things as due process, accountability, democratic processes in the selection of pastors and bishops, an end to discrimination, and involvement of women in ministry.

2) Personhood: Here it supported pro-life activities (of the "seamless garment" variety, of course), programs for the handicapped, the rejection of racism and capital punishment, help in forming one's conscience on sexual expression, homosexuality, etc.,

[9] For a clear summary of the CTA, especially of its final recommendations, see Monsignor George Kelly's account in *The Battle for the American Church* (Garden City, New York: Image Books, 1981).

and an end to civil discrimination against homosexuals (i.e., "gay rights").

3) Family: The convocation called for a fight against anti-family forces, promotion of pro-family legislation, pastoral care for the divorced, separated, and divorced and remarried — including the right for the latter to receive Communion under some circumstances.

4) Neighborhood: Here it came out for small Eucharist communities, neighborhood community groups, community organization (of the Alinsky type, of course — see below), Church assistance for political action programs, etc.

5) Humankind: Here the convocation called for the establishment of diocesan Peace and Justice offices, inviting Third World speakers to speak in our dioceses, the defense of human rights internationally, rejection of multinational corporations, condemnation of nuclear war, amnesty for draft dodgers, solidarity with oppressed people, and so on.

6) Nationhood: It called for programs for peace and disarmament, elimination of poverty and racism, support for the Equal Rights Amendment (ERA), an extensive critique of national policy on any number of issues, and the structuring of ongoing consultation into the institutional structure of the Church.

7) Ethnicity and Race: Recommendations called for support for affirmative action, multilingual education programs, offices for black and Spanish-speaking Catholics, etc.

8) Work: Recommendations called for equal employment opportunity in the Church, efforts to bring about full employment, endorsement of the ERA (again!), teaching of Catholic social doctrine in the schools (but whose?), support for labor unions, amnesty for illegal aliens, etc.

Obviously, there is no need to elaborate on all this. The reader who has followed events in the Church since 1976, however casually, will recognize here the whole mishmash of buzzwords, "code words," etc., that have made up the agenda of the Catholic left all these years. And we all have a pretty good idea what many of these ambiguous words and phrases actually mean when we read between the lines. Clearly, much of what the final recommendations call for is contrary to Catholic teaching — gay rights, for instance. Equally clearly, much of it consists of motherhood and apple pie sloganeering, things which no one could possibly oppose — i.e., programs for the handicapped, defense of human rights. Beyond that, much of the program involves things about which there is no clear Catholic teaching but which honest Catholics can honestly disagree on — as Monsignor George A. Kelly said several years after the Call, "parishioners would consider many recommendations the warp and woof of what separates Democrats from Republicans, not Catholics from each other."[10] What is really important is not the details of this program, so much as the mere fact that a program of this kind got the near-unanimous consent of a convocation claiming to represent the whole American Church, including the "grass roots," and thus in effect got itself institutionalized in the Church to the point where it today has something approaching the status of defined doctrine in the American Church. This was done through a process of deceit and manipulation, and was done with a degree of authoritarianism that the Spanish Inquisition itself might have approved of; that is what will concern us in what follows.

Liberal folklore likes to tell us that revolutions reflect the grass-roots rising up of the masses of the oppressed people against their oppressors — that they are, in fact, the antithesis of authoritarianism. When it comes to the actual revolutions historians must study, however, nothing could be further from the truth. Real-life revolutions are nearly always the work of an elite which manipulates and intimidates the masses into accepting its dominance in place of the previous dominant groups. That is certainly obvious in the case of both the French and the Russian (Soviet) revolutions. It is somewhat less obvious but still, I think, true in the case of the American Revolution, where the new dominant class had the grace to be more benign and less power-mad than the others, largely because it had not been in-

[10] Ibid., p. 385.

fected with anything like the sheer quantity of totalitarian, ideological poison that filled the other groups and made their very presence deadly to any poor souls unfortunate enough to come in contact with them.

The folklore and reality in regard to the Call to Action are similar. The folklore tells us that the Call was a grass-roots movement on the part of the Catholic laity to make itself heard in the American Church, a grass-roots movement which was facilitated by a process of "consultation" in which, at the parish and diocesan levels, ordinary Catholics were able to inform their bishops of their "concerns" and have those concerns reflected at the concluding conclave in Detroit. It sounds very democratic. In fact, in the actual experience of people who took part in the Call, from the "consultations" to the congress itself, nothing of the sort took place. *The Wanderer* warned its readers of this in advance and continued to drive this point home after the Call's final reports and recommendations were in. The reality was a "consultation" process manipulated almost totally by a small elite of Church revolutionaries who saw to it that the various committees in the "consultation" process as well as the concluding conference produced exactly the results they were supposed to, results far, far to the left of the ordinary Catholic in the pews. Numerous *Wanderer* commentators, even during the consultation process, noted that neither the local committees nor the national conference were truly representative of the laity, but only of a liberal elite who set themselves up as spokesmen for a lay population which shared few of its pet ideas. Frank Morriss, writing not long after the conclusion of the Detroit disaster, notes that "the gathering, said to be representative of the grass roots of Catholicism in the United States, was hardly that. About 40% of delegates were priests. A considerable percentage were nuns — for the most, pants-suited and indistinguishable from their non-religious sisters. It could very well be that the laity were in a decided minority. Among those who were lay delegates, however, could be discerned those who are far from representing the Catholics in the pews. Rather, they represent the more active organizations — most of them highly 'progressive' in outlook — or the hangers-on of episcopal favor, the laity who are already part of the Church bureaucracy or who bathe in the diocesan or parochial light of approval."[11] Or, as *Wanderer* editor Al Matt put it, in a column entitled "'These People Don't Represent the Church,'" "...It's basically the same people who have given Catholics in this Country modernist theology, unorthodox Catechetics, far-out liturgies, and situation ethics whom you can thank for the disaster in Detroit."[12] Stanley Interrante, a participant in the conference, commented extensively on the well-organized exclusion of dissent throughout the process, and concludes, using only a little hyperbole, that "if you think for one moment that it is possible, without fantastic organization and patience, to gather together 1,340 delegates from 152 dioceses across the nation, making sure that most of them share a common ideology and mentality which is diametrically opposed to the Church and the Nation, using Church funds obtained from you and me for the purpose of trying to demolish the Church right under the eyes of the bishops, you should capture Heaven by your faith alone."[13]

Clearly, the Call to Action was no grass-roots assembly reflecting the laity's genuine desire for more input into the life of the Church. It was the culmination of the work of a revolutionary elite which had been, for some years, seeking to wrest control of the American Church from her bishops, from the Holy Father, and from allegiance to the centuries old traditions of Catholic Christianity. That being the case, we need to look at that elite's work from several standpoints:

1) Its background in the earlier efforts of the elite to establish a National Pastoral Council in the United States, a Council which would very likely have handed over effective control of the Church to the elite (at least that is what happened in Holland, the model the elite was largely emulating).

---

[11] Frank Morriss, "A Stampede to the Left," W, 11-4-76.

[12] A.J. Matt, Jr., "'These People Don't Represent the Church,'" W, 11-11-76.

[13] Stanley Interrante, "No Dissent Tolerated at the Detroit Convocation," W, 11-11-76.

2) The techniques the elite used to get its way with the Call to Action, after its previous failure with the NPC. The whole organization of the "consultation" process is one big embodiment of those techniques, as *Wanderer* commentators showed again and again from early in the process.

3) The extreme authoritarianism of the elite, an authoritarianism in sharp contrast to its avowed commitment to liberty, to democratic principles, etc. That authoritarianism can, I think, be shown to have its roots in an ideology of the totalitarian left, one which claimed the loyalty of the elite, and had roots, not only in movements such as Marxism, liberation theology, feminism, etc., but in an overarching system of revolutionary theory and "praxis" which we owe to that paradigmatic totalitarian thinker, Saul Alinsky, undoubtedly one of the most corrosive influences on the twentieth century American Church. It was *The Wanderer*'s great accomplishment at the time of the Call, if it could do nothing to stop this totalitarian influence on the whole process, to extensively document its presence, and thus to contribute to a historical record and historical understanding of the events of 1976 which would otherwise reflect only the left's self-understanding, not the historical and spiritual reality of what happened.

Let us take these aspects of the Call to Action one at a time.

2. THE NPC DEBATE — THE FIRST COUP ATTEMPT

The *coup d'église* in the American Church was prefigured by the one that occurred in the Dutch Church a few years earlier. In January, 1969, Catholics in the United States were shocked to hear about the deliberations of a pastoral council held in Noordwijkerhoot, the Netherlands, which ended January 8.[14] That council epitomized the sort of thing we eventually learned to expect here. "The progressivist 'pastoral engineers,' sociologists, psychologists, etc., so dominated the 'council' that the eight Dutch bishops were nothing more [than] 'decorations' whose presence was tolerated perhaps only to lend a certain authenticity to the schismatic circus."[15] Orthodox members of the clergy were not permitted to address the council. *The Wanderer* reported that "the 'schema' contained some absolutely incredible statements — not only against the discipline of the Church but also against dogma and doctrine. The proposals effectively would destroy the sacramental and hierarchical order and basic structure of the Church."[16] The "council" rejected Pope Paul's encyclical *Humanae Vitae*, maintaining that the use of contraception should be left up to the "decision of conscience of married people..."[17] It upheld the notoriously heretical "Dutch Catechism," and what it called the "right to experiment" in ethical areas like homosexuality, abortion, premarital sex, organ transplants, and mercy killing.[18]

This first Dutch "pastoral council" was quickly followed by a second in February, 1970. This one focused heavily on the question of clerical celibacy. "By eighty-three to three, and nine blanks, the

---

[14] "Is the Dutch Church in Schism?" W, 1-23-69.
[15] "Havoc in Holland" W, 1-15-70.
[16] W, 1-15-70.
[17] "Is the Dutch Church in Schism?" W, 1-23-69.
[18] Ibid.

'council' recommended that priests who want to marry or are already married can continue to function fully as priests....By a ninety-four to one vote, and three blanks, they recommended that married men should be eligible for the priesthood...Then, by a ninety-three to two vote, and three blanks, they voted for the [principal] statement that the celibacy rule should be rescinded entirely."[19]

Pope Paul VI spoke out at the time against this council, noting that it committed at least three very serious errors:

"— It misunderstands the mission of the Church to be purely earthly;

"— It misconceives the priest as receiving his office from the Christian community;

"— Its view of religious life is tainted by doctrinal deficiencies and ambiguities;

"— It is anti-papal in that it wishes to diminish the authority that Christ Himself gave to the Pope."[20]

All of this sounds today to us American Catholics like the familiar inventory of "progressivist" Catholic ideas, but in 1969-70 people still had the capacity to be shocked by them. Clearly, at this point, a schism had taken place in the Dutch Catholic Church. *The Wanderer*'s principal comment at that time, one that could fittingly be applied to the progressivists of today, was this: "Truly, the havoc in Holland is so widespread it would seem the only solution would be for Rome to demand that the schismatics accept the teaching and discipline of Rome — or get out of the Church!"[21]

Shocked though traditional Catholics may have been by the mass psychosis in the Dutch Church, it appears pretty obvious that American 'progressivists' could not have been more delighted over what they saw happening across the Atlantic, and began to move quickly to get something similar into motion here. Thus, no later than

---

[19] "Havoc in Holland," W, 1-15-70.

[20] Synopsis by Frank Morriss, "Catholics Must Reject Dutch Council," W, 2-5-70.

[21] "Havoc in Holland," W, 1-15-70.

March, 1970, *Wanderer* readers were informed that "the administrative arm of the National Conference of Catholic Bishops (NCCB) has named an advisory body of bishops, priests, nuns, and laity to study the possibility of creating a National Pastoral Council.... John Cardinal Dearden of Detroit, president of both the NCCB and the U.S. Catholic Conference (USCC) announced the action in Washington on February 20."[22] The advisory panel, according to Cardinal Dearden, was to consist of bishops, priests, religious, laymen, and laywomen from each of ten geographical districts, with the task of discussing the "exercise of shared responsibility in the Church," the "nature of a National Pastoral Council," "how NPC membership would be determined," and "how an NPC would relate to other bodies in the Church"[23] (for instance, would it be a merely advisory body or would it exercise real power?).

In its September 3, 1970 issue, *The Wanderer* published in full the Catholics United for the Faith document entitled "Reflections on a National Pastoral Council."[24] That document is too long to discuss in much detail here, but its principal objections to the NPC could, I think, be summarized as: 1) The fear that the Council would interfere with the prophetic mission of the Church; and 2) the concern that the Council would create an even more bureaucratic Church.

Regarding the first of these concerns, the CUF document has this to say:

> It is one of the Church's God-given tasks to bear prophetic witness of the Kingdom of God as against the Kingdom of the prince of this world. How would the Church be able to discharge this task, to take a stand in favor of any unpopular policy, that is, to take a stand against the world and what the world wants, if her decisions are to be reached under the influence of the very people against whom the Church would have to testify? How would it be possible for a "*democratic*"

[22] "Pastoral Council for U.S. Being Studied," W, 3-5-70.
[23] Ibid.
[24] "Reflections on a National Pastoral Council," W, 9-3-70.

> Council to speak out with any kind of conviction and moral indignation against abortion, for instance, if abortion is daily approved and encouraged by Gallup polls and the newspapers and radio and television? What, indeed, would a National Pastoral Council consider to be its *duty* in such circumstances? To bear faithful witness to her own ancient and authoritative teaching? Or to join the "other-directed" crowd in approval of practices which run counter to the whole tradition of the Christian Faith and its development in history?[25]

Those are genuinely prophetic questions which, sadly, have been all too fully answered since by an American Catholic hierarchy all too willing to take public positions which are popular with the mass media, while apparently terrified to take a stand against a grave moral evil like abortion (with a few honorable exceptions, of course — men like Bishop Austin Vaughan and John Cardinal O'Connor).

As to the second concern, the CUF document states that:

> When the Church makes changes in its external rules and discipline, they may lead its members to a better understanding of the Gospel and what it requires of them. But they may also have an adverse influence on the depth and seriousness of spiritual life within the Church. They may do irreparable damage even though designed to further reconstruction. This danger is especially real in the Church because a man who has developed great administrative abilities seldom retains much spiritual sensitivity as to the consequences of his decisions.
>
> The trouble with that kind of thinking [in support of the Council] is that it ignores the way in which the Council could itself become a means for bureaucratic domination of the life of the Christian people. We all know what severe criticisms have been made of the operations of the Roman Curia, and how much these criticisms were used to justify the transfer of

---

[25] Ibid.

> a greater amount of authority to the bishops in the various national conferences. But what is not sufficiently recognized is the way in which this has simply meant the replacement of bureaucratic authority in Rome by bureaucratic authority in Washington, or the seat of any other national episcopal conference.[26]

To all of which one can only say a resounding Amen!

Eventually, the USCC-NCCB scheduled a consultation on the proposal for a National Pastoral Council, a meeting to be held August 28, 29, and 30 at Mundelein College in Chicago, with representatives of a variety of Catholic groups and organizations in attendance.[27] Fortunately, the use of raw ecclesiastical power to freeze traditionalists out of such discussions had not yet gone as far as it has today, or even as far as it had gone in 1976, and as a result the Catholic right did have representatives at this meeting. These included John Mulloy, a *Wanderer* contributor, representing Catholics United for the Faith; Frank Morriss, another *Wanderer* contributor, representing Catholic Laymen of America, and Al Matt, editor of *The Wanderer*. A real rogue's gallery, at least as far as the "progressivists" were concerned! Already, before the meeting, John Mulloy expressed serious reservations about the procedure for the consultation, first in a letter to Monsignor J. Paul O'Connor, chairman of the Advisory Council Steering Committee, then in a news conference. Mulloy pointed out that the consultation was being held on a very tight schedule, which allowed for little serious debate on the central issues, and that the Steering Committee had plans to get out a booklet almost immediately after the consultation announcing its conclusions. That meant, practically speaking, that there would be no chance for views opposing an NPC to get into the booklet, which would be used in taking the question to the "grass roots." The format appeared to cre-

---

[26] Ibid.

[27] For the account which follows, see Kirby M. Sheridan, "The NPC Consultations...An Unplanned Dialogue," W, 9-17-70.

ate a situation where the only thing the consultation could discuss was the feasibility of a Council, not its desirability, which was precisely the question traditionalists were most concerned about. Mulloy pointed out that "not one of the position papers scheduled for discussion here at Mundelein presents the case for opposition to a National Pastoral Council, or are willing to consider any reasons why the formation of such a Council might be imprudent or ill-advised."[28] Mulloy noted, in words that can be seen in retrospect as truly prophetic, that "not one of the position papers considers the possibility that the present crisis in the Catholic Church might be still further aggravated by the formation of a Council, might make the Catholic laity feel that here was simply one more instrument by which the bureaucrats and those in positions of special power would be able to enforce their will upon the general Catholic populace."[29] Mulloy asked that the consultation process be extended so that more than just pro-Council positions would be included in the booklet to be released. He requested in particular that the CUF document, "Reflections on a National Pastoral Council," be included in the book as well as in the discussion at the Mundelein consultation.[30]

Finally, the day of the much-discussed consultation arrived. Reading about it, for one of today's much-abused and manipulated Catholic laymen, is a delight, because for once things did not go the progressivists' way, though it was not exactly a victory for our side either. But the puppets did not behave as their masters expected them to behave. There seems to have been general discontent, among progressivists as well as traditionalists, over the very tight, closely controlled agenda which allowed no room for discussing the real, underlying issues, but restricted the meeting to hearing the four pro-NPC position papers and discussing them. Very early on, at the opening session on Friday afternoon, Al Matt, not one to be shy or diffident in the presence of people who want to push him around, got up and

[28] "Requests Discussion on Pastoral Council Issues," W, 8-27-70.
[29] Ibid.
[30] Ibid.

stated bluntly that "the only voices heard in these discussions are those which favor an NPC."[31] He asked that the format of the meeting be changed to make it more open and democratic so that all sides of the issue could be heard. Father James A. Coriden, chairing the meeting, pleaded lack of time and refused to consider the request (As was the case later with the Call to Action, one of the methods used for keeping the proceedings under control was to schedule an impossible amount of business into a small amount of time, then use lack of time as an excuse for prohibiting free debate.) Traditionalists present did, however, see that copies of the CUF position paper circulated around the room, and eventually enough pressure was put on the chair so that a decision was made to divide the meeting up into small groups to discuss the issues. At that point, a bit of a revolution began. The groups discussed everything but the four position papers officially approved for a place on the agenda. There was in fact very wide-ranging discussion in the small groups. The problem was that at the end of their meetings, the discussion leaders, "facilitators," or what have you for the groups gave their reports to the general assembly, and those reports were carefully sanitized so as not to reflect the actual discussion that had taken place. In this frustrating situation, the representatives of the lay organizations present met, late Saturday, with Monsignor O'Connor to discuss opening up the meeting. Monsignor O'Connor still refused that request, as well as the closely related request to include the CUF position paper in the booklet being prepared. That was when the fireworks started. As *The Wanderer* described it, "this type of frustration came to a head at the close of Saturday night's session when Mr. Robert Rambush, of the liturgical conference, took control of the mike, immediately after the official session adjourned, and asked for a 'rump' session. Most of the representatives stayed behind with the rump session to express their dissatisfaction with Monsignor O'Connor's agenda, the distortion of their opinions and ideas through the official discussants' reporting, and the lack of receptivity to ideas by the chairman of the Steering Commit-

[31] "The NPC Consultations...An Unplanned Dialogue," W, 9-17-70.

tee." Finally, on Sunday morning, Monsignor O'Connor agreed to completely open up the meeting. Al Matt took the floor and stated that the real issue was not the feasibility of a National Pastoral Council but its desirability. He suggested that, before any decision was made, there be far more regional discussion so that as many people as possible could be involved in the debate. "While many of those present were overjoyed at the prospects of a National Pastoral Council — with the opportunity for having their voices heard while the 'spirit' hovered over their deliberations — there remained a concern in the minds of many — considering the change in agenda during the consultation, the extension of the date to receive feedback from the laity, and the radically different and opposing ideas presented in the open discussions — that perhaps the coming of democracy to the Catholic Church in America at Mundelein College might be the herald of a resurgent and responsible laity."[32] The meeting ended with Monsignor O'Connor agreeing to extend the deadline for grass-roots reaction by six months.

The Mundelein meeting appears, in retrospect, to have been a qualified victory for orthodox Catholics, because the delay that resulted seems to have allowed time for serious thinking about the question of a Council, and, finally, for the whole idea to run out of steam. The progressivists were right in their feeling that the decision to set up the Council had to be made and the Council itself put in place as soon as humanly possible, because the idea might not look so good once people had the chance to think about it. It was therefore imperative that the thing be irreversible before that happened.

After the Mundelein meeting, debate concerning the NPC proposal went on, but gradually petered out over the next year or so. Later in the fall, Frank Morriss summed up the orthodox position:

> ...Although there is nothing necessarily un-Catholic in the concept of a communicative body such as a national pastoral council, this is definitely not the time to initiate one. When a city is under siege or a nation at war, there should be nothing

[32] Ibid.

begun which will divert the citizenry from the struggle for survival. This is particularly true when the war is a civil one.

It seems rather obvious to me that the Church today is a city under siege, and to make the matter even more dangerous, there are elements within the city itself who are in communication with the enemy and quite eager to open the gates to him. It is not the time, therefore, to toy with the idea of setting up a body that could enhance the prestige of those disloyal elements and advance their purpose of surrender.[33]

In September, 1970, a group called POPE (Parents for Orthodoxy in Parochial Education) called on the bishops of the United States to reject a National Pastoral Council "on the grounds that it could destroy the Roman Catholic Church in America by undermining episcopal and papal authority."[34] On June 3, 1971, a letter by John Mulloy which appeared in *The Wanderer Forum*, criticizing a series of articles by Russell Shaw regarding the NPC, mentions that Monsignor O'Connor continued, at that time, to refuse to make the CUF position paper available to the laity or to dialogue with those people opposed to the NPC.[35]

On June 24, 1971, a *Wanderer* article appeared with the headline "Little Interest Shown In A National Pastoral Council."[36] That article discusses a public opinion poll by the *Long Island Catholic* on the subject of the NPC. That poll got very few responses, and the majority of those who did respond felt that the whole idea needed a lot more thought. Then there was a final salvo by the tireless John Mulloy in the form of a letter to the members of the Steering Committee. That letter asked a number of rhetorical questions designed to show that the whole process for getting grass-roots feedback was loaded in favor of a National Pastoral Council, then summed up with the following broadside:

---

[33] Frank Morriss, "Time Not Ripe for NPC," W, 9-17-70.
[34] "POPE Begs Bishops to Reject NPC," W, 10-1-70.
[35] W, 6-3-71.
[36] "Little Interest Shown in a National Pastoral Council," W, 6-24-71.

> The Steering Committee is indeed well named, ladies and gentlemen who compose that body; it has had to steer a circuitous and tortuous route around the rocks of the example of the Dutch Pastoral Council and avoid the open sea of dialogue and genuine consultation, in order to get its frail barque into port. If the helmsman has been somewhat less than forthright in the accomplishment of such a task, if he was forced to rely upon wordy proclamations of dialogue when in reality there could be none if the ship was to survive, he has nevertheless been remarkably expert at achieving his goal. He will end up getting a certain pretense of popular support for a council which no one really wants except a certain minority of radical priests, nuns and laity. These indeed are the ones for whom he has labored. These are the real passengers for whom the Steering Committee has been providing the vessel of a National Pastoral Council — not the American Catholic laity whose name is so often invoked.[37]

I suspect that if I were ever subjected to a critique like the above, I would be tempted to retreat to my home and sit in a corner staring at the walls for the rest of my days. I have no idea whether the members of the Steering Committee were that sensitive, but, considering the ultimate fate of the NPC proposal, perhaps they were.

An August 5, 1971 report in *The Wanderer* indicates that at that time the NPC proposal appeared dead.[38] The Steering Committee had concluded that the NPC was not feasible at that time, and planned to say so in its report to the USCC in September. After this followed a period of total or near-total silence in *The Wanderer* about the whole proposal, followed by one last article in the October 11, 1973 issue, headlined "Bishops Kill Plan for NPC."[39] "According to a statement issued on Oct. 1 by Bishop James S. Rausch, general secretary of the National Conference of Catholic Bishops (NCCB) and

[37] W, 6-24-71.

[38] "NPC Proposal Appears Dead," W, 8-5-71.

[39] "Bishops Kill Plan for NPC," W, 10-11-73.

of the U.S. Catholic Conference (USCC), the American bishops have decided to 'suspend, at least for now, efforts to bring a National Pastoral Council into being.'"[40] The reasons given for this decision included lack of evidence of support for the Council, the opposition of the Vatican, and the fact that other national episcopal conferences had concluded that such councils are not feasible. It appears to me, at least, that the fundamental truth about the matter was that the NPC was one of those ideas which appear highly plausible at a first glance, but which steadily lose that plausibility the longer one has to think about them. The proponents of a Council had hoped, as noted above, to railroad their proposal through before people had time to think, an accomplishment which would have given them, in one fell swoop, the kind of institutional power which, as we shall see, they later consolidated through the Call to Action. It was the not inconsiderable accomplishment of the representatives of orthodoxy at the Mundelein meeting that they rebelled against the agenda foisted on them by the progressives, and thereby forced the Church in America to take a longer look at the whole idea. And that was the end of the first effort at a total takeover of the Church by the progressives. Unfortunately, of course, the story does not end there. In *Luke* 4:13, after the account of Jesus' temptations in the desert, we are told that "when the devil had ended every temptation, he departed from him until an opportune time." We would like to think that the devil goes away permanently after he has tried and failed in one of his projects. Sad to say, he is much more patient than that, and just waits for the next opportunity. For the Church in America, that opportunity was furnished by the movement, already beginning in 1973, for a Call to Action. And that is where our main story picks up again.

[40] Ibid.

3. MANIPULATION —THE NAME OF THE GAME

The openness, the brazenness, with which the conference was manipulated and dissent was suppressed is breathtaking even now, to the reader reviewing the events long after. That kind of blatant, shameless use of raw power is not seen that often. This aspect of the conference deserves to be dwelt upon in some detail, because it so thoroughly exemplifies the whole behavior pattern by which the modernist church has forced its agenda since then down the throats of traditional Catholics. Let us look, therefore, at several examples of the left's high-handed approach to "debate":

There seems to be general agreement, among the traditional Catholics who somehow stumbled into the Witches' Sabbath known as the Call to Action, that even during the planning stages when convocations were held at the Diocesan level, the deck was thoroughly stacked in favor of the "progressives." Jim Wright, telling the story of his involvement in the November 25, 1976 *Wanderer*, reminisced at some length on the diocesan conference he attended earlier in the year: "It was in February that I attended a Liberty and Justice convocation for the Los Angeles Diocese, which then included Orange County. I remembered feeling that there was a certain madness to the whole program — the Marxist tone of the discussion guide, the 'facilitators' that dominated the discussion; the insanity of trying to solve major world problems in a two-hour time allocation; the feeling that the outcome was somehow preplanned — that it could hardly be altered by anything we could do in the amount of time we had allowed. Then there were the recommended actions — the militant outcries that sounded more like demands than recommendations, calling for democracy in the Church and Marxism and pacifism in the country; and the deafening thunderous applause after each militant proclamation. It was a kangaroo court, and the Church, the nation, and the free enterprise system were all on trial."[41] James E. Twyman, reflecting on preparations for the conference, noted that "in Chicago we did not even know via public print who the delegates from our archdiocese were until *after* 'A Call to Action' had assembled and dispersed!"[42] There is massive evidence that the composition of the delegates in no way reflected a cross-section of American Catholics, that it was so heavily weighted toward clergy, religious, and quasi-laity who were actually Church professionals as to make any notion that it was democratic laughable. The ecclesiastical elite got together in Detroit to thunder out their approval of one another's revolutionary projects, and that is all. The very composition of the conference, established beforehand at the parish and diocesan levels where seats were given to those who toed the ideological line, shows that, as noted above, this was a manipulated conference.

If that was the case months before the conference even began, how much more was it the case when the long preparations were over and the main event finally got underway at Cobo Hall on October 21, 1976. The available examples are an embarrassment of riches for the historian.

The basic rules for debate are probably the most dramatic and crucial proof that the conference was manipulated from start to finish. The rules adopted by the conference established that a simple majority was sufficient for a quorum, a simple majority was sufficient to close debate, and roll call votes were forbidden. No one has to be a genius to figure out the effect of these rules. They meant that whatever majority existed at the beginning of a session regarding an issue could simply force its program on everyone without any effective opposition, because there would be no real public debate which would give a dissenting minority a chance to try to change people's minds or even to clarify what the issues were about, an important service which opposition often provides even when it is not able to

[41] Jim Wright, "A Call to Action: The Story of One Delegate," W, 11-25-76.
[42] James E. Twyman, *The Fork in the Road*, Wanderer Press, 1977, p. 12.

prevail. As delegate Frank Teskey, another "Wanderer Gang" member, pointed out afterward, "The two special rules were in plain language a *gag rule*, cutting off debate by a simple majority without accountability. The primary purpose of debate is to enable the minority to convince a sufficient number of the majority so as to bring the minority position to majority status. There is an implicit duty on [the part of] the majority to hold itself open to the possibility of reasonable persuasion by the minority."[43] In effect, the rules guaranteed the blind passage of incompletely understood resolutions by ignorant majorities able to silence their critics. That sounds a lot like a meeting of the Politburo back in the bad old days when the Soviet Union was still a functioning political entity (may it never rise again!). The real purpose of these bizarre rules became dramatically obvious the first time anyone tried to challenge them. A delegate rose and introduced a motion to require a two-thirds majority to close debate (as Roberts Rules of Order requires). Jim Wright, reporting for *The Wanderer*, started up to the mike to argue for the motion, but before he could get there, someone moved, successfully, to close debate, even though the rule for such closure was precisely what was at issue in the motion being considered! Wright attempted to raise a point of order, and was rewarded for his efforts by having his microphone turned off. That was the democratic voice of the People of God in action.[44]

Much of the work of the Call to Action was done in workshops which considered particular areas of concern, then reported to the plenary session. Here, too, there was plenty of opportunity for stacking the deck against anyone who upheld Catholic teaching. Jim Wright again provides us with a beautiful illustration. Wright, after meeting with no success trying to get the workshop on "Humankind" to say something about human rights violations in Communist countries, moved to the "Personhood" group and there thought that he did a little better. That group, by some miracle, seems to have had a

---

[43] Frank Teskey, "First Skirmish at Cobo Corral," W, 12-2-76.

[44] Jim Wright, *op. cit.*

Catholic majority and passed resolutions in favor of the Human Life Amendment and against the Equal Rights Amendment. That, it turned out, was a little too good to be true. Soon afterward, a lot of new people showed up in the room, and the next thing Wright knew, they had successfully passed resolutions reversing the ones previously passed. Obviously, someone had gotten the word out that there was a brush fire needing to be put out in the Personhood group, and a sufficient number of "progressives" was quickly rounded up from the highways and byways of Cobo Hall to take care of the matter.[45]

The commissars in charge of the Call to Action also seem to have had few qualms about such obvious parliamentary tactics as refusing to recognize known dissidents (read: Roman Catholics), turning off people's microphones, etc. At one point, *Wanderer* contributing editor Frank Morriss stepped up to make a point, and found himself being roughly pushed away from the mike by none other than moral theologian Father Charles Curran, one of the more shining examples of the movement toward democracy in the Church. Apparently, there was some technical issue about whether Frank was actually registered as a delegate (he was) and he was finally allowed to speak, but the incident itself speaks eloquently about the atmosphere of this conference.[46]

Finally, the very organization of the conference, the attempt to deal, in three days, with huge issues that a more rational assembly, an Ecumenical Council, for instance, could and would have devoted years to, made it impossible for any real democracy to govern the events. There is simply no way to deal with all that material in three days while allowing for any genuine, meaningful debate or for democratic procedures. The only way the Call to Action could possibly finish all its "work" in such a short time was in an atmosphere where a set of pre-established conclusions were forced down the throats of delegates who often were not even in a position to know what they were voting on. When we add to that the fact that most delegates

---

[45] Ibid.

[46] Teskey, "First Skirmish at Cobo Hall," W, 12-2-76.

were chosen for their compliance with the "progressive" agenda, that just makes the "kangaroo court" atmosphere all the more obvious. Let us, once more, allow Jim Wright to tell us about the atmosphere of the Call to Action: "By the time we registered at Cobo Hall, the intricate workings of the process became apparent. Schedules were arranged so that we were constantly busy from early morning until night. There never seemed to be time for breakfast, and the meetings always interfered with scheduled daily Masses. It was hard not to feel helpless."[47] Frank Teskey recalls that "on the eve of the convention, we [the orthodox Catholic delegates] met almost by chance and agreed that we should make some attempt to challenge the Special Rules of the Convention so that some real debate and discussion of issues could take place at plenary sessions. But this was about the only time we could caucus (or conspire if you prefer) because once the stampede started there was no free time; if we had caucused, we would have been passed up by events."[48] During the plenary sessions, Wright recalls, "There was an hour allocated for each of the eight topics. Each topic had three or four recommendations, and each recommendation had ten or fifteen amendments. It was obvious that there was no time for explanations or serious debate. Most of the amendments were read and instantly voted upon. Some complained that there was not enough time to read the documents (which were distributed just before the meeting started). Still, the voting went on. Any attempts to bring the more radical recommendations in line with the encyclicals and the teachings of the Church were overwhelmingly defeated."[49]

I find it particularly interesting that breakfast and Mass were both sacrificed to the need to keep this breakneck schedule. That meant that simultaneously, on both the natural and the supernatural level, people were deprived of their defenses against manipulation and control by anti-Christian and anti-human ideologues. While there

---

47 Wright, *op. cit.*
48 Teskey, *op. cit.*
49 Wright, *op.cit*

are a few people with weird metabolisms who seem to do just fine without breakfast, most of us find that if we miss that meal, then try to deal with the stresses of just an ordinary day at the office or the factory or wherever we work, we just do not function very efficiently. We are not as alert as we might otherwise be, and we tend to just drag ourselves through the day and "spin our wheels," as the saying has it. It is very easy for people to take advantage of us when we are in such a state. Even more important when people are taking part in an event like the Call to Action, where the life of the spirit is in question, is the need for spiritual nourishment. The orthodox Catholic delegates who took part in the Call to Action found themselves engaged in spiritual warfare, and desperately needed the spiritual strength that comes from prayer, especially from the highest prayer of all, the Eucharist, to struggle effectively against the genuinely and not just figuratively demonic forces that surrounded them. This is an even more important point when we consider that, besides orthodox delegates, there were doubtless many confused Catholics present at the Call to Action, people who were on the fence, not sure exactly what they believed but not yet wholehearted supporters of the "progressive" agenda. Had the spiritual needs of these people been better met, who knows, the conference might have had a better outcome. The fact that the very organization of the Call was such as to deprive people not only of bodily but also of spiritual nourishment, does not necessarily mean that there was a deliberate, conscious conspiracy by the organizers to weaken the opposition in this way, but it certainly underscores the fact that what the Call to Action was about was spiritual warfare. As St. Paul put it, "...we are not contending against flesh and blood, but against the principalities, against the powers, against the world rulers of this present darkness, against the spiritual hosts of wickedness in the heavenly places" (*Ephesians* 6:12).

4. A TRIUMPH OF LIBERAL AUTHORITARIANISM

The fact that the Call to Action left quite a bit to be desired in the way of a commitment to freedom and democracy, the fact that there was something authoritarian, nay, even totalitarian, about the organization and work of the convocation, is pretty evident from its style and methods, documented above. As we have found all too often in this century in our dealings with Communist revolutionary movements, groups which use inhuman tactics, tactics that reduce the person to an organism to be used and manipulated, are not at all likely to be humanistic and personalistic in the substance of their movements. An examination of the Call to Action's methods certainly hints at a totalitarian essence. Having considered those methods, then, we need to go deeper inland and start looking at the social, political, and theological substance of the Call to Action's work.

The fundamental interrelatedness of methods and substance in the Call to Action was first clearly articulated by *Wanderer* editor Al Matt, in an editorial that appeared shortly after the ill-fated convocation: "Let no one be deceived. The 'Call to Action' was a revolutionary assembly in the full sense of that word. It was conceived, developed, and executed with precision and deliberateness. The agents of this revolutionary process (the delegates) were no more representative of the 'People of God' than were the Arians of the fourth century....It is not only the more radical proposals made by the Call to Action which the bishops must reject, it is the process itself by which these proposals have been advanced that must be rejected. There is no doubt that forums should be developed by which the hierarchical Church listens to the voice of the People of God to determine their legitimate needs; but the 'Call to Action' with its ideological slant, its manipulations, its lack of reflection and prudence, its unrepresentativeness, is not the answer."[50]

What, then, is the totalitarian essence of the Call to Action? One clue is to be found, not surprisingly, in the deeply distorted attitude toward personhood which observers of the conference noted in the final resolutions and recommendations. It is, after all, the treatment of the human person which divides totalitarian regimes from all others. Frank Morriss, in a November 11, 1976 editorial, found the center of the Call to Action's distortion of personhood in what he called the idea of personhood as "process":

> Nowhere does the Bishops' Bicentennial Committee on Liberty and Justice for All go more basically wrong than in its presentation on personhood....It is obvious that its very definition of person and personhood is framed within the framework of "process," or evolutionism. And that makes all the difference in the world. For the traditional scholastic philosopher, a "person" is an independent being having intellect and will. The technical definition of human is a rational hypostasis. Though Father Stephen P. Happel of the Catholic University of America, who comments on personhood in the *Liberty and Justice [for] All* handbook, never defines person, it is evident that it is not a being at all, a recognizable entity, but a "becoming." The search for "Who am I?" he explains, is open-ended, going from "Why am I?" through various stages of wonder, with a constant growth process and only hopes for eventual fulfillment. It may be this unfulfilled hope that is helping fill our asylums.[51]

Contrasting this "process" notion of personhood with the Christian understanding, Morriss goes on to note that

> the Master told the rich young man that one saves himself by keeping the Commandments, which is in faithfully keeping

[50] A.J. Matt, Jr., "A Blueprint for a Schismatic Church," W, 11-4-76.

[51] Frank Morriss, "Personhood as 'Process,'" W, 11-11-76.

> to the idea that a person is a definite, formed entirety capable of receiving and obeying commands. Perfection does have to do with possibilities. But sin has to do with realized actuality — what man is, what his nature happens to be, and what God has demanded of him....Persons discovering their dignity in Christ will change the world — and for the better. But if they go on chasing their personhood and thinking they find it or bestow it in a warm squeeze, I wouldn't wait, if I were you, for better days.[52]

A concept of the human person, not as a being having goodness and dignity as a creature and child of God called to eternal life, but as a kind of flux, a sort of indefinite becoming, what someone once called "one damn thing after another," is really the destruction of personhood. It leaves the way totally open for an understanding of the person, not as a free actor who enters into and builds community through love, but as something essentially formless, to be formed and manipulated according to this or that ideologue's blueprint. Paradoxically, that understanding of person as a formless process, something forever indefinite, is in many ways totally congruent with the extreme, atomistic individualism and egalitarianism that characterized many of the Call's positions on moral issues like homosexuality. This is an ideological stance which sees man as naturally good until he is corrupted by social institutions, by law, by morality, etc. That is Rousseau's vision of man. Translated into "process" terms, what Rousseau's pseudo-personalism really means is that it is man's natural (and hence good) state to be something formless, and that society, with its institutions, destroys that natural goodness of the creature who need not be anything in particular, by forcing boundaries on man, forcing him to become something definite, something formed, a being who comes into the world part of a community and already involved in a network of rights and duties which are not his work, and directed toward an end, which is friendship with God in eternity, an end which is also not his work. Rousseau's individualism rejects all

[52] Ibid.

that. "Rousseau," as Morriss points out, "was a noted ingrate. He hated his origins, and he contemned those who listened to him and admired him and helped him. In other words, he turned on those who made him to be. The Detroit delegates — that is, the majority — reacted similarly to the Church that is their mother. They showed notable shame at being Catholics, in an institution they know cannot and will not honor much of what they ask. Like good Rousseauvians they will take pleasure in suffering this rejection, and most will have passed from the scene when those who succeed them are not satisfied with suffering rejection and who supply the revolution that always follows upon romanticism's triumph."[53] As Morriss later summed it up, "2,000 years of Catholic teaching went to the Guillotine."[54] The distortion of personhood, often in the very name of personhood, always does seem to lead to the Guillotine. That distortion is really at the root of the Call to Action's whole program, as I will attempt to show in what follows.

Modern revolutionary movements typically reject the traditional authorities which play such a big role in the formation of the human person as part of a world and not just an isolated atom, "alone and afraid, in a world I never made." In rejecting these authorities, they detach the person from the influence of one kind of authority, but generally only to place him at the mercy of new, totalitarian authorities which aim at the total control of the person, and ultimately the destruction of the person, through such things as social engineering, mass media propaganda, etc. That is why James Eliot Twyman, reflecting on the Call to Action, could suggest that "all this [the work of the conference] combined with something new toward which we have been moving: the surveillance and inspection of everything and everyone by the cultists to ensure that the cult 'goals' are met."[55] The

---

[53] Frank Morriss, "Most Detroit Delegates Were Rousseau's Heirs," W, 11-25-76.

[54] "Most Denver Delegates Agree with 'Call to Action,'" W, 11-25-76.

[55] James E. Twyman, "Saul Alinsky and the Bishops' 'Call to Action,'" W, 10-14-76.

Call to Action basically rejected one of these authorities — that of the institutional Church, especially the Magisterium, the teaching authority of the Church vested in the Pope and the hierarchy.

In rejecting the authority of the hierarchy, what kind of authority, or pseudo-authority, did the Call to Action seek to replace it with? James Eliot Twyman provided a valuable clue to this in a lengthy *Wanderer* essay summing up the Call to Action several months after the fact. His conclusion is that the people (the progressive, middle-management bureaucrats of the Church) who organized the Call sought to replace traditional Catholic authority with the authority of the "People's Organization," a type of organization epitomized by the late Saul Alinsky, a socialist who sought to organize the masses of the people to attack capitalist society and transform the world into a collectivist Utopia. The Call to Action was thus an effort, an at least partially successful one, at a hostile takeover of the Church by people holding beliefs diametrically opposed to Catholic teaching, especially in areas of morality and social justice. As Twyman puts it, "'A Call to Action' which has been presented publicly as a meeting intended to implement the teachings of the Church on social justice is in fact a well-designed, well-orchestrated effort to transform the Catholic Church in the United States into an Alinsky-style 'People's Organization.'"[56] He calls it "the final stroke of the *coup d'église* — that forcible takeover of the Church in the United States by the proponents of a particular point of view, the Alinsky view....What Detroit succeeded in doing was to present a plan using the Catholic Church in this country as a shadow civil government."[57]

In Twyman's view, the whole Call to Action process, from the first organizational steps to the conclusion, was obsessed with power and saw the world almost exclusively in bureaucratic terms. The bureaucratic view of the world is just another aspect of the distortion of personhood. When persons are not real entities, with rights and duties, but merely processes to be manipulated and directed, then social

[56] Ibid., p. 9.
[57] Twyman, *The Fork in the Road*, p. 6.

engineering, the bureaucratic process *par excellence*, becomes everything. "In the Detroit mentality," according to Twyman, "it is structures, not individuals and people, that count. Some might think of this as bureaucracy and some might see in it the Church Organizational thinking that has come to characterize the life of the Church in this country in the last few years. But at the heart of such thinking is a basic orientation that places its trust in structures, groups, and movements — not in men and women, not in individual souls."[58] Reflecting further on the "shadow civil government" idea that seemed to dominate the Call to Action, Twyman suggests that "this theme of alignment of the visible structures of the Catholic culture with the structures of the civil government of the United States at all levels is spread throughout the pages of 'A Call to Action' and in part accounts for the heavy organizational or bureaucratic emphasis that is inescapable in even a first reading of the Detroit papers....The call for community that is insistent these days can be understood at Detroit as a call for the Church as 'People's Organization.' I suggest that *prophecy* nowadays means that the prophet is going to run the show and to tell other people what to do and where to stand and which expressions to hold on their faces."[59] The documents of the Call to Action itself make abundantly clear the orientation of the whole process toward a convergence of Catholicism with the "community organization" movement: "In the final copy of *Neighborhood*, the paper which brings forward all this effort as a five-year plan, comes the statement: 'That the Church should initiate and be actively involved in the development of community organizing projects among all peoples.'"[60] "There is little that Detroit left untouched in its works. Its object is to use the visible and cultural structures of the Church, locally, nationally, internationally, to carry out the social-political designs of a group. And the operative word is always

[58] *The Fork in the Road*, p. 8.
[59] Ibid., pp. 8-9.
[60] Ibid., p. 9.

'organization' in the context of the power-oriented, all-inclusive mass movement."[61]

Twyman is so persuasive in making the case that the totalitarian mood dominated the Call to Action that I think it is worthwhile to quote him at some length as he drives the point home:

> The pattern of coercion under the guise of monitoring — inspection — accountability — examination of lifestyles — enters the working and/or final papers of each of Detroit's eight subject-areas. The emphasis may vary as the shift in wording takes place but the message is clear: the surveillance of everyone and everything to ensure the fulfillment of the objectives of the "People's Organization."[62]
>
> A theme of facilitation, purging, attitudinal control, coercion, and invasion of the privacy not only of mind but of soul builds to such an extent in "A Call to Action" that one finds it novel that the conference puts its unqualified stamp of approval on the 1948 United Nations Universal Declaration of Human Rights which specifically counters "A Call to Action" by stressing freedom to hold opinion without interference and by stating that no one shall be subjected to arbitrary interference with his privacy.[63]
>
> The building of the "People's Organization" within the Church at Detroit manifests itself as an attack on the Church and as an effort to replace the authority of the hierarchy with the authority of the "People's Organization."[64]
>
> The conference that was preening itself as the model of concern for social justice was in fact a crime against social jus-

[61] Ibid., p. 10.
[62] Ibid., p. 15.
[63] Ibid, p. 15.
[64] Ibid., p. 16.

> tice. We all might as well realize it. To think otherwise is to delude ourselves and to immerse ourselves more deeply in the problem of our times. "A Call to Action" was the very model of all that the Popes have been speaking against since 1891.[65]
>
> So detached from the reality of the life of the Church in this country today is it [Detroit] that in pages and pages about social justice not one mention was made of the priests and professed religious who are suffering injustices in their religious houses simply because they seek to maintain the Magisterium.[66]

The Call to Action, from the perspective of those "Wanderer-types" who were present, clearly was not just an exercise in left-wing rhetoric but was an attempt at an *institutional* takeover of the Catholic Church in the United States. Twyman sees it, correctly, I believe, as "the attempted institutionalization of the kinds of perspectives that have publicly and visibly dominated the life of the Church in this country in recent years and which we have taken to calling, erroneously, 'renewal.'"[67] "Both the Church and Nationhood working papers carried the flavor of permanency in regarding 'A Call to Action' as 'a type of national pastoral council' and calling for another such 'consultation' within five years."[68]

The orientation to power as the central goal of all human activity was evident throughout the Call to Action in what Twyman calls the "conflict model of life" at the heart of the documents, a view of life which sees human society almost exclusively in terms of a sort of a Manichaean dualism of good and evil, oppressors and oppressed, exploiters and exploited, etc. Liberal Catholics and progressives may talk till they are blue in the face about Christian 'love,' but in the

---

[65] Ibid., p. 18.
[66] Ibid., p. 18.
[67] Ibid., p. 20.
[68] Ibid., pp. 20-21.

end, for them, power is everything. It is only by the acquisition and use of power, through activities such as community organization, that it is possible for the oppressed and exploited, the victims, to defeat the victimizers, the latter being virtually anyone who owns property, has a position of authority, or is established in any way whatsoever. The possibility that love and mercy might play a role in resolving social injustices never really seems to occur to these people. In the end, for the worldview of the far left so well represented at the Call to Action, every established person or institution or structure in the world is the enemy and must be destroyed. That means endless war against existing governments, against the hierarchy of the Church, against the family, indeed, in the end, against all community. That means that, as Twyman says, "Detroit was anti-social" despite its pretense to be enunciating the social teachings of the Church. For example, as Twyman also points out, the conference, in trying to deal with racial justice, itself falls into racism because it makes race a principal category for evaluating individuals, not personhood. "That paper on Ethnicity and Race is a model of racism and ethnocentrism if by these words one means that 'race' and 'ethnicity' are to be taken as the measures of individuals. On that score, Detroit was racist and ethnocentric to the point of being a crime before God."[69] John Mulloy, looking ahead after the Call to the coming bishops' conference which would have to respond to it, makes this prophetic statement which sums up the whole anti-institutional, anti-community substance of the conference:

> Let the Spirit of Detroit triumph in the bishops' conference, and in the conclusions it arrives at concerning the "Call to Action," and the time is not far off when the Church in this country will no longer be Catholic. Instead, it will be merely a withered and decaying branch, cut off from the Chair of Peter and from the life of Him through whom the Church was first planted and nurtured on these shores of the Americas. If we wish to destroy the great work of the North American

[69] Ibid., p. 29.

> martyrs, and of innumerable other missionaries who spent their lives in the establishment of the Catholic Church in this country, we have only to defend the Detroit assembly and to claim that its results are compatible with Catholic teaching.
>
> Only a repudiation of the entire process of which the Detroit disaster was the culmination, will enable the bishops to begin to repair the terrible damage that already has been done.[70]

Needless to say, that repudiation did not occur, and we are suffering the consequences to this day.

Indeed, the rebellion against human community, human institutions, human order, human love which the Detroit Call to Action of 1976 embodied so fully is really, ultimately, a rebellion against God and His Incarnate Word, Jesus Christ. Monsignor Alphonse Popek, in a homily given on the last morning of the convocation to a group of faithful Catholics, summed up the real situation in words that still speak to us with prophetic power today:

> Before we go back to the convocation, let us think for a moment about our purpose in being here. It has been said that the Church is dying — that Christ, through His Church, is once again being crucified. We hear the loud voices of those at this meeting who sit in judgment over the Church. They are not satisfied with the Church that Christ has given them. Like the early Apostles once did, they want a kingdom of this world; and they want to rule over it.
>
> This morning, we meet one last time here in the catacombs to share this Feast at the table of our Lord. But we know that we cannot remain here where it is quiet. We must go over there, to suffer with our Lord; to face the crowd and to share His pain.[71]

---

[70] John Mulloy, "Bishops' Evaluation of 'Call to Action' Will Be Crucial," W, 12-9-76.
[71] Jim Wright, "A Call to Action: The Story of One Delegate," W, 11-25-76.

The same day, during the session, Jim Wright had an experience that could almost be called a vision:

> While I sat there, I could think only of the beautiful words of the homily that morning. As I listened to the crowd, this strange vision came into my mind. I saw Christ larger than life, hanging upon a giant cross in front of the stands where the delegates were seated. I saw an official-looking man standing at the chairman's podium addressing the crowd. "Shall the amendment to save this man be considered?" I heard him say. "All those in favor, say yes." "Yes," I blurted out, but I realized that my voice was one of a very few. "All those opposed say no," the man added, to which the crowd returned with a single deafening voice: "No."[72]

And thus begins the catacomb age of Catholics in America, struggling to live out their Christian faith in the midst of a Church whose outward institutions are increasingly hostile to them and everything they stand for. If there was a watershed event in this progress toward the catacombs, it was without any doubt the Detroit Call to Action, the historical point where the enemies of Christ took control of the Church's institutions. The ultimate victim of the takeover was none other than Christ Himself, and He will be the ultimate witness against them as well. In the meantime, those of us still left must suffer with Him and fight for Him, seeking to rebuild His city, knowing that we may not see it in our lifetimes but can salute it from afar (*Hebrews* 11:13). Only now can we begin to understand the events in the Church's history that led up to this takeover, as well as those which followed it. As Aristotle would say, let us therefore make a beginning.

---

[72] Ibid.

PART TWO: *HUMANAE VITAE* — THE CHURCH STANDS FIRM

In the parable, the weeds sown by an enemy are allowed to grow with the grain until harvest. Humanae Vitae *seems the first swing of the scythe that harvests the grain of faith and prepares the weeds for burning*

— Frank Morriss

It will be a strange twist if the orthodox Catholic has to join the hippie and the peacenik in civil disobedience, but this could well be demanded of him, as it was demanded in pagan Roman times.

The Roman Catholic Church remains the only organized body in the world today that apparently can or will oppose secular governments in their attempts to control human life without regard to moral principle. That she will *oppose them is now assured; that is the providential meaning of* Humanae Vitae.

— K.D. Whitehead

1. A DECISIVE BATTLE BEGINS

Readers who have just struggled through the account of the institutional takeover of the Church by the 1976 Detroit Call to Action crowd may feel more than a little discouraged. That is understandable. But it is important to remember that institutional power is not the only kind of power. It is not even the principal form power takes within the Church. Before we can understand the agony of the twentieth-century Church, we must transpose the whole discussion to the level of the power of the Spirit. There we see a rather different landscape.

The Call to Action was the Catholic left's great victory when it came to the seizure of social power. Yet, the left may already have lost a decisive battle on the level of spiritual warfare, unlikely though that may seem on the surface. I am talking about the battle over *Humanae Vitae*, Pope Paul VI's encyclical reaffirming Catholic teaching on contraception. The left lost that battle because all its efforts and all its social power failed to get the teaching Church to budge on an issue which is at the very center of man's moral and spiritual life, because it involves the giving and receiving of both love and life. Catholic progressives did indeed succeed in getting millions of Catholic married couples to practice contraception, yet they failed miserably and are still failing miserably in their effort to get a Pope to change the Church's teaching on contraception. What the left needed in the contraception dispute was not merely the power to get people to act in a certain way, but, more important, *legitimacy* for its program. *Humanae Vitae* was, and still is, the great stumbling block to that program. It is the bitter, indigestible lump which the left can neither swallow nor regurgitate. It may well be the stumbling block that will crush them.

Like all the spiritual diseases that afflict today's Church, the disease of contraception was, to use a medical term, "insidious" in its onset. Middle-aged people like me remember when Catholic teaching against artificial birth control was like one of the four pillars that support the cosmos, something fixed and immovable. That being the case, much of the early debate on birth control took place outside the Church, focusing not so much on the morality of contraception *per se*, as on the morality of government involvement in family planning and population control, something that was regarded with horror not only by Catholics, but probably by the majority of Protestants as well. One of the earliest references in *The Wanderer* to this subject was an article in the January 7, 1960 issue reporting that a certain Mrs. A. Powell Davies (have you ever noticed how often people who prescribe family planning for *other* people bear these aristocratic names?) had taken President Eisenhower to task for his opposition to proposals for our government to give birth control help to India and other allegedly "over-populated" nations. Mrs. Davies, speaking for the Unitarian Fellowship for Social Justice, opined that "the social and moral pronouncements of sectarian groups...should not be the criterion for presidential opinions or congressional legislation on this subject."[73] Of course, there was nothing sectarian about the Unitarian Fellowship for Social Justice. Aside from that, the attack was absurd because Eisenhower himself probably had no religious objections to contraception. His opinion was based purely on political concerns — i.e., whether the whole area of family planning was a proper concern for government at all. Yet Mrs. Davies' remarks certainly set the tone for much of the discussion that occupied the next thirty years, a discussion in which proponents of birth control, abortion, euthanasia, and so forth, consistently held to the principle that people making public policy must maintain an absolute divorce between public policy and conscience. We who today see a Church filled with pro-abortion Catholic politicians who continue to be Catholics in good

[73] "Eisenhower Criticized on Birth-Control Issue," W, 1-7-60.

standing are witnesses to the bitter harvest sown back there in the sixties.

The early battles documented in *The Wanderer* on this issue thus were not so much conflicts within the Church herself but conflicts between the Church, with her consistent affirmation of the goodness of the creation and thus of new human life, and the secular world, which was increasingly seeing new life as a curse and as a threat to those who already had life and preferred not to share it — a profoundly anti-Christian attitude. Bishop Fulton J. Sheen, in a *Wanderer* article, took aim at the anti-life mindset in characterizing it as the "birth patrol."

> Birth patrol is a new kind of sentry affecting life. Hitler believed in birth patrol of the Jews; Stalin in birth patrol of Christians; Khrushchev in birth patrol of the Hungarians, Poles, and Ukrainians. Now there are those who would patrol life, not after it became a harvest but while it was seed in the granary. The new kind of vigilance would not wait until the fruit appeared on the tree, as did Hitler and others, but would stifle the blossoms and the buds. They would take up the watch at the border line of love and life and say, 'They shall not be born.'...The attitude of birth patrol is negative, failing to see beauty, truth, love, and life as a whole.[74]

William O. Brady, then Archbishop of St. Paul, Minnesota, put it a bit more colloquially:

> There is nothing wrong with babies but there are many things wrong with grownups. Some love money more than people. Others love cars more than cribs. But the politicians and the economists and the sociologists are right. They know that God loves babies, and that He will cooperate to make

[74] Bishop Fulton J. Sheen, "Coming of the Birth Patrol," W, 6-23-60.

> them His children, even if they should someday grow up to be complaining landlords and critical mothers-in-law.[75]

That sums up, in a gentle, humorous way, the genuine humanism of the Church's attitude toward new life. Unfortunately, since Archbishop Brady's time, the attitude of the "politicians and the economists and the sociologists" has become considerably less benign, with some honorable exceptions. Late in 1960, Colin Clark, an economist, was quoted as expressing some quite positive views on this whole population business, views which his colleagues today would do well to emulate:

> "Countries that surmount the challenge of population pressure emerge with a civilization not only wealthier, but also more cultured, more scientific, and better organized politically than that which went before." Mr. Clark declares that if all the world's arable land were cultivated according to Dutch farming methods, enough food could be produced to accommodate a total of twenty-eight billion — ten times the 1960 population — on a diet equal to that of the peoples of the most prosperous countries today.
>
> And, he adds, if Japanese methods of farming and standards of diet were used, the world could provide for "three or four times as many again."[76]

Though hardly anyone noticed at the time, 1960 seems to have witnessed the first hints of contraception becoming an issue, not only between the Church and the world, but *within* the Church as well. That happened with the appearance of the oral contraceptive *enovid*, now universally referred to simply as "the Pill," and its inventor, a nominally Catholic physician named Dr. John Rock.[77] Dr. Rock appears to have argued that since the Pill, unlike such devices as con-

---

[75] Archbishop William O. Brady, "There's Nothing Wrong with Babies," W, 9-1-60.

[76] "Population Limitation, Bad Economics," W, 12-22-60.

[77] Florence A. Burke, "A 'Catholic Doctor' on Birth Control?" W, 8-24-61.

doms and diaphragms, did not use mechanical means to prevent conception by setting up a barrier, it would not be considered contraception, at least not *artificial contraception.* That reasoning was intended, not to actually reject the Church's teaching, but to do a sort of "end run" around it. (The fact that this position was put forward by someone named "Rock" in opposition to the "Rock" on which Christ built His Church certainly suggests that God is not without a sense of humor, even when pretty grim matters are in question.) *Wanderer* contributors such as Father William Wearsch and Florence Burke lost little time opposing Dr. Rock's sophistic arguments, and Bishop Joseph T. McGucken, in a pastoral letter on the subject, summed up the Church's response to Dr. Rock in saying that "any substantial infringement of the physical integrity of the generative act, or *of the generative powers,* as such, is always immoral and is not justifiable under any circumstances"[78] (italics added). By indicating that the Church's teaching precludes, not merely the mechanical interference with the generative act, but sterilization, whether temporary or permanent, which interferes with the *power* to procreate, Bishop McGucken pretty well disposes of Dr. Rock's arguments. Of course, that prevented no one from advancing these arguments, since, even then, logic never created much of an obstacle for "Catholics" who are out to destroy their Church. The refutation of the arguments for the Pill certainly never prevented people like the ideologues of the *National Catholic Reporter,* Father Arthur McCormack, and others from advocating its use.

In a 1964 *Wanderer* editorial, A.J. Matt, Sr., responded thus to Father Arthur McCormack's argument that "right intention" could justify the use of the Pill:

> And many men and women who enter upon a marriage with the intention of enjoying all the privileges while at the same time deliberately setting aside — by whatever means — the primary purpose of marriage, namely, the procreation of

[78] Bishop Joseph T. McGucken, "The Church Has Not Changed on Birth Control," W, 5-14-64.

> children, for any purpose whatsoever including the perhaps neglected (to quote Father McCormack) "beautiful doctrine of love in marriage" — in reality contract no marriage at all and, worse, perpetuate a caricature and an attempted slap in the face of Almighty God, the Creator and Father of all![79]

In other words, it is not just the method of interfering with conception, mechanical or otherwise, which is the source of disorder, but the very intent to enjoy sex without risk of procreation (even natural family planning is immoral if that happens to be its intent). Matt's article not only brings that out clearly, but also shows us vividly the spiritual and human destructiveness of the contraception mentality and the whole sexual revolution idea of which it partakes, something that, a few years later, will assume the central place in the debate. Contraception, far from advancing the growth and fulfillment of the human person, in fact destroys and dehumanizes the person, and that is what its advocates can only understand, if at all, when that destructiveness catches up with them and leads to despair and perhaps suicide.

The debate on contraception remained a somewhat sporadic thing during roughly the first half of the sixties, something people did not really see as an issue central to the life of the Church. The Council that began in 1962 occupied the limelight, after all. About 1964, the situation started to change. That was the year Pope Paul VI announced that the Church would be doing a complete study of the issue of contraception. Though he warned everyone not to contradict Church teaching while the results of that study were pending, the mere fact that such a project was undertaken at all in regard to what most Catholics had previously seen as immutable moral teaching, led people, consciously or unconsciously, to begin seeing it as an open question. That generated, in the years that followed, a growing mood of expectation that the Pope was about to change the Church's teaching.

---

[79] A.J. Matt, Sr., "What About 'Right Intention?'" W, 2-13-64.

That mood crescendoed in April, 1967, when a certain Father Charles Curran, now notorious for his unorthodox views, was dismissed from his position as a professor of theology at Catholic University of America for teaching that contraception was morally acceptable for Catholics. What made this a critical event was Catholic University's special role as a university directly commissioned by Rome to teach Catholic truth. Unorthodoxy had, of course, been popping up at Catholic universities throughout the nation, but when it cropped up at Catholic U., that directly compromised the Church's Magisterium. The Church could not (in principle, at least) retreat into the position that Father Curran was merely expressing his personal opinions and spoke for no one but himself, least of all for the Church. Father Curran's dismissal provoked a firestorm of protest from students and other faculty members, who took to the streets demanding his reinstatement. *The Wanderer*, needless to say, weighed in against reinstatement. An April 27, 1967 editorial presented *The Wanderer*'s position in no uncertain terms:

> May we add that, from what we have seen and read in the newspapers, particularly the mob scenes and noisy demonstrations at Catholic University, we would be sadly disappointed to see Father Curran reinstated in the University's theology department. First of all, why should a man be reinstated whose personal viewpoints and teachings oftentimes run contrary, as he himself boasts, to the established teachings of the Church? Have not the students, *and especially the parents of those students*, any voice and vote in the matter? Must they accept, willy-nilly, any and all teachers for their youngsters, regardless of their orthodoxy? Is not a theologian, who teaches others, subject like other Catholics, to the teaching Magisterium of the Church in all points touching on faith and morals? Or has mob rule and lynch law come to replace the divine Magisterium?[80]

[80] "Furor at Catholic University," W, 4-27-67.

Unfortunately, that question was answered with an unequivocal yes, when the university bowed to the pressure and reinstated Father Curran. That was the first real victory for the proponents of artificial birth control in the American Church, and was, as a *Wanderer* headline summed it up, a "dark hour for the Church in America." Since then, the institutions have just continued to crumble, a domino effect that never seems to stop.

The Curran affair was a case of a cowardly institution which let a mob of corrupt people with a corrupt leader force it to betray the absolute moral truths that it was obliged, under God, to promote. It is interesting to contrast that case with another removal from office, in another university and in another country. In January, 1968, the well-known British journalist, Malcolm Muggeridge, not yet a Catholic, resigned from his post as rector of Edinburgh University in Scotland, to protest the university's decision to give contraceptives and drugs to the students. No mobs occupied the streets in defense of Muggeridge. He just left. *The Wanderer* printed the text of his resignation speech. A brief quotation will give some idea of the flavor of that speech:

> So now, dear Edinburgh students, I want you to believe that this row I have had with your elected officers is nothing to do with any puritanical attitudes on my part.
> I have no belief for self-abnegation for this, nor do I wish to check any fulfillment of your lives and being.
> But whatever life is or is not about, it is not to be expressed in terms of drug stupefaction and casual sexual relationships.
> However else we may venture into the unknown, it is not, I assure you, on the plastic wings of *Playboy* magazine and psychedelic fantasy.[81]

That is quite a contrast. A gutless institution yielding to mob pressure to let an apostate gut the moral teachings of the Church, versus a courageous individual standing up against an institution's attack

[81] "An Act of High Principle," W, 2-1-68.

on those moral teachings. It is all the more impressive when one considers that this courageous individual was not even a Catholic (he finally became one in 1982) but was merely an honest man who saw, in the institutional subsidizing of contraception, a fundamental attack on the natural law and on the dignity of man. His was the prophetic position. Catholic U.'s was the position of those who, throughout history, have bowed and scraped to the false prophets while persecuting and sometimes killing the real ones. The contrast says it all.

Fortunately, the Church's teaching office, or Magisterium, was not entirely without defenders during this period. Father Lawrence P. Everett, in an April 24, 1968 *Wanderer* essay, ably supported Catholic teaching on contraception while making it very clear that it was precisely this Magisterium which was at stake, an important point to make on what turned out to be the eve of *Humanae Vitae*'s appearance:

> There are times when the Holy Father will instruct the faithful in matters of faith or morals *without intending* that his teaching be infallible.
>
> However, if the Catholic bishops of the world agree that what the Pope says is part of God's revealed word, then the Holy Father's teaching *automatically* becomes a matter of divine and Catholic faith and, therefore, infallible. Technically, this is known as the ordinary and universal *Magisterium* of the Church....An example of a doctrine which is infallible from the teaching of the ordinary and universal Magisterium of the Church is the immorality of contraception.
>
> Pope Pius XI and Pope Pius XII clearly taught that artificial means of birth control are *against the law of God.* However, even if they did not specify their teaching to be infallible, the Catholic bishops of the world agreed with these pronouncements of the Popes. The bishops and their priests taught it to

> the faithful. Consequently, it is infallible that artificial means of birth control are against the law of God.[82]

These events give a pretty good idea where we all were during the period just before July, 1968, when Pope Paul VI gave his landmark encyclical, *Humanae Vitae*, to the world. Unfortunately, not everyone in the world appreciated the gift equally. I know of no single event in the history of the modern Church which provoked quite the amount and bitterness of controversy that this encyclical, reaffirming Catholic teaching on birth control, provoked. What particularly enraged progressive Catholics was the fact that the special commission the Holy Father had appointed to study the issue had, in its final report, recommended that he change Catholic teaching to permit contraception, yet the Pope had chosen to side with the tradition against the commission. To the progressivists, this meant that Paul had put his own private opinion ahead of the findings of a group of experts, something positively un-American. That commission, to the progressives, somehow represented the voice of the people, the voice of the democratic consensus, while Pope Paul's encyclical was, to them, the voice of benighted authoritarianism. The sheer bitterness and nastiness and pettiness of the personal attacks on Pope Paul was one of the sorriest aspects of this whole controversy.

Just to give the reader a feeling for the flavor, the atmosphere, of the bitter controversy which raged in the aftermath of *Humanae Vitae's* appearance (many readers, unlike this author, may be too young to remember it), here is a sampling of *Wanderer* headlines for that period:

> "Pope Paul VI Reaffirms Church's Teaching On Marriage"
> "Prelates Acclaim Encyclical"
> "Encyclical Draws Opposition"
> "Priests Back Encyclical"
> "Conformity to Encyclical a Measure of Catholic Fidelity"
> "Superiors Pledge Loyalty to Pope"

[82] Father Lawrence P. Everett, "The Teaching Church," W, 4-25-68.

"Dissenting Theologians Are Wrong"
"K.C. Chief Deplores Lay Criticism of Encyclical"
"British Priest Dissents from Encyclical — Suspended"
"Irish Theologian Suspended"
"Central Union Vows Loyalty to Paul VI"
"Mexican Bishops Uphold Encyclical"
"Temper Tantrums Don't Sway the Magisterium"
"Theologians Mislead Catholics"
"'Cephas' Supports Pope Paul"
"Priest Dissenters Labeled Traitors"
"No Concessions from Dissenters...Bishops, Theologians"
"Physicians Guild Backs Encyclical"
"Card. O'Boyle Calls Priests to Obey"
"Dissenters Under Fire"
"'Humanae Vitae': The Stubborn Truth"
"Dissent on Encyclical Halts Theology Forum"
"Catholic U. Trustees Meet to Consider Dissent"
"Encyclical Opposition Shocks Bishop"
"Dissenters Distort the Facts"
"Pope Paul VI...Decries 'Corrosive Criticism'"
"Italian, New York Bishops Back Encyclical"
"Columnist Charges Dissenters Try to Undermine Papal Authority"
"Dissenters Interrupt Mass at Cathedral"
"Cardinal O'Boyle Disciplines Dissenting Priests"
"Pope Paul Calls for Loyalty"
"The Nagging Church"
"Cardinal Felici Reprimands Dissenters"
"Obedience to the Church Essential"
"Indian Bishops Support Encyclical"
"Priests Must Accept Papal Teachings"
"14 U.S. Bishops Declare Support of 'Humanae Vitae'"
"The Binding Force of 'Humanae Vitae'"
"Methodist Bishop Hails Encyclical"
"Philippine Bishops Back 'Humanae Vitae'"

"Prelate Raps Dissident Theologians"
"Corrigan-Marra Debate Encyclical"
"The Encyclical Crisis Really Is a Crisis"
"Trahison des Clercs"
"U.S. Bishops' Pastoral Letter...Confesses Binding Force of 'Humanae Vitae'"
"Cardinal Felici Warns Dissenters"
"Dissenting from the Dissenters"
"Pope Paul Denounces Dissident Clergy"
"Scientists Protest Encyclical"
"An Unscientific Declaration"
"Jesuit Says Encyclical Is Infallible"
"Episcopal Commentary on 'Humanae Vitae' Hit by Vatican"
"Pakistani Bishops Praise 'Humanae Vitae'"
"Rhodesian Bishops Support 'Humanae Vitae'"
"Philosophers Affirm Loyalty to Pope"
"Polish Bishops Defend 'Humanae Vitae'"
"'Humanae Vitae' Final and Binding"
"Theologian Declares...Encyclical Dissenters Are Not Authentic Pastors of Christ"

This is not exactly an academic debate among gentlemen who will go out for a beer afterward and forget the whole thing. The parties to this debate are after blood. Clearly, this is a debate that involves the most basic of first principles, a debate in which not only the Church's right to teach, but the very meaning of life and love, and, in a way, of God's creation, is at stake. It is small wonder that the Holy Father himself, in talking about the encyclical, remarked that "never as at this point have we so felt the burden of our office." One gets the impression that, had Pope Paul been able to see his way clear to supporting his commission's recommendation and declaring contraception morally acceptable, no one would have been happier than he. Yet somehow he was not able to take the easy way, the way that would have been, humanly speaking, the path of least resistance. Somehow, his conscience forced him to take the course that he must have known would outrage millions and millions of respected and influential people, inside and outside the Church. If ever there was an event in which the presence of the Holy Spirit protecting the Church from error was clearly evident, this was it. The Christian truth had to be proclaimed in its absoluteness, without compromise, and the masses of respectable, influential people who see truth as a malleable substance to be molded to the desires and needs of the times made no difference when it came to that imperative. When *Humanae Vitae* appeared, we saw a genuine hero of the faith, cursed and maligned and ridiculed by millions, having the courage to speak the hard and difficult and unpopular truth instead of the easy and popular untruth.

The response of the *Wanderer* editorial staff to the encyclical showed a solid grasp of what was at stake. An August 8, 1968 editorial summed it up this way:

> The crisis of the Church in our day is not, in the first place, the question of birth control, nor of priestly celibacy, nor of the relevance of Catholic schools, or the decline of vocations or of the missionary spirit. All these things are mere symptoms, serious enough in themselves, but nevertheless only symptoms of a far deeper crisis: the crisis of belief in the Church as the divinely instituted and infallible teacher of the Word of God and dispenser of His sacramental means for eternal salvation.
>
> It is this crisis with which Pope Paul is most deeply concerned, as his public addresses and pronouncements have borne witness with increasing frequency in recent months. And it is this crisis he has now challenged face to face with the reassertion of the Church's divine commission to be Mother and Teacher of the Nations — first with his magnificent *Credo of the People of God* issued at the closing of the Year of Faith on June 30th, recalling the faithful to the fundamental dogmas of Christian belief, and now with the en-

cyclical *Humanae Vitae*, recalling them to the will of God in the fundamental concerns of human life.[83]

The complete text of *Humanae Vitae* was published by *The Wanderer* on August 8, 1968. If we are to understand why such a ferocious battle raged over a papal document, why the concerns of the encyclical were so absolutely central not just to the Christian life but also to all human life and love, we need to review, at least briefly, the document itself, then look more closely at the ways in which the many parties to the debate, in 1968 and the years since then, have responded to its teaching.

There are, in my view, three aspects of the encyclical's teaching which are of special importance to our times and which *The Wanderer* and its contributors have addressed again and again over the years:

1) The teaching of the encyclical is a profoundly humanistic one, despite all the claims of its detractors to the contrary. The Holy Father's teaching, in this encyclical, is steeped in the genuine Christian humanism which never ceases to affirm the value and dignity of man and of the human person as a child of God. Implicit in this Christian humanism, and constantly present in the encyclical, is an incarnational understanding of man, one which sees man as a true composite of body and soul, not as merely a biological organism, nor as merely a detached intellect or soul, nor as merely both of these accidentally linked together, but as a genuinely incarnate being, an embodied spirit transcending matter but at the same time deeply embedded in and involved in matter, working out its spiritual destiny within and through God's beautiful material creation. All this in contrast to the dualism typical of modern thought since Descartes.

2) The encyclical is an outstanding expression of modern man's struggle against the terrible social and spiritual disorder which has led, again and again, to totalitarian regimes which, in rejecting love and devaluing human life, dehumanize mankind.

[83] "The Challenge of the Magisterium," W, 8-8-68.

3) Finally, *Humanae Vitae* brilliantly upholds and defends the Church's right and duty to teach mankind about the right order and love which are integral to man's vocation as a creature made in God's image, and thus to play the role of the prophet. *The Wanderer*, in the aftermath of the encyclical, defended this right of the Church against a disordered world, and in the process played a truly prophetic role itself.

In the sections which follow, we will look at these aspects one at a time, as seen and witnessed to by *The Wanderer* and its contributors.

2. *HUMANAE VITAE*'S HUMANISM

The critics of Catholic teaching on contraception have always accused the Church of seeing sex and procreation as merely biological processes. In effect, they say this — that the Church looks at the biological process of reproduction and says, on solely biological grounds, that procreation is clearly the purpose of this process. It is immoral to use something for an end other than that for which it was created, and therefore it is immoral to use sex purely for pleasure, or purely as an expression of the love between man and woman. But that, it is argued, means viewing sex and procreation exclusively in their aspect as processes we share with the animals, and not taking their properly human aspect into account. After all, sex is also a way in which a man and woman express their love for each other, and thus has a purpose other than the "merely biological" one of procreation. It also has a spiritual purpose. Perhaps Pope Paul's greatest achievement in *Humanae Vitae* was to deal with that objection head-on, first of all by explicitly affirming the goodness of human sexuality as a composite material and spiritual reality, to be affirmed and loved in both these aspects. Speaking of conjugal love, he says:

> This love is first of all fully human, that is to say, of the senses and of the spirit at the same time. It is not, then, a simple transport of instinct and sentiment, but also, and principally, an act of the free will, intended to endure and grow by means of the joys and sorrows of daily life, in such a way that husband and wife become one only heart and one only soul, and together attain their human perfection.[84]

In a way, the error of those who tax the Church with seeing sex in too biological a way is that they themselves are to some extent involved in a kind of dualism of body and spirit. They themselves see the

---

[84] "The Complete Text of *Humanae Vitae*," W, 8-8-68.

whole issue as one between sex as a merely biological, bodily act, and sex as a "spiritual" act in which love is expressed. Their argument for permitting contraception is, in effect, that when, for whatever reason, the purely biological outcome of the act (i.e., a baby) would be undesirable or inconvenient, the spiritual outcome, the expression of love, remains a good and ought to be pursued. While they might acknowledge that sex is both a bodily and a spiritual reality, they fail to see these two aspects of the one reality as indissolubly bound together, because they are caught up in a dualism between the "merely biological" outcome of the sexual act, and the "properly human," spiritual outcome. When it comes to the situations where the (allegedly) merely biological outcome is seen as undesirable, the contraceptionist can be just as dualistic as any Manichaean in seeing matter as an evil which enslaves man and from which the spirit seeks to escape. What Pope Paul is doing, in contrast, is precisely affirming the properly human way of seeing sexuality. He is saying that, for man, as an incarnate being, there is really nothing "merely biological," nor is there anything "purely spiritual" (that is why the Church sees the doctrine of the Resurrection as so central to our faith — a merely spiritual life with God in eternity would be insufficient because it would not save the whole man but only part of him. Thus we are taught that our life in Heaven after death but before the general resurrection, however happy it may be, will be incomplete as long as our bodies are not there to share in that happiness).

Thus the contraceptionists may accuse the Church of dualism in her teaching, but in reality it is they who are the dualists, and and it is the Church which proceeds from a genuinely integral image of man, an image which denies the possibility of any legitimate separation between body and spirit. Pope Paul makes this very clear when, continuing to speak of conjugal love, he says: "And finally, this love is fecund, for it is not exhausted by the communion between husband and wife, but is destined to continue, raising up new lives."[85] It is thus of the very essence of the love between man and woman, pre-

[85] Ibid.

cisely because it is something integrally human, that it creates new life — love must create, love must give life. The giving of life is of the very essence of love — it is not some accidental appendage which can easily be disposed of. It is the effort to dispose of it that is dehumanizing and violates love.

Pope Paul goes on to spell this out with even greater clarity:

> In the task of transmitting love, therefore, they [husband and wife] are not free to proceed completely at will, as if they could determine in a wholly autonomous way the honest path to follow; but they must conform their activity to the creative intention of God, expressed in the very nature of marriage and of its acts, and manifested by the constant teaching of the Church.
>
> That teaching, often set forth by the Magisterium, is founded upon the inseparable connection, willed by God and unable to be broken by man on his own initiative, between the two meanings of the conjugal act: the unitive meaning and the procreative meaning. Indeed, by its intimate structure, the conjugal act, while most closely uniting husband and wife, capacitates them for the generation of new lives, according to laws inscribed in the very being of man and woman. By safeguarding both these essential aspects, the unitive and the procreative, the conjugal act preserves in its fullness the sense of true mutual love and its ordination toward man's most high calling to parenthood.[86]

What he is saying is that when, by making the sexual act incapable of giving new life, we separate the unitive aspect, the expression of love, from the procreative, the act is diminished, not just as a procreative act, but also as a unitive act. It becomes less fully an expression of love and more an act of egoistic pleasure-seeking on the part of both partners. Thus the Holy Father concludes this part of the discussion by saying that:

---

[86] Ibid.

> ...To make use of the gift of conjugal love while respecting the laws of the generative process means to acknowledge oneself not to be the arbiter of the the sources of human life, but rather the minister of the design established by Creator. In fact, just as man does not have unlimited dominion over his body in general, he has no such dominion over his generative faculties as such, because of their intrinsic ordination toward raising up life, of which God is the principle.[87]

The Wanderer's treatment of the encyclical, which it analyzed in depth, did not fail to appreciate the humanism of *Humanae Vitae*. Archbishop John D. Murphy of Cardiff, Wales, went so far as to call the encyclical a "Magna Carta for mankind": "Make no mistake about this encyclical. There may be a contemporary clamor, drowning the quiet relief of many and the heroic acceptance of the disappointed, but when the history of these days comes to be written, this encyclical will be hailed as the Magna Carta, not merely of all women but of all men and all children."[88] Father John H. Ryder, in an article entitled "'Humanae Vitae': A Work of Divine Providence," argues that there is no conflict between the Church's call for self-discipline and even asceticism in sexual matters, and a genuine humanism:

> More glorious by far than the "updated" license of the "new morality" are those passages of the encyclical where the Supreme Pastor boldly outlines the sanctifying antidote to the (artificially stimulated) lusts of the flesh: "The observance of periodic continence" which "far from harming conjugal love, rather confers upon it a higher human value," which demands continual effort "yet through which husband and

[87] Ibid.

[88] Archbishop John D. Murphy, "The Encyclical...A Magna Carta for Mankind," W, 8-15-68.

> wife fully develop their personalities, being enriched with spiritual values."[89]

Father George A. Floris, in an article appearing October 10, 1968, underscores the fact that Catholic advocates of contraception have undercut their own arguments by appealing to the inseparability of the unitive and procreative aspects of sex: "...The question is inconsistent in its implications by applying a double standard to human nature. It tries to suggest that, whereas we ought not suppress the conjugal act in its unitive capacity, we should be free to suppress it in its procreative capacity."[90]

Joseph Hoeffner, Archbishop of Münster, Germany, bears eloquent witness to the incarnational picture of man which pervades *Humanae Vitae*:

> The teaching of the encyclical does not originate in "biological processes" but in nature as the essential structure of man as such, that is to say, that which metaphysically determines man as man....The objective moral order is determined by the total view of man, that is, by man's essential structure. Naturally, this does not exclude the fact that biological processes play a role in the total human picture. Murder, abortion, and sterilization are intrusions into "biological" realities. Their moral evaluation comes, however, from a total view of man. If the encyclical *Humanae Vitae* were to argue only biologically and physiologically, as it is accused of doing, it would, in order to be consistent, have to end by giving complete approval to free manipulation. With animals, where it would be valid to consider biological-physiological aspects exclusively, *all* manipulation is allowable (artificial insemination, abortion, etc.)....The question of such manipulation of human beings in the sexual sphere must

---

[89] Father John H. Ryder, S.J., "'Humanae Vitae': A Work of Divine Providence," W, 10-3-68.

[90] Father George A. Floris, "The Nagging Church," W, 10-10-68.

> be seen in the larger context of the manipulating of man as such. Whether and to what extent man may be manipulated by intrusion into his bodily (physical and psychological) structure is a fearful problem, especially today in view of scientific and medical possibilities.[91]

The American bishops' pastoral, *Human Life in Our Day*, printed in full in the November 28, 1968 issue, also sought, in giving its support to the Holy Father, to emphasize the humanistic, incarnational teaching of *Humanae Vitae*:

> The Christian ascetic of chastity, within and outside marriage, honors the sanctity of life and protects the dignity of human sexuality. Were there no revelation nor religion, civilization itself would require rational discipline of the sexual instinct. Revelation, however, inspires chastity with more sublime purposes and creative power. In chaste love, the Christian, whether his vocation be to marriage or to celibacy, expresses love for God Himself. In the case of spouses, marital chastity demands not the contradiction of sexuality, but its ordered expression in openness to life and fidelity to love which means also openness and faithfulness to God.[92]

It is important to understand here that the Pope's teaching, notwithstanding the accusations of ignoramuses to the effect that it sees human sexuality solely as a means of producing babies, in reality rejects any separation of the unitive from the procreative, including the separation that seems to favor procreation. Thus the papal teaching, applied to things like artificial insemination and *in vitro* fertilization, clearly teaches that it is immoral in the extreme for people to procreate in a way that excludes the expression of love through the sexual act. When that happens, something is lost, in a way, even from the procreative side. As Joseph Cardinal Ratzinger

[91] Bishop Joseph Hoeffner, "Appreciation of 'Humanae Vitae,'" W, 10-17-68.
[92] "Human Life in Our Day," W, 11-28-68.

pointed out years later, a child has a right to be the product of his parents' love for each other, and a child who is not a product of that love has really and truly lost something. The American bishops' statement makes this clear:

> Both conciliar and papal teaching, therefore, emphasize that the interrelation between the unitive meaning and the procreative meaning of marriage is impaired, even contradicted, when acts expressive of marital union are performed without love on the one hand and without openness to life on the other....The encyclical *Humanae Vitae* is not a negative proclamation seeking only to prohibit artificial methods of contraception. In full awareness of population problems and family anxieties, it is a defense of life and of love, a defense which challenges the prevailing spirit of the times. Long-range judgments may well find the moral insights of the encyclical prophetic and its worldview providential....The encyclical is a positive statement concerning the nature of conjugal love and responsible parenthood, a statement which derives from a global vision of man, an integral view of marriage, and the first principles, at least, of a sound sexuality.[93]

Carrying the debate over the encyclical into 1969, K.D. Whitehead commends *Humanae Vitae* for its affirmation of the goodness and value of the human person as a free moral agent acting in partnership with God in the work of creation:

> [Catholic teaching on contraception] is, in fact, a thread in the seamless robe of God's entire moral plan for men, as revealed in the Scriptures and in the teachings of the Church. Though it flies in the face of much that the modern world accepts as a matter of course about sex and marriage, it is nevertheless consistent with everything the Church teaches about the meaning and purpose of human life and human sexuality.

[93] Ibid.

> Is modern society so successful in meeting human needs that its evaluation of the morality of contraception is to be preferred uncritically to the Church's evaluation?...But in the single area of the creation of new human life, man *does* have a special vantage point; he is in on what God is doing; this is an enormously important fact. And my contention therefore is this: because man and wife make the decision and perform the action in accordance with which God will create new life, their decision and action here should be free moral acts. Especially here, though the same should be true of the other decisions and actions of their lives as well. When God created man, according to the Book of Genesis, He placed him in the world expecting him to act autonomously....The point is that the use of artificial contraceptives is not consonant with the character of a free moral act which should accompany the responsible decision of married couples to allow or limit conception (creation of a new life by God). A decision to limit conception by abstaining from the conjugal act during times when conception might take place, however, is a free moral act of the kind which should characterize the life of the Christian.[94]

Almost ten years later, Bishop Thomas A. Welsh of Arlington, Virginia, picks up this same theme, the profound humanism of *Humanae Vitae*, in a Pastoral letter entitled "Humanae Vitae: A Sign of Christ's Love":

> Among the most common criticisms of the Church's teaching is that it pays too much attention to the "physical act" or the "biological process." The criticism is weak in two major ways. First, there is nothing merely physical or merely biological in man. He is human down to and beyond the DNA. structure. To call an act "physical" or "biological" which strikes so deeply into his personal existence is to ignore the

[94] K.D. Whitehead, "The Mystery of Contraception," W, 6-26-69.

> most significant findings of psychology....Secondly, the criticism is weak because it ignores the indivisible oneness of man. It suggests a separation between body and spirit which might do credit to Descartes, but hardly reflects the best of contemporary scholarship.[95]

In 1980, E. Michael Jones, now editor of *Culture Wars*, gave his own inimitable twist to the issue by showing that contraception violates the human person in violating the very essence of human sexuality, especially the sexuality of women, this despite the fact that so-called feminists advocate contraception as necessary to the liberation of women. Contraception might give people, especially women, a kind of control over their own bodies, but it is a control which is achieved only by treating the body as a machine, as matter to be manipulated, not as the irreducibly bodily-spiritual, incarnate being which is the human person:

> Women "thingify" female sexual nature in order to get control of it, yet once they sacrifice female nature, they as women are no longer in control. If the woman sees her body as an object to be used for her own pleasure, how can she expect men to treat it or her any differently?...Each advance in power means relinquishing a dimension of being female. Abortion nullifies woman as the nurturer of life, contraception her ability to conceive it. Yet each time women relinquish their own sexuality to get power, the power they get only conforms them to the sexual orientation of men. Instead of repudiating an essentially male-oriented, predatory, "hit and run" sexuality, women, in the name of liberation, espouse it themselves. Through contraception a woman changes her sexuality — its demands and its rhythms — to the essentially male pattern of instant availability. Instead of the long-term sexuality of the woman, which includes nurtur-

[95] Bishop Thomas A. Welsh, "'Humanae Vitae': A Sign of Christ's Love," W, 8-10-78.

> ing, giving birth, and breast-feeding, women through contraception are made to conform themselves to the male standard of sexuality, which is intercourse with no lasting effects.[96]

Jones is famous in some circles for his unique ability to say things that outrage liberals, especially feminists, but there is no real secret to this. It is just a matter of stating the obvious truths that most other people are too polite, or too "sensitive," to state, as the passage quoted above illustrates so well.

Humanae Vitae, attacked for 25 years now by people who call themselves humanists, thus turns out to represent the truly humanistic teaching of the Church. That genuine humanism could not help but have profound implications for the social order.

---

[96] E. Michael Jones, "Feminism and Contraception," W, 10-6-80.

3. *HUMANAE VITAE*'S DEFENSE OF THE SOCIAL ORDER

Humanae Vitae outspokenly affirmed the goodness of man as a child of God made in God's image and called to cooperate with God in the work of creating new life. That is what man is in the order of creation, what God meant him to be from the beginning. But of course we know that the order of creation, which includes the presence of the image of God in us humans, has been terribly damaged and disfigured by sin. That harm has meant a disordered, disfigured image of God, one in which those aspects of human life that are supposed to form together an ordered, harmonious whole, tend to be split apart and distorted. Thus the unitive and procreative sides of sexuality, intended by God to be inseparable, do in fact get torn apart by sin. When that happens, people seek the satisfaction of lust to the exclusion of children, destroying both the unitive and the procreative, or they seek to produce children in a laboratory without love. That anyone should attempt either project attests to the presence of spiritual disorder, which darkens and distorts the image of God. Since man is a social being by his very nature, that disorder affects not just his individual life, but the life of the community. Disorder in the soul produces disorder in society. That is why Pope Paul was not content merely to show that contraception produces disorder in the individual person. He also found it necessary to show that it produces tremendous social disorder, culminating in totalitarianism if it goes far enough. Evil, left to itself, keeps on growing (perhaps we should say metastasizing).

Perhaps the most obvious social disorder stemming directly from contraception is the widespread use of sex in a way that neither expresses love nor produces life, but merely exploits other persons for one's own pleasure. Pope Paul, speaking prophetically, made the point in *Humanae Vitae* that "it is also to be feared that the man, growing used to the employment of anti-conceptive practices, may finally lose respect for the woman and, no longer caring for her physical and psychological equilibrium, may come to the point of considering her as a mere instrument of selfish enjoyment, and no longer as his respected and beloved companion."[97] When that happens, there is no longer a community of man and woman, just an arena for combat between them. It is not difficult to see how the worst evils of contemporary feminism came out of that situation. If there is no community of man and woman, then the only thing left is the struggle to decide which of them will run things. The family cannot flourish in that kind of atmosphere. Pope Paul adds that, "in defending conjugal morals in their integral wholeness, the Church knows that she contributes toward the establishment of a truly human civilization; she engages man not to abdicate from his own responsibility in order to rely on technical means; by that very fact she defends the dignity of man and wife."[98]

Archbishop John D. Murphy, emphasizing the destructive effect of contraception on the family, has this to say:

> The Pope has refused to bow to the compassionate plea of those who in a sincere desire to strip woman of her anxieties would strip her of all dignity and status and reduce her to a mere chattel of her lord. He has refused to offer contraceptives to man as a cheap way of controlling his instincts and avoiding his responsibilities....The parents who can do nothing with their children are frequently the parents who can do nothing with themselves. They have looked at the cost of mastery, found it too high a price to pay, and chosen the artificial remedy.[99]

C. Cardinal Journet, discussing the encyclical in an October 24, 1968 article, remarks that "without [light coming from God Himself] this theme remains misunderstood, perhaps even irritating. With it, this

---

[97] "The Complete Text of *Humanae Vitae*," W, 8-8-68.

[98] Ibid.

[99] Archbishop John D. Murphy, "The Encyclical...A Magna Carta for Mankind," W, 8-15-68.

theme opens up a vision of fidelity to God and to His whole Gospel, and consequently of a vast program of restoration of human dignity at all levels — family, social, political; in short, a future of confidence in life."[100] As spiritual disorder begets social chaos, spiritual order begets social order.

On November 28, 1968, just a few months after the appearance of *Humanae Vitae*, *The Wanderer* printed the full text of the American Catholic bishops' pastoral, *Human Life in Our Day*. That pastoral, speaking out against both contraception and its evil offspring, abortion, warns eloquently of the destructive effects on the social order to be expected when man turns against God's laws regarding the transmission of new life:

> At this tense moment in our history when external wars and internal violence make us so conscious of death, an affirmation of the sanctity of human life by renewed attention to the family is imperative. Let society always be on the side of life. Let it never dictate, directly or indirectly, recourse to the prevention of life or to its destruction in any of its phases; neither let it require as a condition of economic assistance that any family yield conscientious determination of the number of its children to the decision of persons or agencies outside the family.[101]

The handwriting was already on the wall in 1968 in regard to the destructive role the state was to play in pushing both contraception and abortion, and thus undermining the very social order it is called to protect. In 1968, the American bishops saw that clearly (would that they had retained that vision and that clarity). The totalitarian possibilities in the situation became clearer in July, 1969, when President Richard M. Nixon called for increased government involvement in population control. A *Wanderer* editorial at that time took the President to task in no uncertain terms:

---

[100] C. Cardinal Journet, "The Light of the Encyclical," W, 10-24-68.
[101] "Human Life in Our Day," W, 11-28-68.

> Behind the humane-sounding phraseology of the President's message is the implicit assertion that the state has a right to intervene into the sacred precincts of the family — into the very soul of a person — to cajole, to persuade, to insist that persons — whom God has made a little less than angels — must descend to a state lower than the animals if humankind is to "save" itself from overpopulation.[102]

Congressman John C. Schmitz, speaking in the U.S. Congress against President Nixon's population bill, underscored the destructive social effects of the contraceptive mentality by showing that the widespread practice of contraception is actually a form of national suicide:

> What we now see is a steady reduction of the birthrate in America, going back to 1957. Accordingly [sic] to the report of the White House National Goals Research Staff, July 4, 1970, ...it has fallen from 2.8 births per mother to less than 2.5 today. If this trend continues and is artificially accelerated by massive government programs such as the bill before us would establish, we may well see not only an end to the "baby boom" of the early 1950s, but an actual population decline resulting from a growing and officially sponsored hostility to conception.[103]

General Thomas Lane, reflecting on the threat to the family of widespread contraception, pointed out the destructive effects the practice had already had in the Protestant churches since the infamous Lambeth Conference in the 1920s gave the green light to contraception:

> Since the Lambeth Conference accepted birth control, immorality has increased....I believe that a serious study of

[102] "Who Will Stand Against This Evil?" W, 7-31-69.

[103] Congressman John C. Schmitz, "The Contraceptive Mentality Invites National Suicide," W, 12-3-70.

> these decades would identify the Christian acceptance of birth control as the breach in the citadel of Christian family life. The Lambeth Conference merely accepted what had been a growing practice in the community; but that church sanction, approving what had theretofore been regarded as sinful, legalized the destruction of the Christian family.[104]

An especially horrendous trend that emerged during the early 1970s was the movement to furnish young people, teenagers, with contraceptives, a movement that has borne horrible fruit in our days in the epidemic of teenage pregnancies, levels of venereal disease previously unheard of, and teen suicide. Charles Rice, writing in the August 19, 1971 *Wanderer*, made a truly prophetic statement about this trend:

> First, if doctors insist on the right to give contraceptives to children, they will also claim the right to perform abortions on them with a similar lack of restraint and parental consent. This will be particularly true when prostaglandins and other types of abortion pills advance beyond their present experimental stage.
>
> Second, the doctor's function will inevitably become that of an advocate. He will persuade, and to some degree implicitly coerce, his young patient to practice contraception or to kill her child by abortion, all without knowledge on the part of her parents.
>
> Third, the result will be another substantial blow at the integrity and privacy of the family.[105]

I am certain that many very orthodox, anti-contraceptive Catholics who read this article must have thought that Rice, while meaning well, had gotten carried away with his own rhetoric and gotten caught up in prophecies of gloom and doom. Yet the gloom and doom he

[104] Thomas Lane, "Birth Control Subverts Morality," W, 6-17-71.

[105] Charles Rice, "Family Integrity Threatened by the Contraceptive Mentality," W, 8-19-71.

predicted then has all come true since. Writing on January 18, 1973, Rice drove the point home yet more forcefully:

> The Planned Parenthood usurpation of parental rights [in giving contraceptives to teens without parental consent] is but one aspect of the massive attack currently waged against the family itself. The encouragement of contraception, among adults as well as children, tends to weaken the family. For contraception involves a basic irresponsibility. It willfully and artificially separates the unitive and the procreative aspects of sex. And it tends to promote irresponsibility in the children of parents who practice it. Parents argue that children should reserve sex for marriage. But this makes sense only if sex naturally has something to do with babies, which of course it has. Many parents today, however, extol the virtues of contraception in marriage. Their children see their parents act as if sex had no essential relation to babies and as if it could therefore be legitimately used for recreation while deliberately frustrating procreation. The children therefore justly regard it as hypocrisy when their parents try to prevent them from using sex outside of marriage. *If it is legitimate to separate sex from life, it is legitimate to separate sex from marriage and ultimately it will be considered legitimate to separate life from the womb through abortion.* (Italics added)[106]

As the debate over *Humanae Vitae* raged on, it became clearer and clearer to those who took the Pope's (and the Church's) side that widespread contraception leads more or less inevitably to the breakdown of the inhibition against taking innocent human life, because, while contraception *per se* does not involve the taking of life, it does amount to man asserting over the process of creation of human life a sovereignty to which only God has a just claim. Once we have put

[106] Charles Rice, "The Remedy Can Be Found in 'Humanae Vitae,'" W, 1-18-73.

ourselves in God's place to the extent of deciding by our arbitrary will when and whether human beings will be conceived, we will find it impossible not to further usurp God's sovereignty by deciding when life shall end. Mary R. Joyce, in a 1974 article entitled "'Humanae Vitae' — Radical and Prophetic," helped clarify for *Wanderer* readers the impossible situation of those who support contraception while opposing abortion:

> While the conscious mind is affirming the practice of contraception and denying the practice of abortion, what message is the subconscious mind receiving? In his explicit thoughts the person might hold that contraceptives merely suppress biology. But his subconscious mind senses that his generative power is part of his whole self, and not just part of his anatomy and physiology. Below the level of consciousness, he "feels" that something totally human is being reduced to biology by contraceptives. At the same time, his subconscious mind strongly intuits the intimate relation between cause and effect. The person tends to think that if the procreative *cause* can be suppressed legitimately by contraceptives, or killed by sterilization, then the effect, new human life, may be similarly treated. In certain individual cases the conscious mind might block this subconscious logic, but no contracepting society has been able to block it. *Thus, a contracepting society spontaneously tends to become an aborting society.* (Italics added)[107]

And that, we all know, is precisely what happened in America. It is a reality we all need to call to mind when we hear "pro-choicers" (no one would ever be so nasty or so crude as to be pro-abortion, after all) telling us that we ought to support birth control because that would eliminate the "need" for abortions. That is the kind of argument that makes a certain sense as long as one does one's thinking at least seven levels of abstraction removed from real life. The only

[107] Mary R. Joyce, "'Humanae Vitae' — Radical and Prophetic," W, 8-8-74.

problem is that, at the level of real life, things don't happen that way. The growth of contraception leads to a growth in abortion, then infanticide, then euthanasia. No small part of the credit for exposing the delusions of the anti-life crowd, both in and out of the Church, goes to *The Wanderer* and its contributors.

A loss of respect for human life is thus one form of disorder clearly attributable to the contraceptive mentality to the extent that the latter becomes widespread in a community. Another casualty is the very institution of marriage. The commitment that a husband and wife make to each other before God is a commitment to total self-giving. That self-giving is simply incompatible with a commitment to avoid procreation, because the will to bring new life into the world is an integral part of the spouse's self-giving. To say, "I love my wife but I draw the line at bringing new life into the world," is to impose a limit on something that by its nature cannot be so limited. It is as if Christ, in the Garden of Gethsemane, had said, "Look — I didn't mind teaching these people and healing their illnesses, but this business of dying for them is going too far." We cannot imagine Christ's love for us imposing such a limit on itself. It is the very nature of Christ's love, as well as of a spouse's love, to give its very life. All genuine love is in some way the communicating of life. Monsignor Vincent Foy, commenting on *Humanae Vitae* in September, 1978, addresses this point directly:

> The more the teaching of *Humanae Vitae* is rejected, the greater the number of invalid or illicit marriages with all the resulting tears, unhappiness, or shattered lives. More and more young people, without having even read the encyclical or the Church's teaching, have been victimized. They come now in ever-increasing numbers, boldly asserting, on the basis of a newspaper article, or panel discussion, or a sermon, that they have the right over their own bodies and will decide when and whether to have children and what means they are going to use. They do not know or understand or accept what the Church affirms.... More and more do not transfer the essential rights of marriage, and so their marriages are invalid

> from the beginning. This is compounded if due care is not taken in the prenuptial investigation or preparation course. So couples often walk from the altar and out of the Church and to their own ruin. It is further compounded when the intention of one party is good and the other bad or invalidating, and one party becomes the victim of the other.[108]

That destruction of marriage cannot help but generate the destruction of the family, and hence the very basis of the social order. Furthermore, contraception creates disorder at the very center of the human person, a disorder which inevitably is destructive to all human order. No one brings this out more bluntly, more shockingly, than does Father Paul Marx, writing in the March 20, 1980 *Wanderer*:

> Theologians sometimes ask me, "What's wrong with contraception?" Invariably, I reply, "What's wrong with anal intercourse?" This retort never fails to knock them off balance. On one occasion, a theologian — after hemming and hawing — looked at me and said, "Well, what *is* wrong with anal intercourse?" It seems obvious that those who condone contraception are in no position to offer any cogent argument against homosexual acts and any other abnormal forms of sexual behavior. In the words of Peter Riga, "If the relationship between sexuality and procreation is only tenuous or accidental, then a homosexual 'marriage' has indeed the same claim to validity and respect as a true marriage."...What, then, is essentially wrong with contraception? Space does not permit a thorough discussion of this question, but one obvious answer is that contraception is a form of sexual perversion.[109]

The Wanderer is thus to be congratulated on the fact that, right from the beginning of the birth-control debate in the post-Vatican II Church, its writers consistently emphasized that contraception is not

---

108 Monsignor Vincent Foy, "A Charter of Life and Love," W, 9-21-78.
109 Father Paul Marx, "What's Wrong with Contraception?" W, 3-20-80.

just a violation of sexual morality but is an attack on the social order itself, an attack which has borne bitter fruit since the 1960s (something one can verify just by looking around). Bishop Joseph V. Sullivan of Baton Rouge, in many ways a martyr to the defense of right order against the contraception mentality, summed this up in October, 1980, in some remarks which could not be more appropriate for concluding this part of the discussion:

> The social consequences of the separation of life and love are all about us to be seen and to cause us grief. It is obvious that what we need now is not a weakening of the Catholic doctrine on contraception, but a reaffirmation of that doctrine in all its purity, all its splendor, and all its potential for showering good upon society. The sexually "liberated society" is an unlivable one. The teaching Church gives us in clear, unequivocal language the key to making that society livable again, and the way to achieve that end is by living the precepts of *Humanae Vitae*, not by undermining them.[110]

---

[110] Bishop Joseph V. Sullivan, "The Benefits of Fidelity to Humanae Vitae," W, 10-16-80.

4. THE MAGISTERIUM UNDER ATTACK

There is yet one more issue that became central in the debate over *Humanae Vitae.* That issue concerns not the substantive truth or falsehood of the encyclical, but the very right of the Holy Father to teach the encyclical's doctrine. The encyclical had hardly appeared when there arose a chorus of voices saying that the teaching was not infallible, that good Catholics could legitimately obey their "consciences" rather than the Holy Father in this matter, and so on.

Almost immediately following the appearance of *Humanae Vitae*, 200 American Catholic theologians, with Father Charles Curran, needless to say, as their ringleader, issued a statement attacking it. Basically, their attack consisted of the assertion that the encyclical's teaching was not infallible teaching and therefore was not normative for Catholics. That being the case, the Pope ought to have yielded to what by then had become majority opinion, at least among the intellectuals — i.e., the opinion that contraception was a legitimate option for Catholics, who therefore ought to be left free to follow their own consciences.

What this attack really reflected was a deep-down incapacity, on the part of Father Curran and his crowd, to even think in terms of the idea of an absolute, objective truth, a truth which is true independently of what individuals or even a majority of the people might happen to believe, and which the Church, represented by the Pope and the bishops in communion with the Pope, is empowered by the Holy Spirit to teach. Like the sophists in the time of Socrates, these people have reduced moral order to a matter of opinion, and cannot seem to understand how the Pope could possibly place his personal opinion ahead of that of the majority of Catholics. As Frank Morriss noted in the August 29, 1968 issue of *The Wanderer*, "the exercise of that competence [the Pope's teaching authority] has gone against one of the unwritten laws of this age, that no one should speak with real authority against what individual opinion may hold."[111] Father John H. Ryder, S.J., in an article entitled, appropriately enough, "'Humanae Vitae': The Stubborn Truth," spells this out even more clearly:

> The indignant ones, then, are in a daze of astonishment that a Pope could, in this way, make himself heartily disliked and distrusted by so many, opening himself at the same time to the scoldings of much of the press. These disillusioned ones assumed that, as do most humans, Pope Paul prefers to be liked rather than disliked. They can understand what he has done only on the assumption that he has acted out of a stubborn clinging to his own opinion — one which, by the way, he only inherited from previous Popes. This, certainly, is not a flattering appraisal; conduct of that kind would ill become a cultured and intelligent gentleman-theologian. But could there not be a better explanation?
>
> Could it not well be that Pope Paul risked the arousing of some animosity because it had no weight with him? Might it not be that he believed that what was at stake was not merely his, some, "theological" *opinion*? Would not such a vigorous step be justified if the Holy Father imagined he was defending and proclaiming anew an immutable divine law? As is plain for all to read in *Humanae Vitae* itself, that is exactly what he did think, and that is precisely the truth.[112]

What particularly offended the contraceptionists was the fact that the Pope had the temerity to place his teaching authority, grounded in two millennia of Christian tradition, in a position of authority transcending the commission that he had appointed to study the issue. We Americans have become devout believers in rule by committee. We are so used to the idea that once a panel of experts, a "blue-ribbon" committee of some kind, has made a recommendation on

---

[111] Frank Morriss, "Inconsistent Contraceptionists," W, 8-29-68.
[112] "'Humanae Vitae': The Stubborn Truth," W, 9-12-68.

something, the matter is ended, that we are actually somewhat scandalized when someone decides to go against such a recommendation. What is at stake here, really, is a conflict between two radically different ideas of authority. Father Rosaire Gagneret, O.P., summed this up in an October 3, 1968 article:

> It is strange to find fault with the Pope for not accepting the advice of the majority of the commission. It was up to the Pope to decide. In this task, the Holy Spirit helps him and he alone assumes the incommunicable responsibility for this decision, since it was on him that Christ conferred the authority to do so and the mission to guide the faithful to life everlasting. This mandate, this authority, this assistance cannot belong to any commission of experts, learned and prudent as they may be. The latter's function is to inform and gather data that may bring light on the decision.[113]

Probably the most frequent argument made against the teaching of *Humanae Vitae*, one that we are still hearing today, is that its teaching is not infallible and hence not binding on the consciences of Catholics. That objection seems to rest on the fact that the encyclical does not take the form of a solemn, *ex cathedra* definition of doctrine, hence is not infallible in the narrowest sense of the word (though one cannot help reflecting that if the teaching on contraception had been promulgated *ex cathedra*, the people who reject it when they find it in the encyclical would almost certainly continue to reject it). Father Curran and his friends are unable to grasp the idea that there is something called the *ordinary* Magisterium of the Church, and that that ordinary Magisterium can possess a degree of infallibility with or without a solemn definition. Infallibility stems ultimately from the fact that Christ promised that the Holy Spirit would protect the Church from error, and that promise would be empty, or nearly so, if it applied only to solemn definitions. After all, how many

[113] Father Rosaire Gagneret, O.P., "The Pope Alone May Decide," W, 10-3-68.

things has the Church ever solemnly defined? This is how I, at least, understand the matter: If the Church, for centuries and centuries, consistently teaches something on an everyday basis, to the point where the teaching becomes part of the Catholic's "world-taken-for-granted," as the doctrine on contraception certainly did, then to state that such a doctrine is not true is to deny that the Holy Spirit protects the Church from error. Now it is true that *Humanae Vitae* broke some ground to the extent that it clarified the Church's historic teaching in some ways, especially as regards the relationship between the unitive and procreative aspects of sexuality, and hence contributed to a genuine development of doctrine, in Cardinal Newman's understanding of that phrase. Nevertheless, it in no way contradicted, but rather resoundingly affirmed, that historic teaching, a teaching which can be traced back to the very early history of the Christian Church. To say that the teaching affirmed in *Humanae Vitae* is not true is thus to deny that the Holy Spirit protects the Church from error, and that would make all the Christian's beliefs on matters of faith and morals a matter of mere private opinion. That is, of course, precisely what Curran and friends want to do.

An unattributed editorial, which *The Wanderer* reprinted in November, 1968, from the Italian paper *Renovatio*, states the following:

> Now we believe that we are forced to accept the following conclusion: The substantive decisions of *Humanae Vitae* are guaranteed by the ordinary Magisterium and are, therefore, irreformable.... The teaching of the encyclical merely recapitulated the old and unchanging teaching of the Church. It appears clear, therefore, that all the conditions governing the infallible ordinary Magisterium are fulfilled in this case. The period of widespread unrest has been so brief, relatively speaking, that it does not materially affect the certitude of so many centuries of universally accepted doctrine.[114]

[114] "The Binding Force of *Humanae Vitae*," W, 11-7-68.

It is still incredible how quickly, during the post-Vatican II era, people who called themselves Catholics adopted the worldview which holds that a human being's only goal in life is to conform himself to the social and cultural world around him, accepting its principles uncritically, as if St. Paul's imperative, "Be not conformed to this world, but be transformed in newness of mind," were not a central text for all Christian living. There seems to be little room, as far as this "liberal" mentality is concerned, for the possibility that it might be a perfectly rational and appropriate thing for one man, the Pope, to stand alone if necessary against the whole world. Father John J. Hartnett, in November, 1968, discussed this aspect of the situation in an article entitled, appropriately enough, "Trahison des Clercs":

> Too many of our articulate Catholics, for one reason or another, ignore entirely the indubitable dogmatic fact that the teaching authority of the Church is a divinely founded and divinely sheltered medium of instruction, the express purpose of which is not to enable the Christian to adjust to the un-Christian environment in which he finds himself by birth and circumstance, but rather to provide guidance for the Christian, in his timeless quest, to rise above his social surroundings in an effective pursuit of divine truth....The fact that the Pope chose to go counter to the majority report (no small scandal to the progressives in the Church) of the commission established to study the question, only emphasizes the more, the irreducible difference between secular, man-centered knowledge, and supernal, God-centered (theological) knowledge, the "wisdom of the saints."[115]

Of course, that is the real crux of the matter. For the theologians who reject *Humanae Vitae* and the Magisterium behind it, there is no such thing as God-centered knowledge, and hence no such thing as an absolute truth that does not vary with the latest fads or the spirit of the

[115] Father John J. Hartnett, "Trahison des Clercs," W, 11-14-68.

age. If there is no truth, then the Pope's claim to be teaching authoritative truth is nothing more than an arrogant pretense.

Father Christopher J. O'Toole, in a 1975 article criticizing an archbishop, no less, who was willing to accept contraception in order to control the alleged population explosion, underscores the relativism which is the central factor in the rejection of the Magisterium by those who do not accept *Humanae Vitae*:

> In sum, there is evident in Archbishop Hurley's observations (1) an implicit acceptance of situation ethics; (2) the practical approval of contraception which leads logically to abortion and euthanasia; (3) the acceptance of relativism in Catholic doctrine and morals. These attitudes may prevent staunch Catholics from being considered the survivors of another age, but at what a price. They will also give comfort to other liberal theologians and to professors in seminaries who maintain that contraception and other issues connected with the Sixth Commandment are morally irrelevant in contemporary society. Finally, they will do a magnificent job of adding to the confusion under which the faithful now labor.[116]

The confusion was very great indeed by the time *Humanae Vitae* appeared. By then, not only had many of the laity pretty well internalized contemporary relativism and lack of conviction on moral issues, but a substantial number of the Catholic clergy, bishops included, had done likewise. That explains the weakness, the "wimpiness," of the Catholic bishops when it came to defending the Pope's teaching. As Joseph Gill put it:

> They [the bishops] have allowed the teaching to be ridiculed and undercut and eroded and savagely attacked in their seminaries and universities, including their own Catholic University of America, with scarcely an episcopal voice raised in its defense. On those rare occasions when one was, he was

[116] Father Christopher J. O'Toole, C.S.C., "Archbishop Hurley and World Population," W, 1-16-75.

> left to stand alone as the others quietly retired to the sidelines and shadows lest they too be torn to shreds for being so imprudent as to stand with Christ.[117]

Of course, then, as now, those who either attacked the Magisterium or failed to defend it often looked for more Catholic-sounding ways of defending their positions than pure, explicit relativism. One of these devices was to take refuge in Cardinal Newman's idea of the development of doctrine. That turned out to be not a very adequate method, as John Mulloy pointed out at the time in criticizing still another Archbishop (where did they all come from?) who was reluctant to accept the teaching of the encyclical:

> Archbishop Quinn's third argument, that the development of doctrine can be used to authorize a change in the papal teaching on contraception, is equally without substance. He simply ignores the fact that there are corruptions in doctrine as well as developments, and that any proposed change must be carefully examined to determine just what kind it is. The only legitimate developments in Catholic teaching are those which are in accord with previous teaching on the subject; all other changes are simply corruptions. They lead to the death of the teaching rather than its greater expansion.[118]

All the elements of the breakdown of the late twentieth-century Church were already implicit in the struggle over *Humanae Vitae*: Moral and theological relativism, self-centered sexual libertinism, and the absolute rejection of any authority beyond the arbitrary will of the isolated individual (referred to by many as "conscience"). Those are the makings of a crisis, spiritual, moral, and social, of the first magnitude. Like all such crises, it produced prophets, true ones as well as false ones. I would like to think that the long-suffering men and women who have put out and written *The Wanderer* during

---

[117] Joseph Gill, "What Can Be Done?" W, 10-16-80.

[118] John J. Mulloy, "Why Archbishop Quinn Wants a Change in 'Humanae Vitae,'" W, 10-30-80.

these years of crisis have made their contribution, however small, to the project of true prophesying in the face of all the false prophecy which the world loves to recognize and praise. No one, other than Pope Paul himself, seems to have spoken quite so prophetically in regard to the issue of birth control than did Joseph Gill, speaking in 1980 about the probable consequences for our bishops if they were ever to get the courage to defend *Humanae Vitae*:

> Of course, the bishops will be savagely dealt with in the media and in so-called liberal progressive circles and by no one more savagely than by those who call themselves Catholic. Their peaceful co-existence with the world will be shattered, as it ought to be. Do they believe, in the face of Christ's own words, that He came among us to bring peace to the world? Do they expect to live better lives and be treated more kindly and graciously by the world than their divine leader was treated, who was put to death in the most ignominious fashion naked on a cross? Do they wish to come to a better end in this world than He did? If they do, they have a shallow and incomplete idea of who He is and what He stands for. And they are overdue for some serious prayer and reflection on just what He expects of them.[119]

And that brings us right to the words of Christ Himself, which could not provide a more fitting conclusion to the history of the struggle over *Humanae Vitae*:

> Blessed are you when men hate you, when they exclude you and insult you and reject your name as evil, because of the Son of Man. Rejoice in that day and leap for joy, because great is your reward in heaven. For that is how their fathers treated the prophets.... Woe to you when all men speak well of you, for that is how their fathers treated the false prophets. (*Luke* 6:22, 23,26)

---

[119] Gill, "What Can Be Done?" W, 10-16-80.

PART THREE: ABORTION — THE GODLESS STATE AND THE GUTLESS CHRISTIANS

1. THE OPENING SKIRMISHES

Readers of the previous chapter may be left with the impression that the debate over contraception largely fizzled out in the Church after the early 1970s. They may be tempted to conclude that the birth control controversy was largely replaced in the public consciousness by the struggle over abortion. That is partly true. A content analysis of *The Wanderer* certainly would show that after the early seventies abortion absolutely dominates over contraception as the subject matter of the articles. Yet I would venture to say that the truth is not so much that contraception was replaced by abortion as *The Wanderer*'s focus of interest, as that contraception was absorbed into a larger frame of reference, which was and is the question: Whose property is human life? In that perspective, abortion and birth control are really the same issue. The people who advocate these practices believe that in the last analysis, man owns the processes of life and death and is free to do what he wishes with them — to bring life into being or not to bring it into being; to preserve life or to destroy it. That is a view in radical contrast to 2,000 years of Christian teaching, which holds that God alone has the right to give and to take life. Contraception and abortion may seem to be different issues, insofar as one practice merely prevents life from starting, while the other kills the already living human being, but the same demonic *hubris* is at the bottom of both — man's arrogation to himself of the rights and the authority of God Himself. When man does this, he sets himself up as a god, and thus he commits the sin of idolatry par excellence.

Only long months spent poring over old issues of *The Wanderer* can really give one a sense of the transformation that its content underwent between the early sixties and the early seventies. Even in quantitative terms, the change is impressive. At the beginning of this period, hardly any attention was given to the subject of abortion. It was possible to go a whole year without seeing a single article on the subject. When the debate did begin to warm up, it was still a question only of a thin trickle of articles, and even these dealt just about exclusively with the question whether abortion could be justified under extraordinary circumstances — for instance, a pretty direct and obvious danger to the life of the mother if the pregnancy were continued, or a strong probability that the baby, if born, would be catastrophically deformed or handicapped. In public, at least, no one was even discussing the idea of out-and-out abortion on demand, for any reason or no reason. For instance, in a 1960 article, Florence A. Burke, R.N., responded to a *Woman's Home Companion* article advocating abortion in certain cases. We know right away that we are looking back at a different universe when we realize that her arguments are dedicated solely to discrediting the "hard case" justifications of abortion, as when she cites an obstetrician who had stated that "anyone performing a therapeutic abortion today does it because he is either ignorant of modern methods of treating the complications of pregnancy, or else he is unwilling to take the time to treat them."[120] Arguments about "choice" just don't seem to have surfaced yet.

Yet the limited debate about abortion in "hard cases" did represent a foot in the door for the abortion mentality. After all, the difference between advocacy for abortion in cases of danger to the life of the mother, rape, and incest, and advocacy of unlimited abortion on demand is a quantitative one, not a qualitative one. The number of abortions in the second case may be much greater, but the essence of the matter is still the same — that human beings are taking upon themselves an authority over life and death that belongs only to God. *Wanderer* commentators seemed to tune in to that reality even at this early stage. That is evident in the *Wanderer*'s response to the Finkbine abortion case. That case involved an Arizona housewife, Mrs. Sherri Finkbine, who in 1962 took a tranquilizer called thalidomide during a pregnancy. Not long afterward, it was discovered that tha-

[120] Florence A. Burke, R.N., "Legal Abortions Are Homicide and Murder," W, 11-10-60.

lidomide, when taken by pregnant women, was causing severe birth defects in many cases — not minor ones, either, but massive deformities, such as a baby being born with no arms or no legs. Mrs. Finkbine attempted to procure a "therapeutic" abortion in the United States, to avoid giving birth to a deformed child, but was prevented from doing so by the then strict laws against abortion. She thereupon went to Sweden, where abortion was legal, and had it done. All this to the accompaniment of a great deal of publicity and public controversy.

Naturally, most people felt compassion for Mrs. Finkbine and could understand the motives for her act. That did not make the act right, however, and that judgment was evident on *The Wanderer*'s editorial page from the beginning. "Wanderer types," then, as now, took the position that, even while we loved and sympathized with the sinner, we had to hate the sin. Thus one guest editorial, which appeared August 9, 1962, made the point that there was far more at stake than Mrs. Finkbine's tragic situation:

> Any public approval of abortion, even in cases of extreme hardship, will only increase the amount of real mischief being done both by unscrupulous hospitals and conscienceless individuals.
>
> ...Compare the Arizona mother's action with the selflessness of so many thousands of parents who have borne and brought up and loved children with physical or mental defects.
>
> Ask them of the sufferings they have undergone and they will tell you of the compensating joys of doing God's will. Can there be any similar joy in willful murder?
>
> Let the child be born. If the natural mother and father are not fit to be its parents, God will provide foster parents to love him, malformed or not.[121]

[121] "Willful Murder," W, 8-9-62.

A second editorial, appearing the following week (August 16) drove the same basic point home in a truly prophetic bit of commentary:

> Once we abandon a moral principle and venture on compromise, there is no point at which the compromise may end. There is a sacred character to human life. If this is overlooked, then who shall decide what degrees of helplessness render this sacredness forfeit? The aged, the infirm, the incapacitated, would hold their lives by sufferance rather than by right.
>
> And out of the world would pass those great qualities of generosity and compassion and sacrifice which touch our race with the spark of the divine, and give significance to all human striving and pain. The earth will not gain in beauty as a result; it will have become a jungle where only the fit survive and the light of a merciful Providence will fall in shadow and in darkness.[122]

The Finkbine abortion issue was pretty much the opening skirmish of the late twentieth century's battle over abortion and the sanctity of human life, a battle which is still raging and which deserves, far more than the Persian Gulf War, to be dubbed "the mother of all battles." As early as August 30, 1962, shortly after the Finkbine abortion, Father John C. Knott, director of the Family Life Bureau of the National Catholic Welfare Conference (then still solidly Catholic), expressed suspicions that the massive publicity given to the Finkbine situation had as its purpose preparing the way for legalized abortion here in the United States.[123] A few years later, Bishop Fulton J. Sheen, in a farsighted letter to the Catholics of the Rochester Diocese, spoke out against the proposed New York law liberalizing abortion, noting that

[122] "Elements of Tragedy," W, 8-16-62.

[123] Father John C. Knott, "Plan Afoot to Relax U.S. Abortion Laws," W, 8-30-62.

> It is only when a civilization begins to degenerate that law and custom permit infanticide and abortion. When Rome became corrupt, a writer of Nero's court justified abortion, saying: "Mad dogs are knocked on the head; the fierce and savage ox we slay; sickly sheep we put to the knife; unnatural children we destroy; we even drown children at birth when they are weakly and abnormal."
>
> Our opposition to the new law, therefore, is not just because we are Catholics, it is because we believe in the sacredness of life.[124]

By the late 1960s, laws liberalizing abortion were being introduced in many states. *The Wanderer* was quick to condemn these efforts, suggesting that they reflected the very mentality which animated Hitler's mass murder of the mentally ill and the retarded. Ominously enough, court decisions too were beginning to go the way of the pro-abortionists. In California, for example, a court refused to prevent Mrs. Nancy O'Beirne from getting an abortion under California's new law, signed by then Governor Ronald Reagan, a law which allowed abortions where they were deemed necessary for the mother's mental health. Her estranged husband, a Catholic, had tried to prohibit the abortion on grounds that it violated his rights as the child's father. In 1968, the American bishops issued a pastoral on abortion, stating that "a human person, nothing more and nothing less, is always at issue once conception has taken place. We expressly repudiate any contradictory suggestion...."[125] "Abortion brings to an end with irreversible finality both the existence and the destiny of the developing human person."[126] In 1969, Juan Ryan, president of the National Right to Life Committee, made a prophetic statement, printed in *The Wanderer*, about what we now call the "slippery slope" — the fact that the early movement for liberalized

---

[124] Bishop Fulton J. Sheen, "Bishop Sheen Urges Opposition to Abortion Law," W, 2-23-67.

[125] "The 1968 Bishops' Pastoral," W, 11-28-68.

[126] Ibid.

abortion laws, horrendous though it was in itself, was really nothing more than a foot in the door for a far more radical agenda:

> Moreover, the proponents of abortion law repeal maintain that they intend not only to guarantee every woman the right to abort her child, but will also work to assure "the availability of abortion services to all women regardless of economic status." Presumably, this will mean that the cost of free abortions will be borne by medical-insurance programs and by government-sponsored health programs. The taxpayers will be called upon to pay for some women's decisions — whether they are responsibly arrived at or not.[127]

During this same time period, unfortunately, we began to see another phenomenon which became all too commonplace in the years that followed — the moral cowardice of Catholics, including their shepherds, on the issue of abortion. In 1970, for instance, we read about Governor Burns of Hawaii, a Catholic who allowed a pro-abortion bill to pass, excusing himself on grounds that to veto it would have violated "separation of church and state."[128] How many times since then have we had to weep and gnash our teeth when we heard that some politician calling himself a Catholic is "personally opposed to abortion but..."? In May, 1970 Frank Morriss had to raise the question why the American Bishops, in their annual conference, had failed to take an uncompromising stand against abortion:

> And why aren't Catholics putting their faith and consciences on the line? Partly, at least, it is because many have been fooled by the liberal assertions concerning the "rights" of error in a pluralistic society. The right of all views to contend in a democratic society has nothing to do with error being justified or acceptable; and certainly nothing to do with the duty of Catholics to oppose such error, particularly when it is

[127] "Abortion on Demand Is Goal," W, 3-20-69.
[128] "An Open Letter to Governor Burns of Hawaii," W, 3-26-70.

> such fundamental error as actually to threaten the life of the innocent.[129]

Fortunately, there continued to be happy exceptions to the Church's general failure to confront the abortion issue. In January, 1971, Archbishop Humberto Medeiros of Boston preached a powerful homily on the Feast of the Holy Innocents. Among other things, he said this:

> My dear brothers and sisters, we cannot condemn Herod for the slaughter of the Holy Innocents and, at the same time, propose abortion as the solution to some of our pressing problems and the legalization of abortion as our legal policy. These are literally "dead-end streets" that do not solve problems but only create larger ones....
>
> My dearly beloved, I beg you to become personally concerned about God's rights over His unborn children and over their right to life and birth. I beseech you to see the legalization of abortion in its true light; it is the denial of God's rights over life and the denial of the unborn's right to be born.[130]

It is evident that very early in the still raging abortion controversy, *The Wanderer* and its orthodox Catholic readers found themselves in a (literally) life and death struggle with their own Church, or at least many of its leaders, over the Church's obligation to speak out prophetically for the sanctity of human life, no matter what the cost (loss of tax exemptions, persecution, etc.), an obligation the powers-that-be in the Church seemed all too anxious to sidestep, even while saying theologically correct things about the sanctity of human life. The conflict between pro-life Catholics and their own Church leaders is a central theme in the history of the abortion battle,

---

129 Frank Morriss, "Why No Call?" W, 5-7-70.

130 Archbishop Humberto Medeiros, "The New Barbarism Is a Summons to Death," W, 1-14-71.

a theme well documented by *The Wanderer* over the years, and we will discuss it in greater detail later.

At the same time, the abortion battle was also clearly a struggle of Catholics and other pro-life Christians (and even some Jews) against a secular state which was and is becoming increasingly anti-life, as it evolves more and more totalitarian programs to regulate all aspects of the American people's lives. The U.S. government, as early as the 1960s, was becoming increasingly active in efforts to use tax dollars to push programs of family planning and population control. The supposedly conservative Nixon administration was no exception. Charles Rice pointed this out in an October 1, 1970 editorial:

> The Nixon administration, through its population-planning and birth-control efforts, is embarking on a regime of extermination that will exceed the Nazi liquidation of the Jews in numbers and calculated cruelty. Abortion is the ultimately indispensable technique of the population-control movement as it is conceived by the administration's planners. If the administration does not pull back from its anti-life policies, no conservative — no American who values freedom and life itself — can properly support that administration any more than a conscientious German could overlook the Nazi murders and support that regime because it was efficient on budgetary matters.[131]

As the confrontation between pro-lifers and the anti-life state intensified, a very interesting phenomenon came into view, one which has, I think, been too little noted by commentators on American society: The shift in the discussion of civil disobedience from the left to the right. All of us who are now middle-aged or older remember clearly the era when there were incessant arguments between mainstream liberals and the far left over whether people trying to change American society, to fight for social justice, had the right to disobey the law. That was a major theme of the sixties — for instance, did people

[131] Rice, "Political Action Is Needed in the Fight for Life," W, 10-1-70.

who believed the war in Vietnam to be illegal or immoral have the right to refuse to serve in that war, to burn their draft cards, to occupy ROTC headquarters, etc.? Or were they obliged, however just their cause might be, to be good citizens and to work peacefully within the system for change? It was, needless to say, the consistent belief of conservatives that the left had better obey the authorities or risk imprisonment. Yet suddenly, right about 1970, we find conservative pro-lifers arguing among themselves about this very question. For instance, on June 18, 1970, we find Paul Weyrich, in an article entitled "On Militancy and Abortion (Some Reflections)," criticizing a group called Action for Life, led by L. Brent Bozell, which had marched on an abortion facility in Washington, D.C., and gotten into a confrontation with the police. Weyrich argued that, while the group may have had good intentions, its methods probably harmed the pro-life cause:

> Catholics and especially conservative Catholics have an obligation to work within the framework of laws and our political system as long as it is possible. Yes, demonstrations and violence bring results on the left. But on the other side, it only serves to bring on repression faster. As Mr. Bozell well knows, the press is not at all inclined to favor conservative (let alone Catholic) demonstrations, while at the same time it often works hand-in-hand with similar activities on the other side.[132]

On July 23, 1970, Michael Lawrence, editor of *Triumph*, responded on behalf of Action for Life in an article entitled "More on Militancy and Responsibility." Lawrence complained that "conservatives," people like Barry Goldwater and George Bush, had largely abandoned the right to life movement:

> This is why militancy, the tactic which Mr. Weyrich so abhors, is essential. Christians have, really, only two options:

[132] Paul Weyrich, "On Militancy and Abortion (Some Reflections)," W, 6-18-70.

> they may pursue the tried and true methods of conventional politics, the petitions and speeches and voting drives and letters to congressmen; or they may be militant.
>
> I believe, Action for Life believes, that the concept of "the Church Militant" has a meaning; a sacramental meaning. It can be understood through a study of the Sacrament of Confirmation. Soldiers of Christ, like soldiers generally, must be prepared to march, to fight, to die. We are preparing. We need a little help from our friends.[133]

John Mulloy, in the same issue, appears to support the militant stand in principle while advocating caution, and stressing the need for militancy to be accompanied by prayer:

> Only that prayer must be real prayer, in trust and perseverance, not demanding immediate results or it will be given up; and the blood of the martyrs must be purged of all self-centeredness and showing off (as the Martin Luther King approach was not), so that one must avoid martyrdom rather than seek it for fear that it is one's own will rather than God's that is being chosen....[134]

But if a truly central theme emerged in *The Wanderer* during this preliminary phase of the abortion battle, it was the clear understanding that the issue of abortion is not, and never has been, merely a disagreement about social policy, one which nice, pragmatic policy-makers can get together and discuss in a gentlemanly manner, and concerning which some sort of workable compromise can surely be arrived at by men of goodwill. On the contrary, the issue was always understood to be one of spiritual order, and, as a result, one of moral and social order. Abortion is a sickness, a disease, of the spirit, and that disease of the spirit inevitably translates into a diseased state of the individual human being and a diseased, disordered state of soci-

---

[133] Michael Lawrence, "More on Militancy and Responsibility," W, 7-23-70.

[134] John J. Mulloy, "When Considering Martyrdom, Be Careful," W, 7-23-70.

ety. Gloria V. Heffernan, M.D., in a July 20, 1972 article entitled "Abortion Exploits Women," effectively and movingly shows us the spiritual destructiveness of abortion and, with it, its tremendously destructive effects on the human person, seen as inviolable by the Church, when it is looked upon as just something to be exploited for pleasure by the secular, murderous society we live in:

> After centuries of being treated as objects, women are being presented the final mechanical insult as a constitutional right.
> The strange compulsion for abortion is in reality the ultimate exploitation of women by immature men: technocrats, generally, imbued with a myopic sense of social awareness and unable to interpret or control their own sexuality.
> The playboys of the Western world and the authoritarian "adolescents" of the socialist world sacrifice their women in order to preserve their dream of libidinal freedom. It is the woman who must go to surgery over and over again to ensure this dream. The whimpering male refused to take responsibility for his sexual behavior.[135]

The struggle over abortion is thus in the end a matter of spiritual warfare. As St. Paul told us long ago, we are not fighting merely flesh and blood, but spiritual powers of evil. If *The Wanderer* had accomplished nothing else during the years this struggle has raged, it would still be able to take credit for keeping this consciousness of the spiritual nature of the struggle alive during a time when our "pragmatists," including many well-meaning but confused pro-life people, have wanted to suppress that consciousness.

It would seem, then, that over three decades *The Wanderer* has documented (as a participant observer) three main aspects of the terrible struggle over abortion:

1) The battle within the Catholic Church, a battle during which Wanderer types have persevered in the effort, against all odds, to put

---

[135] Gloria V. Heffernan, M.D., "Abortion Exploits Women," W, 7-20-72.

an end to the horrible scandal of a Church whose hierarchy has pretty consistently failed to speak out in more than the most timid ways against the horror of abortion, trying to recall the Catholic community to its prophetic mission to proclaim the sanctity of human life to the world and against a secular state and society which have arrogated to themselves the divine prerogative to dispose of human life.

2) The efforts of *Wanderer* commentators, as citizens as well as Christians, to reform and bring back to sanity an increasingly anti-life state which seeks, in totalitarian fashion, to impose the deadly agenda of the population control movement and the social engineers on the American people, efforts made more difficult by lack of support from the leadership of the Church. *The Wanderer*'s efforts, continuing to this day, to come to terms with the issue of civil disobedience in the cause of life, have played a key role in the struggle with the anti-Christian state.

3) The documentation, by *The Wanderer*, of the spiritual disorder embodied in the pro-abortion movement, as well as of the social and moral disorder it spawned. *The Wanderer*'s writings on abortion during the past thirty years have amounted, really, to a history of spiritual warfare.

In what follows, I am going to try to tell the story of *The Wanderer*'s struggle against abortion by examining it in terms of each of these three dimensions of the struggle. I hope that will make what has been happening during these years more understandable to the reader. But before I can do that and make any sense out of the matter, I am going to need to lay one more foundation stone by talking about the one watershed event which, more than any other, made abortion the central issue of social and spiritual order of the twentieth century. That event, the reader will surely have guessed by now, is the infamous *Roe v. Wade* decision of January 22, 1973, which legalized, practically speaking, all abortions. Let us look at that event.

2. A DAY THAT WILL LIVE IN INFAMY

"U.S. SUPREME COURT APPROVES DEATH PENALTY FOR THE UNBORN"

So read the February 1, 1973 front-page headline of *The Wanderer*, a headline which did not, in all likelihood, give the reader any information he had not already heard from the secular press and media, but which certainly put the matter in clear Christian perspective. After years of debate, after the passage of an odd variety of state laws liberalizing abortion to some degree but never giving a completely green light to the practice, after elections in Michigan and North Dakota less than three months earlier which rejected any legalization, the U.S. Supreme Court, a body intended by the authors of our Constitution to interpret the law rather than to blatantly make law, had, in a still breathtaking usurpation of power, decided to veto all state laws restricting abortion and to institutionalize the feminists' revolutionary assertion that a woman has "a right to control her own body" so total as to include the right to kill her unborn baby. That was what we had come to in a few short years. Perhaps it might be best to summarize the story in *The Wanderer*'s own words:

> In a sweeping 7-2 decision, the Supreme Court struck down on January 22 the abortion laws of Texas, Georgia, and all but four of the other fifty states. On the basis of a "right to privacy" allegedly guaranteed by the due process clause of the Fourteenth Amendment, the Court majority ruled that during the first three months of pregnancy, a woman and her doctor have the unconditional right to decide whether she will bear or abort her unborn child.
>
> Moreover, after the first three months, but before the child reaches "viability," the Court ruled, the doctrine of

> "compelling state interest" allows the state to set health care standards for the mother but does not allow any protection to be given to the fetus. After the fetus reaches "viability," occasionally referred to in the decision as "quickening" and loosely assigned to the sixth or seventh month, the states "may regulate or even proscribe" abortions, if they so choose, except that no state may prohibit abortions that are "necessary, in the appropriate medical judgment, for the preservation of the life or health of the mother." It is understood that "health" includes mental health and other intangible factors....[136]

The majority opinion in this bizarre, revolutionary decision was written by Justice Blackmun, with Justices Burger, Douglas, Stewart, Powell, Marshall, and Brennan (a Catholic, and hence, we must assume, "personally opposed" to abortion) concurring, and Justices Rehnquist and White dissenting. The *Wanderer* account goes on to characterize the majority decision:

> Here an extreme intellectual disorder is already visible. If the question of constitutionality can prescind totally from the natural law then the Constitution itself is made to rest on nothing but arbitrary majority will. If philosophy, moreover, religious training, and "one's exposure to the raw edges of human existence" serve only to "color" one's thinking on abortion, as Blackmun suggests, then it follows that the real truth about abortion must come from a source independent of philosophy, religion, and ordinary human experience. But to believe that constitutional jurisprudence can serve as such a source amounts to adopting a thoroughgoing and philosophically untenable nominalism.[137]

---

[136] "U.S. Supreme Court Approves Death Penalty for the Unborn," W, 2-1-73.
[137] Ibid.

After discussing the alleged justification for the decision in a "right of privacy" found in the emanations and penumbras of the Fourteenth Amendment, Blackmun went on to dismiss the so-called fetus's right to life in the following terms:

> The appellee and certain *amici* argue that the fetus is a "person" within the language and meaning of the Fourteenth Amendment. In support of this, they outline at length and in detail the well-known facts of fetal development. If this suggestion of personhood is established, the appellant's case, of course, collapses, for the fetus' right to life is then guaranteed specifically by the amendment. The appellant conceded as much on reargument....The Constitution does not define a person in so many words...(instances of the use of the word "person" in the Constitution and its amendments are then cited [*Wanderer*'s note]) but in nearly all these instances, the use of the word is such that it has application only postnatally. None indicates, with any assurance, that it has any possible prenatal application.
>
> We need not resolve the difficult question of when life begins. When those trained in the respective disciplines of medicine, philosophy, and theology, are unable to arrive at any consensus, the judiciary, at this point in the development of man's knowledge, is not in a position to speculate as to the answer.[138]

The bottom line of this whole argument really comes down to this: We are already committed to legalizing abortion. But if we were to acknowledge that the "fetus" is a person, we would not be able to legalize abortion. Therefore, the fetus is not a person. Aristotle need not have spent much of his life developing a system of logic — not when people like Harry Blackmun can get along so well without it.

There was, of course, opposition to Blackmun's strange reasoning and conclusions from within the Court itself, yet even this op-

[138] Ibid.

position never got at the core issue — the right of the unborn to live. Justice Byron White's dissent, for instance, says this:

> I find nothing in the language or history of the Constitution to support the Court's judgment. The Court simply fashions and announces a new constitutional right for pregnant mothers and, with scarcely any reason or authority for its action, invests that right with sufficient substance to override most existing state abortion statutes. The upshot is that the people and the legislatures of the fifty states are constitutionally disentitled to weigh the relative importance of the continued existence and development of the fetus on the one hand against a spectrum of possible impacts on the mother on the other hand. As an exercise of raw judicial power, the Court perhaps has the authority to do what it does today; but in my view its just [sic] judgment is an improvident and extravagant exercise of the power of judicial review which the Constitution extends to this Court.[139]

We can certainly relate to White's denunciation of the Court's use of "raw judicial power." Yet something is missing here. White, too, sees the life of the unborn as something negotiable, something we have the right to weigh against other goods as if the right to life were not an absolute and hence unconditioned by other goods. The difference is that White sees this weighing as something to be done by state governments rather than by the federal government or the pregnant woman.

Justice Rehnquist's dissent similarly makes some legitimate legal points but misses the main point. He correctly indicates that the right to privacy, at least as the majority on the Court invokes it, is found nowhere in the Constitution, and is certainly not derived from the Fourteenth Amendment, then goes on to say:

> The fact that a majority of states, reflecting after all the majority sentiment in those states, have had restrictions on

[139] "Justice Byron White Dissents from Abortion Ruling," W, 2-1-73.

> abortion for at least a century seems to me as strong an indication there is that the asserted right to an abortion is not so rooted in the traditions and conscience of our people as to be ranked as fundamental.[140]

He suggests that, since many states prohibited abortion at the time the 14th amendment was enacted, clearly the latter was not meant to provide a right to abort.[141] But Rehnquist too fails utterly to discuss the question of the unborn child's right to live, a right many would argue *is* guaranteed by the Fourteenth Amendment.

The *Roe v. Wade* decision has been part of our national landscape for so long now that even those of us who militantly oppose it have to some extent grown accustomed to it and perhaps even a little blasé about it. Because of that, it may be a little difficult for us today to fully grasp the intensity of America's reaction to it, especially when it is Catholic America we are talking about. Again, a sampling of headlines from the *Wanderer* issue that reported *Roe v. Wade* may help to remedy that error of perspective:

> "An Unspeakable Tragedy for Our Nation" — "God's Law Can Never Be Supplanted" — "A Tragic Utilitarian Judgment" — "A National Disaster" — "A Catastrophe for America" — "A Step Backwards" — "The Court Has Gone Beyond Its Competence" — "MCCL to Continue Anti-Abortion Fight" — "License to Kill" — "A Providential Challenge" — "Let Us Repudiate This Denial of Human Rights" — "The Land Will Be Reduced to Desert" — "The 13th Hour" — "A Terrifying Hour for Our Country" — "America Has Been Robbed of Her Conscience" — "Our Prophetic Voice Must Continue" — "A Declaration of War on the Unborn" — "An Indescribable Calamity" — "Christian Principles Must Prevail" — "The Court's Decision Promotes Disregard for Life" — "The Death Knell Be-

140 "Justice William Rehnquist Dissents from Abortion Ruling," W, 2-1-73.
141 Ibid.

gins to Toll" — "We Must Be Ready to Go to Jail" — "Better for Us to Obey God" — "The Court Cannot Take Away God's Right" — "A Mockery of the Moral Law" — "Ill Fares the Land" — "Darkness in the Nation's Soul" — "The Court Cannot Nullify God's Law" — "I Shudder at the Prospects Ahead"

Archbishop Medeiros of Boston, in one of these articles, perhaps sums up the orthodox Catholic response as well as anyone:

> No judicial power nor legislative bodies can make the willful and intentional destruction of the innocent unborn something good....This is a terrifying hour for our country. We are calling upon our heads the just anger of our heavenly Father. Let us plead with Mary Immaculate, the patroness of our nation, to intercede for us and to lead us to repentance. May she inspire all our people with a true horror for the unspeakable crimes about to be committed under the protection of the law so that we may, as a nation under God, reverse the trend to utter corruption and self-destruction as a people. We must work and pray together for a reversal of the Supreme Court's injustice to the unborn which has made Monday, January 22, 1973, a day of infamy in our history.[142]

In stating that "the Court's judgment must be opposed and rejected," the Committee for Pro-Life Affairs of the National Conference of Catholic Bishops came out with a series of recommendations such as restriction of abortions by state governments and efforts to work through the courts to overturn *Roe v. Wade*. Most important, it stated that Catholic hospitals must have nothing to do with abortions.[143] The Committee on Health Affairs of the United States Catholic Conference emphasized that "the Court can nullify laws of

---

[142] Archbishop Humberto Medeiros, "A Terrifying Hour for Our Country," W, 2-1-73.

[143] "'The Court's Judgment Must Be Opposed and Rejected,'" W, 2-1-73.

the states, but it is not within its power to nullify the laws of God."[144] Would that these national Catholic organizations had remained as militant as they appeared to be in 1973. Unfortunately, not long after the statement just quoted, the Family Life Division of the USCC made a point of advising pro-life lawyers not to challenge *Roe v. Wade*.[145] So much for the Church militant!

At least one *Wanderer* commentator, Al Matt, Jr., the editor, did feel at the time that the decision, atrocious though it was, represented an opportunity and not just a disaster:

> Perhaps this is the last opportunity for the Catholic Church in America to restore that unity of faith among its members which was allowed to collapse in the face of the concerted assault upon *Humanae Vitae* by dissident Catholics — a collapse, incidentally, which bears a direct causal relationship to the Supreme Court's abominable decision. In the face of this all-out assault upon morality, the Catholic Church simply cannot afford the luxury of doctrinal and moral dissent within her ranks. It must be, therefore, a matter of first priority for the bishops of this country to assume their collegial responsibility — so admirably demonstrated this week — "to safeguard the unity of the Faith and the discipline common to the whole Church."[146]

It is a great tragedy that a Church in terrible disorder failed to take advantage of that opportunity.

In further reaction to *Roe v. Wade*, *Wanderer* columnist John Mulloy made a valiant effort to call fellow Catholics to action against the decision:

> If Catholics fail to act now, with the greatest urgency and decisiveness, and with action which dramatically focuses at-

[144] "The Court Cannot Nullify God's Law (Statement of the Committee on Health Affairs, USCC)," W, 2-1-73.
[145] "Right to Life Lawyers Advised Not to Challenge Court," W, 2-8-73.
[146] A.J. Matt, Jr., "A Providential Challenge," W, 2-1-73.

> tention on our commitment to the law of God, we will be lost..... As we all know, the Catholic Church has been floundering badly in these last few years, as it has tried to accommodate itself to the mores of a secularized culture and has increasingly dissipated its own spiritual heritage....What this Supreme Court decision means is a chance to reverse that whole tide in which we are being swept loose from our moorings in the Catholic faith and in Catholic morality. But the chance will not come again, neither one so sharply focused nor on so clear and deep a humanitarian issue as this one....Do we mobilize our forces for a full-scale attack upon the advancing armies of abortion, or do we continue our ignominious and disorderly retreat? That is the choice. That is the decision which the American bishops must make.[147]

On February 15, 1973, William F. Buckley compared *Roe v. Wade* to the *Dred Scott* decision:

> The whole of it [the Court's reasoning] is dismal, reaching right down to the neglected cuticles of the Court's language. It is, verily, the *Dred Scott* decision of the twentieth century. One shudders at what a Supreme Court, taking on the responsibility to decide such questions, will feel free to rule upon in the years to come. Woe unto those Americans who, because of their great age, threaten distressfulness upon their children.[148]

Shortly afterward, the American Catholic bishops, in what seemed at the time a promising development, stated in a pastoral letter that

> In effect, the Court is saying that the right of privacy takes precedence over the right to life. This opinion of the Court fails to protect the most basic human right — the right to life.

[147] "'Today If You but Hear His Voice...,'" W, 2-8-73.

[148] William F. Buckley, Jr., "The Dred Scott Decision of theTwentieth Century," W, 2-15-73.

> Therefore, we reject this decision of the Court because, as John XXIII says, "if any government does not acknowledge the rights of man or violates them…its orders completely lack juridical force."….In light of these reasons we reject the opinion of the United States Supreme Court as erroneous, unjust, and immoral.[149]

The bishops went on to state that "Catholics must oppose abortion as an immoral act" and that "no one is obliged to obey any civil law that may require abortion." Finally, the document recommended excommunication for persons procuring abortions.[150]

One final ray of light in the terrible darkness which characterized the winter of 1973: Shortly after the decision was made, Indiana Attorney General John Sendak announced that "until the Supreme Court of the United States or the Supreme Court of Indiana or the Indiana General Assembly deals with Indiana laws, they remain on the books and are valid."[151] How unfortunate that there was not and still is not more of this kind of reaction to intolerable and unjust decisions of our Supreme Court. As far as I know, Sendak was never heard from again on this matter, and probably ended up in some American equivalent of professional Siberia. Yet he had the right idea. The Constitution gives the Supreme Court no enforcement powers, and the authors of the Constitution, discussing the Court's place in the *Federalist Papers*, declared quite definitely that the Court would be the least dangerous branch of government, because it would have no enforcement powers other than persuasion. If, in 1973, enough people in positions of responsibility at state, federal, and local levels, had had the courage to simply reject *Roe v. Wade* and continue enforcing laws against abortion, the decision would have remained to this day a dead letter. Unfortunately, this opportunity too was lost and will never be regained. Instead, we are caught

---

[149] "Bishops' Pastoral Letter…Rejects Court's Abortion Decision," W, 2-22-73.
[150] Ibid.
[151] "Indiana Abortion Law Remains Effective," W, 2-22-73.

up to this day in an uphill struggle to reverse that decision. The material which follows will discuss that struggle in more detail, focusing, as already noted, on the conflict within the Church over abortion, the conflict between Christian teaching and the state, and, finally, the spiritual aspect of the struggle, an aspect which is, really, the essence of the whole thing.

3. THE GREAT WIMPOUT

One of contemporary America's greatest contributions to the development of the English language has been, I am convinced, the creation of the word "wimp," with its variant forms, like "wimpout," "wimpdom," etc. It sums up, in one little monosyllable, a whole range of human behavior, a whole personality type, which we all recognize instinctively but sometimes find it difficult to capture precisely in words and concepts. Perhaps this marvelous word emerged only in the contemporary world because there has been no other age in history quite so dominated by bureaucracy and bureaucrats as the one we live in. Everyone, especially anyone who has ever worked for the government, knows the type: He is the deputy assistant director of nothing in particular. The agency that employs him is having a problem which calls for strong and urgent action. He is placed in charge of the problem, and begins to get ideas and suggestions from his underlings as to what should be done. It soon becomes evident that any proposal that is clear and definite and actually directly addresses the problem is going to be vetoed by this person, who keeps telling you that, "Oh, we can't say that," or "That would offend blacks, or women, or homosexuals, or left-handed sado-masochists." He loves no expression quite so much as "keep a low profile." He ends up with a vaguely worded, bland proposal which indicates that, yes, something really ought to be done about this problem, but is absolutely bereft of the slightest hint of any concrete suggestions for action. He has achieved what every bureaucrat wants: He has succeeded in creating an illusion of taking action but without saying anything that could possibly lead to anyone holding him responsible for anything.

That, sadly, is what the bureaucrats of the Roman Catholic Church (and that category, sadly, includes many of our bishops) have been doing throughout the struggle over abortion. It is part of the great mystery of iniquity that a Church which is, in her essence, the

Mystical Body of Christ and the spotless Bride of Christ, can be so badly contaminated in her external, institutional aspects by fallen men. Historians have never been shy when it comes to telling us about the truly gross instances of institutional corruption in the past history of the Church — e.g., Renaissance Popes with multitudes of illegitimate children and a certain propensity for poisoning people who get in the way of their ambitions. Today, the problem doesn't seem to be so much the truly gross instances of corruption (though these are still real), but the domination of the Church by wimps, by the bureaucratic personality type who is utterly terrified of taking responsibility for anything that might "rock the boat." It is the corruption of the "good" man of whom Edmund Burke spoke, i.e., the man with basically right convictions, who does nothing. The late twentieth century has seen an unparalleled growth of Church bureaucracy — the proliferation of parish and diocesan councils and commissions, the emergence of organizations like the National Conference of Catholic Bishops (NCCB), the United States Catholic Conference (USCC), etc. Satan obviously knew what he was doing when he decided to make bureaucratization the typical form of corruption in the twentieth-century Church. As the secular society around us grows more and more corrupt and dehumanizing, as societies lurch toward totalitarianism, nothing is more desperately needed from Christians than prophetic witness against evil, and that is precisely what the leaders of our Church, with a few honorable exceptions, have been unable or unwilling to give us. And nowhere has the bureaucratic lack of moral courage and prophetic witness been more evident than in the struggle over abortion. Had the Catholic Church, back in 1973, simply refused to make her peace with the institutionalization of abortion, had she encouraged and strongly urged all Catholics to refuse to accept this atrocity and to refuse to obey laws which promoted abortion, the whole history of this issue in America would have been radically different. In all likelihood, the sanctity of human life would by now have been restored as the guiding principle of American society, as not only Catholics, but Protestants and Jews and all men of goodwill, whatever their faith, were moved by the Church's example to fight against the anti-life direction our country was moving in.

Sadly, that did not happen. Yet the situation has not been wholly bleak everywhere. In spite of everything, there have been, here and there, little pockets of resistance, individuals and groups willing to speak out in prophetic witness to the law of God and the sanctity of human life, even when that meant speaking out against our own bishops and against our hypertrophied Church bureaucracies. One of these groups was the one that formed around *The Wanderer*, whose contributors have never stopped, over the years, taking the leaders of our Church to task for their lack of moral courage. Frank Morriss, in a column written after he had attended a regional meeting of the NCCB a few months after *Roe v. Wade*, brought the fundamental issue within the Church to the surface in an editorial entitled, "The Paralysis of Our Shepherds":

> It was an old fighter, once the champion, grown almost helpless; or a knight, once ready for every challenge, now unable to raise lance or barely mount his steed.
>
> That is definitely the impression left with me by observing one of the experimental regional meetings of the National Conference of Catholic Bishops. So inconclusive has the teaching role become, that even with great questions raised in the ridiculous period of two days, there were times when question or comment could not even be drawn out of the delegates, and silent, empty moments passed. There was a total absence of radical (in the sense of root) consideration of the questions from any viewpoint — either progressive or conservative. The delegates simply sat upon their assumptions — that sex education is desirable, youth are being lost to the Church because of some sort of communications gap, a pagan milieu threatens "Christian" values, etc. The situation virtually screamed for some incisive, dogmatic presentation of the truth that applies to each of these things — the Catholic truth as distinguished from mere "Christian" sentiment. But not a whisper was heard, other than a few assertions rec-

> ognizing parental rights regarding sex education and denying that the bishops are divided on *Humanae Vitae*.[152]

Late in November, 1973, Robert Mauro sadly and reluctantly reached the conclusion that the laity would have to lead the fight to restore the sanctity of human life:

> A bruising, bitter fight must be waged to force a reluctant Congress to pass a pro-life amendment. During the November 12 through 16 meeting at the Statler-Hilton Hotel here [in Washington, D.C.], the clear word came forth that the Catholic bishops are not prepared — at least for the moment — to lead such a fight.[153]

That turned out to be an exceedingly long moment which, today, more than two decades later, has not yet ended. On January 3, 1974, as the first anniversary of *Roe v. Wade* drew near, Mary E. Cook raised the question whether Catholics would take a stand against abortion:

> The answer has become painfully clear. Catholics do not want to "impose" their values on a pluralistic society. No matter that the value of a human life is not a Catholic concept alone; that it is the concern of all mankind. To take a stand on abortion is to believe and to be unafraid. Belief is dying; fear the order of the day. And it happened so quickly.[154]

Al Matt, writing in the January 24 edition, stated flatly that "we have lost a year through inaction, timidity, lack of unity. More than a million babies have died. The time has come to call upon our bishops for a plan of action."[155]

The paralysis of the Catholic bureaucracy in the face of abortion was spelled out about as damningly as possible in a June 13, 1974

[152] Frank Morriss, "The Paralysis of Our Shepherds," W, 5-31-73.
[153] Robert L. Mauro, "Laity Must Lead Pro-Life Drive," W, 1-29-73.
[154] Mary E. Cook, "A Private Affair?" W, 1-3-74.
[155] A.J. Matt, Jr., "A Year Lost," W, 1-24-74.

editorial entitled "Catholic Bureaucrats Fiddle While the Unborn Are KILLED":

> It is now clear that one of the key obstacles in the path of those seeking a pro-life amendment in 1974 is a bureaucratic element within the Roman Catholic Church. This bureaucracy is pursuing a "rule or ruin" course. If it cannot dominate all major aspects of the pro-life amendment drive, it appears determined that no pro-life amendment shall be enacted. This bureaucratic element is quietly telling U.S. representatives that they need not or should not sign the Hogan discharge petition, thereby neutralizing letters and visits from pro-lifers to the U.S. representatives demanding they sign the petition.[156]

Scandalous incidents kept piling up during this era, and indeed have not stopped yet. John Mulloy had to comment in July, 1974, on the failure of the Pennsylvania bishops to prevent the nomination of a pro-abortion candidate for governor in that state's Democratic primary.[157] That same summer, in Memphis, a pro-abortion nun, Sister Mary Anne Guthrie, ran for Congress with the consent of her bishop, Carroll T. Dozier. Al Matt most appropriately titled his editorial remarks on this incident "When Will the Scandal End?" Matt acknowledged that the bishops had spoken out against abortion in the sense of making doctrinally correct public statements on the subject, but added that "our concern is not over the failure of the bishops to articulate the moral principles with respect to abortion — this they have done often and admirably — our concern is for the failure of too many bishops to apply these high principles in the practical order."[158] Again and again, we run across headlines like "The Bishops Need a Strategy for Life"; "Catholics Failed at the Polls"; "The Bishops Have No Strategy for Life."

---

[156] "Catholic Bureaucrats Fiddle While the Unborn Are Killed," W, 6-13-74.
[157] John J. Mulloy, "The Catholic Church and the Pennsylvania Primary," W, 7-4-74.
[158] A.J. Matt, Jr., "When Will the Scandal End?" W, 8-1-74.

One ray of light did enter into the darkness of this situation in November, 1974, when the Holy See's Sacred Congregation for the Doctrine of the Faith issued its "Declaration on Procured Abortion," which spelled out Catholic teaching on the evil of abortion about as clearly as anyone could have done. The document gave some real moral support to pro-life Catholics by clearly stating that not only are Christians forbidden to abort, but they are also forbidden to support pro-abortion laws: "Nor can a Christian take part in a propaganda campaign in favor of such a law, or vote for it."[159] That came pretty close to saying that Catholics are forbidden to vote for pro-abortion candidates, since a vote for such a candidate is in effect a vote for abortion. It also came pretty close to saying that Catholics who support abortion in public, as so many Catholic politicians have, to our shame, done over the years without political cost, could be excommunicated. Had the U.S. bishops acted on the Declaration in this way, the whole approach of the American Church to abortion would have changed, and the Church might well have emerged as a powerful force against the continued slaughter of the unborn. But, alas, that did not happen. Instead, the Church bureaucracy became more and more firmly wedded to the status quo of secular society, ultimately making itself quite comfortable by coming up with the approach that later came to be called the "seamless garment": The approach that made abortion just one of a multitude of issues of equal importance. Al Matt described this in a January 16, 1975 article:

> Like racism, hunger, poverty, pornography, and war, abortion now has been added to that list of evils which requires bishops from time to time to deplore and condemn with the most sonorous of declarations. Having thus acquitted themselves by denouncing the latest moral evil, they are free to address themselves to more practical and less prickly issues.[160]

---

[159] "Declaration on Procured Abortion — Given Nov. 18, 1974, by the Holy See's Sacred Congregation for the Doctrine of the Faith," W, 1-2-75.
[160] A.J. Matt, Jr., "Two Years After Black Monday," W, 1-16-75.

John Mulloy diagnosed this situation quite early as a failure of the Church's mission of prophetic witness:

> ...There seems to have developed a gradual acceptance of the accommodationist attitude: a business-as-usual relationship with American society and especially with American government, that will assure the Church of its comfortable status despite some temporary disagreement it may have had with the state on the matter of abortion.[161]

This sadly quite accurate picture of the Church's actual attitude in American society contrasts sharply with what Frank Morriss, in May, 1975, characterized as the attitude God is genuinely calling Catholics to take:

> In many countries this is just what is being asked of Catholics: an open and fearless attitude of resistance — and, if needs be, of rebellion — against unjust and inhuman laws. Their firmness and fearlessness in so acting may be, humanly speaking, the only thing capable of stirring the drugged consciences of so many, and of saving a civilization which seems blindly bent on rejecting the few truly human values left to it, and sinking into barbarism.[162]

Of course, an occasional bishop showed signs of willingness to speak out. In April, 1975, Bishop Leo T. Maher of San Diego issued a warning to the effect that "one who admits publicly to being a member of an organization that promotes abortion, such as the NOW organization, must be refused the sacrament of the Eucharist by priests, deacons, and extraordinary ministers."[163] Even this act of principle, however, was diluted when Auxiliary Bishop Chavez issued a disclaimer to the effect that NOW membership alone would not be sufficient for denial of the Eucharist — that there would have to be evi-

---

[161] John J. Mulloy, "Prophetic Witness, Not Accommodation, Will Defeat Abortion," W, 2-27-75.
[162] Morriss, "On the Necessity of Resisting Unjust Laws," W, 5-29-75.
[163] Frank Morriss, "Confusion Over Bishop's Warning," W, 5-1-75.

dence that a particular member actually favored abortion,[164] a rather silly distinction when we consider that abortion support is practically of the essence of NOW. A pro-life NOW member would be like a Communist who favored free enterprise — a contradiction in terms.

The great tragedy, then, of the post-*Roe v. Wade* era has been the great wimpout by the Catholic Church, or at least of its human representatives in America. Quoting the ubiquitous Frank Morriss once more:

> No party would have dared defy a united Catholic electorate....If Catholics cannot with one voice demand that killing of babies be legally ended, then they hardly have the right to call themselves more than shadow followers of Christ....But where lies the blame for the lack of a united Catholic determination...? It must be placed at the door of the preachers of pluralism who say we must not impose *our* morality on others, as if abortion were merely a matter of *our* morality, and not of divine and natural law and elemental justice.[165]

The bitter fruit of the Catholic failure to stand up to the evil of abortion became all too manifest in phenomena like the "Califano Doctrine," the principle enunciated by President Carter's new secretary of Health, Education, and Welfare, Joseph Califano, who stated that while, as a Catholic, he personally opposed abortion, he would not let his private conscience influence his actions in his new position. Father Mark Pilon, in an article called "A Moral Sellout...The Califano Doctrine," underlined the guilt of Catholic leaders for the triumph of this perverted notion of a purely private conscience which has no place in the public realm:

> The source of this incredible silence [of the Church on abortion], and the moral confusion and compromise it is producing, can only be traced ultimately to one thing. We are pay-

[164] Ibid.

[165] Morriss, "Who Is to Blame for Catholic Disunity on Abortion?" W, 9-2-76.

> ing the price — or rather babies are — for the practical silence of the leaders of the Church on the issue of contraception. Here I am not arguing the logical connection between contraception and these other life issues, although that can be and certainly has been done. What I am arguing is that this effective silence spells toleration of this deviation from Catholic teaching by the hierarchy most often under the aegis of private conscience, and that this has led us to a day when a Protestant notion of conscience now reigns supreme among the majority of Catholics, including, or even especially, among the educated class, like Joseph Califano, Robert Drinan, and Justice Brennan, the tip of an intellectual iceberg of Catholics who may have sold out their faith to the desire for position and power in the going order.[166]

Over the years, *Wanderer* commentators continued the call for prophetic witness against abortion and the other evils spawned by secularist society, though unfortunately without much short-run success (but in the long run, who knows?). Here, for instance, is our intrepid editor, Al Matt, in 1980, decrying the United States Catholic Conference's alliance with homosexual activists and abortionists in defense of the recent White House conference on the "family":

> The Catholic faithful of this country have been patient and long-suffering while the moral authority of the Church has declined precipitously as their leaders succumbed to the lure of a false pluralism. But the time has come for them to call upon the bishops to courageously accept their responsibility as moral leaders and teachers; to regain control of their runaway bureaucracy; and to restore the moral authority of the

---

[166] Father Mark A. Pilon, "A Moral Sellout...The Califano Doctrine," W, 3-2-76.

> Church for the guidance and well-being of Catholics and their fellow citizens.[167]

Once more, sadly, "Wanderer-types" were limited to the role of a voice decrying in the wilderness, having to remember that lack of worldly success in no way takes away the obligation of prophetic witness.

Yet, in the midst of the darkness of this era, there was another shining moment (God seems to know that we need these from time to time if we are not to become totally discouraged and just give up). The October 2, 1980 *Wanderer* tells us that "Humberto Cardinal Medeiros, Archbishop of Boston, issued a letter five days prior to the September 16 Massachusetts primaries, urging voters to vote in the elections, and to work 'to change our nation from its blood-drenched current condition to a sacrificing society that welcomes life at every stage of human development.' He urged voters 'to vote to save our children, born and unborn.'"[168] Frank Morriss, commenting on the controversy this act aroused, stated in the same issue that "voting for pro-abortionists is a type of cooperation with evil that should and must be condemned. There should be some out-and-out teaching from pulpits, chanceries, and in classrooms to the effect that he who votes for an abortionist or pro-abortionist is in effect joining hands with those who do the deed. It is not a remote thing."[169]

Yet, overall, the bishops gave little or no leadership, and seem basically to have made the decision to tolerate abortion. Joseph Gill, in an article entitled, appropriately enough, "One Wonders if They Really Care," contrasts episcopal cowardice on abortion with episcopal enthusiasm for the "peace" movement:

---

[167] A.J. Matt, Jr., "Still More Abandonment of Catholic Integrity," W, 6-26-80.

[168] Robert L. Mauro, "Cardinal Medeiros, the First Amendment, and Abortion," W, 10-2-80.

[169] Frank Morriss, "The Scandal of Catholics Voting Pro-Abortionist," W, 10-2-80.

> It is the official attitude that abortion is only one of a number of equally important right to life and environmental issues to be addressed which has drained official American Catholicism of its credibility in the fight against abortion and made it, if not a laughingstock, then a body not seriously enough interested in the right to life of the unborn to be a force to be respected let alone reckoned with.
>
> If the bishops had the gumption to mobilize the latent power in the sleeping giant which is American Catholicism and to concentrate the moral force on the problem of abortion that they are bringing to bear on the nuclear warfare issue, abortion would likely be a thing of the past. Instead they have dallied and dithered and allowed this force to be diluted and diverted until it has wasted away almost to nothing. As a result, our episcopal leadership has been a hindrance rather than a help in the effort to cure this affliction.[170]

This was about where the debate was when, on December 29, 1982, James Blanchard, the newly elected pro-abortion governor of Michigan, dropped a bombshell by announcing the appointment of Sister Agnes Mansour, a Sister of Mercy, to the position of director of the state's Department of Social Services.[171] Michigan at that time paid for abortions for welfare clients under its Medicaid program, which was administered by the Department of Social Services. That put Sister Mansour in the position of presiding over state funding of abortions, something anyone not blinded by ideology would have seen as an impossible situation for any Catholic, especially a member of a religious order. But of course years of toleration by the bishops of things like the Califano doctrine made it more difficult for Sister Agnes and the rest of the liberal Catholic crowd to see the obvious. Sister Mansour, who had previously run for Congress on a basically pro-choice platform, dutifully indicated that she was "personally op-

---

[170] Joseph T. Gill, "One Wonders if They Really Care," W, 11-18-82.

[171] Frank Teskey, "Michigan Governor Appoints Mercy Nun to High Post," W, 1-13-83.

posed" to abortion, but didn't feel she should impose her values on others, especially poor women.

There was, needless to say, an immediate uproar among Michigan pro-lifers (as a Michigan resident and active pro-lifer, I was myself a minor actor in this drama). Yet it seemed to take some time to get the attention of Church authorities. Archbishop Edmund Szoka of Detroit, in whose jurisdiction Sister Mansour lived, at first brushed off pro-life concerns, indicating that Sister Mansour had to implement the law whether she agreed with it or not. Eventually, he indicated to her that she needed to make some kind of public statement against abortion, something going beyond "personally opposed but," if she wished to keep her public position and remain in the order. Finally, in February, 1983, he did call for her resignation from her post.[172] Many of us suspected at the time that this occurred only as a result of pressure from Rome resulting from the many, many letters pro-lifers had sent to the Holy Father protesting this scandal. Sister Mansour refused to resign, and stuck to her public position that abortion was an evil but not one for which legislation was appropriate: "I don't think you can legislate until you change attitudes, because, if you do you're forcing people against their will and against their conscience to violate the law or to find other means, and I'm afraid that also is evil. I don't think this issue [abortion] lends itself easily or readily to legislative solutions. Unless abortion is unthinkable for people, they'll find a way to do it, whether there's a law or not."[173] Archbishop Szoka indicated that he had hoped she would publicly state her opposition to abortion and thus give a powerful Christian witness in the field of social services. He suggested that if American society had waited for people's attitudes to change on racism before passing civil rights laws, great harm would have been done to black people, and went on to say that

---

[172] "Archbishop Szoka Calls for Nun's Resignation from State Post," W, 3-3-83.
[173] Ibid.

> It is the position of the Catholic Church, and my position, that we must oppose and disapprove of anything that fosters or permits the continuation of the evil of abortion, including Medicaid payments for abortion. Sister Mansour's statement that "more harm could come from halting state funding" for abortions totally disregards the irreparable harm of abortion to unborn infants, a harm that is irreversible for them in their loss of life.[174]

All this, of course, just heated up the public discussion ("uproar" might be a better word), with the Sisters of Mercy and the rest of the modernist nuns attacking Szoka and the Pope, while stridently defending Sister Mansour as a champion of women's rights. *The Wanderer*, needless to say, stayed firmly in the archbishop's column, once he finally got around to acting. Here is what the late Frank Teskey, for many years *The Wanderer*'s Michigan correspondent, had to say:

> Archbishop Edmund C. Szoka is correct both theologically and prudentially in finally demanding that Sister Agnes Mary Mansour, R.S.M., resign as head of Michigan's Department of Social Services. That department administers Medicaid abortion payments; Sister Mansour publicly approves that law — the kind of law which the Church has declared to be evil; and Sister Mansour's actions are causing grave scandal to the faithful. Sister's admitted intention of approving the evil law and the scandal which has resulted leave little doubt that she is in the inexcusable position of materially cooperating with evil whether she admits it or not.
>
> Moreover, the defiance of Sister Mansour and of her ultimate religious superior, Sister Theresa Kane, R.S.M., is by itself another serious scandal.[175]

---

[174] Ibid.

[175] Frank Teskey, "Nun's Insubordination Must Be Put Down," W, 3-24-83.

Shortly afterward, the Sacred Congregation for Religious and Secular Institutes gave the archbishop strong support by ordering Sister Mansour to resign from her position in the Department of Social Services.[176] Sister Mansour's response to this, after considerable maneuvering behind the scenes, was to resign from the Sisters of Mercy while retaining her government position.[177]

That episode left most of us "Wanderer-types" with mixed feelings. We were pleased, of course, that the Church had acted and had not just chosen to quietly tolerate the scandal of a religious sister implementing public funding of abortions. At the same time, it took the Church several months to respond, and then only, one suspects, after considerable pressure was put on the bureaucracy. Governor Blanchard had announced Sister Mansour's appointment on December 29. By December 30, Archbishop Szoka should have called for her resignation. There was nothing complex about this issue. The Church's moral teaching on abortion and on cooperation with evil is really pretty straightforward. Only fear of offending secular society could have motivated the Archbishop's long delay. Furthermore, most of us would argue that, on theological as well as Canon Law grounds, Sister Mansour's administration of state-funded abortions was incompatible, not just with her membership in a religious order, but with her membership in the Church itself, and thus excommunication would have been appropriate. Here is how Joseph Gill summed things up in his retrospective piece on the incident:

> Whatever the past and present bad treatment of religious women, however seriously some communities took the call to renewal (some renewed themselves to the brink of extinction), however influenced they have been by the women's movement, whatever links have been established among communities, the fact remains that no Catholic, religious or lay, has any business doing the grisly work ex-Sister Mansour has chosen to do....It is my conviction that ex-Sister

[176] "Holy See Orders Sister Mansour to Resign," W, 4-7-83.
[177] "Sister Mansour Leaves Order," W, 5-19-83.

> Mansour has been dealt with too gently by the Church. Charity, it seems to me, not only to the millions in the Church and out for whom her action has been a grave scandal, but to her as well would be better served by a public announcement from the Holy See of her excommunication.
>
> We have arrived at the point where a mixed-up, rebellious nun has become a folk heroine because challenge after challenge to sacred teaching and necessary discipline over the last 25 years has been dodged and evaded by authorities. Every time that has happened the stage has been set for even more serious challenges and transgressions in every area of Church life.[178]

Once more, the slowness and weakness of the Church's response may have led to the further entrenchment of the abortion mentality, in secular society as well as in the Church.

From the Mansour incident on, *The Wanderer*'s call for the hierarchy to deal firmly with pro-abortion Catholics, especially those in public life, has gained steadily in volume and clarity. Robert L. Mauro stated in the August 9, 1984 issue:

> I believe the time has come when the Catholic Church must use every weapon in its arsenal to stop the slaughter of innocent children. Bishops of the Catholic Church must confront the Catholic politician who curries favor with Catholic voters by attending Mass every Sunday, and who then publicly supports abortion and funding for abortion.
>
> Excommunication is the most powerful tool the Church can use. It tells the Catholic politician he can no longer have it both ways. On Sunday, attending Mass, and asking implicitly for Catholic votes, and the rest of the week voting to allow the killing of unborn children.[179]

---

[178] Joseph T. Gill, "Let's End the Cover-Up," W, 6-23-83.

[179] Robert L. Mauro, "The Question of Excommunicating Pro-Abortion Catholic Politicians," W, 8-9-84.

1984, one may recall, also brought with it another watershed event of sorts — Geraldine Ferraro's candidacy for vice-president. Once again, the atrocity of someone calling herself a Catholic and rhapsodizing about what a vital part her faith plays in her life, while supporting abortion with the usual disclaimer about personal opposition. The American voters resoundingly let her know at the polls what they thought of this morally unconscionable position, but one of the more long-term consequences of the whole situation was the emergence of New York Governor Mario Cuomo, who came to Ferraro's defense, as an articulate spokesman for the "personally opposed, but" school of Catholic moral thought. That led to Cuomo's invitation to speak at Notre Dame University, where he gave a talk that was a masterpiece of liberal Catholic sophistry. Charles Rice, in an essay entitled "To Be Pro-Choice and Catholic Is a Contradiction in Terms," characterized the Cuomo speech as follows:

> In a way, Mario Cuomo and the Notre Dame Theology Department deserve each other. But the students of the university and their parents who pay the bills deserve better on both counts. What is at stake here is the elementary principle of truth-in-labeling. If one does not accept the teaching authority of the Pope, one ought not to represent his position as Catholic. Every religion has to have a pope, that is, an ultimate authority on religious questions, including the relation between the moral law and the civil law. The Cuomo controversy reminds us that each of us, whether a university or an individual, must decide who is the pope: Mario Cuomo? Geraldine Ferraro? Richard McBrien? Or John Paul II?[180]

At about the same time, Richard Cowden-Guido commented on the episode in an article whose title alone says it all: "Cuomo at Notre Dame...The Song of Pilate."[181] Monica Migliorino, in another won-

---

[180] Charles Rice, "To Be Pro-Choice and Catholic Is a Contradiction in Terms," W, 9-20-84.

[181] Richard Cowden-Guido, "Cuomo at Notre Dame...The Song of Pilate," W, 9-27-84.

derfully titled article, "Cuomo and the Killer State," took Cuomo to task for the contradiction between his support for abortion and his condemnation of capital punishment:

> That justice should compel Cuomo to stop the state when it kills a criminal but does not compel him to do anything as a public official when a preborn child is aborted betrays a lack of understanding on his part concerning the moral value of voluntary acts of commission and omission as they apply to individuals and the state. Cuomo views the Supreme Court decision as essentially a case of the state simply permitting the death of the preborn as if it were in a neutral position concerning their fate. Let us suppose for the moment that Cuomo's assessment of the state's position relative to abortion is correct. Any book dealing with the fundamentals of ethics teaches that a person fails in their moral obligations not only when they perform evil acts but also when they omit performing acts which could have prevented evil. For example, a father would be guilty of killing his son if he knowingly and deliberately fed his son poison. However, the father would be just as guilty if the son was drowning in the bathtub and the father simply stood by and watched when he could reach in and save the boy from death.[182]

So much for Mario Cuomo! The next watershed event (these seem to increase in frequency as time passes) concerning the Church and abortion occurred at about the same time, on October 7, 1984, when the *New York Times* carried an ad in support of abortion by a group calling itself the Catholic Committee on Pluralism and Abortion. The ad said, in essence, that Rome's position on abortion was not the only legitimate position for Catholics to take, that Catholics could validly disagree with Rome's teaching and still remain Catho-

[182] Monica M. Migliorino, "Cuomo and the Killer State," W, 10-18-84.

lic. The signatories included a number of Catholic nuns.[183] This act set the stage for several years of wrangling, as Church officials struggled, with mixed success, to induce religious orders to discipline those of their members who signed the ad. Frank Morriss probably put his finger on the truth when he suggested that the real problem was not so much the individual signers of the ad as the orders to which they belonged, orders which had moved so far away from Catholic teaching and Catholic discipline as to create an atmosphere where atrocities like the ad were bound to occur:

> ...It must be asked if the overseers of these communities are not partially at fault, along with the members of the hierarchy who are required to notice and be concerned with activities of religious orders in their jurisdictions. If those authorities are now awakened from their complacency even the inevitable scandal may be seen as worth it. But it would have been better had greater care prevented what was surely foreseeable, even by those of no great prescience.[184]

As this relentless series of scandals accumulates, a clear picture builds up of a Church that is somehow incapable of really taking a stand against the continuing slaughter of millions of unborn children. Even when the bishops do something right, as when Archbishop Maher announced the refusal of the Eucharist to publicly pro-abortion Catholics, there seemed to be a need, afterward, to backpedal at least a little to avoid giving offense to powerful groups. It is a picture of utter gutlessness. This was spelled out clearly in the January 1, 1987, *Wanderer* in an article entitled "Ecclesiastical Wimpdom: An Accusation," by one George A. Kendall, a newcomer to *The Wanderer*. Commenting on Michigan's gubernatorial election in November, 1986, an election in which a clearly pro-abortion incumbent was pitted against a clearly pro-life challenger, and Michigan's Catholic hi-

---

[183] Robert L. Mauro, "'New York Times' Ad on Abortion Contrary to Church's Declaration," W, 11-1-84.

[184] Frank Morriss, "The Church Must Address the Root of the Rot," W, 1-10-85.

erarchy did no more than utter bland pieties about the duty to get out and vote, not even suggesting that there might be anything morally questionable about Catholics voting for the pro-abortion candidate (as they did in large numbers), Kendall gave vent to the following Jeremiad:

> The hierarchy's refusal to speak out against public officials who murder the innocent is inexcusable. It constitutes a refusal of the Church's mission from Christ to teach the word of God. It is a clear example of the foolishness of believing that one can somehow serve both God and Mammon. One can only wonder how long, some centuries back, our bishops would have had to wrestle with their consciences before managing to manufacture a plausible sounding excuse for burning incense to the Roman Emperor. Perhaps they would have convinced themselves and others that refusing to do so would violate separation of Church and state.
>
> When the shepherds are so easily persuaded to let the wolves have their way, how much hope is there for the sheep?[185]

The gutlessness, needless to say, continued to cloak itself in the highly questionable "seamless garment" formula, made popular by Chicago's Joseph Cardinal Bernardin, a formula which treated abortion as just one in a whole series of (usually) liberal issues. That, as Joseph Scheidler pointed out in March, 1988, saved our bishops from having to take any kind of stance against secular society:

> The true evil of the "seamless garment" is that it provides a specious rationale for naive Catholics to vote for pro-abortion candidates on the theory that a pro-abortion stand can be winked at as long as the candidate otherwise has good liberal credentials. That is precisely the fallacy that has permitted hard-core abortionists to remain in office year after

---

[185] George A. Kendall, "Ecclesiastical Wimpdom: An Accusation," W, 1-1-87.

> year. Catholic voters have kept them there. It is this tragic error that will allow Catholics to support opportunistic turncoats on abortion like Richard Gephardt and Jesse Jackson.[186]

Finally, a note on where that gutlessness has led — not merely to passive tolerance of abortion but to active cooperation. One of the forms that cooperation has taken has been in making Catholic hospital facilities available to abortionists (this is cooperation even if the abortionists do not actually perform their abortions at these hospitals). Charles Rice had this to say about the presence of abortionists on Catholic hospital staffs:

> In the objective moral sense, though not in the legal and criminal sense, abortionists are serial murderers. In no case should such a person be retained on the staff of a Catholic hospital. The free exercise of religion would seem arguably to be infringed by laws that prevent Catholic hospitals from doing something, i.e., firing the abortionists, which their religion would lead them to do if they were not restrained by law.
>
> The bishops' failure even to challenge these laws raises the question of whether, in the era of the "seamless garment," they really do object that much to abortion. Apparently, the prospect of losing federal aid, or even of having to pay to litigate the issue, dictates that Catholic hospitals accept the presence of baby-killers on staff. Money talks. The bishops' surrender on this issue, without even a fight, gives scandal. Their position is a disgrace and it should be reversed.[187]

So there it is. A long, sad story of cowardice on the part of Catholic leaders, a history of betrayal of the Catholic community by the very people it had a right to look to for protection from the evils

---

[186] Joseph Scheidler, "Cardinal's 'Seamless Garment' Theory Is Disastrous," W, 3-24-88.

[187] Charles Rice, "A Disgraceful Policy that Must Be Abandoned," W, 7-7-88.

of our times — its shepherds, its bishops. The great opportunity Al Matt had hoped for back in 1973 was lost, and the result is that abortion has become more and more institutionalized in our society; it has become so integral to the "world taken for granted" by most Americans, and most Catholics, too, that the effort to uproot it will be a labor of Hercules, a revolutionary effort, really. And that takes us to the next part of the story, from the isolated Christian's struggle with his unwilling, spineless Church to his struggle with an increasingly anti-life state.

4. THE ANTI-LIFE STATE AND THE CIVIL DISOBEDIENCE QUESTION

"Wanderer types" are a pretty law-abiding crowd, for the most part. Bearded, long-haired anarchists with the gleam of fanaticism in their eyes are comparatively infrequent in our ranks. Like most traditional Catholics and other Christians, we strongly support the rule of law and carry no brief for civil disobedience in normal times. Unfortunately, we have not been living in normal times the last quarter-century. With the legalization of abortion we found ourselves in a situation where respect for the rule of law was no longer synonymous with respect for the civil authorities. That has happened because our civil authorities, notably our courts, have themselves been acting lawlessly when it comes to the protection of human life. That means that we no longer have a rule of law, and that what purports to be a rule of law is really just institutionalized lawlessness. Thus what may appear to many to be a lack of respect for law on the part of pro-life Christians has in reality been a great struggle to return our country to the rule of law.

It is a pretty basic principle, for Christians living in civil society, that an unjust law, a law violating the law of God, is no law at all, and that disobedience to that law may be not only a right but a duty. As Pope John XXIII said many years ago, "If any government does not acknowledge the rights of man or violates them…its orders completely lack juridical force."[188]

None of that means, though, that we are entitled to go around gratuitously getting into battles with the police over abortion without first making reasonable efforts to resolve the matter peacefully and nonviolently. Pro-life Catholics understood this, and so their first re-

[188] Quoted in "Bishops' Pastoral Letter…Rejects Court's Abortion Decision, Urges Massive Opposition," W, 2-22-73.

sponse to the situation took the form of efforts to amend the U.S. Constitution to protect the life of the unborn child. As early as June, 1973, two Human Life Amendments were already under consideration by the U.S. Congress: The Buckley Amendment, proposed by Senator James Buckley, and the Hogan Amendment, proposed by Rep. Lawrence J. Hogan.[189] Of the two, the Hogan Amendment appears to have been far and away the stronger. The Buckley Amendment contains the following provision:

> With respect to the right to life, the word 'person,' as used in this article and in the Fifth and Fourteenth Articles of Amendment to the Constitution of the United States, applies to all human beings, including their unborn offspring at every stage of their biological development, irrespective of age, health, function, or condition of dependency.

Section 2 then adds an exception withdrawing such protection where a pregnancy endangers the life of the mother. The Hogan petition contains the following language:

> Section 1. Neither the United States nor any State shall deprive any human being, from the moment of conception, of life without due process of law; nor deny to any human being, from the moment of conception, within its jurisdiction, the equal protection of the laws.
>
> Section 2. Neither the United States nor any State shall deprive any human being of life on account of illness, age, or incapacity.

Charles Rice, in his comparison and analysis of these amendments, published in the June 14, 1973 *Wanderer* under the title "The Abortion Amendments — An Analysis," praises the Hogan Amendment for its clarity in definitely protecting life from the moment of conception:

---

[189] Charles Rice, "The Abortion Amendments — An Analysis," W, 6-14-73.

> The test of a constitutional amendment on abortion is whether it will prevent the licensing of abortifacient pills and such items as the intrauterine device which should be excluded from licensing because it is likely to be, though it is not certainly, abortifacient. If abortifacient pills are licensed for use at any stage of pregnancy, even the earliest, it will be impossible to control their use at every stage. In order to prevent the licensing and legal distribution of abortifacient pills, the constitutional amendment on abortion must prohibit abortion at every stage beginning with the moment of conception. And the prohibition must be unequivocal.[190]

The Buckley Amendment, Rice pointed out, failed to specify the application of the equal protection clause of the Fourteenth Amendment to the unborn child, and thus could conceivably be interpreted as excluding the unborn child from equal protection. Furthermore, the Buckley Amendment did not specify when human life begins, whereas the Hogan Amendment did. The Hogan Amendment provided clear protection against euthanasia, something the Buckley Amendment failed to do. The "life of the mother" exception in the Buckley Amendment also presented problems:

> The Buckley Amendment would freeze into the Constitution the allowance of abortion where it is alleged to be necessary to save the life of the mother. It would permanently legitimize, in the process, the psychiatric abortion where it is claimed that the mother needs an abortion because otherwise she will commit suicide.[191]

Clearly, *The Wanderer* came down on the side of the Hogan Amendment. Sadly, as the years went by, the question became a moot one, due in part to the failure of the bishops to provide leadership in the struggle for a Human Life Amendment, and in part, it must be sadly acknowledged, due to disunity among pro-lifers. This

---

[190] Ibid.
[191] Ibid.

ultimately culminated in the lining up of the bishops and much of the right to life movement behind the Hatch Amendment, an amendment which, if passed, would have provided no protection to the unborn, but would merely have placed the issue of abortion back under the jurisdiction of the states. That compromise ultimately failed, too. If you are going to sell your soul to the devil, it is a good idea to make sure he can be held to his end of the bargain.

But even at this early stage, the pressure toward greater militancy, going beyond political activity, was already apparent. Mary R. Joyce, in a November 22, 1973 article provocatively titled, "The Time for Revolution Is Here," delivered herself of the following broadside:

> On January 22, 1973, this great ship of democracy was struck by an iceberg and was torn open all across the bottom. This democratic republic, founded on the right to life, was built to be an unsinkable vessel, [b]ut now it is taking on water and sinking. Many people on deck are taken up in pleasures and luxuries. They do not seem to notice that something is wrong with the ship because the weather is calm and the sky is clear. But other people have come up from below and they cry out, "The ship is going down!" Since these urgent people are disturbing the comfort of their fellow travelers with their unlikely story, unlikely because everyone knows this is an unsinkable ship, they are regarded as emotional, obsessed fanatics. But the fact remains that the ship is taking water fast, and the people aboard soon will be drinking water, too....The time for revolution is here! We have all been violated in the most outrageous manner. Seven judges have declared, in the rawest use of judicial power, that prenatal children can be torn limb from limb and burned inside and out because they are not persons. They have implied that women are too stupid to control their bodies without murderous child abuse. They have insinuated that fathers have no control over the early lives of their own children. Men, women, and children have all been treated as fools and have been raped to the depths of

> their being. And this violation is now part of the establishment! People who know the facts and the truth about men, women, and children will not accept this establishment. We must amend the Constitution![192]

Indeed, much of *The Wanderer*'s commentary after 1973 on the topic of abortion amounted to a continuing public debate on the question of civil disobedience — i.e., when must a Christian obey the law, or at least what purports to be the law, and when is he not only free, but perhaps obligated, to disobey? Clearly, whatever the advisability of prudence in particular situations, it seems to have become the consensus that laws which permit abortion or prohibit interference with abortion are not to be obeyed. Frank Morriss made this consensus clear in a July, 1976 article:

> The Supreme Court has unleashed a bloody pogrom upon this nation, a legally sanctioned massacre that is crushing, burning, tearing life from helpless children unable to protect themselves....Therefore, be it known that no American citizen owes allegiance to such decisions of this so-called High Court. Further, there is the duty for every lover of liberty and all who fear God and honor His decrees to resist the enforcement of these evils by every proper means.[193]

Charles Rice, in a December, 1977 article entitled "Obedience to God, Not the State," also attempted to articulate the first principle at stake here, using the Magi's disobedience to Herod as an illustration:

> It is significant that the Christian era began with an act of disobedience to a godless state. Sooner or later, the Church in America will be faced with the same choice presented to the Magi, who obeyed God rather than Herod. The issue may be the compulsory sterilization of a welfare mother or the elimination, supposedly for his own good, of a senile man who is a

[192] Mary R. Joyce, "The Time for Revolution Is Here," W, 11-22-73.
[193] Morriss, "A Legally Sanctioned Massacre," W, 7-22-76.

> "drain" on the social security system. If it comes to that, and if we read "letters from the bishop" postmarked at Leavenworth Prison, it will be nothing new in the history of the Church.[194]

Of course, Morriss's expression "every *proper* means" leaves a considerable area open for discussion. How do we in fact decide what are proper means — lobbying, demonstrations, bombing abortuaries? J.C. Hauf, writing in September, 1978, took the position that we had already exhausted the reasonable chances of putting an end to legalized abortion by political means only:

> It's time that the field of action was broadened. If it was the Supreme Court and the anti-life demagogues who foisted abortion on demand on this country, it is apparent that a gross defection by Catholics in responsible positions in government, business, and the Church only serves to nullify any effective pro-life movement.[195]

Frank Morriss also clearly implies the need for greater militance without getting into the details in a July, 1979 article responding to a recent Supreme Court decision establishing that minors may secure abortions without parental consent:

> The Supreme Court is in the hands of immoralists and anti-Constitutionalists. It is the nerve center of liberalism at its worst. Through it the most despicable philosophies are put into concrete effect. The natural law has been repealed by these gods on Olympus.
>
> There should be a national outcry against this indecency. Church and civil leaders should decry it and call for a crusade to fight against it. Do not wait for such results, however. Tyranny is imposed upon those who invite it. And the

194 Charles Rice, "Obedience to God, Not the State," W, 12-22-77.

195 J.C. Hauf, "It's Time to Broaden the Field of Action," W, 9-7-78.

> American people have invited this tyranny by their surrender to progressivism.[196]

In May, 1980, Joseph M. Scheidler, one of the most controversial figures in the right to life movement today, wrote in defense of militant tactics like picketing and trespassing on abortion facilities in order to shut them down. His position was that it is absurd to say that such activities are "counterproductive" if particular human lives are saved by them, regardless of the presence or absence of long-term benefits for the movement. After all, saving lives is what we are about:

> Some will never be convinced that sit-ins and pickets are productive because they think they are illegal. They are not. Pickets are an American tradition, and when we can no longer picket, we are no longer a viable democracy. And sit-ins, whether outside or inside the clinic, are legal and are based on a law that takes precedence over trespass laws. The common law of necessity, recognized universally in this country, says that trespass does not occur when someone enters a building to save a life or even property. Nobody sues a fireman for trespass when he enters a home to put out a fire. Nobody sues a police officer who enters a home to stop a burglary. So how can we be trespassing when we enter an abortion clinic to save lives?[197]

Here, for the first time, we encounter the "defense of necessity," destined to play a substantial role in the further legal history of pro-life militancy. What it says in effect is that it is not always illegal to break the law — i.e., that we may sometimes legitimately break a law when it is necessary to do so for the sake of some much greater good than the particular law protects. Thus we may trespass on private property or even damage property in order to save a human life,

---

[196] Morriss, "A Gross Violation of Parental Rights," W, 7-19-79.

[197] Joseph M. Scheidler, "Without a Sit-In, Amy D. Wouldn't Be Here," W, 5-8-80.

which is a greater good than property. Of course, as many pro-lifers have, to their no great surprise, discovered, actually using this defense in a court of law is easier said than done because our courts, basing their judgment on *Roe v. Wade*, generally refuse to acknowledge that a human life is at stake in abortion. Nevertheless, it is of crucial importance for anyone wanting to understand what pro-life "civil disobedience" is about to understand the defense of necessity. The movement does not hold that we may disobey the law in order to save human life. Rather, it holds that we may disobey the civil authorities when they enforce "laws" which, on both constitutional and moral grounds, are unjust and hence null and void. In other words, it is not a matter of disobeying the civil law for the sake of the moral law, but rather of disobeying a pseudo-law which is no law at all. Laws permitting abortion are not just immoral — they are not laws, because no court or legislative body has the constitutional power to enact laws which take away the protection of innocent life. Thus: 1) we may "disobey" a valid but lesser law, like that of trespass, for the sake of a higher law which protects human life; in which case we are not actually disobeying the law, and 2) we may disobey a pseudo-law, like the *Roe v. Wade* precedent, in order to obey the real law, which always protects human life.

Similarly, Christian people who seek to restore the sanctity of life in a society where life has become cheap have to see themselves as people who, in seeking the genuine peace of Christ, have to attack the false peace which Christ came to destroy, a point the ever-present Frank Morriss made in a December, 1980 article commenting on the arrest of one Ned Labato for the crime of "disturbing the peace" by praying at an abortion facility:

> I know he wasn't disturbing the peace as the city ordinance intended that act to be. And I'm glad he didn't have to spend time in jail or pay a fine. Yet somehow I am sorry the jury — speaking for the civil authority — didn't think he was disturbing the peace, for indeed he was if you interpret the peace to be the complacent status quo that can go its way on

> daily business while in the clinic in question (one of thousands) some 2,000 babies die each year.
>
> This defendant had the proper Christian attitude. Christ said He had come to bring a sword, to cast fire upon the earth. He meant He had come to cut His followers asunder from the secular values and worldly measure of esteem. He had come to set raging a spiritual fire that includes intransigence against evil and indignation at its acceptance, particularly its public acceptance. And so Ned Labato, as a follower of Christ, did what all such followers should in one way or another — he made known publicly his disapproval and rejection of killing babies, praying for them and for the souls of those responsible for this abomination.
>
> And he did succeed in disturbing the peace — that is the peace of mind of those who brought the charges against him.[198]

The question of actual civil disobedience, however, remained and remains quite controversial among "Wanderer-types," as Charles Rice's August, 1981 remarks on tactics attest:

> I am convinced that the disruptive tactics are self-defeating and should not be employed. Permissive abortion laws are unjust and so are the laws that protect the murder factories against those who would rescue the victims. The clinics have a legal but not a moral right to exist and the conclusion that they should not be disrupted is not based on respect for the laws that authorize the killing of innocents or those that protect the clinics from disruption. The judgment, rather, is tactical. Disruptive tactics are ultimately self-defeating. The protesters are arrested and prosecuted, they are taken out of circulation by jail sentences or injunctions, they are subjected to potentially ruinous civil suits, and the resources of the movement are disproportionately diverted to unproductive

[198] Frank Morriss, "The 'Peace' Should Be Disturbed," W, 12-11-80.

> legal defense. On the other hand, the lawful rosary vigil, with prayer, literature distribution, and counseling, is a tactic that can bring down the whole structure of legalized abortion.[199]

I feel it necessary to make one comment on this, in my role as an actor, however minor, in this history as well as a chronicler: I believe it is inappropriate and concedes too much to the enemy to say that abortuaries have a legal but not a moral right to exist. The alleged legal right of abortuaries to exist is grounded in *Roe v. Wade*, itself an illegal decision because it involved a usurpation by the Supreme Court of powers it does not have. Whether or not it is a good tactic to disrupt abortuaries, it is not breaking the law, because the abortuaries, in reality, have neither a moral nor a legal right to exist (though of course any courts in which we are put on trial are unlikely to acknowledge this).

The debate over civil disobedience heated up considerably when some activists went beyond sit-ins and picketing to bombing abortion facilities. Late in 1984, four young people in Pensacola, Florida bombed an abortuary, feeling that they were giving a birthday present to the baby Jesus. Richard Cowden-Guido, writing in the January 17, 1985 issue, argued that just war criteria can be applied to such acts:

> In regard to the recent spate of abortion clinic bombings, it should be recalled that just war criteria can sometimes apply to intolerable social situations. That is, the use of force must have a reasonable chance of success. If successful, it must offer a better situation than the one that would have obtained in the absence of the use of force. It must be proportional to the objectives being sought. And the force must be used with the intention of sparing noncombatants and with a reasonable prospect of actually doing so.
>
> Since abortion has been stopped for the time being in Pensacola, Florida, and without loss of life to noncombatants, it can be argued that Matthew Goldsby and Thomas Simmons,

[199] Charles Rice, "Some Observations on Pro-Life Tactics," W, 8-13-81.

> both 21 years old, Simmons' wife Kathy, and Goldsby's fiancee Kay Wiggins, both 18, have met at least some of the above criteria. But there also remains the prudential question. Assuming the bombings have more than just the immediate effect of saving lives in Pensacola (a large assumption), would that effect be to keep the abortion industry thriving longer than it might otherwise have done? Or will it be to make our legislators finally understand that *Roe v. Wade* drove a nail into the side of this nation, and that the bleeding will not stop until the nail is removed?
>
> These, it would seem, are debatable questions.[200]

Charles Rice, shortly afterward, added his own comments in an editorial called "The Bomber as Victim":

> The question of whether one who seeks to save babies ought to sit-in at abortuaries, break up their furniture, or otherwise obstruct their activities, is therefore a prudential, tactical question, unencumbered by any valid claim that the abortuaries have a moral right to exist.
>
> It is not surprising that there are bombings. What is surprising is that they have been so long in coming. The regime of legalized abortion is so contrary to natural justice that it is predictable that some persons would grow impatient with legal and peaceful opposition and would turn to direct, violent action. In this sense, the bombers are themselves victims. The real cure for this problem is to stop the slaughter which predictably leads some people to turn to violence.[201]

Frank Morriss, never one to steer clear of a controversy, weighed in with his own comments in February, 1985. Acknowledging that bombings, as tactics, may be counterproductive, he added that:

---

[200] Richard Cowden-Guido, "Morality and the Pensacola Four," W, 1-17-85.
[201] Charles Rice, "The Bomber as Victim," W, 1-24-85.

> Having said that, I cannot find anything in good ethics or theology that would judge the bombings immoral *per se*, and I dare to suggest some more moral civilization in which abortion is once more recognized as a high crime will memorialize as heroes those who are jailed for doing the bombings.
>
> We can certainly say, paraphrasing Lincoln, that this nation cannot long endure part anti-life and part pro-life. Abortion will be ended, or else there will be major violence in the attempt to end it. Decency demands that, and as long as decency survives, it will wage war on behalf of innocent life. As the means of winning the war are exhausted, others will be taken up. I hope force will be the last means, the final one as dictated by good morals in regard to war, strikes, etc. But let us not be pacifists in regard to abortion. Let us not say that force to end it as a last resort is unthinkable, anymore than war to end slavery was unthinkable to this country as the issues were faced, debated, and finally honestly accepted.
>
> But let us admit that there is a war, even if it is in the preliminary stage. And let us admit that there will be casualties in a war. Already, the casualties on the side of innocent unborn life count in the tens of millions. *That* is the shocking fact — not that some have grown impatient and rushed to arms even at the risk of their own liberty.[202]

More comment on the bombings came on March 28, when Aaron Everett took the position that the bombings were not justifiable, but were understandable:

> We must not sanction the activities of the arsonists and bombers but we must also recognize that their cause is just. The cause is just but the means are unacceptable. It should be clear to those who cry out against this destruction of property that for those attacking the clinics something much greater is

[202] Frank Morriss, "It Is a War that Is Going On," W, 2-14-85.

> involved here: the willful destruction of human lives. Until that is recognized and some corrective action is taken the opposition will and must continue. What those opposed to abortion must do is follow the example of the civil rights activists: picket abortion clinics whenever they are open for business. It may take longer but, in the end, some rights are not denied in seeking to assure other rights.[203]

That point of view seems to ignore the necessity defense (see above), a defense which Charles Rice discussed in June:

> When the history of this time is written, Curt Beseda, Matt Goldsby, Jimmy and Katherine Simmons, Kay Wiggins and others like them, such as Michael Bray, a minister convicted recently of complicity in destroying abortuaries in the Washington, D.C., area, will be rightly regarded as would be a young German who had destroyed the gas chambers at Auschwitz in 1942. My own acquaintance is limited to Curt Beseda and the Pensacola Four. But each of these young people, in human terms, is worth 100 yuppies (or apprentice yuppies in college or graduate school). They put themselves on the line for the right. As one counsel in the Pensacola case observed, "It's the chance of a lifetime, to defend someone who is morally entirely innocent."
>
> As mentioned above, I do not believe that the answer to the abortion problem is to be found in blowing up the murder factories. And I would plead with any person contemplating such action to reconsider and not to do it. The young people in these cases, however, have made a direct appeal to the conscience of America. They are admirable. And they are no less victims of abortion than are the unborn, murdered children. It remains for us to decide whether we will respond to

[203] Aaron Everett, "When the Laws Do Not Protect," W, 3-28-85.

> their sacrifice or whether we will be "good Germans" and close our eyes to the Holocaust.[204]

Rice is saying, in effect, that we must take two views of the bombings, depending on whether we are talking about them before or after the fact. Before the fact, we may certainly hold that, for tactical reasons, bombings are not a good idea. After the fact, however, when it is too late to prevent the bombings, we must acknowledge the genuine heroism of the people who put their liberty on the line to stop the killing of the innocent. There is no room here for the kind of sanctimonious platitudes that "mainstream" pro-life organizations often issue to the press, emphasizing how deeply shocked they are by bombings, and dissociating themselves in every possible way from the bombers, like Peter denying that he even knew Jesus.

In August, Frank Morriss added to what was clearly a growing consensus that there could be no objections in principle to abortuary bombings, but only tactical objections, in an editorial called "No Moral Arguments Against Destroying Abortuaries":

> I fail to understand the reasoning of those, both conservatives and others, who condemn destructive force brought against abortion facilities as immoral. There are many arguments against such actions, but immorality surely is not one of them....There came a time when slavery could no longer be tolerated while legislators and judges and officials failed to prohibit it. But slavery is in some ways a lesser evil than abortion — for its victims could say that while there was life there was hope. The marked victims of abortion face an extermination of hope almost at their beginning, along with their life.
>
> It is more and more apparent that the time of toleration cannot be extended much longer.[205]

---

[204] Charles Rice, "Abortuary Bombing and the Justification Defense," W, 6-27-85.

[205] Frank Morriss, "No Moral Arguments Against Destroying Abortuaries," W, 8-1-85.

The reference to toleration perhaps puts the finger on the key point that all this discussion brought clearly into focus for *Wanderer* readers — that abortion is an atrocity that cannot be tolerated any longer, and the concern for "respect for law" could easily become just an excuse for moral laziness and the flight from all risk. As one *Wanderer* contributor put it in July, 1987:

> Sooner or later, we pro-lifers are going to have to face the fact that our efforts to overturn *Roe v. Wade* by lobbying and education have accomplished little or nothing, and the slaughter goes on. Whether we like it or not, we are at war, and we are losing the war by confining ourselves to these methods. We will turn the tide only when masses of people take to the streets and begin to close down these death chambers.
>
> Whatever one's position on out-and-out civil disobedience, however, the bottom line is that we must stop tolerating the practice of abortion and we must stop implicitly acknowledging the right of abortion chambers to exist. Those of us who do not choose to go to prison must at least be prepared to do everything in our power to aid and defend those who do, and perhaps risk jobs and careers in the process. We have no business treating people like Joan Andrews and Father Edward Markley...as embarrassments and disavowing them as Peter disavowed Christ.[206]

So after all these years, the matter has become clear. As Christians and as citizens, we find ourselves, when we confront abortion, dealing not just with another controversial issue, but with a modern state which has usurped God-like powers for itself, and must be resisted. A state which puts itself in God's place is a totalitarian state, and will create a totalitarian society to the extent that it succeeds in imposing itself on the whole society. That state's tolerance for, and, indeed, pushing of abortion has been an enormously important step in its im-

[206] George A. Kendall, "Human Life and 'Respect for Law,'" W, 7-30-87.

position of a totalitarian order on society. We are at war with that state, and must acknowledge that fact to ourselves as well as to others. Otherwise, we will just add to the confusion of the current situation. The *Wanderer* debate on civil disobedience and the right to life has done a great deal to dispel the confusion.

5. ABORTION AND SPIRITUAL WARFARE

What the secular press and, for that matter, most of the Catholic press, has never seemed very able to understand is that the struggle over abortion is not just about physical evil, the destruction of human life, nor is it just about politics — it is, most fundamentally, about spiritual disorder, and the social disorder which emanates from spiritual disorder because, as Plato recognized millennia ago, disorder in the soul produces disorder in society, which is man (the soul) writ large. Abortion, perhaps more than any of the other evils of our time, destroys the right order in the relationship between man and God. That, in turn, is destructive of the relationship between man and his neighbor, within the human community, and, finally, is destructive of the individual self, the soul.

The spiritual destruction of abortion is an attack on man at the level of the most basic relationships. General Thomas Lane recognized this in an April, 1970 editorial:

> It should be clear that there is no natural justification of abortion. It is not a healing a[c]t. Every woman is better physically and mentally for carrying her child to a natural birth than she would be in aborting him. With modern medicine, we do not choose between the life of the mother and the life of the child: both are saved. Arguments for abortion are an example of the frailty of human reason. They attack the close bond of mother and child, the most basic of all human ties. They were used long ago in Sodom and Gomorrah.
>
> When we speak of a "permissive" society, we mean permissive of evil. No one needs any permission to do what is

> good and wholesome. A permissive society is a decadent society.[207]

The abortion mentality presupposes a radically anti-Christian understanding of man and of the human self, an understanding which sees a human being as an isolated atom within society, an atom which is not bound by either rights or duties, and certainly not by love, for God or for neighbor. This atomistic individual exists only for its egoistic self-gratification, for "self-actualization," for control over its life, and so forth. That means a flat, lusterless idea of human life, it means a human life without love and without courage, without the great adventure to which love summons us. John Hagen said this very well in a May, 1975, editorial called "Liberal View on Abortion Is Bourgeois":

> To be bourgeois is, quite simply, to be an egocentric materialist. It means denying or ignoring the spiritual and social kinship of man, and reducing all human rights and human dignity to the single principle of autonomy. And it is only in a sheerly bourgeois context that the pro-abortion slogans seem unanswerable.[208]

Mary E. Cook's analysis of the pro-abortion worldview in September, 1976, shows how radically that worldview contradicts the 2,000-year-old Christian understanding of man and his dignity as a child of God:

> The attitudes implicit in the Supreme Court decision on pornography helped to pave the way for the abortion decision by lowering the standards of society on the dignity of man....It has been said that what is at stake in the abortion debate is not simply the fate of the murdered children or of the individual woman or even the destiny of individual nations and cultures. What is at stake is the rejection of a worldview

[207] Thomas Lane, "Lawmakers Pervert Society," W, 4-30-70.
[208] John Hagen, "Liberal View on Abortion Is Bourgeois," W, 5-8-75.

> which has sustained a way of life, a mode of being in the world, a pattern of response to the human condition. In essence, an entire system of meaning is at stake, a Christian meaning.[209]

Father Paul Marx, writing in October, 1976, shows us how the destruction of the soul by the abortion mentality is intimately related to human sexuality, which is at the very center of the human personality:

> The gigantic worldwide struggle between pro-life and anti-life forces revolves ultimately around the nature, meaning, and purpose of human sexuality. So all-pervasive is sexuality in the human personality that even the slightest change in emphasis in attitudes toward it will profoundly affect both society and the individual....Widespread contraception is the gateway to abortion, which is not "one" issue, as so many have been brainwashed to believe.[210]

And so we are caught up not just in a political struggle but in spiritual warfare, in a struggle between spiritual order and spiritual disorder. We are in a war for man's very soul. Abortion is a kind of abscess, a kind of focal point of infection from which spiritual disease spreads throughout the person and the world, as Joseph T. Gill made plain in an article titled "The Single Issue Which Bears on All Others":

> My reasoning is simply that a man or woman whose thought processes are so clouded and flawed that he or she does not understand that killing an unborn child is no less heinous a crime than killing someone who has been born is not intellectually equipped to make the right decisions in any other sphere of human activity — political, economic, moral, international relations, what have you.

[209] Mary E. Cook, "Rejection of a Worldview," W, 9-30-76.
[210] Father Paul Marx, "Who Is Really Pro-Life," W, 10-28-76.

> We place our nation and its people in greatest jeopardy when we entrust its affairs to the sort of minds which have difficulty understanding the humanity of unborn babies and their fundamental right to life once conceived.[211]

In truth, abortion is a spiritual cancer which, once it has gotten itself established in the soul, metastasizes everywhere. Sadly, one of the places it tends to metastasize to at times is the pro-life movement itself, to the extent that even some pro-life people do not really grasp the nature of abortion as a spiritual disorder, but see it merely as a political problem to be dealt with by political methods alone. Charles Rice writing in August, 1983, saw the demise of the Hatch Amendment, the ultimate political expression of this misunderstanding of the matter, as a turning point toward a spiritual deepening of the right to life movement:

> These developments can fairly be said to mark the interment of the old pro-life movement, which met its demise when it came under the domination of leaders who could not resist the political operative's temptation to trivialize the issue by treating abortion as a suitable topic for political negotiation, much like a highway appropriation.
>
> Although the old pro-life movement is dead by its own hand, there are signs that a newer movement is emerging which has the potential of real success. For one thing, a hard-nosed, no-compromise political strategy is evident in the work of the American Life Lobby, the March for Life, the U.S. Coalition for Life, and other groups. One of their primary emphases is on the termination of federal funding for abortion and for Planned Parenthood.
>
> ...With developments like these increasing across the country, the real pro-life movement is far from dead. It is just beginning. And if it stays on course, with no-compromise po-

[211] Joseph T. Gill, "The Single Issue Which Bears on All Others," W, 3-29-79.

> litical and legislative action and with the emphasis on prayer and sidewalk counseling, it will succeed.[212]

A particularly virulent, even Satanic, expression of the spiritual disorder of the anti-life mentality came when a "philosopher" named Peter Singer published an article, known to some as the "Pro-Pig Manifesto," which said, in essence, that a healthy pig has greater value and a greater right to life than a human infant with Down's syndrome or some other severe handicap. This is the kind of thing that makes one wonder whether to write a rebuttal or contact an exorcist, but Richard Cowden-Guido adopted the first strategy, writing that

> Baby Doe, in short, *deserved* to die [per Singer] and *Roe v. Wade* made it possible.
>
> Our Lord came to earth to assert precisely the opposite; that a man, even a handicapped one (even a baby girl) is a gift, not of the state, but of God. The state's disagreement with this truth has been responsible for giving the Church many martyrs. It is to be hoped that a vigorous response by the American bishops on the subject of infanticide will obviate such a necessity this time around, but don't count on it....The long-term battle is the one that is always with us; whether we as a nation shall follow the dictates of the Ten Commandments, or the Pro-Pig Manifesto. And may those bishops and politicians who equivocate in this matter win the same respect we afford to quislings who compromised before Hitler's infanticide program of the '30s and '40s, from which the American Academy of Pediatrics has borrowed its thesis.[213]

The struggle against abortion is the struggle against the destruction of the soul. It must be fought with the weapons of the spirit as well as

---

[212] Charles Rice, "Pro-Life Movement Deepening in Spiritual Dimension," W, 8-25-83.

[213] Richard Cowden-Guido, "The Pro-Pig Manifesto," W, 9-1-83.

with the ordinary weapons of political action, and has to be directed at the whole context of man's existence as a spiritual being and a child of God called to eternal happiness with God. An article of mine which appeared in August, 1988, called "A Prophetic Identity," tried to clarify the differences between ordinary action and action in the context of spiritual warfare. At the risk of appearing to be on an ego trip, I will quote it at some length:

> ...Pro-life action in the end makes no sense as action *within* the world, *within* the human community, but only as action *within* the larger community built up out of God's friendship with the whole creation — the community we Christians call the Communion of Saints. Pro-life action makes little sense *within* the world, where results are what counts. But it does make sense as action which manifests the right order between God and the world, the right order which is the norm for any right order in society. It makes sense as action which proclaims, which reveals, the divine truth which both condemns and redeems the world. It is action for and against the world, not action *in* the world....If pro-life action is not normal political action within a normal social order but is action directed at a crisis situation and grounded in principles beyond those that govern the world, then it must be judged in terms of its own proper principles, not in terms of those which govern other forms of action. In crisis situations, what counts is the proclaiming, the witnessing to, the truth, against the untruth which is destroying the human community. This proclamation is a good and a duty whether or not it brings results. Socrates was not able to save Athens from the corruption which was devouring it. Neither was Jeremiah able to save Israel from the idolatry which led to its conquest and to the captivity. Yet there was nothing futile or meaningless about their work, work which survived the destruction of those

> particular societies and became a shining light to all mankind.[214]

John Mulloy, in response to the above remarks, further clarified the spiritual essence which separates the right to life movement from purely social and political movements:

> But we have no reason to assume that saving our society from disaster is what lies in God's providential purposes. However attached we are to our society, we must remember, as C.S. Lewis has emphasized, that only human persons have immortal souls, not societies and civilizations. The basic test of the value of any outcome, therefore, is not whether it tends to the saving of society from disaster, but whether it leads to the saving of immortal souls.[215]

Because it has all too often failed to see the abortion issue in its spiritual dimension, the "mainstream" right to life movement, whatever its good intentions, has often failed to appreciate the depth of spiritual evil which is behind the movement for abortion. It has accordingly tended to see the legalization of abortion as a mistake, not a true evil, and has sought to correct that mistake by education and legislation. Its methods have failed, and are still failing today, in 1997, because they simply are not fitted to the nature of the evil. Again, a quotation from one of my own writings (October, 1988) seems to me to sum up the essence of the matter:

> Only an abyss of love can overcome an abyss of evil, and the evil of abortion is such an abyss. This evil is rooted in a profound hatred of God and, because it is unable to destroy Him, it seeks to destroy His creation. But the true depth of love, the abyss of love, can only mean the giving of one's very self for the one loved, the sacrifice of self to overcome evil....This means that a great evil can only be overcome by

[214] George A. Kendall, "A Prophetic Identity," W, 8-11-88.
[215] John J. Mulloy, "Prophetic Witness and Its Meaning," W, 8-25-88.

> great suffering, not because there is anything intrinsically good about suffering, but because when great love confronts great evil, suffering is the inevitable outcome. Only the giving of self can overcome the absorption in self, the withholding of self, the worship of self, which is evil. Great love means giving ourselves, not just our time, money, or work, it means sacrifice. The depth of evil can't be cured by superficial solutions — education, lobbying. It can only be cured by sacrifice. Education cannot *atone* for abortion, and atonement is what is needed. It is a horrible violation of spiritual order which calls for atonement, and atonement means representative suffering, like Christ's, suffering which individual human beings accept voluntarily for the sake of all.[216]

Pope John Paul II did much to intensify this sense of spiritual warfare when, in 1995, he issued his encyclical *Evangelium Vitae* ("The Gospel of Life") in what must, I think, be regarded as the Church's definitive (and long overdue) declaration of war on the principalities and powers which have tried so hard to erase the sense of the sanctity of human life from the human heart. Here the Holy Father spelled out, in the starkest terms possible, the opposition of the culture of life, rooted in the Good News of Jesus Christ, and the culture of death, rooted in man's rebellion against God and against his own essence as a child of God, made in God's own image. Early Christian literature spoke eloquently of the two ways man must choose between: The way of death and the way of life, and *Evangelium Vitae* is the Church's latest expression of this theme:

> In fact, while the climate of widespread moral uncertainty can in some way be explained by the multiplicity and gravity of today's social problems, and these can sometimes mitigate the subjective responsibility of individuals, it is no less true

[216] George A. Kendall, "Prophetic Witness: The Call to Atonement," W, 10-13-88.

> that we are confronted by an even larger reality, which can be described as a veritable *structure of sin.* This reality is characterized by the emergence of a culture which denies solidarity and in many cases takes the form of a veritable "culture of death."[217]

This culture of death, first and foremost originating in man's rejection of God, has, as its essence, the extreme subjectivism which so characterizes our times. As the Pope says, commenting on the strange contradiction of an age which proclaims its devotion to human rights while attacking the sanctity of human life at every opportunity:

> What are *the roots of this remarkable contradiction*? We can find them in an overall assessment of a cultural and moral nature, beginning with the mentality which *carries the concept of subjectivity to an extreme* and even distorts it, and recognizes as a subject of rights only the person who enjoys full or at least incipient autonomy and who emerges from a state of total dependence on others.[218]
>
> At another level, the roots of the contradiction between the solemn affirmation of human rights and their tragic denial in practice lies in a *notion of freedom* which exalts the isolated individual in an absolute way, and gives no place to solidarity, to openness to others and service of them.[219]
>
> Yes, every man is his "brother's keeper," because God entrusts us to one another. And it is also in view of this entrusting that God gives everyone freedom, a freedom which possesses an *inherently relational dimension*. This is a great gift of the Creator, placed as it is in the service of the person and of his fulfillment through the gift of self and openness to oth-

[217] Pope John Paul II, *The Gospel of Life: Evangelium Vitae* (Pauline Books and Media: Boston, 1995), n. 12, hereafter cited as *EV.*

[218] *EV*, n. 19.

[219] Ibid.

> ers; but when freedom is made absolute in an individualistic way, it is emptied of its original content, and its very meaning and dignity are contradicted.[220]
>
> This situation, with its lights and shadows, ought to make us all fully aware that we are facing an enormous and dramatic clash between good and evil, death and life, the "culture of death" and the "culture of life." We find ourselves not only "faced with" but necessarily "in the midst of" this conflict: we are all involved and we all share in it, with the inescapable responsibility of *choosing to be unconditionally pro-life.*[221]

What throws all discussion of concepts like human rights and human dignity into utter confusion is the fact that modern, anti-Christian thought justifies itself ideologically as *humanism*, while it is in fact profoundly anti-human. In contrast, Catholic moral teaching, while stigmatized routinely as opposed to humanism, is in fact profoundly humanistic because its anthropology is rooted in Christ Himself, the one embodiment of perfect humanity. Hence:

> The life which God gives man is quite different from the life of all other living creatures, inasmuch as man, although formed from the dust of the earth..., *is a manifestation of God in the world, a sign of His presence, a trace of His glory....*[222]
>
> This involves above all proclaiming *the core* of this Gospel. It is the proclamation of a living God who is close to us, who calls us to profound communion with Himself, and awakens in us the certain hope of eternal life. It is the affirmation of the inseparable connection between the person, his life and his bodiliness. It is the presentation of human life as a life of

[220] Ibid.
[221] *EV*, n. 28.
[222] *EV*, n. 34.

> relationship, a gift of God, the fruit and sign of His love. It is the proclamation that Jesus has a unique relationship with every person, which enables us to see in every human face the face of Christ. It is the call for a "sincere gift of self" as the fullest way to realize our personal freedom.[223]

In contrast, the culture of death, with all its humanistic pretensions, is in fact deeply anti-human in its implications:

> Within this same cultural climate, the *body* is no longer perceived as a properly personal reality, a sign and place of relations with others, with God, and with the world. It is reduced to pure materiality: it is simply a complex of organs, functions and energies to be used according to the sole criteria of pleasure and efficiency. Consequently, *sexuality* too is depersonalized and exploited: from being the sign, place, and language of love, that is, of the gift of self and acceptance of another, in all the other's richness as a person, it increasingly becomes the occasion and instrument for self-assertion and the selfish satisfaction of personal desires and instincts. Thus the original import of human sexuality is distorted and falsified, and the two meanings, unitive and procreative, inherent in the very nature of the conjugal act, are artificially separated: in this way the marriage union is betrayed and its fruitfulness is subjected to the caprice of the couple. *Procreation* then becomes the "enemy" to be avoided in sexual activity: if it is welcomed, this is only because it expresses a desire, or indeed the intention, to have a child "at all costs," and not because it signifies the complete acceptance of the other and therefore an openness to the richness of life which the child represents.[224]

---

[223] *EV*, n. 81.
[224] *EV*, n. 23.

> To claim the right to abortion, infanticide, and euthanasia, and to recognize that right in law, means to attribute to human freedom a *perverse and evil significance*: that of an *absolute power over others and against others*. This is the death of true freedom: "Truly, truly, I say to you, every one who commits sin is a slave to sin" (*Jn* 8:34).[225]

The destruction of humanity thus ends up being the one thing to which the culture of death, paradoxically, gives birth, a process Father Paul Marx traced in some detail in an editorial in the May 18, 1995 issue of *The Wanderer*:

> Once you have contraception, legal abortion often follows eventually, if for no other reason, given the failure of contraception. Also contraception steps up irresponsible sexual activity; people become careless about their sexual activity, leaving in its wake ever-more unwanted pregnancies. Therefore, anti-life people argue that we must have "backup" legal abortion. Further, if parents contracept, they have lost their role as parents to exemplify chastity and to teach it to their young. So now you get ever-more irresponsible teen intercourse, ever-more unintended pregnancies, ever-more venereal disease, and ever-more sterility later among married couples. Sexual morality evaporates, as we get recreational sexual activity.
>
> Additionally, with legal abortion, adoption services dry up. Despite widespread contraception, ever-more illegitimate births occur, and venereal disease often escalates out of control. With legal abortion comes the prostitution of the medical and legal professions; the family is destroyed, as are birthrates, and with that comes the dying of the nations.[226]
>
> Babies are the only future that a nation has; babies are the only future the married couple has; what is left of any mar-

[225] *EV*, n. 20.
[226] Father Paul Marx, O.S.B., "The Gospel of Life," W, 5-18-95.

> riage in old age but children who come to visit at Christmas and Easter, and rush to their deathbed from all parts of the country to pray them into Heaven, where, we hope, they will join them in Heaven for all eternity. Non-replacement birthrates create many problems. I became acutely aware that every worthwhile cause one can think of assumes the continuation of human life.[227]
>
> Today, the whole Western world is dying out. Italy has the lowest birthrate in the Western world with 1.2 children per completed family (needed for reproduction: 2.2); the Russians have the lowest birthrate in the world, with 1.1 children; last year, they had 800,000 more coffins than cradles, as the blunt Germans put it. Meanwhile, one billion Moslems are poised to take over Western Europe.[228]

Father Marx accordingly sees *Evangelium Vitae* as a kind of manifesto declaring the Church's unconditional opposition to this terrible downward trend:

> The encyclical is truly a remarkable document. It is a Magna Charta for the Church and mankind on life and family issues. The immediate attacks and rejections from Planned Parenthood, the pseudo-Catholics for a Free Choice, and others only prove how the Pope has zeroed in on the most vital questions of our time.
>
> But will the world listen: Will the bishops in the Western world act? Will our many dissenting theologians follow through? Will they finally see that contraception is the root of so many evils in the destruction of youth, family, Church, and state — and act? Will our bishops now revamp the many sick marriage preparation programs and promote natural family planning as well? Sterilization has become the most

[227] Ibid.
[228] Ibid.

> widespread means of birth control in the United States and the world. Will natural family planning continue to be the great secret in the Catholic Church? Will sex ed continue to destroy our youth?[229]
>
> One of the great tragedies of our time, as *The Gospel of Life* so well demonstrates, is that the Church obviously has the truth about God's great gift of human sexuality, marriage, and the family, but it has not been able for whatever all the reasons to instill this in the young, in those getting married, and in those who as parents could be living examples of loving chastity, without which there can be no authentic human love and a healthy family or society.[230]
>
> This encyclical is a Godsend. It presents the only remedy for the sex mess that pervades the whole affluent West and other parts of the world, influenced by the money and media of the wealthy nations. But will Christians and men of goodwill listen and change? The future of the Church and mankind depends on it.[231]

The culture of death, destructive as it is to right order within the human soul and thus to human dignity, is, by that very fact, destructive of the social and political order. The giving of self, and the existence in community that follows from that gift, is, in the Holy Father's understanding, of the very essence of our humanity. The culture of death rejects the gift of self and hence rejects all genuine human community, though, again, it tries to present itself as the promoter of human community, by way of some notion such as the "New World Order." Nothing could be further from the truth:

---

[229] Ibid.
[230] Ibid.
[231] Ibid.

> In this sense, abortion goes beyond the responsibility of individuals and beyond the harm done to them, and takes on a distinctly social dimension. It is a most serious *wound* inflicted on society and its culture by the very people who ought to be society's promoters and defenders.[232]

> If, at the end of the last century, the Church could not be silent about the injustices of those times, still less can she be silent today, when the social injustices of the past, unfortunately not yet overcome, are being compounded in many regions of the world by still more grievous forms of injustice and oppression, even if these are being presented as elements of progress in view of a New World Order.[233]

What *Evangelium Vitae* finds especially reprehensible is the fact that this terrible spiritual and moral disorder, this violation of the most elementary principles of justice, has become institutionalized and embodied in the "laws" of so many nations, not least the United States. One of the great strengths of this particular encyclical is that the Pope makes it quite clear that laws permitting or promoting such practices as abortion and euthanasia have no legitimacy — they are not merely unjust laws, they are not laws at all:

> Laws which authorize and promote abortion and euthanasia are therefore radically opposed not only to the good of the individual but also to the common good; as such they are completely lacking in authentic juridical validity. Disregard for the right to life, precisely because it leads to the killing of the person whom society exists to serve, is what most directly conflicts with the possibility of achieving the common good. Consequently, a civil law authorizing abortion or

[232] *EV*, n. 59.
[233] *EV*, n. 4.

> euthanasia ceases by that very fact to be a true, morally binding civil law.[234]
>
> Abortion and euthanasia are thus crimes which no human law can claim to legitimize. There is no obligation in conscience to obey such laws; instead there is a *grave and clear obligation to oppose them by conscientious objection.*[235]
>
> In the case of an intrinsically unjust law, such as a law permitting abortion or euthanasia, it is therefore never licit to obey it, or to "take part in a propaganda campaign in favor of such a law, or vote for it."[236]

Thus, the Holy Father clearly and unequivocally takes a stand for civil disobedience where laws clearly violate the law of God concerning the sanctity of human life. Paul Clark, in a January 4, 1996 editorial, notes that many commentators have ignored this all-important aspect of *Evangelium Vitae*, and expands on it at some length:

> The assertion that an unjust edict has no force of law is a long-established principle in Western thought. Cicero insisted that true law is based on justice and the common good; statutes which were unjust, he wrote, "no more deserve to be called laws than the rules a band of robbers might pass." The Catholic Church has long taught this, but also has taught that the Holy Father is the ultimate arbiter of the justice or injustice of civil law. Up through the last century, it was common for Pontiffs to declare laws, and sometimes entire regimes, illegitimate.[237]
>
> In *Evangelium Vitae*, however, the Holy Father goes beyond the general statements that unjust edicts are not laws, and

[234] *EV*, n. 72.
[235] *EV*, n. 73.
[236] *EV*, n. 73.
[237] Paul Clark, "'Evangelium Vitae': A Call For Resistance," W, 1-4-96.

declares invalid particular laws. The fact that the Holy Father so forcefully and explicitly declared invalid laws supporting abortion, contraception, euthanasia, and other sins against life is a surprising and highly significant turn. Pope John Paul repeatedly insists that civil law derives its force from the natural moral law and therefore edicts which support evil have no moral force.[238]

Catholics have a moral obligation to actively resist and disobey unjust laws. I see no other alternative but that Catholic officials from police officers to governors have a moral obligation to refuse to enforce laws which support abortion and other "rights" to do wrong. In the case of governors or mayors, it would even seem to follow that such officials have an obligation to enforce the demands of the common good and reject federal mandates protecting and encouraging inherently unjust activities.[239]

Pope John Paul II quotes *Pacem in Terris* as saying that "any government which refused to recognize human rights or acted in violation of them would not only fail in its duty; its decrees would be wholly lacking in binding force" (n. 71). In the context of *Evangelium Vitae*, it is not clear whether Pope John Paul wants this quotation to indicate that all of the decrees of such a government lose their authority, or only the unjust decrees. If we look to *Pacem in Terris*, however, it is clear that Pope John XXIII is declaring that such governments become illegitimate and lose their moral authority to make law. Prior to this quotation, Pope John had made the case that unjust laws are no law; then in the part of the document from which the quotation is taken, Pope John is now speaking of regimes which do not serve the common

[238] Ibid.
[239] Ibid.

good at all by reason of their level of injustice. He directed this criticism primarily against Communist regimes which had slaughtered so many millions of their own people. It seems clear that Pope John Paul II is similarly distressed by the systematic slaughter of millions of innocents in Western democracies, and he makes it quite clear that the governments are at least as much to blame for the deaths of these innocents as the doctors who perform the murders.[240]

Is Pope John Paul all but declaring the liberal democracies to be illegitimate? Early on in the document, John Paul says that any government which allows the slaughter of innocents "effectively moves toward a form of totalitarianism. The state is no longer the 'common home' where all can live together on the basis of fundamental equalities, but is transformed into a tyrant state which arrogates to itself the right to dispose of the life of the weakest and most defenseless members, from the unborn child to the elderly, in the name of a public interest which is really nothing but the interest of a part" (n. 20).[241]

...The legislation of a right to murder invalidates more than just those specific laws, but all other laws which indirectly support this evil. I think, for example, that laws requiring the payment of taxes would cease to be morally binding. Since conscientious objection becomes a moral requirement, and tax protest is a way to practice this objection, it must be morally licit to disobey laws demanding payment of taxes.

But does not the Holy Father's call for conscientious objection and civil disobedience lead to civil war? The Holy Father tells us quite explicitly that the rejection of morality and the practice of injustice on such a mammoth scale of millions

---

[240] Ibid.
[241] Ibid.

> of deaths laid at the doorstep of liberal democracy is de facto civil war.[242]
>
> If no authority can permit this injustice, then it seems that Catholic governors, indeed all governors, have a moral obligation (though presumably within the confines of political prudence) to refuse to permit abortion within their states.[243]
>
> Of course, the question we must ask is whether more visible and widespread civil disobedience as the Holy Father demands is politically prudent. This depends on particular circumstances, but I think that the Holy Father himself has given us some guidance on this issue. At the beginning of the encyclical he explains why he thinks it was now necessary to put out such a strongly worded (if not outright incendiary) document. He says that despite all of his past exhortations, respect for life has been growing steadily worse in the liberal democracies (n. 17). I think that the Holy Father has come to the point at which he believes that the situation warrants more than preaching. Only through nonviolent civil disobedience, which is forceful and uncompromising, will the Western democracies wake up to the realization that we are on the brink of a new barbarism.[244]

This is quite a contrast to the timidity of the kinds of statements we are used to getting from our bishops and episcopal conferences on the sanctity of human life. Not only is civil disobedience permitted in this area, but it may be positively obligatory. If Church leadership here in America had shown such guts in 1973, when *Roe v. Wade* entered the picture, we might not be today a society where abortion is taken for granted as a right, and be on the verge of judicially proclaiming a right to kill the old and the infirm under the guise of "compassion."

---

[242] Ibid.
[243] Ibid.
[244] *EV*, n. 62.

Besides settling the issue of civil disobedience, *Evangelium Vitae* also settled definitively the question of the legitimacy of dissent within the Church against Catholic teaching on the sanctity of human life. It thus addressed the spiritual warfare going on inside the Church as well as between the Church and the world. It did this by stating, as infallible teaching, the Church's condemnation of abortion and euthanasia. Thus:

> Therefore, by the authority which Christ conferred upon Peter and his Successors, in communion with the bishops — who on various occasions have condemned abortion and who, in the aforementioned consultation, albeit dispersed throughout the world, have shown unanimous agreement concerning this doctrine *[I] declare that direct abortion, that is, abortion willed as an end or as a means, always constitutes a grave moral disorder*, since it is the deliberate killing of an innocent human being. This doctrine is based upon the natural law and upon the Written Word of God, is transmitted by the Church's Tradition and taught by the ordinary and universal Magisterium.[245]
>
> Taking into account these distinctions, in harmony with the Magisterium of my Predecessors and in communion with the bishops of the Catholic Church, *I confirm that euthanasia is a grave violation of the law of God*, since it is the deliberate and morally unacceptable killing of a human person. This doctrine is based upon the natural law and upon the Written Word of God, is transmitted by the Church's Tradition and taught by the ordinary and universal Magisterium.[246]

Of course, Catholic dissidents like the misnamed Catholics for a Free Choice have not and will not hesitate to deny that this is infallible teaching, but the message could not be any clearer.

---

[245] *EV*, n. 65.
[246] *EV*, n. 65.

In the great battle over abortion, which has raged for so many years now and rages on, *The Wanderer* has, I think, been nearly unique in seeking to understand it, not just as a battle with flesh and blood, but as, above all, a struggle with spiritual evil, a struggle to overcome an evil which, in Christ's own words, "can only be driven out by prayer and fasting." If, in the process, *The Wanderer* gang has done even a little to bring the battle ultimately to a victorious close by clarifying, for all of us, what it means, that is no mean accomplishment.

PART FOUR: THE MASS — A GIFT REJECTED

I hate, I despise your religious feasts; I cannot stand your assemblies...Away with the noise of your songs! I will not listen to the music of your harps.

— *Amos 5:21,23*

Is it a mere coincidence that the unholy doings and omissions which are plaguing the Church today broke out after we had all but abandoned our once-fervid prayer and devotional life? Of course not. It is a spiritual law that as prayer and devotional activities build up the supernatural life of the Church, casting them aside tears it down.

— *Monsignor M.B. Molloy,* The Wanderer, *February 25, 1971*

1. WHERE GOD AND MAN MEET

The Mass, as all Catholics used to know, is the Church's central act of worship. More than any other worship, it is the point where Christ and the Church meet. And this is not merely some kind of nebulous "symbolic" meeting, it is the direct, immediate contact of Christians with God, the very Presence, bodily as well as spiritual, of the Second Person of the Trinity, the Logos of God made flesh. If we take this reality seriously, if we allow ourselves to think through its full implications, we cannot help but experience awe, even a measure of fear. That is perhaps why people so frequently yield to the temptation to dilute the reality, to "spiritualize" it, to demythologize it, if you are truly sophisticated — anything to blunt its impact on people who would rather not have their comfortable lives upset by mysterious supernatural presences that insist on intruding themselves into those lives.

One implication is obvious right away: If the Mass is the point of immediate contact between God and the Church, and if the Church in some way represents, not just its members, but all mankind, then the Mass is truly the point of contact of mankind as a whole with God. It is, to use T.S. Eliot's wonderful phrase, "the point of intersection of time and the timeless." In the Mass, mankind meets its God, whether or not particular individuals or even most of mankind are aware of it. But the One who meets man in the Mass is Christ Himself, the Second Person of the Blessed Trinity, the Logos of God. It is through that Logos, Scripture tells us, that all things come to be. That suggests that in some way the whole creation is involved in the meeting of Christ and His Church in the Mass. The Logos of God is the source of all order in the creation, whether that means the old creation *Genesis* tells us about or the new creation in Christ, the world made new by Christ's sacrifice on Calvary and made new again and again by His sacrifice in the Mass. Christ is the one source of the world's order, and the central meeting between Christ and the world occurs in the Mass. The world-order itself depends upon the Mass. If the Mass is disturbed, the whole world is disturbed and thrown into disorder.

But how is the Mass disrupted? How are disorder and confusion introduced into it? In our time, that process has started with the denial that the Mass is a *sacrifice*, a sacrifice in which the infinite, transcendent God becomes immediately, physically as well as spiritually, present to us, a sacrifice which, by its very nature, evokes a response of reverence and awe in the presence of a great mystery. That idea of the Mass has been largely replaced, at least among "progressive" Catholics, by the notion of a kind of communal meal in which Christ is present only symbolically. According to that view, the bread and wine do not truly become the very substance of Christ (transubstantiation), but merely assume a kind of sign value they did not have before ("transignification" is the most common expression "progressive" theologians use for this). This notion of the Mass has its source in a theology which rejects the vertical axis of human life, the reaching up of man toward God and God's reaching down to us, in favor of the horizontal axis, in which human beings reach out to one another. Our modernist brethren seem to have some notion that the Church in the past rejected the horizontal axis, but that is not so — she has merely taught that the vertical comes first, that our relationship with the infinite, transcendent God is what makes possible the love of neighbor which is the horizontal axis. In other words — we have communion with one another because first we have communion with God. The modernist idea of the Mass wants communion with one another to the exclusion of communion with God, and in fact destroys both. That is why the real fruit of the reduction of the Mass to the human community meeting in prayer has been, not the tranquillity of order which one might naively associate with the idea of community, but the horrendous uproar and scandal of a great multitude of sects and cults fighting it out among themselves for supremacy in a Church which seems, at times, to have become no more than a merely human institution, one which is in deep trouble, at that.

Another way to say it is that the Mass, as the Church truly understands it, is a sacrifice in which the infinite, transcendent God becomes immanent to us through the power of God Himself, not through human power. It is the continuation of the Incarnation in the life of the Church and of the universe. In contrast, the progressive elite's notion of the "new Mass" implies either an outright denial of transcendence, or some notion of transcendence becoming immanent by the power of man, by the "People of God," as if we could somehow pull God down to our level. The God who gets pulled down ends up being an idol and not the real God at all. People who see the Mass in this way are really deifying and worshipping the human community.

It is the second idea of the Mass which now reigns supreme in the Catholic Church in America and, indeed, throughout the industrialized world. How such a tremendous disturbance of order came about is indeed a great mystery. Those of us who are now middle-aged or older remember that a number of years ago, in the 1950s and 1960s, there was an intense and enthusiastic movement for renewal of the liturgy, a movement to enhance the beauty of the Mass and bring its meaning home more powerfully to the people, involving the people in more intense participation. It was a movement which envisioned an increase in awe and reverence before the mystery of the true Presence of Christ in the Eucharist. Yet, somehow, after the ecumenical council which legitimated and exalted this movement of liturgical renewal, the movement underwent a radical transformation, a change in its very substance — indeed, one might say, a kind of evil "transubstantiation" that, in a horrible way, mimicked the mystery of the Eucharist. The end result of this deformed movement was that the Mass was reduced, not enhanced, becoming merely a kind of social meeting of the "People," characterized by informality, irreverence, horrible new liturgical music which made the Mass look like a sick joke, and so on. Somehow, a movement to build up and renew the Mass turned into a movement to destroy and tear it down. I doubt that we will ever totally understand how such a thing happened, but we can at least trace the history of the event and cast a partial light on how it happened if we go back and look at *The Wanderer*'s involvement, which began with the liturgical reforms of the Second Vatican Council and continues today. In the pages of *The Wanderer*, we see thirty years of consistent witness to the reality of the Mass and against its destruction by a liturgical revolution which still has not come to an end.

2.LITURGICAL REFORM OR LITURGICAL REVOLUTION?

Few people quite understand that the liturgical revolution we have suffered since the 1960s not only was not mandated by the Second Vatican Council but contradicts the very wishes of the Council. This is the case in part because so many Catholics today are too young to remember the era of the Council. But even those of us now middle-aged or older who lived through those years as adults often have our memories rather clouded by things that have happened since. As a result, we often think we know things about the events of those years, things which we could not possibly know because they are not true. To take one of the most crystal clear examples, almost all of us are quite sure we know that the Second Vatican Council abolished the Latin Mass, doing so with considerable urging by Pope John XXIII, regarded by many today as a great liberal Pope.

This belief, which has become part of the Catholic "world-taken-for-granted," could hardly be further from the truth. In fact, the Council's *Constitution on the Sacred Liturgy*, set forth by the Council as the foundation of the liturgical reform it hoped for, affirms in no uncertain terms that Latin is to continue to be the liturgical language of the Church. Archbishop Leo Binz of St. Paul, writing in the December 19, 1963 *Wanderer*, notes, in explaining the Council's directives on the liturgy, that Latin was to be retained in the Roman rite, but that *permission* for limited use of the vernacular was given. Archbishop Binz expressed his hope that in America, English could be used for some parts (not all) of the Mass:

> The general legislation on the language of the liturgy is set forth in article 36 of the constitution. The principle is stated that "the use of the Latin language is to be preserved in the Latin rites."

> At once, however, the authorization is given to "the competent territorial ecclesiastical authority" to approve within certain limits the use of the mother tongue.
>
> The bishops of the United States met in Rome to consider what viewpoint they would follow. It was our all but unanimous decision to make full use of the vernacular concessions permitted by the Council.[247]

The Council also noted that, in liturgical music, Gregorian chant was to continue to hold "pride of place." There was never the slightest hint, in the decrees of the Council, of such bizarre phenomena as guitar Masses, polka Masses, liturgical dancing by nuns in leotards, and so on *ad nauseam.* As to the allegation that the beloved Pope John XXIII had anything to do with the abandonment of Latin, the Pope, as late as March, 1962, forbade anyone to write *against* the use of Latin in the Mass:

> Historical reasons lead us to do honor to the Latin language and to remain faithful to its usage....
>
> But We want especially to point out here the importance of this language at the present moment of history when, together with a sincere desire for unity and understanding among nations, individualistic expressions are not found wanting.
>
> The language of Rome, used in the Latin rite of the Church, can still render noble service today in the work of peace and unity. It can also render service to the new nations, which are confidently entering international life. It is, in fact, not linked with the interests of any nation.
>
> It is a source of doctrinal clarity and certainty....It is above all an instrument of mutual understanding.[248]

---

[247] "Archbishop Binz Explains Vatican Council's Constitution on the Sacred Liturgy," W, 12-19-63.

[248] "*Pope Forbids Writing Against Latin in Liturgy* — Reaffirms Latin as Official Church Tongue," W, 3-8-62.

So, when we move away from the assumptions so many of us have come to make about the Church's efforts to reform the liturgy and look at the historical facts, we find that the Council, far from suppressing the Latin liturgy, positively *required* its preservation, while giving *permission* for *limited* use of the vernacular. Unfortunately, what often matters in the world is less what really happened than what people think happened, and the liturgical revolutionaries, during the past 30 years, have managed to convince millions of people, including their opponents, that the Council fathers wished for the absolute reverse of what they actually decreed — the abolition of the Latin Mass and the enforcement of the vernacular everywhere. As Hitler understood, if you tell a big enough lie and repeat it often enough, people will believe you because they will take it for granted that no one would ever dare to tell such a monstrous lie. Social power and truth are often very far apart.

Indeed, if we look at the historical record of the events of the mid-1960s, we find that the perception most Catholics had of the situation was that the traditional Latin Mass would continue to exist alongside the vernacular Mass. In the February 18, 1965 *Wanderer*, we find a story entitled, "Dubuque Diocese Fosters Retention of Latin Mass." The plans of the Dubuque Diocese reflect, I think, what most thoughtful Catholics of the time expected from the liturgical reform, as well as what the Council fathers undoubtedly had in mind:

> Regulations concerning the use of the vernacular in the Mass in the Archdiocese of Dubuque (*Witness*, February 11) embody an integral observance of the decree of the Holy See, especially of article 36 of the constitution and of article 59 of the instruction, both of which enjoin that the Latin Mass must be preserved alongside of the vernacular.
>
> Accordingly, the archbishop of Dubuque has promulgated the following rules: All private Masses are to be in Latin; low Masses with servers and congregation may be in Latin or English; so too high and solemn Masses. Masses celebrated with lectors or deacon, acolytes, and congregation, are to be in the vernacular. Every religious community in the archdio-

> cese must have one Latin Mass each week. No permission is granted for offertory processions. Religious and the faithful are urged to use their Missals during Mass. Though he is free to do so, no priest is to be forced to offer Mass facing the people. There is to be no remodeling of sanctuaries without the express permission of the Archbishop.[249]

Similarly, an April 15, 1965 story quotes the Los Angeles Archdiocesan Liturgical Commission as directing that

> The introduction of English, particularly in the historical and instructional parts of the Mass, is permitted in accordance with the decrees of the Constitution on the liturgy and in accord with the granted petition of the National Conference of the Bishops of the United States. This usage is now in practice in the archdiocese.
>
> *The introduction of English into parts of the Mass is permissive and not mandatory* (Italics added).[250]

Yet by this time, Catholics who supported the explicit command of the Council for retaining the Latin found themselves already on the defensive against the growing power of "progressivists" who wanted to suppress the use of Latin. Thus, on May 6, 1965, Cathaleen Hindmarsh, a spokesman for the Latin Mass Society, had to say that

> Those asking for a Latin Mass are not asking for a return to an exclusive Latin liturgy.
>
> We are not reactionary, cranky, or spiritually indolent.
>
> We accept, and are grateful for, the spiritual renewal which, we are told, is spreading through the Church through the use of the new liturgy, and with this we are fully prepared to cooperate.

---

[249] "Dubuque Diocese Fosters Retention of Latin Mass," W, 2-18-65.

[250] "Liturgy Group Stresses Use of English in Mass is Permissive, not Mandatory," W, 4-15-65.

> We ask merely that we be given the opportunity of attending a Sunday Mass in the language we have been accustomed to all our life and which we have come to love.
>
> Yes, we are a minority. But equally we are members of the Mystical Body, people of God and loyal children of the Church.[251]

"Yes, we are a minority." Sad words, indeed, yet the truth. One of the great ironies which abound throughout this sad period of Church history is that so-called liberals, who have consistently justified their own activities in terms of the rights of conscience and the duty to be open-minded, have practiced such consistent and extreme intolerance of the ideas and wishes of those who venture to disagree with them. It was never enough for these progressive types to have the option of an English Mass — it was necessary that the revolutionary liturgy they created have no competition. They must have realized, even at this early date, that if there *were* competition, they would be the ones to be in the minority.

By 1966, there could be little doubt about the revolutionary nature of what was still being passed off as liturgical "reform" or, still more dishonestly, "renewal." Vincent A. McCrossen, writing on August 18 of that year, gave this summary of the situation:

> The pressure for the use of the vernacular in the liturgy for us Latin-rite Catholics came from a very small, tightly organized, and vociferous minority, principally in Bohemia, Germany, Holland, England, and the U.S. — interestingly enough the very lands whence so much dissension against the unity of Western Christendom has traditionally always come. It has been promoted with a plethora of specious reasonings and inadequate scholarship. It is decidedly not correct to say it was promoted by Vatican II or Pope Paul VI or John XXIII. For the first section of Article 36 of the Constitution

[251] Cathaleen Hindmarsh, "Must We Say Goodbye to the Low Mass in Latin?" W, 5-6-65.

> on the Sacred Liturgy of the Second Vatican Ecumenical Council establishes Latin as the basic language of our liturgy. Sections 2 and 3 of article 36 simply permit the use of the vernacular in local areas. Permission never is enthusiastic promotion or urging. Permission is cautious, circumspect tolerance upon the part of authority, ordinarily of something far from a desideratum, and by its very nature is quite probably temporary and can always be withdrawn. Pope Paul VI on April 10, 1966, calls Latin "still the official language of the Catholic Church" and prophesies "Latin will live again with greater impetus, despite fears for its survival." John XXIII calls Latin "the immutable language of the Western Church."[252]

In fact, the very people who had earlier been the pioneers of genuine liturgical renewal soon found it necessary to disown their illegitimate offspring, as an editorial on July 28 made clear:

> For, let it be said bluntly: the reforms envisaged by a St. Pius X, by the Benedictines of Solesmes and Maredsous, by the Apostolate of Klosterneuburg — and lastly by Vatican II, far from seeking after superficial novelties, were totally devoted to *renewal* of the venerable traditions of the liturgy in order that priests and people might better understand and more profoundly appreciate the riches of these treasures and thus come to drink more deeply of the life-giving waters of grace flowing from the Holy Sacrifice of the Mass and the seven sacraments.
>
> Those who stood at the cradle of the liturgical renewal are, almost to a man, horrified to contemplate much of what is being done today by impious hands in the name of a move-

[252] Vincent A. McCrossen, "The Vernacular Chaos, and the Latin Mass," W, 8-16-66.

> ment of such promising beginnings and such splendid first-fruits![253]

By 1980, when Joseph T. Gill published a *Wanderer* article entitled "The Conspiracy to Stamp out Latin in the Mass," so many people had been given the impression that the Latin Mass was now forbidden that it had become necessary to unearth the truth of the matter, much as an archaeologist unearths an ancient and previously unknown civilization:

> The fathers of Vatican Council II directed the introduction of the vernacular into the Mass as a service and a convenience to those who might then be assisted in understanding the Mass better than as celebrated in the Latin. Not at all did they intend that the vernacular should become the norm to the exclusion of Latin. They made it perfectly clear that Latin remained the official language of the Church for this purpose as well as others. But as with so many other details of discipline and practice the option quickly became the norm, to the confusion and distress of millions of people to whom the Latin had a special meaning....What irritates me more than anything else is that those — and there are many — who find a special meaning in the Latin are deprived of it by professional liturgists who are permitted by their bishops to lie not only about the so-called "spirit of Vatican II" but about the actual words appearing in its documents, in order to wipe out Latin from the Mass. To allow these scandals such a stranglehold that they are able to subvert the intent of the Council and of the Popes is a real crime, so far as I am concerned.[254]

Here again, we see the tactic of the "big lie" so useful to Hitler. The professional liturgists and the bishops who supported them succeeded

---

[253] "Liturgical Derailment," W, 3-28-68.
[254] Joseph T. Gill, "The Conspiracy to Stamp out Latin in the Mass," W, 8-21-80.

in for all practical purposes outlawing the Latin simply by letting people believe it had been outlawed.

In 1982, more nails appear to have been put in the coffin of the Latin liturgy when the Vatican released the results of a survey which showed that the Latin Mass was becoming increasingly rare, in the United States and elsewhere:

> The survey report was published by the Sacred Congregation for the Sacraments and Divine Worship in the December issue of *Notitiae*, its official journal....
>
> The report revealed authorized Latin Masses are being celebrated with some frequency in only seven U.S. dioceses and occasionally in 87 others. Fifty-seven dioceses reported no authorized Latin Masses; 108 bishops said they received no requests for such Masses, and 43 reported occasional requests. Latin Masses may be authorized by local bishops, but must be said according to the rite authorized by Pope Paul VI in accordance with liturgical changes of the Second Vatican Council.[255]

The degree of confusion which had evolved by the 1980s is illustrated by the fact that people had come to believe that they needed the local bishop's permission to celebrate a Latin Mass, even though it was said according to the New Order of the Mass, not the by now suppressed Tridentine rite. If the Church never in fact prohibited the use of Latin, why should anyone need permission to use it? But by this time the liturgists had become so all-powerful that hardly anyone raised the question.

Monsignor Richard J. Schuler, writing in the February 4, 1982 *Wanderer*, tried to clarify the meaning of this survey, which was being cited by the liturgists as showing the success of the liturgical "reforms." After all, if no one wanted to change anything, the system

[255] "Holy See's Survey...Shows Use of Latin in the Liturgy Is Fast Disappearing," W, 1-14-82.

must be satisfactory. Monsignor Schuler suggested that there might be a different interpretation:

> Truly, rather than saying that the survey shows the "success of liturgical reform," it quite obviously shows that the reform demanded by the Council fathers has not been achieved, but instead it has been deliberately impeded. If the fathers ordered the use of Latin in speaking and singing by the people at Masses celebrated in Latin, then the survey shows that the will of the fathers has been thwarted. By whom? Obviously by those who have taken credit for the demise of Latin and so gleefully proclaim the triumph of their own version of the place of the vernacular, which the fathers *permitted* in certain parts of the Mass at the same time that they *ordered* the use of Latin.[256]

The use of the Latin language in the Mass is of course not an absolutely central matter. It is true that the central mystery of the Mass, the very Presence of the Word made Flesh under the accidents of bread and wine, is there no matter what language one might use. Yet, there is no doubt that Latin, as the common language of the Western Church, was a powerful sign of unity in the Church. It is also true that Latin was an integral part of a centuries-old tradition which incorporated a whole attitude of reverence and awe in the presence of the mystery. You do not throw away such a tradition for any light reason. To do so is really a crime against both God and man. It robs the human community of a kind of access to the sacred which is a basic human need. Granted that the sacred may still be present under new forms. Yet, psychologically and culturally, it may be enormously difficult for people to find it under a new form which is not necessarily well adapted to the manifestation of the sacred. That kind of access may be a problem even where the new forms *are* adequate ones. Cardinal Newman once used, as a metaphor for such questions,

[256] Monsignor Richard J. Schuler, "'Success' of the Liturgical Reform," W, 2-4-82.

what happens when we transplant a plant. We may take the plant out of its native soil and place it in soil which is just as good in the sense that it has all the nutrients the plant needs, etc. Yet often the plant will die because it is weakened by being uprooted and cannot make the adjustment to different soil. In casually throwing away the Latin Mass, our liturgists uprooted many human souls and put them in soil which, even if it had been of good quality, would have been difficult for them to adjust to, and they were weakened by the process of uprooting. The liturgical revolutionaries may be held responsible for the fate of many souls when judgment day comes and they are called to answer for the results of their meddling.

Of course, the harm was not all done by the suppression of Latin. The situation was greatly aggravated by another factor, the replacement of Latin with absolutely horrendous English translations. One would like to be charitable and assume that the bad translations were purely the result of incompetence on the part of the translators. Yet that does not seem probable. The translations have been so bad that it is inconceivable that such superlative incompetence could be possible among people who, obviously, had some kind of scholarly credentials. And when we consider that the consistent effect of the bad translations has been to remove all sense of reverence and awe as well as poetry from the liturgy, and that they have also pretty consistently tended to water down Catholic doctrine concerning the Mass, one has to conclude that the terrible quality of the translations was at least to some degree deliberate.

The practice of translating the liturgy badly did not begin with the ICEL (International Commission on English in the Liturgy) translation so justly cursed in recent years. As early as 1965, Bishop Robert Dwyer complained of the inadequacy of the English versions in use at that time:

> The liturgy, in a word, still has to be "put across." And if experience has anything to offer us worth listening to, it will not be "put across" by reducing its language to the lowest common denominator of intelligibility, or by stripping it of all verbal grace and dignity, nor by phrasing it according to

> the canons of the "Yoo-Hoo" school of liturgical composition.
>
> It may be a small point to belabor, but who was it that first sold the liturgists on the idea that *Thou* and *Thine* were no longer correct usage when addressing the Deity?
>
> Who was it that originated the curious notion that the Holy Ghost was no longer a proper name for the Third Person of the Blessed Trinity?
>
> Could it be that we have fallen into the clutches of the editors of that fascinating column, "Picturesque Speech," or "Towards A Brighter English"?
>
> It is one thing to couch the vernacular Liturgy in antiquated phraseology, beyond the ken of all but specialists and the erudite, but it is quite another to bring it down to the sudden bathos of vulgarity.[257]

This vulgarization of the Mass, what we would now call a "dumbing down" process, appears to have been one of the first fruits of the derailed liturgical renewal. Though the essence of the Mass remains intact after such a vulgarization, the accident of vulgarized language can only make it more difficult for the participants to actually benefit from the graces present in it. The overall effect is a spiritual loss and a more casual, offhand attitude by the faithful toward the Church's supreme act of worship.

Aside from this "dumbing down" aspect, if the liturgy is in fact the Church's supreme act of worship, then I think it can safely be said that it ought to be beautiful. Outward beauty may be accidental, but it is a very important accident. If outward beauty is there, it is a kind of window for the spirit to look through and see the deep inner beauty of the Mass. Yet the effect of the degradation of liturgical language was to rob the liturgy of beauty. Bishop Dwyer again says it well:

---

[257] Bishop Robert Dwyer, "Is Liturgy in Vernacular a Problem or a Panacea?" W, 1-28-65.

> ...We are gradually losing (or perhaps it would be more accurate to say that we have already lost) all feeling for poetry. Ours, in all likelihood, is the first generation of Western civilization to come to maturity without any realization of the wonder and mystery of the poetic impulse....We have been casting an appraising eye over the supply of hymnals in the vernacular now hurtling from the presses in a febrile effort to keep up with the multiplying orders.
>
> It is not a cheering experience. For here is found not only a poverty of musical inspiration but a dolorous lack of the least poetic sensitivity.
>
> Some of the verses, Heaven help us, would be shocking even on the lowest level of tub-thumping evangelicalism — the early nineteenth-century variety. The disjunction between words and music, between the ideal of the Church praying and singing, and the dull pedestrianism of verse and melody simply underscores the obsessive distemper of our times.
>
> It is not that the Catholic Church in America is peculiarly at fault; it is that our American culture as a whole has effectively denied the relevance of beauty to life.[258]

By 1967, the situation had gotten so bad that Giacomo Cardinal Lercaro, president of the Liturgical Consilium, called for a new authorized English translation, a call which ultimately led to the ICEL translation. "The translation," according to the cardinal, "must be literal and integral. One must take the texts as they are, without mutilations or simplifications of any sort. The adaptation to the nature of the spoken language must be serious and proper."[259] Needless to say, that is not the translation we ultimately got.

In October, 1967, Cardinal Dearden announced that the English translation of the Canon of the Mass prepared by ICEL was ready,

---

[258] Bishop Robert Dwyer, "Vernacular Hymns Lack Sensitivity of Poetry," W, 2-18-65.

[259] "New Vatican Warning Against Liturgy Experiments," W, 8-31-67.

and that its use on an experimental basis was to begin October 22.[260] The new translation provoked an immediate and loud response by traditionalists, one which nevertheless went largely unheeded. Paul Hallett, in an October 19 editorial entitled, appropriately enough, "Is This Translation?" made the following comments:

> The most remarkable thing about the new translation of the Canon of the Mass is not its "simplicity" but the omission of equivalents for key words in the original. This is verified in almost every paragraph....If this official text does not pretend to reproduce the thought of the Latin, it should not be called a translation. Even so, how can the translators justify the omission of such important statements of doctrine as "Mother of God" after the Virgin's name, or "always" before it? As we pray, so we believ[e], to give a free translation of *lex orandi est lex credendi.* Time out of mind, the liturgists trumpet that the liturgy itself is a school for the faithful, and one of them has even said that the liturgy could take the place of Catholic schools. How can it do this if it does not reflect right doctrine?[261]

On February 20, 1969, Pope Paul VI was quoted by *The Wanderer* as calling for perfection in the anticipated complete ICEL translation: "To work well means to elaborate to perfection — I emphasize to perfection — the translations of the liturgical texts. All the more so now that we are entering the august, austere, sacred, venerable, tremendous bourne (boundary) of the Eucharistic prayers, which in ancient times the 'discipline of the arcane' long sought to protect from indiscretion and the profane gaze. They therefore deserve the most sensitive attention of piety, of doctrine, of literary expression in the common tongue."[262] The ICEL translators must have

[260] "English Mass Canon Ready," W, 10-5-67.

[261] "Paul H. Hallett, "Is This Translation?" W, 10-19-67.

[262] "Emphasizes Perfection in Liturgical Texts," W, 2-20-69.

forgotten to read that week's *Wanderer*, and thus didn't get this important message.

Father Ralph March, writing in the April 3, 1969 issue, asked the question so many of us have asked over the years: "What happened to the liturgy?"

> Beauty has all but disappeared from the parish high Mass. All this devastation came about in less than five years. The drastic elimination of beauty was accomplished with a total lack of consideration and charity toward the feeling and the artistic and spiritual need of large sections of the community.... The iconoclasts have performed their demolition with savage efficiency, totally dominating the press and other communication media to achieve a clean, methodic, devastating sweep in the shortest time. Before the faithful had a chance to awaken and realize what was happening, the massacre was already over and only smoldering ashes were left of the centuries-old ceremonies, once surrounded by an aura of beauty and dignity. By and large, vulgarity reigns supreme in the Mass today.[263]

Again, one of the most remarkable things about the radical takeover of the Church in the past generation was how totally the orthodox were blindsided, simply because the events that took place were so bizarre that anyone who had predicted them a few years before they actually happened would have been regarded as a candidate for a rubber room.

In May, 1969, Pope Paul VI officially promulgated the New Roman Missal, containing what is now known as the *Novus Ordo* of the Mass.[264] This was indeed in some ways a "new Mass," but not in the revolutionary sense of the word "new" that many people mistakenly attribute to it. The "new Mass," it should be noted, was in Latin and was very much in continuity with the Tridentine liturgy as well

---

[263] Father Ralph March, "What Happened to the Liturgy?" W, 4-3-69.

[264] "Pope Promulgates New Missal," W, 5-15-69.

as with the reforms undertaken by Pope Pius XII. It represented reform, not revolution. In August, Benno Cardinal Gut, O.S.B., prefect of the Congregation for Divine Worship, stated (prematurely, alas!) that the era of experimentation with the liturgy following the Council was now at an end: "The cardinal urged the revival of Latin in the Mass and he indicated that the celebration of Latin Masses every Sunday in certain churches or cities will be proposed."[265] Once again, the intent of the genuine reformers was totally contradicted by the spurious reformers, especially by the translators of the ICEL version.

July, 1970 saw the formation of a group called the Laymen's Commission on the English Liturgy, numbering several distinguished scholars and writers among its members.[266] The commission sought to respond to the mess ICEL had made of the liturgy by producing its own translation. This group will be discussed in more detail when we take up the traditional Catholic reaction to the liturgical revolution.

In July 1971, Father Jerome Docherty, in "An Open Letter to All English-Speaking Bishops," left no doubt about what he thought of the ICEL translation:

> In this essay I try to show from sound linguistics that the rejection of sound grammar and linguistics leads to the rejection of sound doctrine.
>
> In translation fidelity to the originals is the prime requisite, not always to the exact words, but always to the exact original ideas. In the text of the Sacred Liturgy such words as *Deipara — God-bearer; Substantia; Consubstantialis; Incarnatus* need the most delicate handling on account of their doctrinal content. But to be told that words like *Supplex — on bended knee* or *most humbly,* carry no thought content,...or that you may not have an adjective attached to a noun in the vocative, on the grounds of sound spoken English, or that "better English style seems to reject words like

[265] "Says Liturgical Experimentation Is Over," W, 8-14-69.

[266] "Laymen Set Goals for Commission on Liturgy," W, 7-30-70.

> *Blessed, Holy*, which do not add to the meaning, and are largely decorative and honorific,"...is too much to swallow, especially as we happen to know that Die Herren ICEL have an extreme allergy for all such words, and cart them away as so much "religious jargon!"[267]

Sadly, despite the torrent of criticism of the abominable ICEL translation, that version of the Mass quickly institutionalized itself in America, and the passage of years did nothing to dislodge it, but on the contrary, merely entrenched it more thoroughly. The addiction of the liturgists to constant tinkering with the Mass also did nothing but worsen. In November, 1980, Al Matt, editor of *The Wanderer*, called on the laity to resist liturgical tampering:

> It seems high time for Catholics to voice their concern about this constant liturgical tampering and ask the Holy See to intervene in the matter. It would be reasonable to expect, considering all of the criticisms expressed about the present English translation of the Mass and other liturgical texts, that more worthy translations be commissioned by the Holy See. The piecemeal approach, for less than substantial motives, being pursued by the American bishops threatens to result in texts which will be a tattered patchwork, lacking even a stylistic coherence, much less an adequate expression of the Mystery of the Faith.[268]

Clearly, one of the principal fruits of the liturgical revolution has been the production of liturgical language which seems almost designed to truncate the life of the spirit, to replace true spiritual experience with the flatness and dullness of the profane world. I tried to get that across in a 1987 article, using such verbal atrocities as

---

[267] Father Jerome Docherty, O.S.B., "An Open Letter to All English-Speaking Bishops," W, 7-1-71.

[268] A.J. Matt, Jr., "The Laity Should Protest Liturgical Tampering," W, 11-27-80.

"eternally begotten of the Father" and "we praise you for your glory," as illustrations:

> Good liturgical language, whether Latin, Greek, English, or anything else, needs to function something like a stained-glass window, refracting the light of Christ to us as the window refracts the sun's light, mediating to us the many-colored, many-faceted beauty and mystery of the light of Revelation, mediating to us the many possibilities of that light. This means that the language used in the liturgy is not there merely to point to factual truths of some kind, but is there to actually show us, make us see and hear and feel, the depth and breadth and mystery and glory of our God. The English liturgy which we use today fails dismally in this. Its language is flat and insipid and tasteless; it is language for a flatland liturgy....Contemporary liturgy does away with the images which express the experiences of height and depth, of mystery and radiance and splendor which are at the center of our lives as Christians, and replaces them with flat, insipid, "wimpy" images. It is language for the flatlands.[269]

The *de facto* suppression of the Latin liturgy, combined with the adoption of the appalling ICEL translation (something which really amounted to the suppression of good English in the liturgy), had the overall effect of making it nearly impossible for the faithful to experience reverence and awe in the presence of the sacred; it suppressed a whole dimension of spiritual experience. Much of this suppression was initiated by liturgical revolutionaries who, in utter disobedience to Church law, engaged in what is known as "liturgical free-lancing." The January 5, 1967 *Wanderer* quoted a newsletter put out by the Liturgical Commission of the Diocese of Pittsburgh denouncing "free-lancing": "The Faithful are seriously scandalized by sensation-minded priests who are using English in the Canon, who are offering

[269] George A. Kendall, "Liturgical Language: A Call for Restoration," W, 4-2-87.

Mass without vestments, who eliminate the use of the maniple, burse, or pall in the Mass, who distribute Holy Communion under both species beyond the limits authorized by the Vicar of Christ, who offer Mass in laundries, bedrooms, barrooms, and other indecorous places."[270] In a September, 1966 incident at St. Charles Borromeo Seminary in Pennsylvania, three seminarians were expelled for holding an experimental Mass late at night in a locker room, with the priests wearing street clothes, using ordinary baker's rolls instead of hosts, and so forth.[271] What is really sad is that today most of us wouldn't even turn a hair on hearing about something like this, because the prevalence of such practices has desensitized even the orthodox. Circus-like liturgies, often celebrated even by bishops, have become commonplace. In the traditional liturgy, the faithful left behind the everyday, profane world and entered into a realm of the sacred which in a true sense was outside everyday space and time. They were caught up in an encounter with a transcendent reality. No one has said this better than the philosopher Dietrich von Hildebrand in a March 30, 1967 article:

> *The basic error of most of the innovations is to imagine that the new liturgy brings the Holy Sacrifice of the Mass nearer to the faithful*, that shorn of its old rituals the Mass now enters into the substance of our lives. *For the question is whether we better meet Christ in the Mass by soaring up to Him, or by dragging Him down into our own pedestrian workaday world.* The innovators would replace holy intimacy with Christ by an unbecoming familiarity. The new liturgy actually threatens to frustrate the confrontation with Christ, for it discourages reverence in the face of mystery, precludes awe, and all but extinguishes a sense of sacredness. What really matters, surely, is not whether the faithful feel at home at Mass, but whether they are drawn out of their ordinary lives into the world of Christ — whether their attitude is the

[270] "Free-Lancing in Liturgy 'Scandal of 1966,'" W, 1-5-67.
[271] "3 Seminarians Expelled After Experimental Mass," W, 12-1-66.

> response of ultimate reverence: whether they are imbued with the reality of Christ (italics in original)....A Catholic should regard his liturgy with *pietas*. He should revere, and therefore fear to abandon the prayers and postures and music that have been approved by so many saints throughout the Christian era and delivered to us as a precious heritage. To go no further: the illusion that we can replace the Gregorian chant, with its inspired hymns and rhythms, by equally fine, if not better, music betrays a ridiculous self-assurance and lack of self-knowledge....The fundamental laws of the religious life that govern the imitation of Christ, do not change according to the moods and habits of the historical moment. The difference between a superficial community experience and a profound community experience is always the same. Recollection and contemplative adoration of Christ — which only reverence makes possible — will be the necessary basis for a true communion with others in Christ in every era of human history.[272]

It of course goes without saying that, with the triumph of the attitude of matter-of-factness and profanity which came to characterize the celebration of Mass by the late sixties, sacred music suffered horribly. Gregorian chant was unceremoniously dumped in the trash can. It can be argued that, even in the case of purely secular cultural traditions, those of classical music or great poetry, for instance, no one would have the right to do such a thing. Such traditions are the work of many generations of human beings, some of them men of genius, and it is an unspeakable atrocity when they are casually discarded and trampled upon by people too small, mentally and spiritually, to be capable of creating anything comparable. When it is a cultural tradition tied to worship, the atrocity is just that much more atrocious.

The principal tradition to go into the trash can was Gregorian chant, which for many centuries was normative for Catholic liturgical

[272] Dietrich von Hildebrand, "The Case for the Latin Mass," W, 3-30-67.

music. Its suppression can only be explained by the atmosphere of iconoclasm that had invaded the Church. The change to an English liturgy did not in and of itself make it necessary. For one thing, there was never any valid reason why certain parts of the Mass could not continue to be sung in Latin, an arrangement which the Council fathers clearly favored. But even assuming some compelling reason to eliminate Latin entirely, there is no reason why an English version of the prayers could not be adapted to Gregorian chant. The Byzantine Rite Catholic Church sings most of the Mass in an ancient chant which has a lot in common with Gregorian. When the Byzantine rite in America began using English in the liturgy instead of Slavonic, they retained the traditional chant, and I for one can testify that it is very beautiful (of course, the Byzantines also translated their liturgy into beautiful, reverent, poetic English). Monsignor Richard J. Schuler, a distinguished musicologist, summed the situation up in a 1969 article in which he responded to people's concerns about the desolation wrought by the suppression of traditional sacred art and sacred music:

> These and other questions are frequently on the lips of Catholics who are more and more bewildered by the artistic desolation that is exhibited in most [of] our churches today. The spirit of iconoclasm is working to destroy the musical art as well as the other ecclesiastical handmaids of the liturgy — sculpture, painting, needlework, and silver and gold art. In the place of art we now find whitewashed interiors adjusted to the sounds of folk groups and combos that could not even find employment in second-rate bars but are welcomed into the most sacred of places, the sanctuary. But why not, if one denies the distinction between the sacred and the secular? Why not, if one makes entertainment the reason for music in

> church? Why not, if man replaces God at the center of worship, which has become now "a truly human experience"?[273]

That is a devastating comment on the liturgists' attack on the sacred. The remark about man replacing God at the center of worship brings us to the issue most central to today's liturgy — the impact of the revolutionary changes not just on the externals of the Mass, but on the very theology of the liturgy, following the time-honored principle, *lex orandi, lex credendi.* How we pray and how we believe are inseparable. Accidents and substance do not exist in separation from each other. Rather, accidents *inhere* in substance and manifest substance. When the externals of worship express a distorted form of worship and a distorted relationship of the worshipper to God, then it is likely that the substance of what the worshippers believe is also distorted. The theology of the Eucharist cannot be separated from its outward form.

When we compare the traditional Catholic liturgy with the contemporary "Protestantized" liturgy, we find two fundamental differences in the whole idea of what happens at Mass:

1) The traditional liturgy is founded on the doctrine of transubstantiation, which sees Christ as truly present under the accidents of bread and wine, whereas the contemporary version implies a notion that the bread and wine are mere signs or symbols for Christ, who is present principally in the gathered people themselves.

2) The traditional liturgy implies the doctrine of the Mass as a sacrifice, whereas the contemporary one implies that the Mass is a kind of sacred meal shared by the "People of God."These doctrinal concerns reflect the fundamental conflict underlying all the concerns about the externals of liturgy — music, language, etc. Let us take a little time to discuss them in more detail.

---

[273] Monsignor Richard J. Schuler, "An Answer to the Problems of Sacred Music Today," W, 11-20-69.

3. TRANSUBSTANTIATION OR TRANSIGNIFICATION?

The clear, centuries-old teaching of the Church on the Eucharist holds that in the consecration of the Mass the entire substance of the bread and wine becomes the Body, Blood, Soul and Divinity of Christ. Christ is not just somehow lurking somewhere behind the accidents of bread and wine — He is truly present *in* those accidents, as every substance is in its accidents. This is the doctrine of transubstantiation, which Pope Paul VI stated for our times in his encyclical *The Mystery of Faith*, published in its entirety in the September 23, 1965 issue of *The Wanderer*. After acknowledging some positive results of contemporary theological efforts to understand the Eucharist more deeply, the Holy Father went on to say this:

> ...It is not allowable to emphasize what is called the "communal" Mass to the disparagement of Masses celebrated in private, or to exaggerate the element of sacramental sign as if the symbolism, which all certainly admit in the Eucharist, expresses fully and exhausts completely the mode of Christ's Presence in this Sacrament. Nor is it allowable to discuss the Mystery of Transubstantiation without mentioning what the Council of Trent stated about the marvelous conversion of the whole substance of the bread into the Body and of the whole substance of the wine into the Blood of Christ, speaking rather only of what is called "Transignification" and "Transfiguration," or finally to propose and act upon the opinion according to which, in the consecrated Hosts which remain after the celebration of the Sacrifice of the Mass, Christ Our Lord is no longer present.
>
> This Presence is called "real" — by which it is not intended to exclude all other types of presence as if they could not be "real" too, but because it is presence in the fullest sense: that is to say, it is a substantial presence by which Christ, the

> God-Man, is wholly and entirely present....It would therefore be wrong to explain this presence by having recourse to the "spiritual" nature, as it is called, of the glorified Body of Christ, which is present everywhere, or by reducing it to a kind of symbolism as if this most august Sacrament consisted of nothing else but an efficacious sign "of the spiritual presence of Christ and of His intimate union with the faithful members of His Mystical Body."
>
> This voice [of the Church]...assures that the way Christ is made present in this Sacrament is none other than by the change of the whole substance of the bread into His Body, and of the whole substance of the wine into His Blood, and that this unique and truly wonderful change the Catholic Church rightly calls Transubstantiation. As a result of Transubstantiation, the species of bread and wine undoubtedly take on a new meaning and a new finality, for they no longer remain ordinary bread and ordinary wine, but become the sign of something sacred, the sign of a spiritual food. However, the reason they take on this new significance and this new finality is simply because they contain a new "reality" which We may justly term Ontological. Not that there lies under those species what was already there before, but something quite different; and that not only because of the Faith of the Church, but in objective reality, since after the change of the substance or nature of the bread and wine into the Body and Blood of Christ, nothing remains of the bread and wine but the appearances, under which Christ, whole and entire, in His physical "reality" is bodily present, although not in the same way that bodies are present in a given place.[274]

Transignification and similar doctrines reduce the True Presence to subjectivity. What they amount to is the assertion that after the con-

---

[274] "The Mystery of Faith: Complete Text of Pope Paul's Third Encyclical," W, 9-23-65.

secration, the worshipper *perceives* the bread and wine to have a meaning that they were not *perceived* to have before — that is, to refer to Christ present in His people. Transubstantiation, in contrast, means that Christ is objectively present whether or not I perceive Him there. But that means God Himself, Incarnate in Christ, has come into the world and confronts me, and indeed the entire congregation, as a reality that can make demands on me, not least of which is the demand that I accept Him or reject Him. A mere *perception* makes no such demands. It is nothing more than an opinion I might have about Him, a decision on my part to regard the bread and wine as signs of Him. It doesn't call for a response and can never be proved true or false. One cannot commit a sacrilege by swallowing a "transignified" piece of bread, but one can certainly do so by receiving the very substance of Christ while in a state of mortal sin, an act which insults God Himself and does violence to Him. That is scary, and explains why so many people prefer theories of "transignification" which entail no risks and no responsibility. If Christ is truly present, we are responsible for treating Him reverently because He has in effect placed Himself in our power; if He is not truly present, what we do to mere "transignified" bread and wine really doesn't matter.

It appears, then, that the theology of the Eucharist and the way in which we celebrate it go hand in hand. A false theology is likely to lead to an irreverent celebration, and an irreverent celebration is likely to lead to a heretical understanding of the Mass. Frank Morriss brought this out in a 1978 editorial, commenting on the controversial practice of receiving communion in the hand, authorized by the Holy See not long before:

> The inferences regarding the Real Presence are also many with respect to this change. True, none of the catechesis denies the full import of that doctrine. But praxis is a different matter. The carelessness that is concomitant with the introduction of the change indicates a wide infection of the notions of transignification and transfinalization. There is little

> worry about either conscious or unconscious desecration of the particles of the consecrated Host — not simply because there is trust in the faithful, or because such worry can indeed be carried to the extreme of scrupulosity, but because many have accepted the idea that it is the faith of the receiver, the effect upon the communicant, that involves the true Presence of Christ. Surely, that crumb is not *actually* Christ's flesh and blood![275]

Certainly, a Protestantized liturgy, by lending itself so well to a watered-down notion of the Real Presence, inevitably leads us to water down our idea of the Incarnation, making it an abstraction and depriving us of the full sense of the concrete reality of God, in Christ, entering into our lives. It is a way to keep the God who gives Himself to us at arm's length. This is what an unattributed editorial of January 17, 1980, titled "Transubstantiation and the Real Presence," gets across:

> It is possible to drift toward a notion of our Lord as present in some vague and nebulous fashion in the Eucharist, and then to think of that vague notion as more "spiritual" than the flesh and blood reality.
>
> But it was through His flesh and blood humanity that He redeemed us, and that same humanity exists under the whiteness that looks like bread and the redness that looks like wine. He is as really present there as He was when He walked with His disciples in Galilee, and as He is now in Heaven. We come to see this more clearly by pondering the Church's teaching on transubstantiation.[276]

A liturgy which de-emphasizes transubstantiation is not just de-emphasizing an abstract doctrine — it is de-emphasizing, undermining, the Incarnation, for Christians the central event in human history.

---

[275] Frank Morriss, "Granting of the Option Was News of Great Significance," W, 2-23-78.

[276] "Transubstantiation and the Real Presence," W, 1-17-80.

The problems many of us "traditional Catholics" have about the modern liturgy are not just nitpicking about externals by people with a nostalgia for the past, but go right to the center of the Christian faith and, indeed, of the meaning of human life.

4. SACRIFICE OR COMMUNAL MEAL?

Perhaps it is a slight oversimplification, but I believe it is correct to say that when we think of the Mass, first and foremost, as a sacrifice, we are placing God Himself at the center of the Mass. The Mass is a gift of God, a gift which we have no power to create or give, but can only receive. That is how nearly two thousand years of Catholic tradition thought of the Mass, and how genuine Catholic teaching even today thinks of it. The Mass, in that perspective, is first and foremost a sacrifice in which God Himself is the victim. The Mass is the central locus, the central place, of God's self-giving love. It is the place where St. John's statement, "God is Love," becomes a concrete reality in time and history. The Mass is first of all God's sacrificial gift of Himself to us, and only then is it our gift, as we, the assembled community, join our own gift of ourselves to God's gift which alone gives our gift value. The communal meal idea of the Mass turns the traditional understanding upside-down. For that idea, the meaning of the Mass is the Christian community assembled together to celebrate itself. It is the people giving themselves to one another in Christian love. God still has a place, of course, but a secondary one, insofar as in the Mass the people in some way make Christ present in their midst by their love for one another. This focus on the community fits in best with the transignification idea of the Real Presence discussed above — for this notion Christ becomes present in the bread and wine because the people, in offering the bread and wine with the priest there as *their* representative (not God's), confer on the bread and wine the meaning of the presence of Christ. Deep down, this type of Mass is really the community deifying and worshipping itself. The God who becomes present is really the community itself.

We have to be careful how we formulate this, because the Church in no way rejects the togetherness of the community as a real and important part of the Mass, anymore than she rejects symbolism as an aspect of the Real Presence. But the Church, in the Mass as well as in other matters, always makes the vertical axis of existence, man's reaching upward to God, primary, and the horizontal, man's reaching out to his fellowmen, secondary. For the Church, these are inseparable realities. It is only man's vertical relation to the transcendent, all-holy God that gives man the power to love his fellow human beings. Love of God and love of neighbor are inseparable, but love of God comes first. Pope Paul, in *Mysterium Fidei*, tried to make this clear:

> We desire to recall at the very outset what may be termed the very essence of the dogma, namely, that by means of the Mystery of the Eucharist, the Sacrifice of the Cross, which was once offered on Calvary, is remarkably re-enacted and constantly recalled, and its saving power exerted for the forgiveness of those sins which we daily commit.
>
> We should also mention the public and social nature of every Mass…, a conclusion which clearly follows from the doctrine We have been discussing. For even though a priest should offer Mass in private, that Mass is not something private; it is an act of Christ and of the Church. In offering this sacrifice, the Church learns to offer herself as a sacrifice for all. Moreover, for the salvation of the entire world she applies the single, boundless, redemptive power of the Sacrifice of the Cross. For every Mass is offered not for the salvation of ourselves alone, but also for that of the whole world. Hence, although the very nature of the action renders most appropriate the active participation of many of the faithful in the celebration of the Mass, nevertheless that Mass is to be fully approved which, in conformity with the prescriptions

> and lawful traditions of the Church, a priest for a sufficient reason offers in private....[277]

Advocates of the communal notion of the Mass have almost invariably rejected the whole idea of adoration of the Eucharist outside the Mass, as in the Forty Hours devotions of the old days. They do this basically on grounds that this is a private devotion which is not in accord with the communal idea. For this perspective, it is the gathering of the community which is at the center of the Eucharist, and thus it is only in the context of that gathering that the consecrated bread and wine should be worshipped. If it is the community at prayer that consecrates the bread and wine and makes Christ present, then that Presence has no reality outside the gathering. Pope Paul tried to deal with this too in *Mysterium Fidei*:

> ...The Eucharist is reserved in the churches and oratories as in the spiritual center of a religious community or of a parish, yes, of the Universal Church and of all humanity, since beneath the appearance of the species, Christ is contained, the Invisible Head of the Church, the Redeemer of the world, the Center of all hearts, "by Whom all things are and by Whom we exist" (*I Cor*. 8,6).
>
> From this it follows that the worship paid to the Divine Eucharist strongly impels the soul to cultivate a "social" love...by which the common good is given preference over the good of the individual. Let us consider as our own the interests of the community, of the parish, of the entire Church, extending our charity to the whole world, because we know that everywhere there are members of Christ.[278]

Eucharistic adoration, in other words, does not contradict the importance of the community, but it does mean that the community must be Christ-centered, not man-centered. It is Christ's presence

---

[277] "The Mystery of Faith: Complete Text of Pope Paul's Third Encyclical," W, 9-23-65.
[278] Ibid.

precisely that creates the Christian community. The liturgical modernists have reversed this relation, making it, in a real sense, the community that creates Christ.

The traditional, sacrificial understanding of the Mass was well set forth by Father Michael D. Forrest in a December 9, 1965 editorial:

> But the Catholic Church emphatically teaches that the Eucharist is not only a *sacrament*, a sacred banquet, but also a *sacrifice*, which cannot be defined as a meal or a banquet but as the *offering* of a divine Victim (the Lamb of God) immolated on the altar for love of us in the sacramental garb of death (the separate consecration of the bread into His Body and of the wine into His Blood). After the consecration Christ lies on the altar (a lamb "as it were slain") offering to His Eternal Father the infinite adoration, thanksgiving, atonement, and petition which He offered on the cross (while we unite our suffering with His). The Mass is Calvary in sacramental garb.[279]

Bishop William L. Adrian's explanation of the traditional Mass in August, 1966, makes it easy to understand why the modernists feel so threatened by the old Mass and are so anxious to suppress it:

> Now the very *essence* of the Mass is that it is a *sacrifice*; — and a sacrifice in the liturgical sense is (1) the offering up of some real, material thing, (2) effected by its real or mystical destruction (burning, killing) (3) by a priest, (4) unto God, (5) as a lawfully instituted symbol of the adoration and honor and obedience which man owes to God, his Creator....Since sacrifice is an outward symbol that expresses what takes [place] spiritually — (like water in Baptism denotes cleans-

[279] Father Michael D. Forrest, M.S.C., "False Notion of the Mass Exposed and Refuted," W, 12-9-65.

> ing) — it must indicate the complete dependence of man on God.[280]

It is hard to imagine anything more anathema to the modern secular mind-set than "complete dependence on God."

Not only does the traditional Mass involve Christ's sacrifice, but it is also sacrificial insofar as it calls for man's sacrifice, epitomized in loving obedience to the God who gives Himself for us in the Mass. Father William G. Most made that clear in a September, 1968 article, in which he argued that Christ's sacrifice, re-enacted in the Mass, is the expression of His obedience to the Father, an obedience which we are called to imitate:

> Since, then, obedience is the condition of the New Covenant, a condition already fulfilled by Christ, those who belong to Christ must imitate Him in His obedience. The point to which they bring their obedience is the Mass, the renewal of the New Covenant, as the Council says. We can see now how Pope Paul can say that obedience is "an understanding of the principle which dominates the entire plan of Incarnation and redemption," and why it "becomes assimilation into Christ who is the divine obedient One."
>
> What, then, should we say of those who think they are attaining the true meaning of the Mass by disobeying not only the authorities in the Church, but also by seeking a celebration that will, as Callahan says, "liturgically act out this kind of parallel [i.e., non-subject] relationship with God." They are not only not finding the meaning: they are fleeing at full speed from it.[281]

Writing in October, 1975, Frank Morriss found it necessary to call attention to the replacement of God by the people as the object of

---

[280] Bishop William L. Adrian, "The Mass Is a True Sacrifice," W, 8-18-66.

[281] Father William G. Most, "The Mass: A Center of Obedience," W, 9-5-68.

worship in the Mass, responding to a situation which had developed at Georgetown University:

> When we are given the Georgetown Campus Ministry's explanation of what the Mass really is, it becomes clearer: "In the Roman Catholic Mass, we come together to experience and celebrate the Lord's presence in the Bread and Wine, in his Word, in the Celebrant who presides over the ceremony, and in the People themselves gathered there."
>
> Note the first important word is "experience." Nothing about worship or sacrifice. Next we have the theological monstrosity of putting on a level Christ "in" the Bread and Wine, in His Word, and in the Celebrant and People. (The people's divinization apparently has reached the point of allowing them a capital "P.")[282]

That kind of thing was still a little shocking in 1975. Today we listen to such blasphemous nonsense from the pulpit or in the "commentaries" of the Mass and hardly turn a hair. We have become desensitized.

Finally, the Church's ability, in her teaching on the Mass, to incorporate both aspects, sacrifice and communal meal, while keeping them in their right order, was exemplified in Pope John Paul II's 1980 apostolic letter, *Dominicae Cenae*:

> The Eucharist is above all else a sacrifice....The celebrant, as minister of this sacrifice, is the authentic *priest*, performing — in virtue of the specific power of sacred ordination — a true sacrificial act that brings creation back to God. Although all those who participate in the Eucharist do not confect the sacrifice as he does, they offer with him, by virtue of their *common* priesthood their own *spiritual sacrifices* represented

[282] Frank Morriss, "Denigrating the Holy Sacrifice of the Mass," W, 10-9-75.

> by the bread and wine from the moment of their presentation at the altar.[283]

The record of public debate about the liturgy, epitomized in the selection of *Wanderer* commentary assembled in this section, shows pretty conclusively, I think, the absolute contradiction between the liturgical reform and renewal desired by the Council, and the liturgical revolution that actually took place under the direction of modernist ideologues who could not have departed further from both the letter and the spirit of the Council when they worked their many iniquities. Archbishop Robert Dwyer, in a July 22, 1971 article entitled, appropriately enough, "The Liturgy Has Been Dismantled," sums up, better than I can, this contradiction and the state of chaos which has been the end product of the revolution:

> The liturgy needed reform by 1965; there was no call for dismantling it. It was intended that the vernacular would enhance the Latin, not supplant it. It was not, emphatically, the mind of the Council fathers to jettison Gregorian chant or to encourage the banal secularization of Church music, so as now to surpass in crudity the worst aberrations of the Howling Pentecostals....But the broad permissiveness granted or even encouraged by the Sacred Congregation and by various episcopal conference committees, has led to what must be described, without exaggeration, as a state of chaos. Everyman is now his own liturgist, just as he is his own pope; the parish liturgical commission, made up, for the most, part of good and well-meaning folk whose liturgical competence is on the kindergarten level, legislates for all the world as though it were the Sacred Congregation itself. Or perhaps, what is by no means unthinkable, with far greater assurance and authority.

---

[283] "Pope Stresses Ever-Living Tradition in Apostolic Letter on the Eucharist," W, 3-27-80.

> How long, do you suppose, will it take for another Hercules to clean up these Augean Stables?[284]

Archbishop Dwyer's concluding question has not gone without at least some attempts at an answer. How successfully it has been answered will be the topic of discussion in the next section, dealing with the responses of traditional Catholics to the revolution so rudely forced upon them.

[284] Archbishop Robert Dwyer, "The Liturgy Has Been Dismantled," W, 7-22-71.

5. COUNTERREVOLUTION IN THE CHURCH: ORTHODOXY VS. RIGHT-WING SECTARIANISM

The battle over the liturgy has this in common with the rest of the battles chronicled in this volume: It started out with an ambush. To put it bluntly: The "good guys" were blindsided. Traditional Catholics were almost totally unprepared, in the early 1960s, for the liturgical revolution that suddenly engulfed them. Granted that there had been talk for several years about the possibility of a vernacular liturgy, but the signals from Rome all seemed to contradict such an expectation. Pope John XXIII, as we saw earlier, in his public statements, consistently upheld the place of Latin in the liturgy, calling Latin "a manifest and splendid sign of unity." Furthermore, almost everyone assumed that if a vernacular liturgy came to be adopted, it would be purely and simply a translation of the already existing liturgy, something which would probably have been acceptable to most traditional Catholics, even if they did feel a little nostalgia for the Latin. Most expected something similar to the Anglican liturgy (as it was then, not today), not the chaotic mess of guitar Masses, clown Masses, liturgical dancing, flat and banal wording, etc., that soon grew like a kind of giant fungus in the Church. The changes were expected to be minor and accidental, not touching on the essence of the Mass. Alas, it was not to be thus. That was evident as early as 1965 to an anonymous pastor who wrote in his parish bulletin that

> The changes authorized by the Holy See in the liturgy affect only the externals and accidentals, not the essentials of the Mass. The fact that Mass has always been validly offered in different languages and different ceremonies shows that we

> are dealing with something secondary. The sad and unfortunate feature of the present life of the Church in our country is the introduction of unauthorized, undignified, and sometimes almost frivolous changes into the Church's worship; it is the pushing of change into the essentials, into the Church's infallible, unchangeable, and changeless teachings; it is the inciting of disrespect for, and rebellion against, the Holy See, and against the Holy Father who by Christ's will is the universal ruler of the whole Church. All this can lead only to internal and eventually to external defection from the faith. Again, we must remember that there is a very close connection and interplay between bodily actions and mental ideas. The placing or the omission of certain ceremonies may easily weaken the *faith of the people in the Holy Eucharist*, the very center and heart of the whole liturgy. What would happen to our faith if, for example, we stopped genuflecting before the Blessed Sacrament?...As far as your parish church is concerned, our Lord will be removed from the main altar to the sacristy only over the pastor's dead body.[285]

That is a prophetic message, and expresses very well the mixture of bewilderment and outrage in the hearts of traditional Catholics as the reality that a revolution was occurring in the liturgy began to cross their threshold of consciousness.

The earliest traditionalist response to this situation was not to directly attack the "new Mass" but to espouse a "live and let live" approach, tolerating the new liturgy but asking that the old Latin Mass be allowed to coexist with the new. That is the kind of arrangement that the Dubuque Diocese attempted to work out (see above).

The Catholic Traditionalist Movement, one of the earliest organized efforts at a liturgical counterrevolution, basically sought tolerance for those who wanted the old liturgy more than a suppression of the new. In March, 1965, the Movement issued a *Catholic Manifesto*

---

285 "'Unauthorized, Undignified UpDating': An Appeal to Reason," W, 2-25-65.

which incorporated a number of "suggestions" submitted to the Bishops. These, according to the *Wanderer* coverage at the time, included:

> Full option and adequate opportunity to assist at Mass in the traditional Latin form; an end to mandatory "regimented" group participation at Mass, and instead full permission for individual silent participation; elimination of practices or hymns with "non-Catholic overtones"; continuation of such Catholic customs as genuflections and kneeling before the Blessed Sacrament; encouragement of the "eminently Catholic" devotion to the Blessed Virgin Mary; "mature loyalty and filial obedience" to the Pope; and only those changes in nuns' dresses which "will still allow the Sisters' uniform to remain indicative of their special dedicated position among God's people."...The manifesto also states that "liturgical progressivism is increasingly and alarmingly appearing to many as only the first phase of a broader scheme intent to 'Protestantize' the entire Church." It deplores what it calls "progressivist agitation in the liturgy," which it claims is leading to "increasing polarization of the radical minority and the traditionalist majority among God's people."[286]

These are suggestions most of us "reactionary" types would support enthusiastically. Unfortunately, the Catholic Traditionalist Movement (CTM) ended up being less than effective as an advocate for these ideas due to a history of problems centering largely around the personality of its leader, Father Gommar DePauw. Father DePauw, a 46-year old theology instructor at Mt. St. Mary's Seminary in Emmitsburg, Maryland, had been spiritual leader of the movement. In April, 1965, however, he was ordered by his bishop, Lawrence Cardinal Shehan of Baltimore, to dissociate himself from it. At the time, Father DePauw chose to obey Cardinal Shehan's orders and not to ap-

[286] "'Traditional Catholic' Group Calls for Restraint in Liturgical Changes," W, 3-25-65.

peal to Rome, but did, ominously, leave open the possibility of changing his mind if circumstances so warranted. At that time, *The Wanderer* praised him for his obedience.[287]

Apparently, this did not prevent the CTM, whether or not at Father DePauw's urging, from launching personal attacks on Cardinal Shehan. In an editorial entitled "More Dialogue, Less Diatribe, Please!" *The Wanderer* expressed agreement with the group's goal of seeking more of a place for Latin in the liturgy, but criticized it for allowing itself to be diverted into personal attacks:

> As observers sympathetic to the objectives expressed in the first manifesto of the "Catholic Traditionalist Movement" we are deeply saddened by this regrettable diversion of a promising and constructive movement into the bypaths of personal and sterile invective which can only do harm to the Movement itself and to the genuine reform of the liturgy which all Catholics so earnestly desire. We sincerely hope that cool heads may prevail and that the Traditionalist Movement may yet perform the providential function of purifying the ferment so that it may ultimately yield a good wine.[288]

Father DePauw was back in the news in January, 1966. He had apparently decided to appeal his case to Rome after all, and on December 31, 1965, had sent a letter to the bishops of the United States, in which he indicated that

> As a result of this appeal to Rome I am no longer subject to the authority of the cardinal-archbishop of Baltimore. Instead, I am now a canonically incardinated priest of the Diocese of Tivoli-Rome, a diocese directly subject to the Holy See. With the full permission and the encouragement of my new ecclesiastical superiors I have returned to the United States and am resuming the public leadership of the Catholic Traditionalist Movement which is now a corporation organ-

[287] "Father DePauw Plans No Appeal to Rome at Present," W, 4-22-65.

[288] "More Dialogue, Less Diatribe, Please!" W, 5-13-65.

> ized and existing under the laws of the State of New York....[289]

Father DePauw also stated that the CTM had given Rome a report of the findings of a survey on "The True Feelings of American Catholics Concerning Their 'Updated' Church in General and the New Liturgy in Particular." The survey showed that less than 25% of Catholics approved of the changes.[290]

Unfortunately, the headline of the article reporting these events was "Pope Paul OK's Work of 'Catholic Traditionalist' Priest-Leader." That turned out to be more than a little premature, as was the title of Walter L. Matt's editorial in the same issue, "A Vindication for the Traditionalists."[291]

It soon became clear that there were some questions about the precise canonical status of Father DePauw, and that perhaps the situation was not quite as simple as he had indicated. Walter Matt, in a January 20 article, tried to sidestep the issue in stating that:

> As far as the editors of *The Wanderer* are concerned, let this be clearly understood: We hold no particular brief for Father DePauw or for the Catholic Traditionalist Movement to which the Holy See has or had, apparently, given its blessing. To this very moment, we have not met Father DePauw in person, nor have we ever applied for or received personal membership in the CTM. We do know, however, that, whatever else may be said either for or against him, Father DePauw is a Roman Catholic priest in good standing, that he is *not* — repeat *not* — a priest in any way rebelling or fomenting rebellion against either the Pope or the divinely ordained teaching Magisterium of Holy Mother the Church, or

---

289 "Pope Paul OK's Work Of 'Catholic Traditionalist' Priest-Leader," W, 1-13-66.

290 Ibid.

291 Walter L. Matt, "A Vindication for the Traditionalists", W, 1-13-66.

> the official decrees or decisions voted upon at the Second Vatican Council.[292]

This is what is, I believe, called, in media jargon, "distancing oneself," in this case probably a prudent step.

By late January, a situation of total chaos had developed in regard to Father DePauw's status.[293] The January 27 *Wanderer* reports that earlier in January Cardinal Shehan had ordered Father DePauw to report to him, apparently not accepting the latter's claim to be outside the cardinal's jurisdiction. The Most Rev. Egidio Vagnozzi, apostolic delegate to the United States, supported Shehan, and advised him not to grant the excardination. Vagnozzi stated that Bishop Faveri of Tivoli-Rome, whom Father DePauw claimed as his bishop, had agreed to state that Father DePauw was not validly incardinated. On the other hand, Bishop Blaise S. Kurz, exiled prefect apostolic of Youngchow, China, who had been Father DePauw's immediate superior through the years of the Vatican Council, issued a statement on January 17 to the effect that he had personally delivered the decree of incardination from Bishop Faveri to Father DePauw. He added that "*I consider any attack on Father DePauw, at whatever source or with whatever person that attack may originate, as an attack on my personal integrity as a bishop of the Catholic Church. I most solemnly declare that the statements released by Father DePauw to the communications media and particularly to the* New York Times *contain the truth and nothing but the truth.*" Bishop Kurz also indicated that, as Father DePauw's immediate superior, he had ordered Father DePauw *not* to return to Baltimore.[294]

A February 3 editorial in *The Wanderer* expressed the concern that the substantive issues relating to Father DePauw were being allowed, by elements in the liberal Catholic press, to be overshadowed by character attacks on him — accusations that he was fomenting

---

[292] Walter L. Matt, "The Case of Father DePauw — Smears vs. the Truth," W, 1-20-66.

[293] Walter L. Matt, "The Case of Father DePauw," W, 1-27-66.

[294] Ibid.

schism, for instance. People were accusing Father DePauw of disobedience to his ecclesiastical superiors, when precisely the issue was who these superiors were. *The Wanderer* noted that writers like Bernard Casserly were concerned about the possibility of Father DePauw's actions leading to a schism, but "to permit any substantive dialogue to deteriorate into vilification and character assassination is to court the very disaster which Mr. Casserly and others fear: an outright schism which may set the Church in the United States back by decades if not by centuries."[295]

In a February 10 editorial, *The Wanderer* developed this theme a little further, noting that, whatever the Church's ultimate decision about Father DePauw, the truly important divisions in the American Church were very deep and went to central matters of teaching, where Father DePauw's criticisms related to more peripheral matters. There was a rumor that Father DePauw had said he would ignore a decree of excommunication. *The Wanderer* indicated that such an act on his part would be very wrong, but at the same time called attention to the fact that dissidents on the left were constantly defying ecclesiastical authority with impunity.[296]

On March 10, *The Wanderer* indicated it had not "backed away" from Father DePauw, but wanted the issues surrounding his status resolved soon and the confusion ended:

> We suggest, however, that in justice and fairness to Father De Pauw, all the canonical — i.e., legalistic — discussions pertaining to his excardination from the Archdiocese of Baltimore be *not* dropped, as Father Geaney seems to be saying, but rather that all of the canonical documents pertinent to his case be turned over to the proper ecclesiastical court, or courts, at the Holy See, and that unless or until the final verdict by such court or courts is rendered, Father De Pauw must be presumed to be a priest in good standing, a priest who if he defied an order by one bishop claiming to be his

---

[295] "Threat of Schism?" W, 2-3-66.
[296] "Modernists, Si, Father DePauw, No?" W, 2-10-66.

> superior in Baltimore, has done so only because of his obedience to another bishop — the Most Rev. Blaise Kurz, who publicly and explicitly ordered him *not* to return to Baltimore. In short, this seems to be a case where a man must be presumed to be innocent until he is proven guilty. Meanwhile it is rank injustice to call him names and to make him out as a renegade priest.[297]

Several months later, in August, 1966, *The Wanderer* indicated that it continued to support the goals of the CTM, but took no position on Father DePauw's canonical status.[298] Finally, the December 22, 1966 *Wanderer* reported that the Vatican had found Father DePauw's excardination invalid:

> According to an AP dispatch from Vatican City last week, Father Gommar DePauw, Belgian-born Baltimore priest who founded the American Catholic Traditionalist Movement, has been judged still bound by Canon Law to the Baltimore archdiocese.
>
> The Associated Press said that a special commission appointed by the Vatican's Congregation of the Council, which has had charge of Catholic diocesan affairs since the 1663 [sic] Council of Trent, made the decision affecting Father DePauw.
>
> The Associated Press further reported that Father DePauw has challenged the commission's ruling, arguing that it "was not competent" to deal with his case. He claimed it should be handled either by Pope Paul VI or the Roman Rota.
>
> The communiqué from the Congregation, according to the Associated Press, said the special commission, "after hearing the interested parties and examining documents submitted by them," ruled September 30 that the incardination claimed by Father DePauw — to the Diocese of Tivoli, Italy — is "not

[297] "This and That," W, 3-10-66.
[298] Walter L. Matt, "The CTM and Father DePauw," W, 8-11-66.

> valid." Hence, Father DePauw remains, with all canonical effects, subject to the archbishop of Baltimore.[299]

One gets the impression, reading the record, that *The Wanderer* badly wanted to support Father DePauw, that its editors suspected then, as I do now, that this was a classic case where people who support Rome and orthodoxy get hung out to dry — i.e., that Rome backed away from an arrangement it had originally sanctioned after the bishops' "good ol' boy" network got into the act. Whatever the case, however, *The Wanderer* held that, in the end, we have to accept the Holy See's decisions even when we may feel they are unjust, and not fall into the Protestant habit of private judgment in such matters. Hence:

> We strongly suggest, therefore, that those of us who choose to call themselves conservative, orthodox, or traditionalist Catholics, should be the very last ones indeed ever to defy the rightful moral authority and juridical institutions of the teaching Magisterium of Holy Mother Church. Our responsibility, particularly in the storm-tossed, revolution-swept world of today, is infinitely greater than that. Loyalty to Christ and to His Vicar here on earth demands something more of us than grudging lip service. It demands of us, as it did of Him, perfect obedience, humility, and loyalty — and, of course, the atoning spirit of forgiveness and sacrifice for the sins of men, even for those who again today would stoop to betray Him and send Him to the cross.[300]

Unfortunately, Father DePauw did not accept the decision in that spirit, but instead attempted to do what amounted to founding a new Church. A *Wanderer* report of September 7, 1967 states that:

> According to an NC News Service dispatch from New York, Father Gommar A. DePauw, president of the Catholic Tradi-

---

[299] "Vatican Rules Father DePauw Case 'Not Valid,'" W, 12-22-66.
[300] Walter L. Matt, "A Word About Frs. Nugent and DePauw," W, 1-19-67.

> tionalist Movement who was suspended last year by Lawrence Cardinal Shehan of Baltimore, says he has sent a twelve-page letter to Pope Paul VI asking for the establishment of a "traditionalist Latin rite" in the United States.
>
> He said he also asked the Pope to appoint a bishop to head the rite and to authorize the consecration of other Bishops for the rite.
>
> The letter also carried what amounted to a virtual ultimatum:
>
> If his demands are not granted, said DePauw, or if he is not given a chance to discuss them, he and 156 other priests who belong to the Traditionalists will open up storefront churches and offer Latin Masses.
>
> The Traditionalist leader gave the Pope a month to comply with his requests. The letter was written August 15th.[301]

That is not exactly the spirit of filial obedience, as the September 14 *Wanderer* pointed out. It also noted that Father DePauw's public utterances were filled with contradictions. For instance, he had initially indicated full support for the Second Vatican Council, stating only that he opposed certain abuses perpetrated in the name of the Council, yet in his ultimatum to Rome he declared the Council a grave mistake and called on the Pope to repudiate it. He had also refused to appeal his case to the Roman Rota. *The Wanderer* added that traditional Catholics, even more than others, needed to have the spirit of obedience to Church authority:

> It is deeply deplorable that, despite these and many other admonitions given to Father DePauw over the past two years, he has allowed himself — directly contrary to his most solemn earlier assurances and directly contrary even to his public oath "before God and men...that we traditionalist Catholics will never leave the Holy Roman Catholic Church"...to be driven into his presently wholly unwarranted and unten-

[301] "Father DePauw Asks Latin Rite," W, 9-7-67.

> able position. If today Father DePauw in fact forgets his solemn oath by disloyalty or even schism to the Holy See, he will of course bring disgrace not only upon himself but, far worse, he will render a tremendous disservice to the cause of sound Catholic tradition, Church discipline, and religious orthodoxy.[302]

The article expressed the belief that Father DePauw was indeed treated shabbily by the authorities, but indicated that he was nevertheless without excuse for his current actions, and called on him to turn away from these actions.

On October 5, *The Wanderer*, in an article called "A Final Word on the DePauw Case," gave its analysis of the legal issues in the case. It appeared that what had probably happened was more or less as follows: That Cardinal Shehan, writing privately to Bishop Faveri, had asked him to incardinate Father DePauw in the Tivoli Diocese, then had changed his mind, perhaps on finding out that Father DePauw intended to return to the United States, and had never sent the document of excardination from Baltimore. That being the case, the document of incardination to Tivoli was null and void:

> In short, it appears to us that Father DePauw, whatever the admitted validity and orthodoxy of the Catholic Traditionalist Movement, is anything but on solid ground insofar as his priestly credentials are concerned. He has insisted ever since January, 1966, that he is or was a duly incardinated priest of Bishop Faveri's diocese, not of Cardinal Shehan's. But Bishop Faveri himself, as we see here, not only flatly denies this but completely disowns him. So did Cardinal Ottaviani. So did Archbishop Vagnozzi. So did Archbishop Cicognani. They all, in fact, put the full burden of proof on Father DePauw either to produce the "missing document" from

[302] "Father DePauw's Threatened Break With Rome," W, 9-14-67.

> Baltimore, or, failing that, obediently return to his post as a duly incardinated priest of that diocese.[303]

This is a sad case and, unfortunately, seems to have established the pattern for many later confrontations between Catholic traditionalists and Church authorities. It is certainly a classic case of the cold-bloodedness and dishonesty with which Church authorities so often deal with individual human beings, making agreements in private, then publicly disavowing them when pressure is brought to bear. One cannot help but feel sorry for Father DePauw, who was treated very badly. At the same time, however, the case set the pattern for some future confrontations in another way — as a classic case of Satan's ability to undermine the work of the orthodox by getting at the leaders through their egos. Like many such leaders, including the late Archbishop Lefebvre, to be discussed later, Father DePauw seems to have reached the point of seeing himself as God's special representative who was so morally pure as to be above the rules binding on ordinary mortals, particularly the obligation to obey Church authorities, even when one feels they are unjust. He seems, like Martin Luther, to have almost made a kind of little god out of himself. With less ego, Father DePauw might have reached the sensible decision to let go of the Catholic Traditionalist Movement, knowing that no one is indispensable and knowing that, if it was God's will that the group continue, surely God would raise up a leader for it, perhaps a lay person not subject in the same way to ecclesiastical authorities. The decision of the authorities, just or unjust, may well have meant that it was not God's will for Father DePauw to lead the movement. But instead, Father DePauw decided to place his retention of leadership ahead of the movement and the Catholic orthodoxy for which it stood, and both were lost.

What is really important about the DePauw case, for readers of *The Wanderer*, is that it illustrates the kind of tightrope *The Wanderer* walked again and again when it came to confrontations like this between the "orthodox" and the authorities in the Church. *The Wan-*

[303] "A Final Word on the DePauw Case," W, 10-5-67.

derer has consistently opposed the kind of mass insanity, especially in the liturgical area, which has turned the Catholic Church in America largely into a liberal Protestant Church At the same time, it has steered clear of the kinds of traditionalists who end up rejecting Church authority, particularly that of the Holy Father, and thus contradicting the very orthodoxy they set out to defend. Orthodoxy that rejects Rome is no longer orthodoxy. *The Wanderer* supported Father DePauw as long as it appeared that he was ready to obey the Church no matter how it decided his case, and dropped him when he rebelled against the Holy Father and tried to set up his own church. It is not always easy to walk such a tightrope, but that is what genuinely orthodox Catholics are called to do in troubled times like these.

The challenge to defend what was legitimate in the traditionalist cause, especially when the integrity of the liturgy was at stake, while at the same time supporting without reservation the authority of the Holy Father to teach and to legislate in these matters, faced *The Wanderer* on a larger, international scale when it came to the conflict between Rome and Archbishop Marcel Lefebvre. This conflict had as its focal point the changes in the liturgy following the Second Vatican Council, changes which included the suppression of the centuries-old Tridentine rite in favor of the *Novus Ordo* promulgated by Pope Paul VI. *The Wanderer* expressed much sympathy with Lefebvre but in the end broke with him when his activities led to out-and-out disobedience to the Pope.

Archbishop Lefebvre, who had for some years been superior general of the Holy Ghost Fathers, missionaries to Africa, first emerged as a spokesman for traditionalism in the late 1960s. It is interesting, in light of all that has happened since, to look at an article of Lefebvre's published in *The Wanderer* on August 8, 1968, entitled, "Some Light on the Church's Present Crisis." In this article, Lefebvre says some quite orthodox things about the Church and her Magisterium, things which today seem ironic in light of his later behavior. For instance:

> It is this unity in multiplicity that allows the Church's divine teaching to reach out to all times and places with an unvary-

> ing continuity that has ever been a source of wonderment to men of every sort. *Entire branches have separated themselves from the trunk; and yet the trunk itself has not been affected either in structure or doctrinal substance by that loss.* (Italics added)[304]

Yet, not that many years later, Lefebvre put himself in the position of saying, in effect, that the trunk had separated itself from the branches and fallen into heresy, and that his particular branch, the Priestly Fraternity (or Society) of St. Pius X, was now the trunk. His article does hint at such a development, when it asserts that such things as collegiality, the proliferation of bishops' conferences, and so forth, have weakened the Magisterium and made it ineffective.

Lefebvre's St. Pius X Society, along with its offspring, his seminary at Econe, Switzerland, had, by the mid-1970s, become the international headquarters for his movement of restoration. Lefebvre had become more and more outspoken in his public criticisms of Pope Paul VI and the Second Vatican Council, a situation which led Bishop Pierre Mamie, in May, 1974, to withdraw canonical approval from the Society and from the seminary at Econe.[305] Lefebvre ignored this decision and continued operating the seminary. In July, 1976, he brought matters to a head when he ordained 13 priests from the seminary after Pope Paul VI had expressly forbidden him to do so. Pope Paul responded to this act by suspending Archbishop Lefebvre, thus taking away his faculties for administering the sacraments, including ordination. Despite the suspension, Lefebvre went on ordaining priests in the years that followed. These events made the issue no longer one of tradition versus updating, but one of obedience to the Holy Father, as far as *The Wanderer* was concerned. An anonymous editorial of July 29, 1976 made this clear:

---

[304] Archbishop Marcel Lefebvre, "Some Light on the Church's Present Crisis," W, 8-8-68.

[305] Father John W. Flanagan, "The War Against the Pope," W, 8-12-76.

> It would seem self-evident that those who reject the authority of Pope Paul and Vatican Council II, place themselves outside the Catholic community of faith. To reject magisterial authority in the name of tradition is no less erroneous than to reject it in the name of theological modernism.[306]

Throughout these years, Pope Paul again and again wrote to Archbishop Lefebvre, urging him to accept the authority of the Council and of the Pope's acts implementing the Council, especially in the area of liturgy, and to obey the Pope and be reconciled. These letters either went unanswered or got responses from Lefebvre in which he verbally indicated his loyalty to the Holy Father, then went right ahead and continued his pattern of disobedience. Thus he continued in a state of practical schism with Rome. As Father John W. Flanagan pointed out in an editorial of August 12, 1976, "Anyone who can read and reflect on the papal letters will see that the basic fault with Archbishop Lefebvre was and is disobedience to the Holy Father and to the Holy See."[307]

Father Flanagan pointed out that, while Lefebvre and his supporters held the view that the *Novus Ordo* was not mandatory but was just an option available to Catholics in addition to the Tridentine liturgy, which, in their view, the Holy Father had no authority to abrogate, in fact, the *Novus Ordo*, whatever feelings one might have about it, *was* mandatory, and the Tridentine liturgy, however one might love it, was forbidden by Pope Paul. Father Flanagan's article challenged every Catholic to ask himself:

> If I am free to reject the mandatory nature of the constitution promulgating the *Novus Ordo*, how can I be resentful or critical of others who reject papal authority in another matter, e.g., as exercised in *Humanae Vitae* or the *Credo of the People of God?*[308]

---

[306] "The Schism of Archbishop Lefebvre," W, 7-29-76.
[307] Father John W. Flanagan, "The War Against the Pope," W, 8-12-76.
[308] Ibid.

In December, 1978, Archbishop Lefebvre again brought things to one of their frequent boiling points when he ordained another group of priests just before Christmas. This prompted *Wanderer* editor Al Matt, in an editorial, to call on Archbishop Lefebvre to make a major change in attitude and be reconciled with Rome:

> The Lefebvre movement has been one of the most tragic developments in the aftermath of Vatican II. Perhaps its most damaging effect has been to divert attention from those who are the real subversives in the Church — the neomodernists and their secularizing allies. We pray that Archbishop Lefebvre will be moved by God's grace to submit to the supreme authority of the Church and that Pope John Paul II will be as generous as possible in his terms for reconciliation.[309]

But nothing changed. As time passed, Lefebvre continued defying Rome by saying the Tridentine Mass, by administering the sacraments, and particularly by ordaining new priests and deacons. The situation still had not led, however, to out-and-out excommunication, and the rumor was that there was an understanding that excommunication would occur only if Lefebvre began consecrating bishops, something he had not done thus far. That situation could not remain stable indefinitely, however, if only because Archbishop Lefebvre was getting older and had to think about what was going to happen to his traditionalist movement after his death. That consideration apparently led him, in 1982, to begin seeking some kind of terms for reconciliation with Rome.[310] In August of that year, Lefebvre announced that he planned to retire as head of the Society, and sought permission from Rome to consecrate a bishop to take his place. He indicated that otherwise he would remain available to ordain priests. By December, 1982, Lefebvre was in Rome having meetings with Cardinal Ratzinger.[311] Apparently, these meetings led nowhere, be-

---

[309] A.J. Matt, Jr., "Reconciliation for Archbishop Lefebvre?" W, 1-25-79.

[310] "Archbishop Lefebvre Says He Seeks Reconciliation With Rome," W, 8-5-82.

[311] "Archbishop Lefebvre Confers at Vatican," W, 12-23-82.

cause in July, 1983, we find that Lefebvre had indeed retired as head of the Society but that, at the Mass held to celebrate his retirement, he had ordained 20 more priests.[312] In June, 1985, Lefebvre appeared to reject reconciliation with Rome, at least if we assume that a letter to the Holy Father from Father Franz Schmidberger, the new superior general of the Society, reflected Lefebvre's thinking. In that letter, Schmidberger said, among other things, that "only the cessation of 'enemy occupation' of Rome, a condemnation of the 'destructive liberal principles' of Vatican Council II, and an unconditional return to Tradition' are the way willed by God [for reconciliation] and 'befitting the dignity of the Church.'"[313]

In January, 1986, Archbishop Lefebvre raised new concerns in Rome when he indicated he might consider ordaining bishops:

> Archbishop Lefebvre recently turned 80. If the movement is to live on after his death, there must be bishops to ordain new priests. Will he do it or won't he? "The future is in the hands of God," he said. "The situation in the Church is very grave....If it gets worse I will consider the possibility."[314]

Lefebvre indicated at that time that he was pleased with the new Vatican policy that made it possible for people to have the Tridentine Mass with the approval of their bishops, but objected to the conditions, especially the fact that people wanting the old Mass would be required to acknowledge the doctrinal correctness of the new Mass. Clearly, the basic issues had not changed.

In late 1987, Archbishop Lefebvre was again having meetings with Cardinal Ratzinger, and accepted the appointment of Edouard Cardinal Gagnon as apostolic visitor to the Society of St. Pius X.[315]

---

[312] "Archbishop Lefebvre Retires, but Will Continue Ordinations," W, 7-14-83.

[313] "Lefebvre Appears To Reject Any Reconciliation With Rome," W, 6-13-85.

[314] "Archbishop Lefebvre Says He Will Consider Consecrating Bishops," W, 1-30-86.

[315] "Archbishop Lefebvre Accepts Apostolic Visitor," W, 10-29-87.

There were genuine grounds for hope at that point that a reconciliation might be brought about in 1988. Sadly, that was not to be.

On April 4, 1988, Pope John Paul wrote to Cardinal Ratzinger expressing his wish that everything possible be done to permit the existence of the Society of St. Pius X in union with the Church and in communion with the Holy See. Extensive meetings were held in April between experts from the Congregation for the Doctrine of the Faith and representatives of the Society to work out the details of such an accommodation. On May 5, Cardinal Ratzinger and Archbishop Lefebvre met and signed a protocol to regularize the status of the Society in the Church, subject to final approval by the Pope. In that document Lefebvre stated his loyalty to Rome and to the Holy Father, as well as his acceptance of the teachings of the Second Vatican Council. On May 24, Ratzinger and Lefebvre met again, and at that meeting Ratzinger informed Lefebvre that the Pope was willing to nominate a Bishop for the Society, to be consecrated August 15. At that meeting, Lefebvre insisted that the date be changed to June 30, and that *three* bishops be consecrated. In a letter of May 30, Cardinal Ratzinger informed Archbishop Lefebvre that he would have to give up the June 30 date. On June 2, Lefebvre sent a letter to the Holy Father, stating his objections to the spirit of Vatican II and "false ecumenism," and citing the need for several bishops who agree with him on these matters to protect the Society from compromise: "This is why we ourselves will provide the means to continue the work which Providence has entrusted to us, assured by the letter of His Eminence Cardinal Ratzinger of May 30 that the episcopal consecration is not contrary to the will of the Holy See, since it has been agreed for August 15." On June 9, Pope John Paul responded to Lefebvre in a letter which warned him not to go ahead with the planned consecrations.[316]

On June 15, Archbishop Lefebvre held a news conference in Econe, Switzerland, at which he announced his intention to conse-

[316] "Chronology of the Vatican-Lefebvre Discussions," W, 7-14-88.

crate four bishops on June 30.[317] Rome responded to this announcement with a letter of June 30 from Bernardin Cardinal Gantin to Lefebvre, warning him that he would face automatic excommunication if he proceeded with the consecrations.[318] Lefebvre proceeded with the consecrations, and Rome proceeded with the excommunication.[319]

A sad ending for a drama that began, apparently, as a legitimate effort by a prelate of considerable ability and, it would appear, of considerable personal sanctity, too, to defend the Mass against what virtually all orthodox Catholics would regard as horrendous abuses, abuses extensively covered in this chapter. Fortunately, the outcome of this episode was not an entirely negative one from the standpoint of orthodox Catholics who love the Mass. Pope John Paul seems to have understood that the popularity of Archbishop Lefebvre's movement was not just an unaccountable aberration, it was not just an expression of the rebellion of some stubborn persons against the lawful authority of Rome, but also reflected aspirations with deep roots in the Catholic faith itself: The deep love of the Catholic faithful for the Mass as the encounter between man and the Incarnate God, an encounter deserving to be protected by profound reverence and awe and by an atmosphere of beauty. Hence the Holy Father did not simply excommunicate Lefebvre and leave it at that, but also made an effort to grant the legitimate wishes of Catholic traditionalists.[320] In his *motu proprio Ecclesia Dei*, the Holy Father spelled out his wishes in regard to Catholics who wanted the Tridentine liturgy, indicating that these persons should be treated as good Catholics and every effort should be made to allow them to have the old Mass celebrated for them. He suggested, in particular, that bishops ought to be much more liberal in granting permission for the Tridentine Mass under the indult granted in 1984. A *Wanderer* editorial of July 28 summed up the content of *Ecclesia Dei*:

---

[317] "Archbishop Lefebvre Set To Consecrate Bishops," W, 6-23-88.
[318] "Holy See Warns Lefebvre," W, 6-30-88.
[319] "Lefebvre Excommunicated," W, 7-7-88.
[320] "After Archbishop Lefebvre's Excommunication...Holy See Moves To Limit Spread of Schism," W, 7-14-88.

> It is clear from his language that the Pope is very supportive of Catholics who desire a traditional liturgy and who practice traditional devotions. He calls for "a new awareness, not only of the lawfulness but also of the richness for the Church of a diversity of charisms, traditions of spirituality, and apostolate, which also constitutes the beauty of unity in variety: of that blended 'harmony' which the earthly Church raises up to Heaven under the impulse of the Holy Spirit."
>
> And, in announcing the formation of a commission to advance the reconciliation of supporters of Archbishop Lefebvre with the Church, Pope John Paul goes far beyond his concern for followers of the archbishop when he declares that "moreover, respect *must everywhere* be shown for the feelings of *all* those who are attached to the Latin liturgical tradition, by a *wide and generous application* of the directives already issued some time ago by the Apostolic See, for the use of the Roman Missal according to the typical edition of 1962." (emphasis added)[321]

Monsignor John F. McCarthy also suggested that the Lefebvre schism might have positive effects in the long run, by stimulating a renaissance of awareness of the whole Catholic liturgical tradition within the Church, as well as a new sensitivity to the needs and rights of traditional Catholics:

> We do indeed find reason for deep gratitude to our Holy Father for this benevolent response to the needs of the Catholic faithful who hold dear to their hearts the precious dogmatic, moral, and mystical tradition of the Church. A living tradition is one that constantly renews itself in the fonts of its origin, while adapting itself to the real needs of the time. The call of Pope John Paul II to theologians and other experts in the ecclesiastical sciences to study more deeply the continu-

[321] A.J. Matt, Jr., "The Lefebvre Schism: What It Means for Faithful Catholics," W, 7-28-88.

> ity of contemporary interpretations of the Council with the past of Catholic Tradition will be received with varying degrees of fervor, but it is like the sound of a trumpet for us. And the challenge lies in this, that many theologians and other experts of our time have failed to perceive the full presence of Tradition in the decrees of the Council. Hence, a major reworking of contemporary theology needs to be done.[322]

Cardinal Ratzinger, a central actor in these events, stressed their importance for a return to true renewal in an address given in Santiago, Chile on July 13:

> One of the basic discoveries of the theology of ecumenism is that schisms can take place only when certain truths and certain values of the Christian faith are no longer lived and loved within the Church....
>
> The Second Vatican Council has not been treated as a part of the entire living Tradition of the Church, but as an end of Tradition, a new start from zero....
>
> We ought to get back to the dimension of the sacred in the liturgy. The liturgy is not a festivity; it is not a meeting for the purpose of having a good time. It is of no importance that the parish priest has cudgeled his brains to come up with suggestive ideas or imaginative novelties. The liturgy is what makes the thrice-holy God present among us; it is the burning bush; it is the alliance of God with man in Jesus Christ, who has died and risen again. The grandeur of the liturgy does not rest upon the fact that it offers an interesting entertainment, but in rendering tangible the Totally Other, whom we are not capable of summoning. He comes because He wills. In other words, the essential in the liturgy is the mystery, which is realized in the common ritual of the Church;

[322] Monsignor John F. McCarthy, "A Light at the End of the Tunnel?," W, 8-4-88.

> all the rest diminishes it. Men experiment with it in lively fashion, and find themselves deceived, when the mystery is transformed into distraction, when the chief actor in the liturgy is not the Living God but the priest or the liturgical director.[323]

Cardinal Ratzinger's remarks stand right at the dividing line between the pseudo-orthodox reform rightly condemned by the Church, and the genuinely orthodox movement for restoration of the liturgy in its full integrity, a reform which, with the Lefebvre fiasco and the promulgation of *Ecclesia Dei*, at last began to get significant support from Rome. *Ecclesia Dei* represents the point at which those of us who seek genuine liturgical reform, yet have no wish to separate ourselves ever from the divinely instituted authority of the Holy Father, became re-enfranchised, or, if that is an over-statement, at least saw the beginning of that re-enfranchisement. The Lefebvre schism, in contrast, represents the definitive bankruptcy of the pseudo-orthodoxy which was willing to abandon the Body of Christ rather than give up its agenda or practice the virtue of patience (a very difficult virtue). The pseudo-orthodoxy of Archbishop Lefebvre as well as of Father DePauw is, as noted earlier, absolutely typical of the way in which Satan gets his foot in the door with orthodox Catholics, working on their egos and convincing them that somehow they are so exceptionally holy and righteous that they are authorized to take ecclesiastical authority upon themselves while rejecting the authority established by Christ. It is amazing how easy it is for these people to begin saying to themselves, "Lord, I thank thee that I am not as the rest of men — modernists, idolaters, desecrators of the liturgy, etc." Whatever the validity (and it is considerable) of their particular criticisms of the establishment, they are ultimately led into a kind of spiritual pride in which, without realizing it themselves, they put themselves in God's place as final judges of the Church and her authority. And that inevitably leads to an illusion of personal in-

[323] Joseph Cardinal Ratzinger, "Some Lessons to Be Learned from the Lefebvre Schism," W, 9-8-88.

dispensability by the leaders of these movements. We have seen how Father DePauw became apparently so certain of the inability of the Catholic Traditionalist Movement to function without his wisdom and leadership that he was ready to disobey the Holy Father himself rather than give up that leadership. Similarly, it appears that the principal motive for Archbishop Lefebvre's consecration of bishops in 1988 was his concern that his people might be left spiritual orphans upon his death. He was not willing to leave it to divine Providence to see to the preservation of his movement or at least of what was true and valid in it, but had to replace it with his own purely human providence, a providence which, in the end, foundered on the rock of human egotism and the merely human propensity of his followers to fight among themselves and fall into various types of sectarianism. Father DePauw's movement seems to have pretty much disappeared from public visibility over the years. The Society of St. Pius X does not quite seem to have done that yet, but the evidence is that since Archbishop Lefebvre's death a spirit of bizarre sectarianism has taken it over. Some of its leaders have fallen into anti-Semitism and developed strong neo-Nazi sympathies. One of the bishops consecrated by Lefebvre has said that he believes the Nazi Holocaust to have been a hoax. He has also asserted that it is a waste of time to hear women's confessions because women cannot be saved. "Whom the gods would destroy, they first make mad," as the Greeks used to say. (I strongly recommend E. Michael Jones' studies of the Lefebvrite movement in the U.S. in *Fidelity* magazine on this matter.) The Lefebvre and DePauw episodes are a grim reminder to all of us of how Satan can get at and lead astray even very holy persons (as both Lefebvre and DePauw appear to have been at one time). Christ's warning to be watchful at all times is one for us orthodox Catholics to take with great seriousness, and not just use as a stick to beat the modernists with.

At the same time, the Lefebvre excommunication and the issuance of *Ecclesia Dei* is a sign to all of us that it is time to abandon any sympathy for basically escapist reform movements and get on with the genuine, hard work of true reform within the limits of orthodoxy and a submission to the authority of the Holy Father. It is time to forget the derailed counterrevolution and get on with the real revolution, at least if we want to have God's blessing for our work.

Of course, the legitimate, orthodox movement to restore the liturgy did not just begin with *Ecclesia Dei.* Since quite early in the post-Vatican II era, Catholics with a love for the Mass have worked in a variety of groups to restore the tradition. As early as 1965, the Latin Mass Society was formed under the leadership of Sir Arnold Lunn to fight for the right of Catholics who want the Latin Mass to have it as an alternative. This is how Sir Arnold outlined its aims:

> The Latin Mass Society has been formed in order to seek the preservation of the Latin liturgy. It is not contended that the use of the vernacular should be discontinued; only that the liturgical language which since the earliest centuries has bound the Western Church in a single bond of spiritual unity, and which is today the cherished Catholic heritage of thousands, may remain in us and may not be lost to future generations.
>
> The aims of the society are:
>
> 1. That all who desire it may be able to attend a wholly Latin low Mass, daily if possible, and at a convenient hour.
> 2. The retention of the established form of high Mass.
> 3. The preservation of traditional music of the Church.
> 4. That it may provide a means whereby the faithful may in such matters communicate their needs and desires to the Hierarchy.[324]

This, of course, was always an important focus of the genuine restoration movement — to raise the question: Why can't people who still want the traditional Mass have it, without in any way trying to keep others from having a vernacular Mass? The tremendous struggle of the progressive liturgists and their ilk against any concessions whatsoever to the traditional Mass makes very clear the totali-

[324] "The Latin Mass Society States Its Objectives," W, 6-3-65.

tarian spirit of their movement. Traditionalists are willing to live and let live — not so the revolutionary modernists, for all their pretense of liberalism and open-mindedness.

One of the most eloquent appeals for preservation of the old liturgy came in 1967 from another traditionalist organization, one called *Una Voce*, in a letter of May 25 of that year to the Holy Father:

> The Catholics who, once again, have asked *Una Voce* to speak for them, thus ask, prostrate at the feet of Your Holiness, that their Supreme Pastor will deign to be good enough to make provision so that the conciliary constitution *Sacrosanctum Concilium* — which asserts the permanent nature of the traditional Roman liturgy, with its consecrated language (the only one "which we can call truly Catholic") (Pius XI, apostolic letter *Officiorum Omnium*), and its own music, does not become a dead letter. They ask and implore that side by side with the liturgy of community type in the vernacular, for the future imposed everywhere beyond all the limits imposed by the constitution there shall be solidly assured the existence of the Latin-Gregorian liturgy, which is the proper form of the Roman rite: a liturgy that is irreplaceable, the center pearl of the marvelous many-colored crown of the Catholic rites, the proper form, not only of our religious rite, but also — with its linguistic, musical, architectural, artistic, and artisan tradition — the proper form of the whole civilization of the West.
>
> May Your Holiness deign to be good enough so to dispose, then, that this patrimony, which does not belong only to the Church, but to the whole world of the mind and of culture, may not be suppressed by the arbitrary judgment of the ordinaries of certain places, who have no right, by the very terms of the constitution, to *forbid* its celebration, as happens only too often.
>
> Your Holiness has often deplored, in recent times, the weakening, in certain places, of faith in the Christian dogmas and

> in the doctrinal Magisterium of the Church. But are not the liturgy as a whole and the Mass at the center of the liturgy "a continual and explicit profession of Catholic faith"? (Pius XII, *Mediator Dei*) How is each individual Catholic to be put on his guard against the infiltration of heresy if all the visible signs of his faith are taken away from him one after the other?
>
> It is not indeed a matter of chance that the great heresies of history have always been introduced through a reform of the liturgy, which tended gradually to diminish its sacred character until it should be reduced to pure symbolism and thus be left wide open to arbitrariness and caprice. The suppression which is aimed at — this has, indeed, been openly admitted — is the frontier between the sacred and the profane. But the true Catholic for whom the Incarnation of the Word has always signified the descent among men, not of a man like ourselves but of the perfect Man, perfected Image and Resemblance of the heavenly Father, cannot understand the matter thus. For true Catholics, holy things remain holy, holy mysteries remain mysteries, and God's ministers must remain figures of God, the Supreme Pontiff and Priest.[325]

The Wanderer's editorial position throughout these years has been to work for a restoration of the full Catholic liturgical tradition while at the same time upholding the authority of the Holy See to legislate in this area. With the promulgation of the *Novus Ordo*, *The Wanderer* thus had no choice but to urge its readers to obey the Holy Father, in spite of its own reservations about the changes:

> It must be admitted that the promulgation of the new Ordo comes at a time when the faith of millions of Catholics has been sorely confused, if not shaken to its depths by changes and innovations on all sides. Some of them indeed were initiated and authorized by the Magisterium of the Church for

[325] "An Appeal to the Holy Father," W, 9-21-67.

> carefully considered pastoral reasons. Many more, however, were instituted and propagated by self-appointed "reformers" bedeviled by a lust for novelty and change for change's sake. To the faithful torn from accustomed styles of thought as well as modes of personal devotions and liturgical piety, almost *any* change now comes as a new assault on their sensibilities if not their faith.
>
> For our part, though we confess our own regret over the passing of the long-cherished Tridentine Ordo with its beautiful prayers and stately rubrics, we must accept the new Ordo from the hands of the Magisterium, and we call upon all our readers to join with us in this acceptance, for the honor of God, the peace and prosperity of Holy Mother Church, and the salvation of souls.[326]

Some readers did challenge *The Wanderer*'s editorial position on the *Novus Ordo*, citing Pope Pius V's bull *Quo Primum*, issued at the time of the promulgation of the Tridentine liturgy. This decree appeared to many to rule out any departure from the old liturgy. It said, in part:

> By this Our decree, to be valid in perpetuity, We determine and order that never shall anything be added to, or omitted from or changed in the Missal...ordered by the Sacred Council of Trent, and encompassing all that is necessary to preserve a pure and universally uniform way of worshipping God....
>
> We herewith declare that it is in virtue of Our apostolic authority that We decree and determine that this Our present order and decree is to last in perpetuity and can never be legally revoked or amended at a future date.
>
> And if anyone would nevertheless ever dare to attempt any action contrary to this order of Ours, given for all times, let

[326] "The New Ordo Missae," W, 12-4-69.

> him know that he has incurred the wrath of Almighty God and of the Blessed Apostles Peter and Paul.[327]

That sounds more than a little daunting. Nevertheless, *The Wanderer* pointed out in an "Our Readers Ask" column of April 9, 1970 that the bull cannot have been understood to rule out any liturgical modifications whatsoever or any other rites, since Pius V himself permitted the retention of the Eastern rites, and numerous modifications had been made in the Roman Missal in the centuries since Pius V. Clearly, the Pope retains the authority to regulate the liturgy. The article went on to say:

> This principle, acknowledged by Trent, and by the Popes sanctioning the decrees of Trent, is in no way in opposition to the encyclical of St. Pius V, under whose jurisdiction the Missal for the Mass was decreed. No one can deny that over the years many changes have come into that Missal: new feasts, new prefaces, new prayers, new gestures, even the allowing of older rites to continue. Vatican II was simply complying with the will of the Sovereign Pontiff that the changeless remain as such and that the changeable be studied and be made conformable with the intent and the expression of the changeless.[328]

The editorial quoted above, calling readers to accept the *Novus Ordo*, did, however, note that while acceptance of the *Novus Ordo* was mandatory, the ICEL translation of the liturgy was still open to debate:

> Holy Mother Church has decided for pastoral reasons that Mass in the vernacular will be the general rule. Can those whose appointed task it is to deepen the love of the Catholic people for the Mass be satisfied with anything less than a vernacular liturgy which expresses — as the Latin Mass did

327 Quoted in "Our Readers Ask," W, 4-9-70.
328 "Our Readers Ask," W, 4-9-70.

> so well — the reverence, beauty, and nobility of the worship due the Most High God![329]

The Wanderer also had to deal with the claim by many readers that the new Mass was invalid. The focal point for this accusation was the wording of the English translation of the words of consecration, which, in the official versions, says that Christ's Blood is shed "for you and for *all men*." The Latin "pro multis" would be literally translated "for many," not "for all." Many held that this change in the words of consecration (a change found in the ICEL translation but not in the Latin *Novus Ordo*) invalidates the English Mass. A *Wanderer* editorial of March 12, 1970, entitled "'For All Men' (A Licit and Valid Form)," quotes, in refutation, a recent Vatican document which asserted that

> ...According to the exegetes, the Aramaean word, which was rendered by "pro multis" in Latin, has the sense of "pro omnibus": the multitude for whom Christ suffered death is without any limitation, it is why it is right to say: Christ is dead for all....
>
> In no way is the doctrine of the *Roman Catechism* to be held as obsolete: its distinction about Christ's death sufficient for all, but efficacious only for many, retains its value.[330]

Many seemed to reject the "for all" wording on basically Jansenist grounds that Christ died only for the elect, not for all men. A March 12 "Our Readers Ask" column addressed this issue, indicating that it is heretical to assert that some are excluded in Christ's act of redemption:

> You make it appear that Christ was deliberately ruling out other "some" intentionally in the wording He used. This is contrary to the reason for Christ's coming, to save mankind. That not all would cooperate with Him and His graces gained

[329] "The New Ordo Missae," W, 12-4-69.
[330] "'For All Men' (A Licit and Valid Form)," W, 3-12-70.

> for them He knew, but did He will their damnation? No one is in Hell except under his own power and his own perverse will turned against God. Did Christ will such by His words?[331]

Finally, in an April 23, 1970 editorial entitled "Unity in the Mass — Unity With the Pope," *The Wanderer* made unequivocally clear its support for the Holy Father on the new liturgy, denouncing as scandalous the position of some traditional Catholics that the new Mass was invalid even though supported by Papal authority:

> Some of the difficulties which are accompanying the implementation of the new rite of the Mass in this country must be attributed, however, to the failure of many American bishops to: (1) Provide an adequate catechetical instruction on the Mass which explains its theology and doctrine; (2) Make clear that the new rite and instructions were promulgated by Pope Paul in Latin and that the rubrics and language of the vernacular Mass must conform in letter and spirit to the *Latin ordo*; (3) Make clear that the new legislation does not preclude the celebration in this country of the new rite of the Mass in Latin (including Gregorian chant and other traditional sacred music)
>
> Whatever problems individual Catholics had, or continue to have with the new rite of the Mass, should be subordinated for the sake of that unity which the Church so desperately needs; for those many souls who are scandalized — some to the point of leaving the Church; and as an affirmation of love and belief in the Mass and acknowledgment of Pope Paul as Christ's Vicar. We therefore appeal:
>
> -for an end of the futile and divisive debate about the new Ordo.

---

[331] Father James A. McInerny, O.P., "Our Readers Ask," W, 3-12-70.

-to our bishops to strengthen the faith in, and deepen the love for the Mass by truly pastoral catechetical instruction on the Holy Sacrifice.

-to our priests for their example of fidelity to the letter and spirit of the new rite of Mass by demonstrating their faith in the Real Presence of Christ as they celebrate at the altar of sacrifice and the banquet of the Lamb.

-to our fellow Catholics to accept with faith in Christ and confidence in His Vicar the Mass which — however changed in appearance — remains the mystery of our Faith, the ineffable instrument of our salvation."[332]

That is a crucial document in the history of *The Wanderer* and its readers, one which, I believe, deserves to be quoted at length. It also needs to be noted that this editorial stance was by no means without cost to *The Wanderer*. In fact it cost *The Wanderer* several thousand subscribers, a substantial portion of its readership at the time, and seems to have left a permanent residue of at least mild resentment among those who did not cancel their subscriptions. I can testify from my own experience that expressing the opinion, in the pages of *The Wanderer*, that the new Mass is valid can get a writer some interesting letters, usually with a copy of *Quo Primum* enclosed. From a worldly standpoint, it is not wise for a periodical to alienate people who can ordinarily be counted upon to be its friends, yet it is difficult to see what else could have been done in this case. Loyalty to papal authority, whatever our reservations about the prudence of some decisions, is probably the most basic first principle underlying *The Wanderer*'s apostolate.

In regard to the liturgical changes, *The Wanderer* called Catholics to obedience to the Holy See, but not to blind, thoughtless obedience. On two points in particular it made clear the need for thoughtfulness in our obedience:

[332] "Unity in the Mass — Unity With the Pope," W, 4-23-70.

1) On the importance of using an accurate and beautiful English translation of the new Mass, a condition which had not then been met and, as the reader knows, still has not been.

2) The fact that the implementation of the *Novus Ordo* did not and does not preclude the celebration of Latin Masses.

In both of these areas there has been room for legitimate traditionalism, and *The Wanderer* has consistently supported those who sought reforms in these areas.

In July, 1970, a group of Catholic scholars and writers met in Washington, D.C., to found an organization called the Laymen's Commission on the English Liturgy (LCEL). The founding members included John Mulloy, chairman; Dr. James Lucier; Dr. William Marra; A.J. Matt, Jr.; Frank Morriss; Dr. William Roberts; Paul Weyrich; and Father James McInerny, O.P., spiritual advisor. The commission saw its purposes as "preparing a critical study of the English translation of the *New Order of the Mass*; making certain positive proposals in regard to the translation; submitting these to the American bishops for their consideration."[333] Paul M. Weyrich, in an August 20 article, added that:

> The newly elected Laymen's Commission on the English Liturgy, recognizing that the English translation is clearly reformable, has invited comments from the faithful. The Commission's goal is to persuade the American bishops to adopt as the vernacular norm an English liturgy which is a faithful translation both in word and spirit of the reformed *Ordo Missae*, promulgated by Pope Paul VI in the apostolic constitution Missale Romanum.[334]

I particularly like the diplomacy inherent in the statement that the ICEL translation is reformable. Less diplomatic people (myself, for instance), would have said, "It stinks." But that is not how to win friends and influence people.

---

[333] "Laymen Set Goals for Commission on Liturgy," W, 7-30-70.

[334] Paul M. Weyrich, "At Last the People Have a Say," W, 8-20-70.

By September, LCEL had begun making its own translation, and by April, 1971, LCEL representatives had begun discussions with representatives of the National Conference of Catholic Bishops' Committee on the Liturgy.[335] Sadly, LCEL got little cooperation from this committee, which appeared irrevocably committed to ICEL. John Mulloy summarized the situation as of July, 1971:

> Under present circumstances, there is no real effective way in which the American bishops can or will hear objections to the ICEL translation. It has become a *fait accompli*, whether or not the bishops realize it, and whether or not they were told it was to be something other than that at their November, 1969 meeting. In effect, the bishops gave what amounts to a permanent acceptance of ICEL at that meeting. They cannot have second thoughts on the advisability of their action in accepting this ICEL translation, so long as the present membership of the Bishops' Committee on the Liturgy remains what it is.[336]

In other words, the bureaucracy had the bishops where it wanted them, because they were unwilling to admit openly to having made a mistake when they gave the bureaucracy *carte blanche* in preparing the translation. This was certainly one of the great tragedies of the postconciliar era in America, because, at the time LCEL was doing its work, most traditional Catholics were willing, in principle, to accept the idea of an English liturgy, no matter how sad they might be over losing the beauty and majesty of the old one, provided the English liturgy was written in beautiful, reverent English, consistent with the Catholic understanding of the Sacrifice of the Mass as a great and awesome mystery. They asked for bread, and were given a stone — or was it a serpent? When the bishops insisted on forcing the ICEL translation of the Mass on the Catholic people of America, they so-

---

[335] "Discussions on Liturgy Begin Between LCEL and NCCB Representatives," W, 4-15-71.

[336] John J. Mulloy, "The Liturgy and the Bishop's Committee," W, 7-29-71.

lidified the antagonism and resistance of a very large number of traditional Catholics not only against the English Mass but against the *Novus Ordo* itself. Who knows how many people, over the years, have left the Church and perhaps lost their faith completely because of this act of official intransigence? We do know that statistics which became available in November, 1973 showed a catastrophic decline in Mass attendance, from 61% in 1972 to 48% in July, 1973. The fact that two events are correlated does not establish a causal relationship, of course, but it certainly makes one think.

It is also worth noting that the promulgation of the *Novus Ordo* did not, in itself, imply a prohibition on Latin in the Mass. It did, of course, prohibit the Tridentine Latin liturgy (though this prohibition was modified by the 1984 indult), but that is another matter. In fact, in July, 1974, James Cardinal Knox, prefect of the Sacred Congregation for Divine Worship, issued a letter urging continued use of Latin and Gregorian chant. Among other things, he said that:

> ...This reform [vernacular in liturgy] cannot and does not repudiate the past. It tries to "guard carefully." This means evaluating the contents of our highly cultured and artistic tradition and fostering those elements within it that outwardly express and serve the unity of believers. To have a minimal repertoire of Gregorian chant would be fully in accord with this need and would make it easier for Catholics to associate themselves in worship both with their brethren of today and of past centuries. For this reason, then, the encouragement of congregational singing must consider Gregorian chant seriously.[337]

As a result, traditional Catholics, here and there, have continued over the years to promote the Latin Mass in the *Novus Ordo* as an alternative to the vernacular. In August, 1975, a group called the Latin Liturgy Association was formed in St. Louis under the temporary chairmanship of historian James Hitchcock. Hitchcock pointed

---

[337] James Cardinal Knox, "'Jubilate Deo,'" W, 7-18-74.

out that "most Catholics, including priests, are unaware that Latin remains the official liturgical language of the Church, and that no special permission is ever needed by a priest to celebrate the Mass in Latin, provided the new rite is used."[338]

In a May 11, 1978 article, Rupert J. Ederer submitted, for the consideration of *Wanderer* readers, "A Proposal for a Latin Mass." In it, he pointed out that the Church has never legislated against the use of Latin:

> Since many of our pastors seem so responsive to all of the new ideas their parish councils and various parishioners propose to them for putting "new life" into the liturgy, here is a proposal that would be brand new for most parishes. How about having one Mass each Sunday in Latin, in the new, approved rite, of course? Wouldn't that be a nifty innovation for all of God's people who are tired of the same old thing every week?...
>
> Surprised? You shouldn't be. It wasn't Vatican II or Pope John or even Pope Paul who banned Latin Masses, it was, in effect, our dilettante liturgists. What better way to defuse the ongoing deceptive appeal of the traditionalists who lure good people from the Catholic Church just by offering them a Mass in Latin. Offer them a weekly Latin Mass right in the bosom of Mother Church! There's nothing wrong with the Tridentine Mass, obviously, or the Church would not have used it for four centuries. But there is a whole lot wrong with a public act of disobedience to the lawmaking authority of the Church, and that is what Archbishop Lefebvre and his followers are about. There is also nothing wrong with the Latin Mass in the new, approved rite as anyone who has ever experienced it can testify. The trouble is that most Catholics have never experienced it, and that is one of the tragedies of our present anglicized Catholicism. Light a fire under your

[338] "Group Will Promote Celebration of Mass in Latin," W, 8-28-75.

> pastor before he forgets his Latin altogether — with a Roman candle maybe![339]

What has of course most unfortunately happened is that the Latin Mass has come to be for most practical purposes prohibited in many places due to a combination of disuse, the widespread but mistaken perception that it is forbidden, and, finally, the enormous social power of liturgists in most dioceses today. Monsignor Richard J. Schuler discussed this in a February, 1981 article:

> The Latin Mass has all but died out in the United States, despite the clearly stated and frequently repeated orders of the Church that it be fostered. Factors in this demise are unquestionably the suppression ordered by some diocesan authorities, the conviction of most parish priests that the Council had outlawed or at least outmoded Latin, and the apathy of the faithful or at best the willingness of Catholics to do as their pastors prescribe. The basic reason why such a situation has come about lies in the false propaganda of the '60s, spread throughout the country by liturgists and their organizations and publications, proclaiming that Latin had been suppressed by the Council. This false propaganda was accepted even by some diocesan authorities and almost totally by the parish clergy who came to think that it was ordered by the bishops. It was taught in seminaries. Thus, today, 15 years after the promulgation of the Constitution on the Sacred Liturgy, the exact opposite of the Council's order is the rule in this country.[340]

This is an area where I would suggest that some renewed militancy by traditional Catholics is in order. It seems to me a that lot of time and energy has for some years now gone into efforts to bring back the Tridentine Mass, when it might better have gone into working to

[339] Rupert J. Ederer, "A Proposal for a Latin Mass," W, 5-11-78.
[340] Monsignor Richard J. Schuler, "Why the Latin Mass Has All but Died in America," W, 2-5-81.

make the Latin Mass in the *Novus Ordo* more widely available. In 1984, following the issuance of the Tridentine indult, Monsignor Richard J. Schuler again tried to clarify this issue:

> The truth is that the new Mass of Pope Paul VI may be celebrated in Latin or in the vernacular; it may be celebrated at an altar *versus populum* or at an altar of traditional construction....At the Church of St. Agnes in St. Paul, Minnesota, solemn Mass is celebrated each Sunday according to the Missal of Pope Paul VI, in the Latin language, and at the traditionally oriented high altar. The music is the Gregorian chant and the Masses of the Viennese composers with orchestra. This is the "new" Mass. It is in a direct line with the development through the centuries of the Missa Romana cantata, which was the will of the Council fathers who wanted to purify the liturgy of accretions meaningless to our age and present to us the unencumbered gem that the Roman liturgy is, adorned with the beauty that all centuries have contributed but not overgrown with unnecessary accumulations.[341]

What the *Wanderer* coverage of liturgical issues during the post-Vatican II years has made unmistakably clear is this: That a counter-revolution in the liturgy is badly needed, as it is in most other areas of Church life, too, but that there is a right and a wrong way to do it. Some efforts at counterrevolution have failed because they were derailed by the very spirit of disobedience to Church authority that they were so quick to condemn in their modernist adversaries. That is what happened to the work of Father DePauw and Archbishop Lefebvre. The Lefebvrite movement in particular, so arrogant in its claim to be *the* true Church against an allegedly apostate papacy, is now rapidly turning into an insignificant sect, something like the Old Catholics or the Feeneyites. The real counterrevolution has got to

[341] Monsignor Richard J. Schuler, "Confusion Over Liturgical Law Resurfaces With 'Tridentine' Indult," W, 1-10-84.

have its roots in a source from which it can draw life, and only the Roman Church itself can be such a source for it. Accordingly, there are ways of working for reform in the liturgy that can be grounded in the Roman Church because they involve doing things which are not only not prohibited by the Church but are positively prescribed by the Council and the papal documents on the liturgy: restoration of Latin and Gregorian chant within the "new Mass," and the struggle for an accurate and beautiful English version. *Ecclesia Dei*, for many of us, restored some hope that true reform of the liturgy is possible. In a December, 1988 editorial, entitled "Join in the Restoration of the Sacred Liturgy," Al Matt tried to instill that attitude in *Wanderer* readers:

> We encourage every reader who desires a broad restoration of the traditional Latin Mass to participate in this important endeavor....There is much to be done if a genuine restoration of the sacred liturgy (whether in the vernacular or in Latin) is to take place in this country. The encouragement provided by the Holy Father in *Ecclesia Dei* and by Cardinal Mayer in his letter to Archbishop May requires a vigorous response on the part of every faithful Catholic.[342]

The Wanderer has done a lot since the Council to keep the Church's liturgical memory alive in America. Now it is time, indeed, past time, to forget our fears of despotic liturgists and modernist bishops, and begin the work of restoration in earnest. We will take some hard knocks as reward for our efforts, but when hard knocks are punishment for faithfulness to the Lord's work, they are nothing to fear or be ashamed of.

---

[342] A.J. Matt, Jr., "Join in the Restoration of the Sacred Liturgy," W, 12-15-88.

PART FIVE: SPIRITUAL DISEASE

SECTION I — THE CORRUPTION OF THE INTELLECT

Much learning does not teach understanding...
— Heraclitus

1. THE ATTACK ON CHRISTIAN WHOLENESS

Those of us who have witnessed and even participated in the Church's struggles against totalitarian ideologies, the rejection of the sanctity of human life, and the destruction of the Eucharist, mankind's principal act of worship of God, find it not melodramatic at all but only the sober truth to see themselves as witnesses to a great and perhaps unprecedented growth of evil in the Body of Christ. Perhaps the best analogy for this process is that of a spiritual disease, a kind of cancer, which has invaded that body and seems in the process of destroying it. A malignant growth in the body generally starts in one organ and then spreads, metastasizes, to the whole organism. In the case of the Body of Christ, I would suggest an analogy with a cancer which starts in the brain and then metastasizes to the rest of the body. The spiritual cancer which afflicts the Church seems to have started with the intellectual elite of the Church, the brain, in a manner of speaking, and then spread to the rest of the faithful by a process of indoctrination or catechesis which continues today.

The spiritual disease afflicting the Church since the 1960s has two aspects, in accord with the two principal powers of the soul, the intellect and will. Both follow the pattern outlined above:

I. The corruption of the intellect, by two processes:

A. The destruction of orthodox Catholic teaching by intellectuals using as tools contemporary "new" theology grounded in existentialism and other anti-Christian ideologies, and contemporary biblical scholarship aimed at reducing Scripture to merely human literature and totally undermining it as a witness to the revealed Word of God. The chief focus of both of these attacks is the doctrine of the Incarnation, the absolute core and center of God's revelation to man, a center without which there is no Church.

B. The corruption of the minds of the young through catechesis which embodies these new, false teachings and suppresses traditional Catholic doctrine, particularly as it relates to the person and work of Christ.

II. The corruption of the will:

A. By an attack on Catholic moral teaching, especially in regard to sexual morality. This attack too has been led by intellectuals — moral theologians, psychologists, educators, etc.

B. The corruption of the young by sex education classes which embody the "new morality," otherwise known as the "sexual revolution."

All disease tends to destroy the wholeness of the body, its integrity. Hence the spiritual disease of the contemporary Church tends, again and again, to destroy what I would call Christian wholeness. That is why the Incarnation of the Word of God is the principal target of the new theologians when they deal with matters of faith, because the Incarnation is God's act of healing the separation of man from God. By God's assumption of a true human nature into His divine nature in an unbreakable unity, the rift between God and His creation brought about by sin has been healed, and wholeness has been restored to all things, at least the beginning of wholeness. The new theology, with its multiple devices for separating the humanity of Jesus from His divinity — by asserting, for instance, a historical Jesus who is merely a great teacher or something of that sort — attacks that wholeness and in the process does its best to bring the Church down in ruins.

The attack on wholeness is also apparent when we talk about moral teaching. Catholic moral teaching presupposes the wholeness and integrity of the human person, as a composite of body and soul, spirit and matter, forming a unity which is not to be broken. It is probably in the area of human sexuality more than any other that we see this union of spirit and matter, which parallels the union of divine and human in Christ, most fully realized, so that is the area the disease targets more than any other. By attempting to separate sexual pleasure from procreation, as well as from any genuine gift of self to the other in the sexual relationship, the new morality creates an image of a human being as an autonomous, isolated self and thus is terribly destructive of the integrity of the human person.

Eric Voegelin once defined ideology as "existence in rebellion against both man and God." The spiritual cancer in today's Church certainly fits that definition, with its twofold attack on the Incarnation of Christ and on man's condition as an incarnate being, an incarnate spirit. Let us look at these one at a time.

2. THE DISEASE — ORIGINS IN THE INTELLECT

It has always been easy for skeptics to conclude that the endless debates in the Church's history over such things as the relation of the two natures and the one person in Christ, whether Christ and the Father are of the same substance or merely of similar substance, the exact role the Bible plays as the authoritative word of God, and so forth, were just so many hair-splitting scholastic debates, of little practical importance — just games intellectuals play. Indeed, these skeptics like to remind us that at the verbal level the conflict over consubstantiality depended on the presence or absence of one letter, an iota, the smallest letter in the Greek alphabet. Yet, apparently abstract questions can be of earthshaking significance. Some very abstract equations, incomprehensible to the vast majority of us, made it possible to develop nuclear weapons. Similarly, the debates in the twentieth century Church over Christology and Scripture have gone to the very heart of what is at stake in a human being's choice to be or not to be a Christian. In a way, the very structure of reality is at stake.

This might best be understood in this way: In the beginning of our life as human beings, there is a world, and ourselves living in the world. This means a basic set of data is available to all humanity and has been available throughout history. There is a basic, core situation of man living in a world. From the beginnings of history, people have speculated about what this situation is about, what is its meaning, what is it all for, and, of course, how to be happy, how to in some way achieve one's end. In other words, people have interpreted the data. As it happens, the nature of the data is such that no one interpretation is forced on our minds. There are many possible interpretations, not mutually exclusive but reflecting different aspects of the data themselves: Hence we have interpretations like Buddhism, Hinduism, Greek mythology, Greek philosophy, etc. Students of religions or worldviews can compare and contrast these interpretations, and perhaps even conclude that some of them are superior to others, but none has an exclusive claim on the truth. What we have is a body of data, unchanging in its essentials, and a multitude of interpretations of the data.

But what Christians hold is that something happened in history which did not merely add one more interpretation to those which had already accumulated, but in fact changed the very nature of the data to be interpreted. We hold that at a particular point in history, God acted to save us from our situation in a world which turned out to be a fallen world, that God entered into history, became man, and suffered and died for us to save us from sin and death, that God *revealed* Himself. That means that God is not just one more passive part of the data we are given to interpret, but that God really and truly acts. In acting, He has changed the world, He has changed the structure of reality by becoming an active part of the world and history, present to the end of time in His Church. That means that the things we believe about Christ, for instance, that He was born of a Virgin, was put to death, and rose from the dead, are not just stories or myths expressing a certain interpretation of the world — they are real events which changed the world to be interpreted.

That is disturbing to many people, especially intellectuals, because it leaves them no longer free to just interpret the world any way they wish. Suddenly, what matters is no longer man's many interpretations, but God's acts. I am no longer free to be a Buddhist, a Hindu, a Confucian, an Aristotelian, a Platonist, or whatever, at no cost to myself, because there are no right or wrong answers. Instead, I am confronted with God's act for me, and must choose to say yes or no to it, with an infinite cost if I make the wrong choice. That is, to say the least, a scary situation, and the temptation, when I find myself in it, is to engage in denial. The most obvious form of denial is simply to reject the whole belief that God has intervened actively in human history. If I do this consistently, I will reject Christianity and join up with one of these other religions, or perhaps make up one of my own. But if I happen to be in a social and cultural situation where I have something to gain by continuing to call myself a Christian (if, for instance, I am a Catholic priest, or even a professor of Catholic theology), then what I will be tempted to do is to reduce Christianity to the level of the other religions. That means to hold that Christianity is simply one more interpretation of the world, but that the world itself has not changed and that God has never acted redemptively in the world. The beliefs that seem to say that God did intervene in the world have to be reinterpreted as in reality just expressions of a "Christian" interpretation of the world, not assertions about events that are supposed to have actually taken place. They are "myths" or "theologoumena" or something like that. Thus, when we see the Bible asserting that Jesus rose from the dead, we can conclude that this story is only a mythical way of saying that the Apostles believed that, in spite of His death, the ideals that He stood for (loving one's neighbor, for instance) were still alive. The story of the virginal conception was just a way of saying that, somehow, Jesus was really rather unique and "special." And so on *ad nauseam*. Of course, I can still call myself a Christian, by the simple expedient of saying that, while Christianity is just one more interpretation of the world, it is in some way the best interpretation, or at least the best one to come along yet.

If we look at all closely at the ideas of our theological modernists, demythologizers, biblical critics, and so forth, what we find is that it is just such a radical redefinition of Christianity that they are trying to bring about. They are trying to reduce Christianity to the level of just one more interpretation of the world, just one more human effort to understand the human condition, in direct opposition to a two-thousand-year-old Christian tradition which says that God's revelation in Christ is something radically new in the world, never heard of before and never to be repeated. It is a reality which calls for our consent and our cooperation, and eternity is at stake — eternal life or eternal death. It is a lot less frightening to just see it as a way of looking at things, and forget that it is *God*'s way of looking at things and leaves no more room any more for *our* way of looking at things.

In 1979, Philip Trower, a scholar who did not throw in his lot with the modernist intellectuals and their ilk, did a great service in arming *Wanderer* readers for this debate by publishing a series of articles entitled "The Church Learned and the Revolt of the Scholars," in which he traced the growth of the modernist movement in the intellectual history as well as the current crisis of the Church. For Trower, that current crisis was made possible by widespread but largely secret unbelief among the "higher clergy" (the intellectuals) during the years prior to the Council. That unbelief was a kind of underground river flowing from the first Catholic modernist movement, which was suppressed, at least publicly, by Pope Pius X in the early twentieth century. That modernism was itself traceable to the influence of liberal Protestant biblical scholars and theologians, who, by the nineteenth century, had managed to cast doubt on the very idea of revelation. Here is how Trower sums up their influence:

> The mystery of the Incarnation of the Word of God in literary form which we call the Bible has always posed certain problems, which scholars down the ages have tried to answer. But the critical approach characteristic of modern times, and which began in the seventeenth century, has this special quality: it was inspired by and has received its driving force from men intensely hostile to religion or the idea of revelation. Before their investigations begin, three assumptions have been made. God had nothing to do with the composition of the Bible; supernatural events do not take place and descriptions of them are, therefore, the product of imagination; all peoples of the past were of a lower order of intelligence than men and women of modern times and incapable of preserving historical facts accurately and faithfully. The whole movement has been colored by these three prejudices, which seem rapidly to infect anyone who approaches it.[343]

[343] Philip Trower, "The Church Learned and the Revolt of the Scholars," Pt. II, "The Roots of Modernist Unbelief," W, 1-11-79.

Once Scripture is understood in this way, it becomes quite difficult to believe that there is such a thing as revelation if by revelation we mean God's initiative toward us, rather than our initiative in trying to understand God. But if Scripture is merely an expression of man's effort to understand reality (including "ultimate reality," or God), then we are thrown back on a completely subjectivistic notion of truth. "Since there can be no certainty about what God has revealed, the source of religious knowledge is inner 'experience,'" Trower goes on to say. "... Doctrines — or those at least which the modernists found 'difficult,' or as would now be said, 'lacking in credibility' — should not be regarded as statement of fact, but as in some sense 'symbolic.' Exactly what they symbolized remained to be determined."[344]

The deep-down subjectivism of modernist thinking has, in recent years, been aided and abetted by a philosophical current known as existentialism, an ideology which sees the autonomous self, acting in a vacuum without any objective criteria for his "free acts," as the only reality:

> Man finds himself "thrown into the world" without knowing how or why he is there and with no real way of finding out. His basic states are those of Care (he is condemned to preoccupation with pointless worldly tasks) and Dread (like Kierkegaard, he has constantly to make decisions, but every situation is different and there are no rules to guide him. At the same time he is responsible for the remotest consequences of his smallest acts). So he moves through life, haunted by the flight of time, burdened by guilt, trying to reach "self-understanding" through the experience of his "present situation," and "projecting himself into the future" as he endeavors to "realize his possibilities," until he reaches death, the last of his "possibilities" which will put an end to him. As his present situation is never quite the same today as it was yesterday, he is ever having to change his understand-

[344] Ibid.

> ing of things and make a new beginning. Not surprisingly, the existentialist decides that life is meaningless and absurd.[345]

It is hardly difficult to see the effect of such bizarre thought processes on the very notion of an objectively valid revealed truth:

> Imitating the existentialist, the neomodernist Christian seeks to realize *his* ever-changing existence and spiritual and material needs, in the light of *his* ever-changing "present situation." Through ongoing revelation God sends messages about how to do it. God's messages are received interiorly through "religious experience," and exteriorly through the circumstances of the moment. There has been no other revelation.[346]

"Modernism," says Trower, "should now be seen as a new and powerful 'fourth denomination' whose members are scattered among already existing Christian bodies and are fighting to take them over."[347] Trower identifies three main "syntheses," three systems of modernist thought in present day "Christianity": Teilhard de Chardin's evolutionary system, which turns Christianity into man's evolutionary ascent toward the "Omega point," a point of this-worldly perfection where man will, in effect, have become God; liberation theology, which reduces redemption to the history of class struggle leading to an earthly utopia; and Bultmann's system, "based on the existentialist view of man as a self-creating free will, knowing only the light provided by his 'present situation,' with the Bible symbolically reinterpreted for each generation in terms of that situation."[348]

> At its heart, and holding the system together, were still those interlocking principles we looked at to begin with. 1) No public Revelation by God; neither the *Bible* nor the Church

[345] Ibid., Pt. IV, "Existentialism — The Ugly Intruder," W, 1-25-79.
[346] Ibid.
[347] Ibid., Pt. V, "The Essence of Our Present Day's Tragedy," W, 2-1-79.
[348] Ibid.

> are trustworthy; 2) Science and modern thought the highest and only certain source of knowledge; religion must adapt to them; 3) "Revelation" (insofar as it exists) through inner experience; 4) The Church's doctrines to be understood symbolically as the evolving expression of man's religious needs, or (in the up-to-date version) of his own self-discovery.[349]

Staying with the spiritual disease analogy, a body is most likely to fall victim to disease when its immune mechanisms are for some reason weak. Trower basically argues that the Church's immune system, her mechanisms for fighting spiritual disease, were weakened through sin. Heresy today can, indeed, be seen as a kind of spiritual AIDS, a case of a body weakened by its own sins being devastated by a disease which even further destroys its ability to resist disease. Trower's analysis of this process in the contemporary Church is worth quoting at length:

> Modernism could never have spread and succeeded as it has if the rest of the Church Learned had put up a stronger fight. Why hasn't it?...There can, I think, be only two answers: (a) they are no longer able to see quickly and clearly what is heresy or tending that way, and what isn't; or (b) heresy does not seem particularly dreadful or serious. Probably both answers are applicable.
>
> This being so, the reason will in the first place be a spiritual one, of the kind I considered at the outset of these articles. In regard to most of the Church Learned we have, I believe, to make the same distinctions I made elsewhere in connection with bishops between the "bad" — those who, through sin, have lost the faith; and the "sad" — those who have not utterly lost it but, also through sin, are, in regard to faith, afflicted with a kind of twilight of the mind and apathy of the will. These latter, like their counterparts in the episcopate, from lack of spiritual vitality, are lying listlessly about like

[349] Ibid.

> wounded commanders bleeding to death (intelligence officers rather than generals this time) while the leaderless troops are massacred. It is necessary to refer to sin in this connection, otherwise loss of faith is likely to be attributed to accident, or worse, to God.[350]

One could, in fact, compare modernism with those "opportunistic infections" characteristic of AIDS (Trower was writing before the onset of the AIDS epidemic, and did not have this metaphor at his disposal, but it does cast light on the matter). AIDS patients frequently die from infections caused by microorganisms that are always present in the environment, perhaps even present in the body, but which are easily controlled by the healthy body's immune system. But when the AIDS virus has destroyed the immune system, these ever-present organisms can take advantage of the situation to attack the body and destroy it. The virus of modernism has been present for many years — indeed, it could be argued that it has, in some form, been present throughout the Church's history, but prior to the Vatican II era, the Church's defenses were generally adequate to deal with it:

Of course, for the higher clergy as a whole, modernism did not "reappear" in the sense that it did for everyone else, like the ghost of someone dead. In their world, anyone who was anybody had known all along that modernism was still in the house and in reasonable health even if having to live in a closet under the stairs and be let out for exercise in the middle of the night. What must have surprised the higher clergy, orthodox and unorthodox, was the welcome modernism received from so many of the ordinary faithful once it was able to get out of the closet, come upstairs, and make its appearance in the state apartments.[351]

---

[350] Ibid.

[351] Ibid.

3. FATHER BROWN'S ASSAULT ON THE BIBLE AND THE INCARNATION

One of the principal battlefields on which the war against the Incarnation has been fought is the Bible. The scholarly study of the Bible is in itself a valuable pursuit in the great enterprise by which the Christian's faith seeks understanding, a pursuit which the Church supports and encourages. The problem is that a good deal of what passes itself off as biblical scholarship is in reality biblical reductionism, a discipline which seeks not to explain its object but to explain it away. A look at the history of the conflict over Scripture during the past generation will show, I think, that what the contemporary biblical scholar wants most of all to explain away is the Incarnation. He wants to explain away Christ Himself. The presence of Christ on the scene as the sign of contradiction, as an overwhelming reality to which we have finally to respond, to accept or reject, is more than the twentieth-century unbelieving intellectual can tolerate. So he reduces Christ to myth or symbol, to anything but a historical reality. This is something the believing Christian cannot and will not do, as John Mulloy pointed out in a 1981 article:

> Thus when the Christian, in celebrating Christmas, insists upon the reality of the historical events in the Gospel narrative, he is in fact standing firm against the collapse of the Christian story into mere myth, mere sentimentality. For this would mean the death of Christianity, the effective ending of the Good News which Christ came to announce to the world. Strip the Gospel of what seem to be dispensable factual elements in its narrative, and you find yourself left with no reason for believing the doctrines which are inextricably intertwined with this account. Once you have made the historical facts into a symbol rather than a reality, the doctrine itself becomes merely symbolic.

> Let us therefore rejoice that the Gospel fulfilled the yearning of the mythological stories by being real.[352]

For the anxious intellectual terrified by the possibility that Christianity might turn out to be true, no news is good news, and good news diluted into myth or symbol is almost as good as no news at all.

Perhaps no scholar in the contemporary Church has so epitomized this reduction of the revealed Word of God, in which the good news about Jesus Christ is embedded, as has Father Raymond Brown. Father Brown's writings and lectures have consistently tried to demonstrate such things as the assertion that Jesus, in His human knowledge, was capable of ignorance, that Jesus did not know He was the Messiah, let alone the Son of God, that supernatural phenomena like the miracles found in the Gospel narratives did not really occur, and so on. Father Brown's career has been particularly important in the eyes of "Wanderer types" because he has somehow managed to do all this while hanging on to a reputation for orthodoxy and moderation. As a result, *Wanderer* writers over the years have been especially anxious to unmask Father Brown as the thoroughgoing modernist he is. The furor over Father Brown reached a boiling point in April, 1973, when he delivered an address to the National Catholic Educational Association entitled, "The Current Crisis in Theology as It Affects the Teaching of Catholic Doctrine." In that speech, Father Brown attacked the conservative Catholic press in such a way as to make it obvious to anyone knowing how to read between the lines that *The Wanderer* was a prominent target. *The Wanderer* thereupon challenged Father Brown to a debate. Getting no response, the editors went ahead and published the complete text of Father Brown's speech in the June 7, 1973 issue, along with responses by Edith Myers, Father Jerome Docherty, John Mulloy, Charles Pulver, and Carol Jackson Robinson. This collection of articles ended up being a key document in *The Wanderer*'s continuing battle with biblical modernism, and I will therefore summarize it at some length.

---

[352] John J. Mulloy, "Historical Fact and the Infancy Narratives," W, 1-1-81.

Father Brown's address states that the history of theology should be understood, not as a river flowing peacefully along, but as one which is placid at times, but at other times is filled with floodwaters from its many tributaries — for instance, at St. Thomas Aquinas's time, when a great deal of new knowledge resulting from contact with the Islamic civilization had to be incorporated into the tradition. For Brown, the current era, with the flood of new scientific knowledge about the Bible, is another such time:

> This understanding of the irregular, spasmodic growth of theology in the past, with its accompanying hostile divisiveness, may enable us to grasp a little better the period of tremendous theological change in which we are living — a period when another tributary, that of knowledge flowing from recently developed sciences, pours its waters into the Christian mainstream of thought.[353]

Father Brown maintains that in the light of our new knowledge about the Scriptures, we need to make a distinction between the divine component in revelation, and a human component which is a kind of prism through which we see revelation but which can change in response to the knowledge available in the current culture. Thus modern scientific biblical criticism changes our understanding of the Scriptures and hence changes the human component in revelation. This is a change that Father Brown feels the Church should not resist, and criticizes those who are still on the defensive against it. Here is his summary of the theological implications of the new biblical criticism:

> In the speech with which he opened the Council (October 11, 1962), Pope John XXIII made one of the most important magisterial admissions of modern times, "The substance of the ancient doctrine of the Deposit of Faith is one thing, and the way in which it is presented is another." In other words,

[353] Father Raymond Brown, "The Current Crisis in Theology as It Affects the Teaching of Catholic Doctrine," W, 6-7-73.

> the Pope opened the possibility of distinguishing between a revealed doctrine and the way in which it has been formulated.
>
> The key to biblical criticism was the recognition that, while the Scriptures are the Word of God, they do not escape the limitations of history. Rather the Scriptures reflect the limited views current in specific periods of human history, and this historical context must be taken into account in interpreting the weight and import of their inspired message. And now the Pope's statement led many theologians to the conclusion that the doctrinal statements of the Church were under a similar historical limitation. While doctrinal formulations of the past capture an aspect of revealed truth, they do not exhaust it; they represent the limited insight of one period of Church history which can be *modified* in another period of Church history as Christians approach the truth from a new direction or with new tools of investigation.[354]

There is, of course, an element of truth here, insofar as new knowledge may cast new light on Church teachings, enabling the Church to clarify those teachings and perhaps formulate them more precisely. This actually happens in the history of the Church, but it presupposes that there is no contradiction between the old formulations and the new ones, that the new ones build on the old ones without abolishing them. If the Church teaches infallibly, then new knowledge is not going to show that old teachings are incorrect. If the latter is possible, then Father Brown has found the proverbial loophole that one can drive a truck through, and every generation can manufacture new doctrines and throw out old ones with reckless abandon.

Father Brown, as noted above, took some time to go after the conservative Catholic press which ventured to question his teachings, remarking that "with increasing frequency, ultra-conservative or fundamentalist Catholics are usurping the authority of the Magisterium by trying to condemn as heretical all theological speculation that

---

[354] Ibid.

shows any sign of nuance with regard to past doctrine."[355] Father Brown apparently felt he was delivering the death-blow to so-called fundamentalists when he indicated that these people (meaning us) had been shut out of respectable academic institutions and periodicals and so had been forced to become journalists. The possibility that Catholic traditionalists get shut out of the institutions, not because they are lacking in skills or credentials, but simply because they are not in accord with majority thinking in these institutions, is one that he studiously avoids considering. What does disturb him profoundly is that people who are not professional scholars with the necessary anointing by the academic institutions deemed to possess the authority to rule in such disputes should have the effrontery to question the orthodoxy of the anointed ones:

> I have said above that the arch-conservative section of the Catholic press has usurped the authority of the Church's Magisterium to judge what is orthodox in theology — these propagandists think they can condemn theologians as heretical. But more seriously they are trying to usurp the bishops' authority to determine what can be taught as Catholic doctrine to the youth. They do not hesitate to denounce catechisms approved by the bishops with an incredible demand to return to the *Baltimore Catechism*.[356]

It is fascinating to see how readily intellectuals who pride themselves on their liberal and democratic attitudes will fall back on arguments from authority when it is their own arrogance which is under attack.

The *Wanderer* truth squad which replied to Father Brown's speech left him with little ground for such arrogance (though I doubt that he saw it that way). Edith Myers, commenting on the presumption he seemed to make throughout his speech in favor of theological innovation, made the following observation:

---

[355] Ibid.
[356] Ibid.

> Through the centuries, Father Brown says, there have been controversies over new contributions to theology. He fails to mention, however, that many of these "contributions" were never accepted, but were flatly declared heretical. He lays great stress on "new knowledge" — he repeats this phrase over and over — and deplores opposition to it, thus implying that all the supposed new knowledge (some presented as "new" is really very old) is valid. There is nothing to support this assumption.[357]

Father Docherty accuses Father Brown of "attempting to hide behind magisterial coattails," and reduces to nonsense his claim to support by Pope John XXIII by quoting in full that Pope's statement about the relationship between doctrine and its expression:

> This is what the great Pope said, with its context: *This certain and changeless doctrine, to which we must yield loyal obedience*, must be examined and explained in the manner demanded by our times. *That ancient Deposit of the Faith, by which I mean the truths that are contained in our venerable Christian doctrine*, is one matter (thing, consideration), the method of presentation another, *always, of course, maintaining the same meaning and the same thinking.*[358]

That is a far cry from the kind of doctrinal relativism that Father Brown attributes to Pope John. "All he [John XXIII] was saying," according to Father Docherty, "was that in the pedagogical and pastoral approach to doctrine, we must adjust and adapt to the audience we address. Nothing more elementary in catechetics."[359]

John Mulloy's response focused on Father Brown's dismissal of his critics as lacking in scholarly respectability, and is quite devastating:

---

[357] Edith Myers, "The Strange Case of Father Brown," W, 6-7-73.

[358] Father Jerome Docherty, O.S.B., "An Attempt to Hide Behind Magisterial Coattails," W, 6-7-73.

[359] Ibid.

> ...If he believes that only those possessed of what he terms "scholarly respectability" have the right to criticize or disagree with him when he is presenting some new viewpoint of what the Church teaches, should he not reserve such novelties in teaching only for their eyes and ears?[360]

In that case, Mulloy suggests, he should not be presenting his ideas to groups of people who are not professional scholars, such as the schoolteachers present at the NCEA convention:

> Father Brown must give up this dishonest attempt to have it both ways: if he is going into the marketplace to gain as wide a currency as possible for his novelties in teaching, he must be prepared to meet criticism by journalists and other members of the People of God. And he must be prepared to meet those criticisms with specific replies, not try to dodge behind the bishops for protection or retreat into the *sanctum sanctorum* of the scholar. Let him remember that the teaching of the Gospel and the Catholic Tradition is a common possession of all the Catholic faithful, not the private preserve of himself and other learned theologians whom he deems of "scholarly respectability." When any member of the faithful sees Catholic teaching being eroded or undermined or mutilated, it is his right — indeed it is even his duty — to speak out in protest against this.
>
> ...It is not the right of the theologians, or of bishops who may acquiesce in their views, to decide that certain parts of the teaching of the Gospel and Catholic Tradition are now antiquated and may be dropped — and then to protest against usurpation of their authority when the faithful demand that they receive the whole Word of God.[361]

Charles Pulver, picking up on this concern, notes that in "going public" and thus abandoning whatever privilege the academician

---

[360] John J. Mulloy, "The Theologian and the Catholic People," W, 6-7-73.
[361] Ibid.

does have to speculate freely, Father Brown's theorizing gets him involved in responsibility for the real human consequences of such speculation:

> ...Like others of the new breed of experts, Father Brown displays no apparent concern for the pastoral consequences (i.e., the loss or weakening of faith) of his biblical theorizing. Now that "progressive" priests and nuns are so specialized in sociology, psychology, biology and other secular fields, they seem to have forgotten about the faith they are serving — supposedly their prime concern and reason for being. Popes through the ages, and especially in recent times, have warned theologians *not to scandalize the faithful* by their speculations. And, of course, our Lord suggested a rather shocking form of capital punishment for those who scandalize the faithful. (A fate which today seems identified with the hapless victim who crosses the mob and ends up in the river wearing "cement overshoes.") It's hard to imagine Father Brown on a shopping spree just to buy a millstone for himself.[362]

Carol Jackson Robinson appropriately entitled her contribution to this symposium "The Credulity of Father Brown," because what her rebuttal brings out is that often the arguments modernists construct to explain away the supernatural involve hypotheses inherently even harder to believe than that of supernatural intervention. Here is her characterization of the way biblical scholars like Father Brown deal with the scriptural texts:

> It works this way: The books of the Bible are literally true. But where are they? Surely, we can't consider the *Gospel of St. Matthew*, for instance, as a book in the ordinary sense. Scripture scholars know (because of their esoteric studies) that it is a compilation of many separate fragments written by

[362] Charles Pulver, "The Make-Believe World of Father Raymond Brown," W, 6-7-73.

> many different authors at different times. Which of these authors was inspired? In which of these contributions is the literal truth to be found?
>
> Assuming it to be in the earliest of them, the scholars begin an onion-peeling process, by which they disassemble the whole and then sort out the separate contributions in chronological layers. They find that the oldest, the core document, is what contains the literal meaning of the Gospel. Unfortunately, this is missing entirely. They must figure out what it must have been like by starting with the earliest interpretation of it. The earliest interpretation is the most unvarnished record they can reconstruct; itself a product of theological reflection on real events of which we have no written record. However, it doesn't matter that we don't have the original because faith bears not on real happenings but on the changing products (formulations) of theological reflection. These products are myths, for myth is the language of religion.[363]

This kind of thing has always made me think of Beetle Bailey, on KP for the 10,000th time, peeling a potato while he daydreams and ending up with several feet of potato peelings and no potato. That is what reductionism does — it reduces and reduces, and it stops only when there is nothing left to reduce. Robinson does a rather thorough job of summing up what Father Brown's allegedly scientific approach to biblical study is really about:

> My case against Father Brown is as follows:
> 1) He has lost his faith.
> 2) He won't admit he has lost his faith.
> 3) He is working to destroy our faith.
> 4) His heretical views do not trace to special scholarship as he claims. (This is my great discovery.)

[363] Carol Jackson Robinson, "The Credulity of Father Brown," W, 6-7-73.

> 5) The locus of his errors is metaphysical, and his competence in the field of philosophy is not remarkable.
> 6) Father Brown is sunk in metaphysical credulity.
> ...When you examine the matter closely you discover that the critics are not forced to their interpretations of Scripture by the weight of their specialized learning; rather they are using this learning to promote and camouflage ideas of an ideological and philosophical nature. Quite often unconsciously. Or from spiritual blindness....But when they were finished dismantling the Gospels, what had been discredited? Every single evidence of the supernatural: all miracles, the Virgin Birth, the Resurrection, the prophecies....Nothing was left but some purely natural fragments of information about a man named Jesus.[364]

Robinson theorizes that biblical scholars like Father Brown get into this position because they are stuck in nominalism, a philosophical position which rejects metaphysics and hence denies the possibility of any objective knowledge about reality (subjectivism again). She reviews the various substitutes for metaphysics which the various schools of "philosophy" have attempted over the centuries, then gives her verdict on Father Brown:

> I think Father Brown is using the scientific method itself, in its Bultmann pseudo-mystical form, as a metaphysics....This, then, is Father Brown's credulity, which he would like to impose on us. He doesn't believe that the sun is God, or that a rabbit's foot will bring him luck; he believes that a Bultmannized scientific method will, for those committed to it in faith, gush forth a never-ending stream of revelation.[365]

John Mulloy, in a February, 1977 article, "The Bible, the Magisterium, and Father Brown," shows clearly the extent of the dogmatism underlying Father Brown's supposedly anti-dogmatic

---

[364] Ibid.
[365] Ibid.

work, as well as the extent to which the Incarnation itself is the target of that work:

> That is the measure of the distance which separates Father Brown from the teaching of the *Dogmatic Constitution on Divine Revelation*. On the one hand, the Vatican II document follows the plain record of the documents themselves, in which the Apostles are portrayed, with a realism which is most convincing, as uncertain and hesitant, coming gradually to an understanding that their Master was the Messiah and a Person in some way uniquely united to God the Father; falling back from that insight and then advancing toward it again, but not having full understanding until after the Spirit had been sent upon them at Pentecost. In Brown's exegesis, on the other hand, the Apostles had no knowledge whatever of the messiahship or divinity of Jesus during His public life, nor even after the Resurrection or Pentecost. Thus they did not know that this was the eternal Son of God, but interpreted His messiahship in terms which ignored His divinity — His pre-existence with the Father from all eternity — or as Father Brown derisively put it..., "his pre-career." Consequently, anything we find in the Gospels which testifies clearly to the divinity of Jesus must have been put there by a later generation of Christians; since neither Jesus Himself nor the Apostles were aware of it.[366]

"The fact of the matter is," Mulloy adds,

> Brown is not really a scholar, but an advocate, a lawyer aiming to present only that evidence which favors his side of the case, and aiming to distort whatever evidence he cannot easily ignore. For this reason, the only sensible way to allow Father Brown to lecture would be in an adversary relationship, such as exists in a court of law. That is, the lawyer for

[366] John J. Mulloy, "The Bible, the Magisterium, and Father Brown," W, 2-3-77.

> one side is counterbalanced by the arguments of the lawyer for the other side. In the case of Father Brown's lectures, the other side never really does get presented, and thus his audience is left in ignorance that there is an other side except Brown's.[367]

Father Brown's method of scriptural exegesis, which starts from the assumption that the Gospels are not reliable as historical documents, leaves us with an impoverished and watered-down version of the Incarnation, indeed, with no Incarnation at all, if we get right down to it. Mulloy, in contrast, was able, in still another of his many articles criticizing Father Brown, to paint a vivid and beautiful picture of what we get when we take the Gospel accounts seriously and allow them to speak for themselves:

> Once allow for the figure of Jesus in the Gospel to be the reality which the disciples witnessed[,] the Person they heard and saw, the One deeply engraved upon their imaginations and their hearts, and things fall into place; and we see why the Gospels give this overpowering sense of reality, and why they possess an inner psychological unity. In whatever way the memories of Jesus came to be collected by the Evangelists (whether they were themselves eye-witnesses or consulted those who had been with Jesus during His lifetime), it was the dominance of the living reality of Jesus in the minds of the Apostles and disciples which accounts for the picture which results. The methods by which the accounts in the Gospel were brought together become wholly secondary; the primary and governing influence throughout the whole of the process is the reality of Jesus Himself.
>
> It is to be feared that Father Brown and others like him, who emphasize a contrast between the "idealized" Jesus as we have Him in the Gospels and the "real" Jesus as He was in His ministry in Palestine, have in fact missed the wood for

[367] Ibid.

> the trees. They are so intent upon the process of form criticism and redaction criticism which fills their minds, that they have little time to see the overwhelming reality of the Figure with which they are dealing, its vital unity, and its sense of transcendent power.[368]

Mulloy is in no doubt that, despite Father Brown's claims to orthodoxy, it is the very divinity of Christ which he seeks to undermine:

> ...Father Brown makes a great fuss by declaring that, in our secularized world, it is important to reassert our belief in the fact that Jesus is the Son of God. But in speaking of this, Father Brown said that Jesus was the Son of God from "the moment of conception." Is this meant to imply that He was not the Son of God before He was conceived in the womb of Mary? In other words, does Father Brown suggest that the Person of Jesus Christ is not that of the eternal Son of God, living with the Father and the Holy Spirit before all ages? Does it mean that God adopted Jesus as His Son, and that therefore what we have in Jesus is a human person who was allowed to enter into a closer relationship with the Father than the ordinary man? Does Father Brown believe that Jesus is simply a creature, and that His position therefore is somewhat similar to that of the Blessed Virgin Mary?
>
> ...Father Brown tells us that Jesus was simply a Jew of the first third of the first century, with all the limitations of worldview and with all the customary beliefs of a Jew of that particular period of time. Now if Jesus was indeed only that, why bother to call Him the Son of God?[369]

---

[368] John J. Mulloy, "Father Brown on the Historical 'Truth' of the Gospels," W, 3-10-77.

[369] John J. Mulloy, "What Is Father Raymond Brown Really Saying?" W, 2-2-78.

Furthermore, *The Wanderer* made it clear at every opportunity that the beliefs of Father Brown and others as to the historical unreliability of the Gospels were not necessarily the results of genuinely scientific exegesis, and were in fact often contradicted by the results of such exegesis when done by respected scholars who did not share Father Brown's modernist, anti-supernatural biases. Thus, during the '70s and '80s, we witnessed the rise of a number of scholars, especially in France, whose studies increasingly undermined modernist reductionism. The indefatigable John Mulloy, in a 1984 article, made the point that the case for the historical reliability of the Gospel narratives is, on the face of it, at least as plausible as the case against it, and probably more so. Scholars today tend to acknowledge that the Gospels were probably written before A.D. 80, and possibly much earlier, placing them within a time period when many of the principal witnesses to the events were still living. In addition, the Jewish society at that time still had a strong tradition for the oral transmission of information, so the assumption that, within a generation or two, whatever Jesus actually said and did was totally swallowed up by a wave of mythmaking and perhaps just plain lies, inherently lacks plausibility. Too many people would have been around to object. Furthermore:

> The modernist view concerning the fabrication of events and sayings of Jesus by the early Christians is dependent on the idea that the early Christians had no great interest in learning the facts of the life of Jesus, but were completely freewheeling when it came to deciding what they would believe concerning Him. But this is a view reflective of the biblical critic's own attitude toward Jesus, and manifests the arrogance of the skeptic rather than the humble faith of the believer.[370]

[370] John J. Mulloy, "Demythologizing the Modernist Myth of the Gospels," W, 5-17-84.

4. THE TRIUMPH OF SUBJECTIVISM

Clearly, the rejection, by the modernist biblical scholar, of the historical truth of the Gospels as well as of that of the Incarnation to which they testify, is rooted, not in the demands of scientific method, but in his own unbelief. But what is the source of that unbelief? Probably no one answer to this question will ever really be sufficient, but I would venture to suggest that a major part of modernist unbelief is traceable to the unwillingness, perhaps even inability, of the modernist mind-set to acknowledge the reality of anything outside the mind or even the feelings of the thinker. As this aspect of the matter is of tremendous importance for the understanding of modernist catechesis, it will be worthwhile to take a little time to explore it.

The centrality of subjectivism to the modernist attack on faith is amply attested to by the fact that Pope Paul VI, in his "The 'Credo' of the People of God" (June 30, 1968), found it necessary to remind us that:

> It is important...to recall that beyond scientifically verified phenomena, the intellect which God has given us reaches *that which is*, and not merely the subjective expression of the structures and development of consciousness; and, on the other hand, that the task of interpretation — of hermeneutics — is to try to understand and extricate, while respecting the word expressed, the sense conveyed by a text, and not to re-create, in some fashion, this sense in accordance with arbitrary hypotheses.[371]

This is Christian realism. It is also one aspect of the Christian wholeness discussed earlier. What Pope Paul's statement tells us is that the alienation of the mind and the world from each other, an alienation which is almost the essence of modern thought, is, in the end, an il-

---

[371] Pope Paul VI, "The 'Credo' of the People of God," W, 7-18-68.

lusion, a nightmare from which it is possible to awaken. And this awakening can lead to a genuine restoration of the community between mind and world, knower and object, a community which was part of God's plan when He created both.

The nightmare of subjectivism was analyzed in great depth by Philip Trower in a July 9, 1987 article entitled "Experience, Feeling, and Revealed Truth." Trower sees theological subjectivism as the attempt to make "experience," consciousness, feelings, or what have you, rather than objective reality, the object of thought. He sees the source of much of this "experientialism" in an understandable reaction against a sterile rationalism which seemed to turn reality into abstractions. "Rationalist influence," according to Trower,

> eventually bred a deep and irrational prejudice not only against abstract ideas, but against any kind of clear systematic thought in religion. Abstract ideas came to be regarded as falsifying reality rather than illuminating it, as enemies rather than servants of truth, and unequivocal formulations of doctrine as intolerable restrictions on liberty.[372]

Unfortunately, in rejecting a kind of sterile objectivism which seemed to draw the very life out of the objects of knowledge, too many modern thinkers rejected the very idea of a reality distinct from experience. They thus rejected not only Cartesian rationalism but the great tradition of realist philosophy which, in Trower's words, "starts from the premise that the primary object of perception is not thought but things. Only after first having had knowledge of things do we know we have thought about them."[373] In contrast,

> The philosophies of experience all have in common the fact that they make the whole range of man's conscious and semiconscious states of mind — not just thoughts and sense impressions, but feelings, moods, intuitions, desires, impulses, instincts, imaginings as well, usually called "the

[372] Philip Trower, "Experience, Feeling, and Revealed Truth," W, 7-9-87.
[373] Ibid.

> contents of consciousness" — their subject of investigation.[374]

Trower stresses that the emphasis on experience is not necessarily a bad thing in itself. It is of great importance for the Christian life that the Church's teachings come alive for us experientially, and are not just abstract formulas, but the emphasis on experience to the exclusion of objective reality can only create spiritual and intellectual disorder:

> ...The important thing is that experience is only the stuff from which knowledge is made. It is not in the full sense knowledge itself. Through experience, one could say we touch the surface of the real, but if we are to penetrate deeply into it and grasp its meaning we have to think about it, reflect on it, which necessarily involves to some extent the formulation of propositions and the use of abstractions. The idea that experience (whether objective or subjective) can be a way of knowing better than or in opposition to the formulation of ideas, conclusions, and judgments in the mind is quite simply preposterous.[375]

For knowledge to be complete, in Trower's view, we need to unite experience, understood as feelings, emotions, etc., with the objective, "rational" component in such a way that we are truly experiencing, in a rich, vital way, a reality which is, at the same time, not dependent on our experiencing it that way, and which needs all the tools of reason to be known adequately. Trower brings this home in an eloquent statement which is itself an experiential presentation, in the best sense:

> Revelation is not a book of instructions for working a machine, or a set of plans for an expedition into the Amazonian jungle. Revelation is the unveiling of a whole world of per-

[374] Ibid.
[375] Ibid.

> sons, places, and powers, a whole panorama of activities and events, natural and supernatural, past, present, and to come, which are meant by God to be the believers' spiritual homeland. It is not a question for the believer of living in two worlds, but of seeing the two worlds, visible and invisible (or no longer visible) as one. He should learn to see the crowds of angels as well as shoppers in the supermarket, not to mention the odd demon or two. He should come to recognize in the garage mechanic or waiter not just a sociological type or even a fellow human being, but a soul redeemed by Christ. He should be trained to think of grace as a power of infinitely more importance to the welfare of society than electricity or the water supply. The principal figures of the Old and New Testaments should be as familiar to him as his family and friends. And finally, while glorifying God for the splendor of the visible world, he must learn to account the invisible one the more real and enduring.[376]

Just as there is no knowledge without both subject and object, knower and thing known, in an unbroken wholeness, so it is vital that we both know what we experience and experience what we know. Modernist theology, unfortunately, breaks up this wholeness and tries to reduce Christian thinking to subjectivity, with predictably disastrous results:

> The modernists, having lost their belief in a Revelation with an unchanging content, and adopting instead the notion of ongoing revelation through experience, see experience as the final court of appeal. What does not fall within the compass of man's experience (objective or subjective), is and always will be incomprehensible to him. The Church's philosophy and theology must therefore be given an idealist foundation and doctrine altered to fit experience. But this cannot be openly stated. So the philosophies of consciousness are used

[376] Ibid.

to emphasize the discordances between doctrine and experience in a way that discredits the former and enhances the attractiveness of the latter. Doctrines are to be made to sound as outlandish or inimical to human welfare as possible, in order to make the case for altering them to seem more plausible.[377]

[377] Ibid.

5. THE NEW CATECHETICS — THE CANCER METASTASIZES

Perhaps the bitterest fruit borne by the subjectivist version of the Christian faith has been the role it gives something called "modern consciousness." Modern man, say the theologians, has patterns of thought peculiarly his own, patterns formed by such influences as modern science, technology, and democracy, and he is incapable of understanding or in any way dealing with ideas and teachings which are not in harmony with those categories. Thus, according to Rudolf Bultmann, no one who uses electricity can possibly believe in the Resurrection. Modern man sees all phenomena as having scientifically ascertainable causes, hence he cannot possibly take miracles seriously.

It is at this point that the relevance of subjectivist theology for catechetics, that is, for the teaching of the Christian faith to adult converts or children, becomes obvious. If we are to teach someone the Christian faith, we must teach it in a way he can understand, can "relate to," as the current jargon has it. That of course is true if it means that, without changing the content of Christian teaching, we should present it in a way that the person being taught can understand. The problem is that when we bring in the "modern consciousness" idea we end up saying that much of the *content* of the Christian faith is such that modern people cannot relate to it, and therefore, if we are to teach the faith in a way that is "meaningful" to modern man, we must actually change the faith itself. If the proponents of the "modern consciousness" idea were truly consistent and honest, they would simply say that modern man cannot relate to Christianity, and therefore we should stop trying to teach him Christianity and instead teach him a new religion that he *can* relate to, that is, the religion of secularism. But instead, they try to get us to believe that they are merely changing the method of presentation, not the faith itself. That this is patently untrue was brought out by John Mulloy in a July, 1987 article:

> It may readily be granted that religion should appeal to a deeper than intellectual level, and that the heart and soul of the believer should be touched. But is this what is the usual result of the attempt to experience religion through modern catechetical efforts? Or do we have an attempt to fit the Catholic faith into modern life, so that the child is not confronted with anything which would give him a different outlook from that of the secularized culture which surrounds him? Is not much of modern catechetics committed to the view that it is the Christian faith which must conform itself to the world in which we live, instead of having that faith serve to leaven the world and open up to modern man new dimensions of reality and meaning?
>
> ...When we ask why it is that we are losing our youth to fundamentalist Protestant churches or to a general indifference to religion, we have here the answer to that question. The Catholic faith under these circumstances has nothing to offer, for it has denied its own reason for existence in order to make itself a part of the modern environment.
>
> This is not, however, necessarily the outcome of any effort to experience Catholicism as a living reality. Instead, it is the result of a completely misguided attitude based upon a fear of being thought odd and different from one's neighbors, which consequently leaches out of Catholicism those things which make it distinctively what it is.
>
> ...Catholicism has always had a wealth of means by which to support a religion of experience. But the experience is not of the desacralized environment of a secularized culture, but of the transcendental truths of the Christian Revelation.[378]

[378] John J. Mulloy, "Experiential Catechetics: Counterfeit or Authentic?" W, 7-9-87.

When Mulloy wrote this, he was looking back at a generation of catechetical experimentation starting in the mid-1960s, a time when bewildered people, parents in particular, began to notice that there was something a little peculiar about the catechisms the children were bringing home from school. The Baltimore Catechism they were not. An anonymous editorialist, writing in the September 7, 1967 *Wanderer*, appears to have been appropriately scandalized after his first look at a catechism in the *Word and Worship* series. The book contained almost no doctrine, ignored the supernatural almost entirely in order to focus on the social gospel, and made heroes out of such people as the Rev. Martin Luther King, Jr., and the existentialist theologian Paul Tillich:

> In the face of what we have seen and read from the *Word And Worship* series, we can only conclude that the religious formation of children is here being sacrificed for the sake of a senseless experimentation from which the fundamentals of religion have been all but totally expunged. Obviously, this is a series in which the dogma of original sin or, for that matter, of actual sin, is so little in evidence that one can readily understand why it is devoid even of the ordinary rudiments of reality and common sense. In short, it is a series which, though striving throughout for religious "relevancy," fails miserably in the attempt to relate to the realities of life in its natural as well as supernatural totality.[379]

Dietrich von Hildebrand, writing later in the same year, was even more blunt in his attack on the new catechisms, noting in particular that the *Word and Worship* series distorts the humanity of Christ, makes Him "just a nice guy," etc. The title of his article, "The Corruption of Souls by the New Catechisms," in itself spells out his attitude pretty clearly:

> Catholic parents should not be distracted by pedagogical arguments. The pedagogy put forward to justify the new cate-

[379] "This Is Christian Doctrine?" W, 9-7-67.

> chisms is false. But what we are confronted with here is not a question of pedagogy. Written all over these textbooks which are this very day poisoning the souls of little children is a hatred of the sacred and of the supernatural. This demands more from Catholic parents than arguments: it demands action. The rights of Catholic parents in these matters were reaffirmed by the Second Vatican Council. Their duty in the present hour is clear. They must not tolerate their children's being force-fed a secularized Christianity. They must insist that these texts be removed from the Catholic grammar schools, and they must withhold their children and their financial support from these schools until such vicious books as the *Word and Worship* series are removed.[380]

In a 1969 article, von Hildebrand continued his attack on the (then) new catechisms and at the same time outlined criteria for genuine Christian education:

> It has become very urgent today to ask what are the marks of a true Christian education. Every faithful Catholic who has eyes to see and ears to hear cannot but notice that we are facing a radical destruction of the transmission of Catholic faith in Catholic grammar schools, high schools, and colleges. We need only think of the horror of so many new catechisms, such as the Benziger catechism (in which Christ is represented as a mediocre, jolly-good fellow), or of the Sadlier and Paulist catechisms, in which the narration of the Gospel is arbitrarily falsified and Christ is, at best, a humanitarian reformer. The Decalogue is dismissed, and an un-Christian, "New Morality" replaces it.
>
> ...In truth, only that person has the right to teach religion in the frame of the Catholic Church who accepts unconditionally the Creed of Nicaea — as well as the Creed of Pope Paul

---

[380] Dietrich von Hildebrand, "The Corruption of Souls by the New Catechisms," W, 12-7-67.

> VI; the dogmas, the official teaching of the Church about morals, and the infallibility of the Pope as defined in Vatican Council I and reaffirmed in Vatican Council II.[381]

Von Hildebrand notes that the new catechists often justify their aberrations by noting that the older catechists were frequently guilty of the ultimate, unforgivable sin — something called "negative thinking." He loses little time in disposing of the modernist claim to be teaching positive thinking (from a standpoint of logic, these people rarely have much chance against thinkers of von Hildebrand's caliber, but unfortunately, when the votes are counted, they usually win):

> This slogan of "the positive approach" has a magic influence on many. In truth, however, it conceals many grave confusions. There is no attitude toward an object which, in itself, is positive. The "no" spoken to error is as positive as the "yes" spoken to truth. It is only the reverse side of the "yes" to truth. It implies the same objectivity, the same love for truth, the same reverence before reality, the same transcendence.
>
> Whether we should say yes or no depends exclusively on the nature of the object. To say "no" to truth and "yes" to error is the real negative attitude. The truly positive answer is the one which is dictated by the nature of the object. It is the same in the field of truth as in the moral field. To say "no" to a disvalue is as positive as to say "yes" to a value. Thus the claim to take a positive attitude toward errors, especially when divine Revelation is at stake, is nonsensical. This allegedly positive attitude is, in reality, a most negative one.[382]

Having thus established the critical importance of going after errors rather than preening oneself on "positive thinking," von Hildebrand proceeds to outline the principal errors of the contemporary cate-

[381] Dietrich von Hildebrand, "The Marks of a True Christian Education," W, 4-17-69.
[382] Ibid.

chisms. These include "the myth of 'modern man,'" (what we have called "modern consciousness"), whose nature is supposed to be so different from that of his ancestors:

> In reality, man's nature does not change in history. You need only read Plato's dialogues or Herodotus to *see* that man remains always the same in his basic structure. There is but one radical *change* in history: the advent of Christ, the redemption of man through His death on the cross, the gift of the life of grace through Baptism. Thus, by his vocation to holiness each man is called upon to effect this change in himself.[383]

The second error is the whole atmosphere of constant experimentation in religious education, an attitude rooted in a "fetishization of natural science." Thirdly, the catechisms have a "wrong concept of vivification," an understandable but nevertheless erroneous reaction against an arid, merely conventional Catholicism:

> As soon as we have understood the true nature of a living existential religion which is the real antithesis to a mere conventional religion, we easily see that the attempt to blur the difference between the natural and supernatural is precisely the way to conventionalize religion and to undermine the possibility of a true lived Christianity. The shortcomings of the past were rooted precisely in the fact that religious truths were presented in an abstract, conceptual way. The awesome reality of the supernatural, and its complete difference from the natural, were never elaborated upon in the correct style and manner — one, namely, which would afford the student an intuitive living awareness of the great things before him.[384]

Finally, the new catechisms reflect a confusion about the true nature of success in catechetics:

---

[383] Ibid.
[384] Ibid.

> These pedagogues congratulate themselves on the brilliant success of their "new approach" to religious teaching; it never seems to dawn on them that the attractiveness of their method was purchased by their repudiating the very truths and supernatural realities which they supposedly aimed at imparting. Their "success," then, is comparable to that of the surgeon who boasts: "The operation was a brilliant success — but the patient died." Thus the end at which they aim and which gives the operation its meaning is sacrificed for the sake of the brilliancy of the operation.[385]

Subjectivism always involves a great reluctance to deal with propositional truth, i.e., with any statement purporting to say something about a reality independent of the thinker's own mind or experience. When people with this mentality write catechisms, they naturally avoid doctrine like the plague, and the result is books which are not necessarily heretical in a strict, formal sense, but which are just hopelessly vague about Catholic teaching. K.D. Whitehead, in a 1970 article, showed this in regard to the Sadlier series, focusing on the way it deals with the Sacraments:

> The Teacher's Guide to the series says that the book will concentrate on "their social aspect as actions of the risen Christ with the body of His Church," and, of course, the social aspect of the sacraments is undoubtedly important. But not to the exclusion of understanding what the sacraments are in themselves. How can a fifth-grader understand even their social aspect if he doesn't understand what they are?
>
> Yet, it is extremely difficult to understand what a sacrament is on the basis of the treatment encountered in this book. Nowhere are the sacraments clearly defined, named, or enumerated. The text mentions once in passing that there are seven of them; otherwise it would be difficult, if not impos-

[385] Ibid.

> sible, to know this on the basis of the information given therein.[386]

The result is a text which no one can possibly pin down on any matter of Catholic teaching:

> Just about everything in this book flows imperceptibly into something else. The Spirit, of course, is a favorite and recurring theme as is the Word. Other themes are person, unity, community, loving, sharing, concern — undoubtedly Christian themes that need to be imparted to the children, but wasn't this particular textbook supposed to be about something else? In actual fact, the sacraments seem to be among the things that interest the writers least.
>
> ...Never mind that no child can enter into a proper relationship with Christ without knowing who He is. Children have to be told who He is, as they have to be taught that there is, in fact, a God. They *cannot* learn these truths merely from "experience." The evidence of Christ's divinity, as of God's very existence, is so far beyond the experience of a child, or even of an adult for that matter, that it was perhaps for that very reason God saw fit to *reveal* these truths for the salvation of man. Such considerations seem unimportant in the world of this textbook, which never really gets around to explaining who Christ is, as it should be explained and as Christ Himself did in the Scriptures, but believes it has made a significant statement for the fifth-grader by explaining that He is "Someone-for-us."[387]

---

[386] K.D. Whitehead, "A Radical Failure to Present Catholicism," W, 2-5-70.
[387] Ibid.

6. THE EVALUATION INSTRUMENT

In late 1970, the National Conference of Catholic Bishops (NCCB) assigned to its Division of Research and Development in Religious Education the task of evaluating the textbooks then in wide use. This division prepared something called the *Instrument for the Evaluation of Religion Textbooks,* which set forth criteria to be used in the evaluation. It soon became evident to *Wanderer* types and other "fascist pigs" that this was a classic case of hiring the fox to guard the chicken coop, because the criteria used by the *Instrument* were such as to pretty much guarantee that faithfulness to Catholic doctrine would not be considered in the evaluation. The authors of the *Instrument* basically did an end run around issues of doctrine by deciding that only books with an imprimatur would be evaluated. Apparently, that took care of doctrinal matters as far as they were concerned, because of course it could be presumed that any book with an imprimatur was free from doctrinal error. As John Mulloy said in an October, 1970 article, an imprimatur today tells us very little about the doctrinal content or absence of same in a textbook:

> ...An *imprimatur* does not testify to the fact that the book contains any substantial content in doctrine at all. It only asserts that the book is formally free, in the opinion of the censor, of doctrinal or moral error. But one could write a book intended for use in Religion classes in which the doctrine would be largely omitted, and some kind of psychological and sociological speculations might be given in place of teaching on Catholic faith and morality.[388]

A book could thus be free of formal heresy simply by avoiding doctrine entirely. Furthermore, as everyone knows, it is members of the bishops' bureaucracies, and not the bishops themselves, who make

[388] John J. Mulloy, "Examining the Evaluation Instrument," W, 10-29-70.

the decisions on imprimaturs, hence bishops frequently give the imprimatur to texts they haven't even read. By a clever device, the authors of the *Instrument* had managed to rule out of court any discussion of the doctrinal soundness of the books, and forced evaluators to limit themselves to issues of methodology, pedagogics, etc.:

> Thus if the evaluator should find what he believes to be a considerable gap between what is presented in the book — or more likely what is omitted from the book — and the basic doctrines of the Catholic faith, he must not therefore assume that it is his task to point out that fact, and to make clear that there has *not* been achieved an effective, clear and adequate expression of the Catholic faith. He must rather pause and consider whether he is not being pedagogically naive in expecting that the book should do anything of this nature. After all, there is such a plurality of theories in religious education, that one should not really find the book deficient in any way, as it is simply achieving the goals of its own particular theory; and who is the evaluator to quarrel with the expertise of the textbook, especially when that book has an imprimatur and is used in many dioceses already.[389]

K.D. Whitehead's evaluation of the *Instrument* zeroes in on the same issue. "The *Instrument,*" he remarks, "assumes from the start that there is nothing basically, i.e., morally and doctrinally, wrong with any of the new textbooks; at any rate, its questions are not framed to *find* anything morally or doctrinally wrong with them, if there is anything. In a word, the jury empaneled to render a verdict on these textbooks appears to be a packed jury."[390] He goes on to note that the ideas about the very nature of Christian faith which seem implicit in the *Instrument* are obviously ideas of a secularist order, and as such are in no way derived from Christian tradition:

---

389 Ibid.
390 K.D. Whitehead, "'Lord, Make Me an Instrument,'" W, 11-5-70.

> Nor is the religious duty of man primarily a duty of "apprehending the faith," "thinking about the world," and "coming to a sense of values," as the *Instrument* implies. Rather, man's religious duty involves first *repenting* and *believing* — as Christ Himself taught in the very first words He preached (*Mark* 1:15).
>
> ...Moreover, the basic aim of all Christian education is not, as the *Instrument* seems to think, the "development" or "maturity" of the human person. These are psychological terms, as used by the *Instrument*; they are unknown to Scripture or Tradition.
>
> ...We get no sense whatever from this *Instrument* that a transformation in Christ is the aim of Christian education.[391]

John Mulloy, writing again in November, 1970, stresses that the *Instrument*, in common with the books it is supposed to evaluate, betrays the very essence of Christianity by de-emphasizing transcendence as opposed to immanence. It does not so much reject transcendence as just completely ignore and dismiss it:

> In actual fact, in all of these doctrinal points, what is required for orthodox Christian teaching is neither a transcendent nor an immanent approach, nor even a dialectic one (sometimes transcendent, sometimes immanent), but rather the meeting of the transcendent and immanent in an encounter between God and man which is what Christianity is about. One cannot teach Christianity as though one can choose one of these elements at the expense of the other; and to try to set up the structure in the way this *Instrument* does is to make certain that there will be a continual chasing back and forth from one extreme to the other. This may suit the preference of certain present-day "new" theologians who wish to emphasize immanence today, and thus need to claim that only transcendence was emphasized before; but to accommodate textbooks

[391] Ibid.

> to their preference means the scrapping of any teaching that is specifically Christian.[392]

But by simply leaving transcendence out of consideration, the *Instrument* and the textbooks suppress the very notion of Revelation:

> The use of the term Revelation is extremely important to any statement of the Catholic faith. If a clear sense of its meaning is not maintained, and it is used indiscriminately to apply to anything which has provided us with spiritual inspiration, then we shall have to seek some other word to signify what was previously meant by the term Revelation. But why should this be made necessary...unless indeed it is deliberately intended to destroy the specific character of Revelation, and to substitute in its place an indeterminate product that has no definite form whatever? Why attempt to scrap a perfectly good term for a clearly understandable concept, unless we do not like the idea of what Revelation involves and therefore wish to deprive it of any substantial meaning?
>
> ...Revelation in the proper use of the term testifies to the existence of the transcendent and the supernatural: it is God Himself coming down to man and telling man what He requires of him and what are the conditions necessary for man's salvation. Whether it be to Moses on Mount Sinai, or later to the prophets of Israel, or finally and in the fullness of time through the sending of God's only-begotten Son, the fact of revelation breaks in upon man's world of limited self-sufficient existence and tells man things he could not possibly know on his own through his natural faculties and means of knowledge. Even more than knowledge, it impinges upon man's will — it directs him toward a morality that may reject the way of life his society already possesses. Revelation

[392] John J. Mulloy, "Errors Compounded and Perpetuated," W, 11-12-70.

> stands over against man's will to fashion an image of God that will serve his own purposes rather than God's.[393]

Above all, according to Mulloy, the new textbooks, in their presentation of Jesus, simply ignore the Incarnation, and the *Instrument* does not appear even to see this as an issue for the evaluators. Mulloy's comment is rather devastating:

> ...To the Division of Research and Development in Religious Education which prepared this *Instrument*, all of the struggle of the Christian Church over nineteen centuries to teach and maintain the central doctrine of the Christian faith is a lost cause. One can, with a perfectly good conscience from their standpoint, choose to ignore the significance of the Incarnation in the writing of a religion textbook for Catholic school children, and there is nothing which will not be found acceptable in what you have to offer. ...There is no direct challenge posed to the divinity of Christ, you simply ignore its crucial significance, and congratulate yourself on how well you are adapting your teaching to the modern cultural milieu.[394]

William Marra faults the *Instrument* for ignoring the matters of faith at the roots of the textbook controversy, and focusing exclusively on issues of methodology, which are rather accidental compared to issues of faith:

> When now it is proposed that the entire matter of catechetics be aired, the least we might expect is a thoroughly honest confrontation with the issues of faith and orthodoxy...documented so brilliantly and so forcefully by many true Catholic believers. But, as we have come now to expect with resignation and revulsion, the proposed remedy, the so-called *Instrument for the Evaluation of Religion Textbooks*,

[393] Ibid.
[394] Ibid.

> cynically disregards the only substantive question and brazenly chats about pedagogy.[395]

Mulloy, in still another article on this topic, takes issue with the educators on their use of educational psychology as a method taking precedence over the substance of religious education, which is the learning of the revealed truths taught by the Church. Books are considered good because they employ the latest trendy ideas in psychology, not because they teach Christian truth:

> In approaching the methods to be used in teaching children, one should recognize certain important psychological principles. Number one is the desire of the child for straight answers — he wants to know the truth, to get at the facts, to be brought into contact with reality. He does not want to be given a lot of indefinite and uncertain answers which proclaim the ignorance of the teacher and thus show his unfitness for teaching....But when teachers and textbooks emphasize precisely the opposite viewpoint, that there is no substantial reality to the knowledge with which the Catholic faith is concerned, they have set the students on the road which leads to rejection of the Christian faith and to the abandonment of membership in the Catholic Church. Thus if methodology is thought to be a substitute for content, it means the end of Catholicism as a vital force in contemporary society. And this comes through the disregard of some of the most fundamental principles of pedagogy: that what you are teaching is true and deserves to be learned, not toyed with in dilettante fashion for whatever incidental satisfaction it may afford you.[396]

Mulloy goes on, in a January, 1971 article, to take issue with the way in which the religious education establishment seems to absolu-

---

[395] William Marra, "That Which Thou Dost, Do Quickly," W, 11-19-70.
[396] John J. Mulloy, "The Instrument and Educational Psychology," W, 12-24-70.

tize its *methods* while relativizing the *content* of the teaching: "Thus the emphasis shifts from the doctrines revealed by God to the pedagogical methods devised by man; and the latter apparently now possess an unquestioned character which was formerly reserved for the Word of God."[397] This in effect insulates the elite from rational argument about what it is doing, and gives its work the status of a kind of new revelation to today's Church.

That new religion is extremely short on doctrine, but seems to devote a lot of attention to concepts of love and freedom, never clearly defined:

> It may be that the fullness of love is not possible for the individual until he has been detached from sin by the realization of the ills it will bring upon him, including the punishments which God visits upon man's sinfulness. To speak of love without the prior purification of the sentiments may be for most people an invitation to falsehood and pretense, in which talk about a religion of love covers over an unwillingness to make the sacrifices required by love of God and neighbor.
>
> ...Freedom which has to be exercised in disregard of the realities of the moral order and of the sanctions attached to its transgression is not a genuine freedom at all; it is empty of any real substance.
>
> ...In addition, there is lost a sense of the meaning of life, and the result is a sense of drift, with the teaching of the Christian religion itself becoming a part of the meaningless flux of existence, as it substitutes a flabby sentimentality for a vigorous grasp of the fundamental truths which Christianity came to proclaim.
>
> ...To refrain, therefore, from teaching the child either a creed or a code of conduct is one of the most unnatural things in the world. It can only lead the child to have scorn for the

397 John J. Mulloy, "Examining the Evaluation 'Instrument'...Freeing the Child From the Creed," W, 1-7-71.

> teacher when he finds that the teacher has no faith himself and no definite moral standards, that he talks about weighing moral values and personal choice because his mind and heart are a spiritual vacuum on these issues which are so important to the child's own needs.[398]

Mulloy sees the incessant spirit of innovation in the teaching of religion today as reflecting, not a concern for adapting the message to the needs of children (as the educators claim), so much as adapting it to the lack of faith and spirituality of the educators, usually priests or nuns:

> Is it not strange that those who have the greatest difficulty in retaining commitment to their vocation are regarded by many as the greatest experts in telling children what the true meaning of Christian commitment is?
>
> ...If there is no time for the contemplation of God, the teacher is simply drowned in a whirlpool of sensations. No one is able to give that which he does not have. If there is no inner well of quiet springing up within the soul, the teacher becomes a barren cistern and an empty well.
>
> ...Such teachers will seek a thousand and one novelties because they do not have the patience and the docility to listen to the Spirit of God and hear what is really being said in God's Revealed Word; or if they do hear it, they reject it because it is not stimulating enough....Where Elijah found the presence of God in the gentle breeze, they find it only in the whirlwind and the earthquake.[399]

Edith Myers, in a January, 1971 article, sums up pretty definitively what bothered orthodox Catholics so much about the *Instrument* — the fact that the one thing it failed to deal with was the one thing that mattered, the question of the orthodoxy of the books:

---

[398] Ibid.

[399] John J. Mulloy, "Tailoring the Message," W, 1-14-71.

> The *Instrument* states (p. 2) that the criteria to be used *"do not represent a checklist of doctrines against which the books are to be measured."* Without such a checklist, any real evaluation is impossible. Virtually all of the protest against the "new" catechetics has been on grounds of omission or distortion of doctrine....The only thing tested appears to be the manner of presentation — not the matter presented. The *Instrument*, indeed, takes an entirely different direction when it asks evaluators to judge catechetical presentation on the basis of "the aim of the work"; for the aim of some of our catechetical "experts" seems hardly to be the teaching of all the truths summed up by Pope John. One of them, Brother Gabriel Moran, whose books are constantly recommended to our teachers, says doctrine *should not be* taught to children; that Christianity has no definite message, no "set of truths."[400]

To no one's great astonishment, when the USCC's Textbook Evaluation was finally published in May, 1971, it consisted principally of a whitewash of the heretical textbooks now used almost everywhere. Given the criteria outlined in the *Instrument*, no other result was possible. In addition, the evaluation was extremely critical of orthodox textbooks, dismissing them as too "rigid," "too content-oriented," while being quite friendly in its review of books that presented Jesus as merely a human person.

---

[400] Edith Myers, "The Basic Question Is Ignored," W, 1-14-71.

7. THE NATIONAL CATECHETICAL DIRECTORY

Continuing our tour of great *Wanderer* battlefields (dangerous places where the careless visitor may still stumble over the odd land mine), we come to the conflict over the National Catechetical Directory. In early 1974, the bishops of the United States announced their intention to engage in a broad-based consultation aimed at establishing a set of criteria for the content and methods of catechesis in America. This was an attempt, of course, to resolve the crisis in catechetics that we have been talking about, but, sadly, like many of the U.S. bishops' initiatives, it ran aground due to the bishops' tendency to try to please everyone, and the predictable result was that it pleased no one. When the first draft of this document appeared in early 1975, Frank Morriss was very quick to label it "a disaster on the way to happening." In all too many crucial areas, the document seemed to amount to a capitulation to modernist catechesis. Morriss found serious problems in three areas: 1) The way it handled the confrontation between Catholic and American values; 2) The absence of an epistemology which said that man can know reality; 3) Its surrender to behavioral psychology and related ideologies in its approach to teaching children:

> The first area is the confrontation of Catholic and what are called American values, in which the draft comes up with a picture that is more fiction than reality....
>
> In the second area there is a virtual absence of recognition of the absolute need for a new type of conceptual epistemology, that is, the establishing of the necessity for insisting man can know reality as it is. In the third area, that of teaching Catholic truth to children, the draft makes an abject surrender to

> behavioral psychology and its gray eminence — existentialism.[401]

The NCD, in Morriss's view, simply failed to address even the possibility of conflict between Catholic teachings, especially in the area of morality, and contemporary American values. That would be far too uncomfortable to deal with. "The point for consideration in the teaching of Catholicity," says Morriss, "must concern a moral absolutism that may demand a separation from the community at large. It is the very failure to make such a separation that is aiding the triumphant forward march of abortion today."[402] Unfortunately, America has not escaped the influence of secularist, anti-Christian ideologies:

> America, perhaps because of its geographic and economic isolation from Europe, escaped the immediate impact of the atheists and libertarians of the French Revolt. But the influence of such persons rode the winds of the Romantic philosophies to this country, and planted the weed of license in regard to thought and truth.[403]

In order to really address the crisis in catechetics, the NCD needed to spell out in no uncertain terms that God's revelation to man is an objective reality which man can know, not a matter of myth or subjective experiences. That would have amounted to affirming the centrality of scholastic-Aristotelian thought in Catholic teaching:

> The philosophy of the scholastics...is not the philosophy of the Catholic Church by accident. It is Catholic philosophy because it upholds the claims of the Catholic Church to have a knowable revelation that can be transmitted to men in a definite and consistent way. This should be established as an

---

[401] Frank Morriss, "A Disaster on the Way to Happening," W, 2-6-75.
[402] Ibid.
[403] Ibid.

> indispensable part of Catholic teaching in our day. But the proposed *Catechetical Directory* ignores this problem.
> The Catholic liberals already have served notice of their intention to ignore the *Directory*. This rejection is based philosophically on the idea that no one can tell another what is truth or what is the proper manner of dispensing truth. The Catholic liberal is compounded of barely baptized subjectivism and rugged intellectual individualism. If we do not educate a new generation of Catholics who once again follow an objective epistemology and metaphysics (in the context of a type of Thomistic psychology) then we simply will be educating a generation to ignore what they are being taught. The *Directory*, in other words, will be committing suicide.[404]

The failure to stand up for the position that there is such a thing as reality and that it can be objectively known led the NCD straight into the trap of subjectivism, something implicit in the psychological theories that formed the basis of its approach to teaching children. The draft basically accepted the behaviorist idea that children are a kind of *tabula rasa*, a sort of clay, perhaps, which is passively formed by its environment, or, in the present case, by the enlightened modern educator, when in fact children, like all other human beings (except modern subjectivists) work very hard at trying to reach out and grasp truth:

> ...Sadly enough [for the *Directory*], the child is an experimenting little primate. Between six and ten, says the draft, "the child's intellectual capacity expands gradually from viewing the world exclusively in terms of the concrete and experienced to the point where generalized concepts can be formed from these experiences."
> The draft quickly cautions, however, that "education specialists generally agree that teaching at this stage should remain largely experiential and should relate the concepts introduced

[404] Ibid.

> to the experience provided." A blunter term for this is "conditioning." If there were respect for the nature of concepts no attempt could be made to relate them to "experience," for concepts are derived from the experience of reality and should not be enslaved to experience. By ten a normal child should be introduced to philosophizing, syllogizing, debating, learning the nature of fallacy. The behaviorists, however, will have him experiencing unity by holding hands in a classroom circle.[405]

These problems outlined by Morriss basically persisted during the months and years that the Directory continued to be debated. When the bishops adopted the final draft during their annual meeting in November, 1977, significant improvements had been made as regards the Directory's orthodoxy on specific doctrinal questions, but the overall document still failed to address the central issues Morriss had called attention to three years earlier. Some sound doctrine had, in John Mulloy's view, been put back into the Directory concerning such things as continuing revelation, the Church's understanding of mortal sin and her rejection of the fundamental option idea, her understanding of baptism, and so on, yet overall the document embraced a catechesis which refused to confront contemporary anti-Christian ideologies and remained hopelessly vague on all too many issues. In one particularly important area, the bishops rejected amendments which would have called on Catholics to obey Vatican directives on the necessity of first confession before first Communion. Much of this seemed to derive from the fact that the real power in the American Church had largely shifted from the bishops to the Church bureaucrats:

> The basic reason why the bishops refused to act to implement the Vatican decrees on First Confession was that they were up against the entrenched power of their own catechetical bureaucracy in their dioceses, and what reinforces and feeds

[405] Ibid.

> that bureaucracy on the national level — that is, the Education Department of the United States Catholic Conference. Doctrinally sound for the most part when they are not challenged, the bishops yield and cave in whenever the opposition to authentic Catholic teaching or practice is strongly mounted. The bishops have for so long a time allowed their religious education directors to run their catechetical programs, that most of them feel incapable or unwilling to take on these powerful forces in their own dioceses. And the First Confession issue was one where there was bound to be a head-on collision with their own bureaucrats; so the bishops backed away from it.[406]

In the end, the National Catechetical Directory embodied all too well the weakness of the bishops, their lack of the will to take a stand for Catholic truth when doing so would require a confrontation with well-organized and aggressive bureaucrats:

> But even when the bishops do set down the authentic Catholic teaching, as in many parts of this *Directory*, it remains to be seen whether what they have done is not simply to create a paper document. For the overcoming of the catechetical crisis, and also the religious crisis, within the Catholic Church in America today, is not primarily a matter of the intellect, but of the will. Consequently, the ultimate question is this: Do the bishops have the will to undertake the necessary actions by which the Catholic faith can be handed on to the next generation, or will they be content with theoretical statements devoid of implementation? Their decision concerning First Confession does not augur well for the outcome.[407]

---

[406] John J. Mulloy, "The Bishops and the Catechetical Directory," W, 12-1-77.
[407] Ibid.

That question, sadly, is one that has been answered all too clearly since John Mulloy asked it in 1977.

Because of its failure to take a stand on anything, to take the risk of displeasing any group, the Directory ended up being a monument to tepidity and, in consequence, not only pleased no one, but made no impression whatsoever on anyone. As a result, it became, not an exercise of the bishops' authority to teach, but a stillborn document. At least ninety-nine out of a hundred Catholics today, if asked what they thought of the National Catechetical Directory, would respond with blank stares because, after not all that many years, they have not even heard of it. That says it all.

8. METHODOLOGY AND FAITH

The commonest defense of contemporary catechetics is that the new approach does not change the content of the faith being taught but is merely a change in the methods used to teach that content. That is a fraudulent claim, as a look at any of the new books will show. The problem is that sometimes methodology is not all that easy to separate from content. A means (in this case, pedagogical method) may in fact determine the end (the content to be taught) to some degree. A method may simply be more suited for one end than another. If a teaching method is grounded in an educational psychology that embodies subjectivism and relativism, then it can hardly be used to teach truths which claim to be objectively true. If one were to try to do this, the method itself would constantly undermine the content being taught. We would be teaching Catholic doctrines and at the same time implicitly telling the children that they need not accept these doctrines unless they feel disposed to do so. It is easier to give up entirely trying to teach Catholic doctrine, and that is exactly what happens. "The truth is," says James Likoudis in a September, 1975 article on "Methodology in the New Catechetics," "that some new methods and procedures utilized by modern religious educators radically *inhibit* and *negate* the communication of authentic Catholic doctrine to children and youth. The use of certain psychological methods and techniques can, in effect, injure or destroy faith."[408] Likoudis notes that, in particular, the use of Harvard psychologist Lawrence Kohlberg's theories of moral development, which are radically relativistic, seeing truth and right basically as a matter of the individual child's decision, has resulted in catechesis which cannot possibly teach any recognizably Catholic doctrine. Likoudis sees Kohlberg's theories as the source of most of what was wrong with

---

[408] James Likoudis, "Methodology in the New Catechetics", Pt. I, W, 9-25-75.

the first draft of the National Catechetical Directory, discussed previously:

> The presence of Kohlberg's *Theory of Moral Development* on the modern catechetical scene is further evidenced by the fact that the first draft of *The National Catechetical Directory* (*NCD*) is literally saturated with it. The unhappiness of many observers with the *NCD*'s first draft is in large measure the result of their perceiving that, though the U.S. bishops' *Basic Teachings* document does appear in Chapter Five, Kohlberg's methodology is persistently relied upon to prevent solid doctrine from being taught at practically every grade level![409]

It is quite understandable, Likoudis suggests, that educators committed to such theories become nearly apoplectic at even the mention of the old Baltimore Catechism:

> Their entire catechetical approach has undergone a radical transformation. They are now, in Father Newton's words, "concerned with process rather than content, with the future rather than the present, with the ability to grow rather than the faithful approximation of a conventional model of Christian behavior." No longer are Catholics to be produced "who were oriented toward obedience and authority, law and duty, and to obeying a rather specific and fixed moral code" — for this again is to retard the spiritual, moral, and intellectual growth of Christians. Modern catechists, as Father Newton goes on to sympathetically explain, "interpret their task as helping their students to think in a manner that will allow them to discover their own answers to questions rather than encouraging them to accept ready-made answers."[410]

[409] Ibid.
[410] Ibid.

(Likoudis's reference is to an article in the 3-15-72 issue of *America* by Father Robert R. Newton, S.J., entitled "Religious Education in Transition.")

It is hard to be clearer than that. The new catechesis rejects the very notion of fixed truths, and instead focuses exclusively on the student's free decision about the faith, whether that free decision is Christian or anti-Christian in its content. It is interesting that Kohlberg's "Fourth Stage of Moral Development" is the stage of orientation to authority, law, and so forth — that is, orientation to the idea of a fixed order which we are called upon to accept and to conform ourselves to. To Kohlberg and his followers, this is an immature stage of development, which we are to transcend by going on to an autonomous stage where *we* determine what is true and false, and the only order is the order we ourselves impose upon our lives. That appears to be the outlook of Kohlberg's catechetical disciples, too. But it is clearly not compatible with anything earlier generations understood to be the content of the Catholic faith:

> The questionable behavioral insights of a Lawrence Kohlberg have been used to buttress an experiential catechesis downgrading any need to know the specifics of Catholic dogma and morality. This subtle undermining of Catholic dogma and the Church's norms of objective morality in favor of "openness, growth, and flexibility" (the rhetoric, by the way, of entrenched progressivist secular educators) only leads to teachers and students being unable to articulate or defend the teachings of the Church.[411]

[411] James Likoudis, "Methodology in the New Catechetics", Pt. II, W, 10-2-75.

9. A LIGHT IN THE DARKNESS

The horror stories detailed above give little ground for optimism. During the past few years, however, there has emerged one genuine ray of light in the darkness. That light comes from the new *Catechism of the Catholic Church*, released in French in 1992 and in English in 1994. This catechism, put together in response to the Synod of 1985, is perhaps the most clear and orthodox statement of the Catholic faith since the *Catechism of the Council of Trent*. It is now the authoritative Catholic document on catechesis, coming directly from the Holy Father. While the modernists of course reject it, it is difficult for them to deny that it is the teaching of the universal Church which they are rejecting, and those of us engaged in the struggle for restoration of the Catholic Church now have a powerful weapon to use, as the always outspoken Malachi Martin, quoted by *The Wanderer* on April 8, 1993, pointed out:

> "While the institutional Church limps badly in its decline, showing little sign of getting better, we are being given a great consolation in the new *Catechism of the Catholic Church*.... Look upon it as a temporary restraining order.[412]
>
> "When Bishop Untener of Saginaw, Mich., and Archbishop Weakland of Milwaukee insist on discussing women priests, we can say, 'Your Excellencies, the catechism.' When Sister Theresa Kane presents her usual mixture of blasphemous wicca and the goddess Sophia, we can say, 'Sister Theresa, the catechism.'
>
> "When theologian Father Richard McBrien speaks about his hopes that one day he will see Mrs. Pope standing on the balcony of St. Peter's — he does say this — blessing the crowd

---

[412] Henry V. King, "Malachi Martin Cites 'Endless Uses' of New Catechism," W, 4-8-93.

> with her husband, Mr. Pope, we can say, 'Richie, go home, read your catechism.'
>
> "When Father McNulty concelebrates with a nun, a woman, at daily Mass, we can say, 'It's a long, long way to Tipperary, as the Pope told you, and read your catechism.'
>
> "When Father Charles Curran of the Catholic University proposes masturbation or homosexuality or anything else that makes you feel good, we can say, 'Charlie, the universal catechism.'
>
> "When the Jesuits propose using enneagrams to foster devotion to the Holy Spirit, we can say, 'Fathers, *Circe Jesu*, read the catechism.'
>
> "When Cardinal Lustiger of Paris says we shouldn't preach to Jews because they have a separate covenant, we can say, 'Your Eminence, please read the catechism.'
>
> "When Bishop Walter Sullivan of Richmond, Bishop Gumbleton of Detroit, Bishop Quinn of Sacramento, and Bishop Hughes of Covington, Ky., all say homosexuality can be a healthy experience, we can say, 'Excellencies, read that catechism.'"'[413]

Pope John Paul II himself, in a statement reported by *The Wanderer* early in 1993, introduced the catechism and its purpose to the world:

> A gift for everyone: This is what the new catechism is meant to be. In regard to this text, no one should feel a stranger, excluded, or distant. In fact, it is addressed to everyone because it concerns the Lord of all, Jesus Christ, the one who proclaims and is proclaimed, the Awaited, the Teacher, and the model of every proclamation. It seeks to respond to and satisfy the needs of all those who, in their conscious or unconscious search for truth and certitude, seek God, "even

[413] Ibid.

> perhaps grope for Him, though indeed He is not far from any one of us" (*Acts* 17:27).[414]

Certainly, the "conscious or unconscious search for truth and certitude" has rarely been a more anxious or more critical one than in these decades of doctrinal confusion in the Church, and a response has rarely been so sorely needed. The sense that the catechism helped fulfill the felt need for a restoration of order to this ecclesial confusion was captured by Father John T. Zuhlsdorf in a series of articles he wrote for *The Wanderer* on the catechism:

> With the arrival of the catechism we now have a completed set of the tools needed for the restoration of the three great pillars upon which our lived Catholic faith must always rest: cult, code, and creed: *Cult*, because how we pray has a reciprocal relationship with what we believe; *code*, because Holy Mother the Church must defend the faithful, guide them in the daily living of their faith, and promote communion within the Christian community; and now *creed*, a bold witness and confession of the Catholic faith directed toward future generations while maintaining an unbroken connection with the past.[415]

What is perhaps most crucial about the new catechism, from the perspective of the orthodox Catholic, is that it spells out with great clarity the doctrines of the Church taught for nearly two millennia now, thus helping us to deal effectively with the many heterodox, and destructive, opinions circulating around the Christian community today under the guise of "renewal," while at the very same time formulating these clear teachings in a way that responds to central concerns of modern man having to do with human dignity, human rights, and the need for a *lived* faith, not merely the rote faith which characterized

---

[414] Pope John Paul II, "Catechism Is Truly Gift to the Church," W, 1-7-93.

[415] Father John T. Zuhlsdorf, "'What Is Old and What Is New': A Preparatory View of the New Catechism of the Catholic Church," Introduction, W, 1-14-93.

what the late John Mulloy sometimes called the "arid catechetics" of the old days. Thus:

> The catechism presents "things old and new" (cf. *Matt.* 13:52), the faith which is always the same and is a source of light which is ever new. The catechism embodies the old Latin phrase *non nova sed nove*...not new things but in a new way.[416]

> The novelty in the new catechism is not new dogma or commandments. It is a new organic and unifying vision of the faith, of man and of his destiny.[417]

> Now we distinguish the terms "faith" and "doctrine." Although one cannot limit oneself to this all too brief explication, "presents the faith" means that the Catechism *proclaims* Christian faith. It is *kerygma*, a word in Greek meaning "proclamation" in the New Testament sense. The catechism proclaims our faith to the entire world and is thereby a gesture of outreach to Christians strengthening their existing faith and to nonbelievers who have yet to find it. *Kerygma* must have a content able to be proclaimed, something teachable. As it "presents...Catholic doctrine," the Catechism gives us a thorough exposition, approved by the highest authority, of the content of that faith which the Catholic Church proclaims, as it is based on the supports of the authority at the foundation of our faith, Scripture, Tradition, and Magisterium.

The catechism introduces, of course, no new doctrine — it does, however, incorporate an important *development of doctrine* in allowing a central role, in the explication of the faith, to the kind of Christian humanism found in the documents of Vatican II as well as in the numerous writings of the present Holy Father, both before and after

---

[416] Zuhlsdorf, Part III, W, 2-4-93.
[417] Ibid.

his succession to the Chair of Peter. Father Zuhlsdorf summarizes it in this way:

> The present Holy Father is well known for his defense of the human person and his beautiful theology which has as its foundation the concept of the human person made in the image and likeness of the divine person of the Father, his Creator. Jesus Christ, our God in His divinity and our brother in His humanity, came both to save us as well as to "reveal man fully to himself" (*Gaudium et Spes*, n. 22; a favorite quotation of the Holy Father. It is said that during the Council he had a hand in its composition). Because the human person is created to act as God acts, to know and will, to love and be loved, man has an inherent God-given dignity written into his very being. This dignity is inviolable and in all our human acts must be respected, both in ourselves and in others. A glance at the index of the catechism shows instantly how vital this concept is for a proper reading of its entire contents. Remember that the catechism is an "organic expose of the whole of the Catholic faith. It must be read as a unity" (cf. prologue, § 18). This theological concept, that the human person is the image and likeness of the divine person, is fundamental in the catechism's unity.[418]

Of course, anything like a synopsis of the contents of the new catechism in this narrative would be an impossibility, for practical purposes. The synopsis would have to be a synopsis of the entire Catholic faith, which is precisely what the catechism is. Thus readers who want such a synopsis would be well-advised to follow Malachi Martin's suggestion, and "read the catechism." Suffice it to say that the arrival of this catechism on the scene has meant a ray of hope in the midst of near-despair for those of us who have tried to uphold the integrity of the Catholic faith since the 1960s.

---

[418] Zuhlsdorf, Part IV, W, 2-11-93.

Of course, it goes without saying that the catechism has not made its appearance without generating plenty of opposition from Catholic dissidents, many of them in positions of power in the Church, who have done and are doing their best (or their worst) to undermine it, as they have worked to undermine every other doctrinal initiative the Holy Father has taken in recent years. A book by Monsignor Michael J. Wrenn and Kenneth D. Whitehead (no strangers to *Wanderer* readers), entitled *Flawed Expectations: The Reception of the Catechism of the Catholic Church*, has focused on these efforts. In a lengthy review of that book, William Doino, Jr., summarized some of what it said about the history of resistance to the Catechism here in the United States:

> Initially, the dissidents tried to stop the catechism's publication altogether. They argued that the constant changes of life and thought ruled out any dependable catechism, since catechesis had to be constantly written anew to keep pace with the developing modern world. That tactic failed, however, and "once it was clear that the catechism could no longer be stopped, the focus shifted from attacking it outright to somewhat more subtle efforts to belittle its significance and usefulness for the Church of today."[419]

For example, a symposium held by the School of Religious Studies at the Catholic University of America made a show of accepting and receiving the new catechism, yet expressed so many qualifications on the need for "adaptation," "inculturation," etc. etc., that their effort, eventually published in book form, amounted to a pretty thoroughgoing trashing of the catechism. And the participants in the symposium included a substantial portion of the leadership of the Catholic Church in America. This prompted Doino to raise an obvious question in his review:

> Why has the American Catholic hierarchy allowed the implementation of the catechism in the United States to fall into

[419] William Doino, Jr., "Subverting the Catechism," W, 2-6-97.

> the hands of dissidents? Moreover, why is the "national" Catholic university, to which the faithful are asked to contribute, sponsoring and subsidizing the subversion of the Church's catechism?[420]

Of course, we all know the answer, which is that much of the hierarchy is in fact in league with the dissidents, and that those who are not are frequently so intimidated by the bureaucrats who manage their dioceses that they are unlikely to protest the undermining of the faith. As of this writing, the struggle goes on, and it is by no means certain that the powers that be in the American Church are ever going to accept the catechism. Yet Doino, in his discussion, sees grounds for hope:

> Although *Flawed Expectations* often makes for disturbing reading, there is nonetheless an element of hope running throughout it. This is because, in spite of the virulent attacks upon the catechism, its orthodox Catholic defenders are slowly winning the war over its implementation. The very fact that it was published in the first place is a sign of victory; so, too, was the catechism's immediate rise to international best-seller status — an event that shocked and infuriated its critics. Moreover, the bitter struggle over the English translation of the catechism was won, not by those who demanded "inclusive" and vague language (which would have effectively neutralized the catechism's impact in English-speaking lands), but by the Catholic faithful, who fought for, and received, an accurate translation.[421]
>
> If there is one lasting impression the reader will take away from this book it is the immutable essence of the Catholic faith. Perhaps the most frequent criticism against the catechism is that it is "outdated," "anachronistic," and even "medieval." Typical is the disdain Father Gabriel Daly, a lib-

---

[420] Ibid.
[421] Ibid.

> eral theologian from Ireland, expressed about the catechism: "Readers should prepare themselves for something of a cultural shock as they are conveyed abruptly back to the 13th century."
>
> To this sarcastic crack, Monsignor Wrenn and Whitehead reply: Precisely! It is the *glory* of the Catechism that it aims to hand down — and *does* hand down — "the Catholic faith that comes to us from the Apostles." This does not mean that the Catechism "is not also entirely up-to-date in the things it is supposed to be up-to-date on, namely, how the traditional faith that has been handed down from the time of the Apostles has also been developed and interpreted under the guidance of the Magisterium with the assistance of the Holy Spirit."[422]

The times ahead for *The Wanderer* and its readers promise to be, if nothing else, interesting ones.

Throughout the history of Judeo-Christian and even pagan thought (at least in the West), there has been, since time immemorial, a solid first principle according to which there is objective truth about reality, and the human mind is capable, however imperfectly, of knowing that truth. The rejection of that first principle by contemporary theology as well as contemporary catechetics, creates a split in the human mind and soul where previously there was a wholeness. It therefore exalts unwholeness, so it is not surprising if its results are, to put it mildly, unwholesome. The new thought creates fragmented, un-whole human beings who have lost a sense of solid selfhood, and have lost the sense of belonging to any community, earthly or heavenly, which transcends their autonomous selves and has reality for more than just the "existential moment." Even on a purely natural level, that is a catastrophe. But the new catechetics goes beyond merely natural harm, and destroys the unity between man and God that Christ created by becoming man and suffering and dying for us.

[422] Ibid.

The new methods create a Church filled with spiritual orphans, incomplete people trying to live while cut off from the very source of life, Christ Himself. That breakdown in wholeness in regard to the faith and to the intellect's grasp of the truths of faith is disastrous enough, but of course it does not stop there, but goes on to destroy the wholeness of the will. The resulting disorder will be the topic of this book's next and final Part.

PART FIVE: SPIRITUAL DISEASE

SECTION II — THE CORRUPTION OF THE WILL

And they came over unto the other side of the sea, into the country of the Gadarenes. And when he was come out of the ship, immediately there met him out of the tombs a man with an unclean spirit, who had his dwelling among the tombs; and no man could bind him, no, not with chains: Because that he had been often bound with fetters and chains, and the chains had been plucked asunder by him, and the fetters broken in pieces: neither could any man tame him. And always, night and day, he was in the mountains, and in the tombs, crying, and cutting himself with stones. But when he saw Jesus afar off, he ran and worshipped him, and cried with a loud voice, and said, What have I to do with thee, Jesus, thou Son of the most high God? I adjure thee by God, that thou torment me not. For he said unto him, Come out of the man, thou unclean spirit. And he asked him, What is thy name? And he answered, saying, My name is Legion: for we are many. And he besought him much that he would not send them away out of the country. Now there was there nigh unto the mountains a great herd of swine feeding. And all the devils besought him, saying, Send us into the swine, that we may enter into them. And forthwith Jesus gave them leave. And the unclean spirits went out, and entered into the swine: and the herd ran violently down a steep place into the sea (they were about two thousand;) and were choked in the sea.

— *Mark* 5:1-13

1. LOSS OF THE GOOD

The heresies against faith discussed in the previous chapter add up altogether to a concentrated attack upon Christian wholeness. The same can be said for the closely related heresies against Christian moral teaching. The first kind of error is an attack on Christian man's ability to know the truth; the second is an attack on his ability to *do* the truth. In the first case, we lose the wholeness to be found in the relation of the intellect to reality, to being; in the second case, we lose the right relation between the will and the good. A deep loss of human integrity occurs in both cases.

During the 1960s, we witnessed, both in secular society and in the Church, the rise of movements which denied that man can or ought to order his life in accordance with moral principles grounded in the will of God. For reasons which we may never fully understand, these movements focused their wrath on traditional Christian teachings regarding sexual morality. That is not really too surprising, because while, as we know, sexual sins are not the only or even the worst of sins, somehow the sexual impulse, more than any other human drive, is tied to community, and community is the essence of human wholeness. The sexual impulse, properly ordered, is the basis for the love between man and woman which is the foundation for the first form of human community, the family. And that sexual impulse brings about the creation of new life which is the central vocation of the family. This is not to say, as Freud and too many others have held, that sex is *the* center of human life or is its essence. Clearly, man's spiritual, intellectual nature is his essence. Yet his sexuality, if not his essence, is certainly what philosophers have called a proper accident, an accident with such close ties to the center of man's personhood that to abuse or damage it is to abuse and damage the whole human person. The sexual impulse has exceedingly close ties to that in man which draws him out of himself into relation with others. If that bond is broken, the human being ceases to have the wholeness which comes from being part of a continuing community of love, and becomes the atomistic, "autonomous" modern man, cut off from the sources of life and condemned forever to loneliness and isolation.

Because sexual morality seems to have been, with good reason, the principal focus of modern man's attack on Christian morality, an attack which has come to be known as the "sexual revolution," sexual morality will be the principal focus of this section. In it I will try to show how *The Wanderer* responded to the challenge of the sexual revolution by articulating the real meaning of Christian sexual teachings in opposition to erroneous understandings of those teachings, by warning of the human destructiveness of those errors, and by defending chastity as the way for man to recover from that destruction and return to spiritual health.

Probably the biggest error modern man makes in his understanding of Christian teaching on sexual morality is his belief that the Church's teaching in this area amounts to a set of arbitrary taboos, designed to be a sort of test of obedience. Sometimes even people who defend Christian morals seem to see it that way. Again and again, we run into people who visualize the whole situation as one in which a group of sexually starved celibates in the Vatican hands down decrees designed to prevent the rest of us from having a good time. The reality, of course, is that the law of God is not a heavy burden laid on us, either by God or by the Church. It is, on the contrary, the gift of God's loving-kindness. Obedience to that law leads to what human happiness is possible in this life, and to complete happiness in eternity. Disobedience leads to unhappiness and suffering in this world and, of course, to eternal suffering in the next. God gave us the law, not for His sake, but for ours. The rejection of the law leads to a loss of wholeness by persons and communities. Obedience rebuilds that wholeness. That is the perspective we need to start out with and stay with in this presentation.

2. THE POPE SAYS NO TO SEXUAL CHAOS

That perspective was beautifully outlined in 1976, in Pope Paul VI's document, *Declaration on Certain Questions Concerning Sexual Ethics*, a document which appeared at the height of the sexual revolution and is probably still the Church's definitive response to that revolution. What the document takes aim at in particular is the modernist notion that sexual acts, being acts that are merely of the body and thus not "spiritual," are morally indifferent. The essence of this attitude seems to be that it doesn't matter what I do with my body as long as I keep my soul pure. But that is an understanding which actually denigrates the body and denies man's wholeness as an incarnate being, an indivisible composite of body and soul, all of whose actions are fully spiritual. Pope Paul starts out by noting the tremendous breakdown in sexual morality in the late twentieth century:

> In the present period, the corruption of morals has increased, and one of the most serious indications of this corruption is the unbridled exaltation of sex. Moreover, through the means of social communication and through public entertainment this corruption has reached the point of invading the field of education and of infecting the general mentality.[423]

Much of the new thinking reflected an attitude that doing away with allegedly obsolete moral teachings would somehow enhance human freedom and dignity. Not so, says the Church:

> ...There can be no true promotion of man's dignity unless the essential order of his nature is respected. Of course, in the history of civilization many of the concrete conditions and

[423] Pope Paul VI, "Declaration on Certain Questions Concerning Sexual Ethics," W, 1-29-76.

> needs of human life have changed and will continue to change. But all evolution of morals and every type of life must be kept within the limits imposed by the immutable principles based upon every human person's constitutive elements and essential relations — elements and relations which transcend historical contingency.
>
> ...Hence, those people are in error who today assert that one can find neither in human nature nor in the revealed law any absolute and immutable norm to serve for particular actions other than the one which expresses itself in the general law of charity and respect for human dignity.[424]

"Sexual union," says the Holy Father, "therefore is only legitimate if a definitive community of life has been established between the man and the woman."[425] Violations of this principle cannot be rationalized as minor peccadilloes not related to the essence of man's spiritual life, as the modernists would like us to think. On the contrary,

> According to the Church's teaching, mortal sin, which is opposed to God, does not consist only in formal and direct resistance to the commandment of charity. It is equally to be found in this opposition to authentic love which is included in every deliberate transgression, in serious matter, of each of the moral laws.
>
> ...A person therefore sins mortally not only when his action comes from direct contempt for love of God and neighbor, but also when he consciously and freely, for whatever reason, chooses something which is seriously disordered. For in this choice...there is already included contempt for the divine commandment: the person turns himself away from God and loses charity. Now according to Christian tradition and the Church's teaching, and as right reason also recognizes, *the moral order of sexuality involves such high values of human*

---

[424] Ibid.

[425] Ibid.

> *life that every direct violation of this order is objectively serious* [Italics added].[426]

That is a genuinely humanistic statement, one fully consistent with the document's affirmation that "chastity is not a negation of sexuality; it is a way of placing the God-given gift of sex in the context of a full, mature human life, rooted in respect for oneself, others, and the law of God."[427] It is the sexual libertines, not the Church, whose views attack the dignity and goodness of the human person.

[426] Ibid.
[427] Ibid.

3. THE *HUMAN SEXUALITY* DISASTER

It took little time for the enemies of that teaching to make their countermove, in the form of a study commissioned by the Catholic Theological Society of America, published in 1977 under the title, *Human Sexuality*. That study, the work of several authors but under the overall direction of Father Anthony Kosnik, was a virulent attack on virtually any attempt to see as gravely sinful any human sexual act whatsoever. It was even inclined to take a benign view of bestiality, under some circumstances. The only moral principle that the CTSA study recognized was one that it called "the fundamental principle of creative growth toward integration," one that could be used to justify almost anything. The study concluded that such acts as fornication, adultery, abortion, contraception, homosexual relations, and so on *ad nauseam*, could be done at will provided, of course, that they were done "responsibly" and with an eye toward "creative growth toward integration," conditions which the doers of these acts can always find to be present if they feel called upon to justify their actions at all.[428]

The *Human Sexuality* study has to be one of the great cases of Satan overplaying his hand. The study was so utterly lacking in any subtlety in its attack on Christian moral teachings that it could not help arousing wrath from many quarters. Here is how Father Albert J. Nevins, in a June, 1977 article, sums up the study:

> There is an insufferable pride in this book that is both aggravating and frustrating. They write: "From St. Paul through St. Thomas to our own day and the 1975 *Vatican Declaration on Sexual Ethics*, Catholic tradition has consistently judged all homosexual acts against nature." Against all that authority the group comes up with the verdict: "It is our considered

---

[428] A.J. Matt, Jr., "The Coming 'Catholic' Assault on Chastity," W, 6-2-77.

> opinion that Christian sexual morality does not require a dual standard." Therefore, what is permitted to married couples is to be allowed to the unmarried and to homosexuals. Why? They write: "God is present in homosexual relationships." They settle the birth control problem by saying: "The decision to use artificial methods of contraception is both morally responsible and justified." Masturbation is a matter of "prudent choice of values" and to impute any moral malice to the act is nonsense. Regarding transsexualism: "It seems unrealistic to reject this procedure as totally unacceptable because it involves the mutilation of healthy organs." Mention any aberration and it can find some factor to diminish moral culpability.[429]

Monsignor John F. McCarthy played a major role in *The Wanderer*'s response to the CTSA study when he wrote a series of articles on the topic, "Human Sexuality: Theology or Pornology?" A review of his study will do much to clarify what was at stake in this debate.

A key point in McCarthy's critique is that the CTSA study exhibits radical subjectivism on moral principles, probably the deepest subjectivism to be found at that point in moral ideas purporting to be Catholic. It is the very nature of subjectivism to be profoundly opposed to any real human community, just as it is the nature of genuinely Christian moral teaching to support and build up community. The CTSA study, like so much of the "new morality," tries to make conscience the basis of morality. Yet its idea of conscience and the Church's could not be further apart:

> The CTSA report on *Human Sexuality* makes subjective conscience the ultimate criterion for the moral evaluation of sexual conduct. "The well-formed individual conscience responsive to principles, values, and guidelines remains the ultimate subjective source for evaluating the morality of par-

---

[429] Father Albert J. Nevins, "Church Authority Cannot Let the CTSA's 'Human Sexuality' Go Unchallenged," W, 6-30-77.

> ticular sexual expressions...." By principles, the CTSA means exclusively "the fundamental principle of creative growth toward integration that ought to guide all sexual activity."
>
> ...Traditional moral teaching has always acknowledged that the well-formed individual conscience is the subjective norm of moral evaluation. Where it differs from the CTSA approach is in its realization that the well-formed conscience is a conscience formed by an intellectual awareness of objective law. Adam and Eve were left to decide for themselves whether or not to eat the forbidden fruit, but, in choosing to eat it, they sinned against the law of God.
>
> ...The "well-formed conscience" of the CTSA report is the sensuous human individual choosing his own subjective good according to the principle of "creative growth toward integration," which...is nothing more elevated than the unbridled urge to sexual pleasure and genital union.[430]

The modernist conscience is the conscience of the isolated, lust-focused self; the Christian conscience is the conscience of the self rooted in the universal community of redeemed mankind under God, and hence focused on love.

McCarthy goes on to note that the CTSA report not only seems to see no sexual act as sinful in and of itself, but actually goes to the blasphemous extreme of holding that God actually wills and affirms the goodness of acts the Church always previously considered gravely evil:

> [The CTSA study] does not hesitate to illustrate its position by quoting a blasphemy against the Son of God contained in the affirmation that "the *logos* is already incarnate in the sexual impulse," and then calling this blasphemy an expression of "behavioral science." This reducing of the Incarnation to "the sexual impulse" is also a blasphemy against the Spirit of

[430] Monsignor John F. McCarthy, "Moral Evaluation," W, 1-5-78.

> Holiness; it is the essence of the impurity and repugnance to God contained in the pagan fertility rites. Such flagrant lack of Christian sensitivity to the offensiveness of sexual blasphemy shows how little the authors-approvers of the report comprehend or even want to comprehend the spirit of divine Revelation, the holiness of God, the sinfulness of eros-oriented man, and the antireligious, neopagan, and diabolical tendencies of the "will of the flesh" left to prosper on its own. "Do not be deceived: God is not mocked. For what a man sows, that will he also reap. For he who sows in the flesh, from the flesh also will reap corruption. But he who sows in the spirit, from the spirit will reap life everlasting" (*Gal*. 6:7-8).[431]

Of course, the Logos *is* in some sense present in the sexual impulse as God created it; but the authors of the CTSA study are in effect saying that the Logos is present in the disordered sexual impulse created by sin, that God is present in human lust and concupiscence, a terrible blasphemy indeed.

McCarthy also brings home the gnostic essence of the CTSA's idea of sexuality, an idea which radically separates sexual pleasure from procreation and hence from family life and community, once again trying to condemn modern man to a life of alienation and imprisonment within the autonomous self:

> When the CTSA tells us that "in humans, bodily presence in the world has transcended the facticity of the male-female dichotomy" as well as "the notion of complementarity based on gender"...it does not mean that men and women rise above their sexual complementarity in the common and equal exercise of intellectual understanding and spiritual insight. In that sense, for the CTSA "we are [only] our bodies." What the CTSA authorship means is that human beings are capable

[431] Monsignor John F. McCarthy, "Sexo-Biblical Blasphemy and Homophobia," W, 3-9-78.

> of expressing their sexuality outside of its procreative purpose by the "autonomous" practices of masturbation, homosexual intercourse, and copulation outside the species.
> ...The real reason, then, why the CTSA authorship thinks that the homosexual condition is irreversible is because it does not want the homosexual to change his condition as long as he derives phallic fulfillment from it. All the talk about "empirical data" is mere camouflage for an irrational infatuation with the thought of sexual pleasure, by force of which no proper attention is given to the latent power of all concerned — be they authors, approvers, or general practitioners of sexual license — to make use of their God-given freedom to withdraw from erotic excitement and dry their minds out.[432]

The denial that the division of mankind into men and women is in any way fundamental to the structure of the world, is a denial of the goodness of God's creation as radical as any we might encounter among sexual puritans, but here the denial is used to support the doctrine that anything goes. Reality is filled with strange paradoxes, indeed.

The *Human Sexuality* study, Monsignor McCarthy makes clear, is as anti-human and anti-Christian as anything could possibly be, and hence Catholics have a serious obligation to reject it *in toto*:

> Catholic ecclesiastical documents are unanimous in rejecting the sexual permissiveness reflected in the CTSA report, not only with regard to homosexuality, but in all areas of sexuality....Catholic teaching has, indeed, always given explicit recognition to the value of the human person, but Catholic teaching has never submerged the objective values of Christian marriage in the subjective sensuality which the CTSA report identifies with the core of the human person....

---

[432] Monsignor John F. McCarthy, "Bards of a Homosexual Utopia," W, 3-30-78.

> *Human Sexuality* has been published under the auspices of a Catholic theological society, but it is not a Catholic book. It is anti-Catholic, anti-Christian, and anti-biblical. It is the responsibility of every believer to reject this book, mentally and vocally, firmly and constantly, until its evil influence is no more. And it is the responsibility of the Church to lead the way in this exercise of Christian virtue by not allowing pornology to sit in the chair of moral theology.[433]

In August, 1979, the Sacred Congregation for the Doctrine of the Faith, in a letter by its prefect, Franjo Cardinal Seper, entitled "Observations on the Book 'Human Sexuality,'" strongly seconded Monsignor McCarthy's recommendations, condemning the CTSA study not only for its gross immorality but for the intellectual dishonesty and, at times, outright fraudulence of its arguments. The letter notes, among other things, that the study manipulates definitions of sexuality, failing to distinguish between our generic sexuality (that is, the fact that each of us is either a man or a woman, and that men and women are complementary) and genital sexuality. But the moral issues it deals with relate to genital, not generic, sexuality, so that, by failing to distinguish the two concepts, the study's attempts to deal with moral issues create great confusion:

> It is not, however, in this area of generic sexuality that the moral problematic of chastity is engaged. This occurs rather within the more specific field of sexual being and behavior called *genital* sexuality, which, while existing within the field of generic sexuality, has its specific rules corresponding to its proper structure and finality.[434]

---

433 Monsignor John F. McCarthy, "The Responsibility of the Church," W, 5-18-78.

434 "'Observations on the Book "Human Sexuality"' by the Sacred Congregation for the Doctrine of the Faith," W, 8-23-79.

The letter goes on to reject the study's claim that the Second Vatican Council got rid of the traditional hierarchy by which the procreative ends of marriage take precedence over other ends:

> In the view of sexuality described in *Human Sexuality*, the formulation of its purpose undergoes a substantial change with respect to the classical formulation: the traditional "procreative and unitive purpose" of sexuality, consistently developed in all the magisterial documents through Vatican II and *Humanae Vitae*, is substituted by a "creative and integrative purpose," also called "creative growth toward integration," which describes a broad and vague purpose applicable to any generic sexuality (and practically to any human action). Admitting that procreation is only one possible form of creativity, but not essential to sexuality...is a gratuitous change in the accepted terms without any substantial argument, a change which contradicts the formulation used in Vatican II and assumed in *Persona Humana*. This change in purpose and consequently of the criteria for morality in human sexuality evidently changes all the traditional conclusions about sexual behavior; it even precludes the possibility of fruitful theological discussion by removing the common terminology.[435]

Disorder does have this way of creating confusion. Cardinal Seper's letter shows clearly how the radical subjectivism of *Human Sexuality* leads to conceptual chaos:

> The authors pretend that these are not purely subjective criteria, though in fact they are: the personal judgments about these factors are so different, determined by personal sentiments, feelings, customs, etc., that it would be next to impossible to single out definite criteria of what exactly integrates a particular person or contributes to his or her creative growth in any specific sexual activity....The authors nearly

[435] Ibid.

> always find a way to allow for integrative growth through the neglect or destruction of some intrinsic element of sexual morality, particularly its procreative ordination. And if some forms of sexual conduct are disapproved, it is only because of the supposed absence, generally expressed in the form of doubt, of "human integration" (as in swinging, mate-swapping, bestiality), and not because these actions are opposed to the nature of human sexuality. When some action is considered completely immoral, it is never for intrinsic reasons, on the basis of objective finality, but only because the authors happen not to see, for their part, any way of making it so for some human integration. This subjection of theological and scientific arguments to evaluation by criteria primarily derived from one's present experience of what is human or less than human gives rise to a relativism in human conduct which recognizes no absolute values. Given these criteria, it is small wonder that this book pays such scant attention to the documents of the Church's Magisterium, whose clear teaching and helpful norms of morality in the area of human sexuality it often openly contradicts.[436]

And here we see the central contradiction. The CTSA study points to human integration as its criterion for morality. Integration basically means the establishment of wholeness, yet when we get anywhere near the CTSA type of moral teaching, all we ever find is confusion, chaos, *dis*integration. The new morality does not promote, but destroys, human wholeness and hence Christian wholeness.

---

[436] Ibid.

4. THE HOMOSEXUAL MOVEMENT

Perhaps nowhere has this proven to be truer than in the movement to justify and legitimate homosexual behavior, a movement which began in liberal Catholic circles in the sixties and picked up steam during the seventies and eighties. The contradiction is pretty total between a movement which claims that it seeks human integration and a lifestyle, homosexuality, which leads to the disintegration and destruction of the human person. Scripture leaves little doubt about the human destructiveness of homosexual behavior:

> Because of this, God gave them over to shameful lusts. Even their women exchanged natural relations for unnatural ones. In the same way the men also abandoned natural relations with women and were inflamed with lust for one another. Men committed indecent acts with other men, and received in themselves the due penalty for their perversion. Furthermore, since they did not think it worthwhile to retain the knowledge of God, he gave them over to a depraved mind, to do what ought not to be done. They have become filled with every kind of wickedness, evil, greed, and depravity. They are full of envy, murder, strife, deceit, and malice. They are gossips, slanderers, God-haters, insolent, arrogant, and boastful; they invent ways of doing evil; they disobey their parents; they are senseless, faithless, heartless, ruthless. Although they know God's righteous decree that those who do such things deserve death, they not only continue to do these very things but also approve of those who practice them. (*Romans* 1:26-32)

This is hardly a picture of "creative growth toward integration," and hardly describes the idyllic, unrepressed existence which the promoters of the new morality want us to think is located somewhere at the end of the rainbow. It is a picture of hell on earth, and that is the real state of those who practice the homosexual lifestyle. In somewhat more modern, less passionate language, Pope Paul VI has stated much the same thing in his *Declaration on Certain Questions Concerning Sexual Ethics*, already cited above:

> In the pastoral field, these homosexuals must certainly be treated with understanding and sustained in the hope of overcoming their personal difficulties and their inability to fit into society. Their culpability will be judged with prudence. But no pastoral method can be employed which would give moral justification to these acts on the grounds that they would be consonant with the condition of such people. For according to the objective moral law, homosexual relations are acts which lack an essential and indispensable finality. In Sacred Scripture they are condemned as a serious depravity and even presented as the sad consequence of rejecting God. This judgment of Scripture does not of course permit us to conclude that all those who suffer from this anomaly are personally responsible for it, but it does attest to the fact that homosexual acts are intrinsically disordered and can in no case be approved of.[437]

Wholeness is, among other things, order, the proper organization and direction of human acts and faculties toward man's end. Actions which are disordered, which involve a deviation from man's end, can, by definition, only create disorder, and hence unwholeness, disintegration.

If homosexual acts create disorder in the life of the individual, then it is to be expected that, to the extent that these acts come to be tolerated and even protected as "rights" by civil society, they will promote social disorder. Yet that is exactly what the promoters of "happy, holy homosexuality" (!), inside or outside the Church, seek.

[437] Pope Paul VI, "Declaration on Certain Questions Concerning Sexual Ethics," W, 1-29-76.

Plato said that the polis is man writ large, that a society reflects the souls of the human beings who make it up. If a society allows itself to be built on the moral and spiritual disorder of many of its members, if it allows that disorder to be institutionalized, as the "gay rights" people demand, that will mean the destruction of the social order. This aspect of the issue was the focus for a debate in June, 1980, in the pages of *The Wanderer*, between John Mulloy and Father Robert Nugent, a proponent of "civil rights" for homosexuals. That controversy was ignited by a statement issued by a group called the Catholic Coalition for Gay Civil Rights, a group which sought, as does all the homosexual lobby, to equate "gay" demands for rights with the demands made by historically oppressed groups such as blacks for equal rights. Father Nugent made the claim, also rather common to Catholic pro-homosexual groups at that time, that this movement in no way entailed the denial of Catholic moral teaching on homosexuality, a claim which was itself largely disintegrated once Mulloy got through with it. Father Nugent maintained that

> The coalition statement carefully and deliberately avoids taking any particular moral-theological position on the question of the morality of homosexual activity. The signers are well aware of the Church's traditional teaching in this area. Nevertheless, the signers feel that the related issues of human-civil rights and sexual morality can be distinguished much the same way that Catholic social policy treats other questions involving morality and legality in a pluralistic society. Defending and fostering the human and civil rights of homosexual people is not necessarily making any statement about the morality of homosexual behavior any more than guaranteeing justice in law for divorced people is to foster or condone divorce. Asserting the equality of homosexual persons *as persons* in laws about housing, employment, and immigration is not necessarily putting society's stamp of approval on what these people do or refrain from doing in their personal lives.

> ...In the case of employment and "gay rights" there can arise, especially in a teaching situation, a certain apparent conflict of rights between the rights of the gay person and the rights of the parents. This is a complex issue and while it might not involve the myth of child molestation (which Mulloy utilizes) it might involve the issue of role modeling and, in any case, needs much more study.[438]

Basically, Nugent is trying to separate the private moral issue of homosexual behavior from the public moral issue of human rights supposedly inhering in homosexuals as a group. But Catholic social teaching has never made such a distinction but rather, as we have already noted, sees social disorder as rooted in individual moral and spiritual disorder. Mulloy points to the inseparability of these two issues in suggesting that the actual effect of gay civil rights laws would be positively to encourage and support antisocial homosexual behavior, just as laws permitting abortion have had the actual effect of promoting the murder of the unborn:

> The propaganda on behalf of an "oppressed" group — on behalf of mothers wanting an abortion and not being able to procure it — has completely changed the legal structure of our society so as to give support to the murder of the unborn child. Would not the same thing happen with regard to homosexuality?
>
> ...Male homosexuals are not satisfied with consenting adults, but have a natural tendency to engage in homosexual intercourse with youths and young boys. Will "gay civil rights" give the homosexuals a greater opportunity to satisfy these desires?[439]

---

[438] Father Robert Nugent, "Homosexual Behavior and Civil Rights," W, 6-12-80.

[439] John J. Mulloy, "The Case Against 'Gay Civil Rights' Laws," W, 6-12-80.

If a society is to survive, in Mulloy's view, it cannot remain neutral on central matters of right order:

> ...[Father Nugent] disregards the fact that there is a moral consensus upon which every society depends — a consensus which determines its essential character. A society in which homosexuality is given the active support of the laws — the government interfering at federal and local levels to see to it that the homosexuals get their "rights" — will be a different kind of society from one in which normal sexuality sets the standards and defines the ethos which governs the relations between the sexes....Father Nugent's justification of his stand on the basis of how "Catholic social policy treats other questions involving morality and legality in a pluralistic society" is very much in line with the defense that other Catholic priests make in connection with abortion. They tell us we don't need to consider the morality or immorality of abortion — or of homosexuality — because a pluralistic society is the overarching good to which every moral issue must bow....Can the common good of society be achieved by disregarding the moral law of God?[440]

Countering Father Nugent's insinuation that child molestation by homosexuals is largely mythical, Mulloy points out that

> ...a considerable percentage of male child molestation by homosexuals does take place today, when social disapproval and laws are still strong against this sort of offense. Once the bars of disapproval are removed, conditions will favor a great increase in male child molestation. Father Nugent would have us ignore the reality of what is already happening and what that points to in the future once homosexual practice is seen as merely an alternative lifestyle, and when the rights of the "gays" are promoted by government decree. The existence of the powerful and coordinated political constituency,

[440] Ibid.

> referred to by *U.S. News & World Report*, will make it most difficult, once the government is promoting homosexual "rights," to maintain present attitudes of social deterrence against male child molestation.[441]

In the final analysis, in Mulloy's view, the effort to separate the moral issue of homosexuality from the issue of social policy creates only confusion, confusion that could have most unfortunate consequences:

> What Father Nugent has to decide, as he pursues his New Ways Ministry, is just what *new ways* he has in mind. He has to make clear to himself and to others whether he intends to canonize homosexual intercourse as a legitimate form of sexual union. Or is his ministry to be one of drawing homosexuals back to a life lived in accordance with the teachings of the Gospel and the Catholic Church? If he leaves himself in his present ambivalent attitude, he can be a force of great spiritual disaster for those to whom he ministers.[442]

Father Robert E. Burns, a weekly *Wanderer* columnist during these years, regularly made a point of calling attention to the chaos created by homosexuality on the level of the common good of the community. In a 1983 article, in which he commented on the unspeakable organization known as NAMBLA, the North American Man-Boy Love Association, which promotes the legalization of child molestation, Father Burns summed up the issue this way:

> Homosexuals are entitled to exercise their rights, providing they do not jeopardize the safety and well-being of others. However, parents have every right to be concerned about the moral character of those who teach their children. Teachers influence children in more ways than the material contained in textbooks. Homosexual actions involve moral depravity

---

[441] Ibid.

[442] Ibid.

> and homosexuals have a tendency to draw younger people into their sphere of domination. Furthermore, as every criminologist and psychologist must know, homosexual encounters frequently lead to violence....
>
> The shocking increase in homosexual activity in this country is simply further evidence of our decadent society. But God will not be mocked. Perhaps the alarming spread of herpes is just the first warning He is going to give us. Let us fight to protect our children from these moral perverts.[443]

Unfortunately, despite the best efforts of *Wanderer* commentators, confusion was the norm throughout these post-Vatican II years when it came to the issue of homosexuality. "Catholic" pro-homosexual groups tended to promote confusion by their insistence that they existed only in order to help Catholics with homosexual orientation to live Christian lives. But even a casual look at the literature of groups like Dignity and New Ways Ministry, or an hour spent listening to one of their speakers, leaves one in little doubt that they are actually promoting homosexual behavior. As Father Burns pointed out in a 1979 article:

> Some draw a comparison between Alcoholics Anonymous and organizations like Dignity. While there are some similarities, there is one very important vital difference. It is that AA does not and has never condoned or encouraged alcoholism. On the other hand, organizations like Dignity do condone homosexual conduct and demand that it be accepted, not only by the state, but also by the Church, as an alternate lifestyle.[444]

---

[443] Father Robert E. Burns, "Enter NAMBLA," W, 1-27-83.
[444] Father Robert E. Burns, "Understanding 'Dignity,'" W, 11-29-79.

5. THE CHURCH'S RESPONSE TO MILITANT SODOMY

Sadly, the response to the pro-homosexual movement by the Catholic Church in America has, for the most part, ranged from weak to positively supportive. In a March, 1983 article, James Sterling Corum took Archbishop William D. Borders of Baltimore to task for his support of gay rights legislation, going so far as to offer him the "Golden Calf Award" for his activities. In doing so, Corum brought out what was to be a crucial distinction between the compassion and charity Christians owe to homosexuals as human beings, and the kind of false compassion which pro-homosexual social policies embody:

> Since homosexuality is indeed a psychological problem it is certainly cruel and uncharitable to call homosexuals names or to abuse them. Although homosexuality *is* a sin and the people who accept it do so out of their own free will, the psychological factor may be an important extenuating circumstance. Homosexuals have genuine problems and many of them need counseling and proper psychological help. If Archbishop Borders had established a counseling program to help homosexuals, many of whom have had tragic family experiences, it would have been in the Catholic tradition of caring for those with personal problems.
>
> Unfortunately, Archbishop Borders and his ministry to the gays seem unable or unwilling to explain the full teaching of the Church. The Catholic Church emphasizes the importance of the family. God intended man and woman to become one and to create a family. The sexual sins that the Church denounces, including adultery, abortion, and homosexuality,

> are all actions that tend to destroy the family and, hence, God's plan for mankind.
>
> But, ministering to groups is quite different from ministering to individuals. The homosexual organizations, including the ones that call themselves Catholic, advocate and support a lifestyle that is contrary to the teaching of the Church.[445]

Unfortunately, that response was not by and large what American Catholics, looking for guidance on this issue, got from their bishops, though there were honorable exceptions —John Cardinal O'Connor of New York, for example. Happily, after some years of discussion, Rome did finally issue what is probably the teaching Church's definitive response to the moral questions raised by homosexuality and homosexual behavior, in the form of a *Letter to Bishops of the Catholic Church on the Pastoral Care of Homosexual Persons*, prepared by Joseph Cardinal Ratzinger. That response focused strongly on the distinction between homosexual behavior, which is always evil, and homosexual orientation, which may not always be morally evil:

> In the discussion which followed the publication of the *Declaration [on Certain Questions Concerning Sexual Ethics]*, however, an overly benign interpretation was given to the homosexual condition itself, some going so far as to call it neutral, or even good. Although the particular inclination of the homosexual person is not a sin, it is a more or less strong tendency ordered toward an intrinsic moral evil; and thus the inclination itself must be seen as an objective disorder.
>
> Therefore special concern and pastoral attention should be directed toward those who have this condition, lest they be

[445] James Sterling Corum, "Borders of Baltimore Appeases the Homosexual Network," W, 3-3-83.

> led to believe that the living out of this orientation in homosexual activity is a morally acceptable option. It is not.[446]

Cardinal Ratzinger went on to summarize the biblical teaching on homosexuality, and then showed why the Church's teaching on this subject follows necessarily from her teaching on the nature and purpose of sexuality:

> The Church, obedient to the Lord who founded her and gave to her the sacramental life, celebrates the divine plan of the loving and life-giving union of men and women in the Sacrament of Marriage. It is only in the marital relationship that the use of the sexual faculty can be morally good. A person engaging in homosexual behavior therefore acts immorally.
>
> To choose someone of the same sex for one's sexual activity is to annul the rich symbolism and meaning, not to mention the goals, of the Creator's sexual design. Homosexual activity is not a complementary union, able to transmit life; and so it thwarts the call to a life of that form of self-giving which the Gospel says is the essence of Christian living. This does not mean that homosexual persons are not often generous and giving of themselves; but when they engage in homosexual activity they confirm within themselves a disordered sexual inclination which is essentially self-indulgent.
>
> As in every moral disorder, homosexual activity prevents one's own fulfillment and happiness by acting contrary to the creative wisdom of God. The Church, in rejecting erroneous opinions regarding homosexuality, does not limit but rather defends personal freedom and dignity realistically and authentically understood.[447]

This analysis brings out, I believe, what was said earlier: that the law of God is not a set of arbitrary taboos which God, for unknown rea-

[446] "Letter to Bishops of the Catholic Church on the Pastoral Care of Homosexual Persons," W, 11-27-86.

[447] Ibid.

sons, has decided to impose on us, but is the gift of His loving-kindness, a gift given us for the sake of our happiness, not to thwart it. A look at the tremendous unhappiness and misery of so many homosexuals certainly confirms this point, a point Cardinal Ratzinger makes even clearer when he goes on to discuss the duties of homosexuals who wish to live Christian lives:

> What, then, are homosexual persons to do who seek to follow the Lord? Fundamentally, they are called to enact the will of God in their life by joining whatever sufferings and difficulties they experience in virtue of their condition to the sacrifice of the Lord's cross. That cross, for the believer, is a fruitful sacrifice since from that death come life and redemption. While any call to carry the cross or to understand a Christian's suffering in this way will predictably be met with bitter ridicule by some, it should be remembered that this is the way to eternal life for *all* who follow Christ.[448]

Thus, the Church is not calling homosexuals uniquely to suffering, but is calling all to eternal life, regardless of sexual orientation or any other characteristic. In the light of what the Cardinal is saying here, it should be clear that any support by the Church for groups which claim that homosexual behavior is morally acceptable runs counter to this purpose, this call to eternal life. Church support for homosexual acts would be analogous to a doctor telling a cancer victim that cancer is good for him and need not be treated. That approach may give a temporary illusion of compassion, but in fact condemns the person to suffering and death. That is why the Church needs to avoid even the appearance of condoning homosexual acts:

> All support should be withdrawn from any organizations which seek to undermine the teaching of the Church, which are ambiguous about it, or which neglect it entirely. Such support, or even the semblance of such support, can be gravely misinterpreted.

[448] Ibid.

> Special attention should be given to the practice of scheduling religious services and to the use of Church buildings by these groups, including the facilities of Catholic schools and colleges. To some, such permission to use Church property may seem only just and charitable; but in reality it is contradictory to the purpose for which these institutions were founded, it is misleading and often scandalous.[449]

And that is where the American Catholic debate on homosexuality still stands today, with the liberal Catholic press (the *National Catholic Reporter*, for instance) loudly and belligerently attacking Cardinal Ratzinger's teaching, while *Wanderer* commentators at least as consistently (and, some might say, loudly and belligerently) speak out in support of that teaching. Sadly, Catholic parishes and dioceses in many places continue to give more or less active aid and comfort to homosexual groups like Dignity, allowing them the use of Church buildings for meetings, having special Masses for them, etc. But as long as the prophetic witness of "Papist" Catholics like those who read and write *The Wanderer* continues, there is hope.

[449] Ibid.

6. FATHER CURRAN — THE LITTLE POPE

Readers who have struggled through the earlier chapters of this account will remember that, at the height of the debate over contraception in the 1960s, a certain Father Charles Curran, a theology professor at Catholic University of America, played a leading role in the rejection of Catholic teaching on this issue by liberal Catholics. His involvement led to his dismissal from the university faculty, making him, briefly, a martyr in many people's minds. The uproar over his dismissal was so tremendous that, after a short time, the university was intimidated and rehired him. A similar drama was played out in the 1980's, though this time with a different ending. This time, Rome, rather than the university, took disciplinary action against Curran. This second Curran episode became enough of a watershed event in the conflict over Catholic moral teaching as to deserve some attention here.

Following an extensive investigation of Father Curran's writings, Cardinal Ratzinger, in September, 1985, wrote to him to the effect that "in the correspondence exchanged between yourself and this congregation, you have clearly affirmed that the positions you have maintained on various important elements of moral doctrine are in open conflict with the teachings of the Magisterium...."[450] Ratzinger went on to review Father Curran's views on birth control, sterilization, abortion, euthanasia, masturbation, premarital intercourse, the indissolubility of marriage, and homosexual acts, making it clear that in all these areas Curran's views contradicted the clear teaching of the Magisterium. He then summed up with the statement that

> In light of the indispensable requirements for authentic theological instruction, described by the Council and by the

---

[450] "The Present Situation Cannot be Allowed to Continue," W, 3-20-86.

> public law of the Catholic Church..., the congregation now invites you to reconsider and to retract those positions which violate the conditions necessary for a professor to be called a Catholic theologian. It must be recognized that the authorities of the Church cannot allow the present situation to continue in which the inherent contradiction is prolonged that one who is to teach in the name of the Church in fact denies her teaching.[451]

The letter concluded by giving Father Curran two months to reconsider and reply before a final decision was made. Of course, by the 1980s, America was filled with "Catholic" theologians who shared all of Father Curran's erroneous views on moral questions, but what made this incident a crucial one was the fact that Curran was teaching at a Catholic university with a specific commission from Rome to teach Catholic doctrine. That meant that teachers of theology at the university were licensed by Rome to teach. It was clearly inappropriate for a professor like Curran to be licensed by Rome to teach ideas that contradicted Roman teaching.

On March 11, 1986, Father Curran held a press conference in Washington, in the course of which he released the text of a statement defending his position. Here are some highlights of that statement:

> The core of the difference between the congregation and myself concerns the legitimacy of dissent from authoritative, *noninfallible* Church teaching. Note clearly that *I do not disagree with any dogmas or defined truths of the Catholic faith.* [Italics added]
>
> ...At times it is legitimate for a Roman Catholic to dissent in theory and in practice from noninfallible Church teaching. This position has been proposed by many world-acclaimed Roman Catholic theologians such as Karl Rahner, Yves Congar, Bernard Haring. In addition, many United States Roman

[451] Ibid.

> Catholic theologians such as Avery Dulles, Richard McBrien, Richard McCormick, David Tracy, and many others have accepted the possibility in theory and in practice for a Catholic and a Catholic theologian to dissent from noninfallible Church teaching.
>
> ...It is unjust to single me out for disciplinary action of any type when so many other Catholic theologians hold the same basic position. In fact, within the Roman Catholic theological community I am looked upon as a moderate, and there are many people who hold positions much more radical than mine.
>
> ...A disciplinary action taken by Rome which directly affects the status of a professor in a Catholic university in the United States is a violation of the academic freedom, autonomy, and integrity of that institution.[452]

It is a little scary to us reactionaries to hear Father Curran say that in the eyes of most of his colleagues he is a moderate. What would a radical be? Someone who advocates cannibalism, maybe. People concerned about remaining sane will not pursue the question further. One point, however, on which Father Curran is no doubt correct is his feeling that it is a little unfair to single him out for disciplinary action, since his positions are widely held today by "Catholic" theologians. The moral of the story, however, is not that he should not be disciplined, but that we should hang them all.

So much for the fantasies of the orthodox. The crucial issue in regard to Curran's teaching, however, is his insistence that he is not contradicting any *infallible* teachings of the Church. At least one *Wanderer* commentator, John Mulloy, unmasked this as a sophistry:

> What this argument implies is that the Church does not speak with infallible authority on any moral matter, but only on matters of divine revelation. It also means that unless a sol-

[452] "Curran Attempts to Justify His Dissent," W, 3-20-86.

> emn definition of doctrine is handed down, we do not have a teaching which binds the Catholic conscience.
>
> The first thing to recognize is that the kind of infallible teaching which Father Curran is willing to accept has been given only rarely, and then almost always on matters of faith rather than morality. If this argument held up, there would be no moral teaching of the Catholic Church which could not be called into question and made a matter of doubt. Thus the Catholic could practice contraception, masturbation, fornication, adultery, homosexuality, or any other transgression of the moral law, without falling under the penalties of deliberate violation of God's Commandments.
>
> In fact, however, Father Curran overlooks — conveniently for himself — the ordinary Magisterium of the Church — that which the Catholic Church has taught consistently over the centuries concerning the precepts of morality.[453]

And this is really the central issue of the whole Curran case: Does the Church have the right to teach authoritatively on matters of morality?

It is interesting to note that, fairly early in this dispute, the Catholic Theological Society of America (CTSA) came out in support of Father Curran. That is the same CTSA that brought us the study *Human Sexuality.* Hardly an astonishing, though certainly a revolting, development. John Mulloy was quick to comment on the situation:

> So Catholics need not think that the society's approval of Father Curran means anything more than an illustration of group-think on the part of people who have already committed themselves to a degraded — and degrading — conception of human sexuality. It reminds one of the incident in the Gospel where the Gadarene swine plunged down the slope

---

[453] John J. Mulloy, "The Fallible Arguments of Father Charles Curran," W, 4-3-86.

> into the lake to drown there, once the demons had been allowed to enter them. The basic question is whether the theologians of the CTSA will be able to take the rest of the Catholic Church in America down with them, as they continue their own plunge to destruction.[454]

On August 18, 1986, the Holy See officially announced its decision to revoke Father Curran's license to teach Catholic theology. The fact that Cardinal Ratzinger received over 10,000 postcards from *Wanderer* readers against Father Curran contributed, one would like to think, to this outcome. Ratzinger's letter confirmed Rome's decision and pointed out that, contrary to Curran's position, the ordinary Magisterium can teach infallibly without solemn definition:

> In any case, the faithful must accept not only the infallible Magisterium; they are to give the religious submission of intellect and will to the teaching which the Supreme Pontiff or the college of bishops enunciate on faith or morals when they exercise the authentic Magisterium — even if they do not intend to proclaim it with a definitive act. This you have continued to refuse to do.[455]

Cardinal Ratzinger went on to respond to Father Curran's claim that he had not been allowed to confront his accusers:

> ...You publicly claim that you were never told who your accusers were. The congregation based its inquiry exclusively on your published works and on your personal responses to its observations. In effect, then, your own works have been your accusers and they alone.[456]

On the basis of those works, Rome reached its decision on Curran's role as a Catholic theologian:

---

[454] John J. Mulloy, "What Kind of Theologians Support Father Curran?" W, 7-24-86.
[455] "'Not Suitable nor Eligible to Teach Catholic Theology,'" W, 8-28-86.
[456] Ibid.

> In light of your repeated refusal to accept what the Church teaches and in light of its mandate to promote and safeguard the Church's teaching on faith and morals throughout the Catholic world, this congregation, in agreement with the Congregation for Catholic Education, sees no alternative now but to advise the Most Reverend Chancellor that you will no longer be considered suitable nor eligible to exercise the function of a professor of Catholic theology.[457]

Of course, it is one thing for a theologian to be condemned by Rome — it is another thing altogether for that theologian to actually lose his influence and social power among a particular nation's Catholics. It thus rested with the authorities in the American Church to decide how much actual power Father Curran was to continue exercising, something Frank Morriss pointed out at the time, in an article aptly titled "A Flash Point in the Growing Civil War Within the Church":

> Curran can still carry the day (though never the war itself) unless he is faced with a united front of authority. If that united front is presented I am confident there is enough Catholicity left in much of the laity to bring the hierarchy a host of defenders and save the Church in the U.S. If the hierarchy falters now, or simply retreats into neutrality or indecision, there will be no saving of what is left of the true Catholic faith in America.[458]

Fortunately, Archbishop James Hickey of Washington, D.C., supported Rome, and Father Curran was removed from the CU faculty.[459] He of course continues to exercise a great deal of influence in liberal Catholic circles in the United States, especially given his new role as a martyr of the modernist Church. But at least the line was

[457] Ibid.

[458] Frank Morriss, "A Flash Point in the Growing Civil War Within the Church," W, 8-28-86.

[459] David Wagner, "Archbishop Hickey and the Curran Case," W, 9-11-86.

held to the extent that Rome was supported in denying a heretical theologian's right to teach as a Catholic theologian in a university with a special charter from Rome to teach Catholic and only Catholic doctrine. The fact that this line had to be held at all, however, is ample proof of the spiritual disease infecting the American Church when it comes to moral theology and especially to sexual morality. This disease has now spread far beyond the departments of theology where it could be discussed abstractly by professors, and has invaded the Church at her most vulnerable point, her children, as we shall see.

7. *VERITATIS SPLENDOR*: THE POPE STRIKES BACK

It was said earlier that modern subjectivism attacks human wholeness in two ways: First, on the level of faith (doctrine), it denies man's ability to know the truth. Second, on the level of morals, it denies his ability to *do* the truth. In denying that man can do the truth, it tries to justify itself by an appeal to *freedom*, an inherently powerful appeal in a nation which tends to exalt freedom above all other human goods. Contributing to the strength of that appeal is the fact that America is also a predominantly Protestant nation, and Protestant theology has always placed a heavy emphasis on Christian liberty, usually a distorted concept based on a misinterpretation of St. Paul. What subjectivistic moral theology seems to be saying is that if there is any knowable truth about right order, then there is no freedom, and we must have freedom above all else, therefore there is no knowable truth about right and wrong. But the reality is different. Freedom, if it means anything, means the ability to act. But to act is in the very nature of things to act in relation to something, to a world, to the other. But if there is no knowable other, in other words, no truth, then we cannot act. Thus the Church's counter-offensive against moral subjectivism has been to reaffirm the connection between freedom and truth. That counteroffensive has nowhere been delivered more forcefully than in Pope John Paul II's remarkable encyclical, *Veritatis Splendor*, "The Splendor of Truth," which sums up the Church's current situation in this way:

> In fact, a new situation has come about *within the Christian community itself*, which has experienced the spread of numerous doubts and objections of a human and psychological, social and cultural, religious and even properly theological nature, with regard to the Church's moral teachings. It is no longer a matter of limited and occasional dissent, but of an

> overall and systematic calling into question of traditional moral doctrine, on the basis of certain anthropological and ethical presuppositions. At the root of these presuppositions is the more or less obvious influence of currents of thought which end by detaching human freedom from its essential and constitutive relationship to truth.[460]

In sharp contrast, the Holy Father again and again points to the inseparability of freedom and truth:

> God's law does not reduce, much less do away with human freedom; rather, it protects and promotes that freedom. In contrast, however, some present-day cultural tendencies have given rise to several currents of thought in ethics which center upon *an alleged conflict between freedom and law*. These doctrines would grant to individuals or social groups the right *to determine what is good or evil*. Human freedom would thus be able to "create values" and would enjoy a primacy over truth, to the point that truth itself would be considered a creation of freedom. Freedom would thus lay claim to a *moral autonomy* which would actually amount to an *absolute sovereignty*.[461]

Thus truth, understood as the objectively knowable law of God, far from inhibiting freedom, is necessary to it:

> *Human freedom and God's law meet and are called to intersect*, in the sense of man's free obedience to God and of God's completely gratuitous benevolence toward man. Hence obedience to God is not, as some would believe, a *heteronomy*, as if the moral life were subject to the will of something all-powerful, absolute, extraneous to man, and intolerant of his freedom. If in fact a heteronomy of morality were to mean a denial of man's self-determination or the im-

[460] Pope John Paul II, *The Splendor of Truth: Veritatis Splendor* (Pauline Books and Media: Boston, 1993), n. 4.
[461] Ibid., n. 35.

> position of norms unrelated to his good, this would be in contradiction to the Revelation of the Covenant and of the redemptive Incarnation. Such a heteronomy would be nothing but a form of alienation, contrary to divine wisdom and to the dignity of the human person.[462]

Probably the most familiar form this subjectivizing of freedom has taken in the modern Church is the insistence that decisions about right and wrong must be made by the *conscience* of the individual. Thus people looking for guidance on moral issues, especially sexual ones, are routinely told by their priests that they must follow their own consciences, a kind of advice which certainly makes the priest's job easier but is of highly questionable value to anyone else. Pope John Paul shows persuasively that this is a misunderstanding of the true meaning of *conscience*:

> Conscience is no longer considered [by modernist moral theologians] in its primordial reality as an act of a person's intelligence, the function of which is to apply the universal knowledge of the good in a specific situation and thus to express a judgment about the right conduct to be chosen here and now. Instead, there is a tendency to grant to the individual conscience the prerogative of independently determining the criteria of good and evil and then acting accordingly.[463]

The individual must of course follow his own conscience in making moral decisions. But conscience is not the same thing as arbitrary will. Conscience, as the Church understands it, is, if rightly formed, grounded in and formed by the law of God which is known both by reason and by the revelation given by God to the Church:

> The dignity of this rational forum [conscience] and the authority of its voice and judgments derive from the *truth* about moral good and evil, which it is called to listen to and

462 Ibid., n. 41.
463 Ibid., n. 32.

> to express. This truth is indicated by the "divine law," *the universal and objective norm of morality*. The judgment of conscience does not establish the law; rather it bears witness to the authority of the natural law and of the practical reason with reference to the supreme good, whose attractiveness the human person perceives and whose commandments he accepts.[464]

Thus, the dualism between freedom and truth, which frequently takes the form of a dualism between conscience and authority, is not grounded in the reality of who and what man is (keeping in mind that one of this Pope's emphases is that a major part of the Church's mission is to reveal man to himself). If it were, man would be a fragmented being, not an integrated whole. So in man as he truly is, truth and freedom form an inseparable wholeness, as do conscience and authority.

Dualistic ideologies, of course, have a way of being global, that is, they tend to dualize everything they encounter, and the result is that subjectivistic moral theology, which is really dualistic moral theology, tends to introduce dualism into its whole picture of man. Thus *Veritatis Splendor* deals with related dualisms introduced by the modern mentality, among them a dualism of body and soul, a tendency to see things such as sexual morality, which involve the body, as *merely* of the body, and hence of no importance. Few contemporary moral theologians would admit to it, but much of their thinking seems to reduce to some such notion as: We are really in our essence spiritual beings, and so what our bodies do really doesn't matter all that much. I once saw a rather bad made-for-TV movie in which a "Christian" woman tells a man she has slept with, "My body belonged to you for one night, but my soul belongs to Jesus forever." This kind of silliness is really what much current moral theology is about. The Church, in contrast, insists that we are incarnate beings, that our bodiliness is of our very essence, so that what the body does

[464] Ibid., n. 60.

has a human meaning, a meaning for the whole person, not just for the body taken in isolation. Thus:

> Only in reference to the human person in his "unified totality," that is, as "a soul which expresses itself in a body and a body informed by an immortal spirit," can the specifically human meaning of the body be grasped....By rejecting all manipulations of corporeity which alter its human meaning, the Church serves man and shows him the path of true love, the only path on which he can find the true God.[465]

A closely related dualism is grounded in the notion of a conflict between particular and universal, and takes the form of what is called the "fundamental option" theory. This bit of speculation holds that our salvation or damnation, our righteousness, is based on the fundamental choice we make in the course of our lives between good and evil, between God and self, not in particular acts. The Church would enthusiastically agree with the first part of the formulation, that the fundamental choice is what matters, but would deny that this choice is unrelated to particular acts. What so many liberal "Christians" would like to be able to do, in effect, is to say: Sure, I've committed adultery, and fornication, and sodomy, and abortion, and theft, and lying, etc., etc., but I haven't rejected God! This is a meaningless statement. To do those things *is* to reject God, but not everyone wants to see it that way. Pope John Paul in fact does an excellent job of summing up both the truth in the "fundamental option" idea, and the untruth in the way so many people today understand it:

> By his fundamental choice, man is capable of giving his life direction and of progressing, with the help of grace, toward his end, following God's call. But this capacity is actually exercised in the particular choices of specific actions, through which man deliberately conforms himself to God"s will, wisdom, and law. It thus needs to be stated that *the so-called fundamental option, to the extent that it is distinct*

[465] Ibid., n. 50.

> *from a generic intention* and hence one not yet determined in such a way that freedom is obligated, *is always brought into play through conscious and free decisions.* Precisely for this reason, *it is revoked when man engages his freedom in conscious decisions to the contrary, with regard to morally grave matter.*[466]

So in the end, it is the wholeness of the human person, as knower and actor, which is crucial for the Church. As the Holy Father sums it up:

> The *fundamental question* which the moral theories mentioned above pose in a particularly forceful way is that of the relationship of man's freedom to God's law; it is ultimately the question of the *relationship between freedom and truth.*
> According to Christian faith and the Church's teaching, "only the freedom which submits to the Truth leads the human person to his true good. The good of the person is to be in the Truth and to *do* the Truth."[467]

Needless to say, the essential humanism of the teaching of *Veritatis Splendor*, its focus on human wholeness, and with it, the effort to restore some kind of "rule of law" to Christian life, was one *The Wanderer* could warmly endorse, something its contributors lost no time in doing. Thomas A. Droleskey, for example, was quick to underscore the practical importance of the Pope's rejection of subjectivism with its claim of absolute human autonomy, a rejection which was to provide orthodox Catholics with a great deal of ammunition in their continuing war with the modernists:

> Dissenting theologians are already lining up to dismiss such "outdated" concepts without realizing that their dissent would make sense only if humans were not mortals subject to laws they did not create and cannot repeal. In other words,

[466] Ibid., n. 67.
[467] Ibid., n. 84.

dissenting theologians make sense only if human beings are morally autonomous "gods."[468]

The Pope specifically warns the dissenters that the Church is *not* a democracy — and that "dissent in the form of carefully orchestrated protests and polemics carried on in the media" is not acceptable. He also reminds Catholic educational and health care institutions that their Catholic identity is bestowed by the bishops — and it can be *removed* by the bishops "in cases of serious failure to live up to that title." While Vatican spokesmen have said that this statement is not meant to be the principal focus of the encyclical letter, it is nevertheless true that he is challenging bishops to see to it that Catholic institutions are authentically Catholic. One of the positive ways that the encyclical letter's teaching can be promoted is by ending the confusion that dominates our Catholic institutions, a confusion which is giving free rein to all types of moral evils.[469]

...The truths contained in the encyclical letter are not the "invention" of the Church or Pope John Paul II. Truth resides in the person of Jesus Christ, the splendor of Truth Incarnate. Truth is not determined by public opinion polls or by dissenting theologians. The full truth of human existence is meant to set us free from an enslavement to sin and to selfishness.[470]

A.J. Matt, Jr., writing in the same issue, expressed similar hopes:

There is no room left for episcopal dissembling, equivocation, or hesitation about the Church's teaching on morality. As Pope John Paul puts it, there is an "unbreakable bond"

[468] Thomas A. Droleskey, "The Splendor of Truth," W, 10-14-93.
[469] Ibid.
[470] Ibid.

> between faith and morality, and a "close relationship between the moral good of human actions and eternal life."[471]

Of course, that hardly stopped such dissembling, by bishops and others, but it certainly took away its legitimacy, and, like the catechism, gave us an important tool to use in response to such dishonesty.

Paul Likoudis expressed hope that the encyclical would finally goad our bishops into taking action on the disease of dissent from the Church's moral teachings:

> Just as the splendor of baroque art, architecture, and music was the Catholic Church's answer to the iconoclasm of the Protestant reformers in the sixteenth century, so Pope John Paul II's new encyclical on the splendor of truth, *Veritatis Splendor*, is his answer to the equally destructive force of theological dissent afflicting late twentieth-century Catholicism.[472]

> It is not theologians or philosophers or the autonomous self who decide what is right or wrong, but it is God alone who decides. God has revealed His decisions, and it is the Catholic Church which interprets the word of God, "whether in its written form or in tradition."[473]

> Bishop Fabian Bruskewitz of Lincoln, Neb., said the encyclical "provides a guiding light in the darkness of contemporary moral trends. I hope all Catholics as well as other people of goodwill will be able to read and study this fine document and find in it inspiration and assistance."[474]

---

[471] A.J. Matt, Jr., "The Bishops Will be Tested," W, 10-14-93.
[472] Paul Likoudis, "New Encyclical Exhorts Bishops to Put a Lid on Dissent," W, 10-14-93.
[473] Ibid.
[474] Ibid.

> While this encyclical is a profound philosophical and theological treatise that takes aim at what may be the number one problem in the world today — moral relativism — by a man who has seen its fruits — in Nazism, Communism, and their ideological offspring in the neopagan West — it does have a practical bottom line that should impress every North American Catholic: The dissent among Catholics must end.[475]

Frank Morriss echoed this concern that the Church finally do something about the scandal of dissent within the Church, especially on issues like abortion, and extended this concern to relate to the political and legal situation here in America:

> Pope John Paul II's encyclical *Veritatis Splendor* will make it difficult, if not impossible, to claim the compatibility of dissent and the Catholic faith.[476]
>
> Will the Catholic lobbyists and politicians, the Catholic promoters and defenders of these things [abortion, homosexuality, etc.], use the encyclical to correct their consciences in this regard? Now, especially, they must consider that the excuses of freedom of conscience, pluralism, and so on, can no longer justify their disagreement with Catholic moral teaching.
>
> I think particularly of the Catholic politicians who vote for abortion funding, of nuns and lay women who defend the right of a mother to kill her unborn children, of activists who claim the homosexual lifestyle, of theologians and sociologists who say that Catholics know better than the Church when they use contraceptives.[477]
>
> This encyclical demands that all consider the state of ecclesial communion they truly have on the basis of whether they

---

[475] Ibid.

[476] Frank Morriss, "Will 'Veritatis Splendor' Curb the Dissenters?" W, 10-14-93.

[477] Ibid.

> give religious assent of the will to what the document teaches. It is Peter speaking, and surely those of true Catholic heart and mind must consider the causes it addresses to be ruled upon with finality. Not that these dissents had any validity before the encyclical; but it serves a kind of magisterial notice that those in disagreement are in a state of contempt for the Church that amounts to separation.[478]

Veritatis Splendor is still one more document that has given us all hope. What its appearance means is that moral subjectivism has not been allowed to triumph in the Church. It has not been allowed to corrupt the official teaching of the Church, which, we believe, the Holy Spirit protects from error. But of course none of this means that we have definitively won yet or that the subjectivists have definitively lost. We are still very much in the middle of that battle, and whether *Veritatis Splendor* turns out to be its turning point is something only future historians will be in a position to know. James Likoudis, in a powerful editorial published several months after the encyclical appeared, summed up this state of things pretty well:

> As the Pope told the bishops of the Catholic world, we must not be content just to warn the faithful about the errors and dangers of certain ethical theories. We must first of all show the inviting splendor of the truth which is Jesus Christ Himself. But dissenter theologians who have been scandalously contradicting the moral truths of Jesus Christ and busily malforming the consciences of the faithful, must be dealt with and corrected. Let us note, for example, this deplorable judgment on *Veritatis Splendor* by the arrogant dissenters who publish *The National Catholic Reporter*:
>
> "This [encyclical], no matter how one reads it, is a harsh, negative, rigid, authoritarian document. The Christian searches vainly for the positive, affirming, all-embracing, compassionate tone of the Christ in whose name the Pope

[478] Ibid.

> wrote his encyclical; the Christ who said to prostitutes and tax collectors and other rejects to come along and follow him, who was anything but absolute, putting up instead an umbrella big enough for everyone, and suggesting by his wholesome attitude that he respected the intelligence and conscience God had given to people in the first place" (Oct. 15, 1993).[479]
>
> Notably, the entire thrust of *The Splendor of Truth* is directed at refuting the exaggerated idea of *freedom* promoted by individualistic liberals and secularists (and their dissenter allies in the Church) — all of whom give voice to "the world, the flesh, and the Devil" in moral decision making.[480]

Veritatis Splendor clarified some extremely important doctrinal issues having to do with morality. But a great deal yet needs to be done when it comes to the practical applications (as the writers cited above have made clear), and this is nowhere more obvious than in the issue of Catholic sex education, to be discussed next.

---

[479] James Likoudis, "The Splendor of Truth," W, 2-24-94.
[480] Ibid.

8. ANOTHER METASTASIS — THE SEX EDUCATION DISASTER

And he said to his disciples, "Temptations to sin are sure to come; but woe to him by whom they come! It would be better for him if a millstone were hung round his neck and he were cast into the sea, than that he should cause one of these little ones to sin.

— Luke 17:1-2

They promise...freedom, but they themselves are slaves of corruption...

— II Peter 2:19

Sexual morality, as we have seen, cannot be separated from the most basic principles and values governing human existence in community. If that existence, which for the Christian is fundamentally existence in the covenant with God, is to continue and prosper, these central principles must be passed on to each new generation as it grows to maturity. Where these principles impinge on sexual morality, we are dealing with what could be called, in the most basic and general sense, sex education. If that initiation into Christian family life and into sexuality as the gift which men and women give to each other, in the process giving the gift of life to their children, miscarries, if it fails in its mission, the result is the breakdown of the Christian and human community and incalculable human misery. Such a breakdown is precisely what we have witnessed in the generation since the 1960s, and the principal instrument of the breakdown has been something called "sex education," which is in reality sex miseducation, a kind of pseudo-education which has taught a whole generation to see sexuality in a twisted and distorted manner, in a manner inconsistent with human wholeness because it separates sex from love and from community life and makes it the property of the isolated, autonomous individual. Such an approach destroys love, and while loudly proclaiming freedom, deeply violates the dignity and liberty of the human person before God.

Pseudo-sex education began as a threat primarily from the secular state, but as the modernist Church came to be more and more infected with secularist ideas, it became a threat to the Catholic community from within the Church herself. Parents who placed their children in Catholic schools in order to protect them from the destructive "sex education" which was sweeping the public schools, found to their horror and outrage that, in many cases, the same poison was being fed to students in the Catholic schools. Sometimes the dosage was even more concentrated — after all, there is no zealot like a convert.

The Church, indeed, had always favored sex education in the first sense discussed above, education which initiated children into the mystery of sexual love and Christian family life. But the Church also taught that such sex education was first and foremost the right and duty of parents, not of the state and not of the schools, whether public or private. The Church has also consistently taught that such education ought not to be carried out in the classroom, because no two children are alike, and each has unique needs which must be addressed. There is no place for a "one size fits all" approach here. And certainly it is not to be carried out in mixed groups. The sex education which swept both Catholic and public schools in the sixties and seventies flagrantly violated all these principles. The threat of such sex education to the rights of parents and to the Christian family was noted by James Likoudis in a June, 1968 *Wanderer* article:

> The pathetic abdication of parental rights by many parents themselves, and, as we shall see, the absorption of these rights by agencies of the state, is one of the most alarming moral and spiritual problems confronting the Catholic Church in America today. Indeed, no greater threat is posed by secularism to the Catholic Church (as well as the other

> churches) than the growing disintegration of the family consequent upon the steady denigration of parental authority and the virtues peculiar to the family. For it is not only that immense social evils (with which, of course, the Church is always vitally concerned) follow in the wake of the collapse of the family. But the moral welfare of the family is indissolubly linked to the vitality of religion itself.[481]

The decline of the family, of which the current cult of sex education is such a reliable indicator, is, as far as Likoudis is concerned, tied, in its very essence, to the rise of the total state. E.K. Roosevelt took the position, in a 1969 article, that sex education is indeed a quasi-religious cult, and a state-sponsored one at that:

> The inalienable right of parents to teach their own values and views on morality to their children was once unquestioned. Indeed, prayers are banned from public schools on the grounds that this would constitute a violation of the principle of the separation of church and state.
>
> But recently there has grown up a religious cult in our schools that is not only being tolerated but actively encouraged by the U.S. government — the teaching of sex as a required classroom subject.[482]

Unfortunately, this state-sponsored cult, which one would expect to have been resisted to the death by the Catholic Church, was, in many cases, all too eagerly welcomed into the Catholic schools by the Church's own school bureaucracy. In April, 1969, James and Ruth Likoudis tried to warn the Church about the dangers of this development, in a letter addressed to the American Catholic bishops meeting in Houston April 14-17. In the process, they provided a pretty good overview of the genuinely Catholic approach to sex education:

---

[481] James Likoudis, "Sex Education: The Latest Outrage...Parents and the Benevolent Leviathan," W, 6-6-68.
[482] E.K. Roosevelt, "The Mystique of Sex Education," W, 4-3-69.

> We wish to express our grave concern at the introduction and spread of naturalist-progressivist sex-education courses in public schools affecting the spiritual welfare of Catholic children, and the serious injury done the rights of Catholic parents in similar (often "experimental") classroom programs in the parochial schools of many dioceses throughout the nation. We, therefore, wish to bring to your attention the profound sense of consternation we have felt at the silence of the Church in the face of compulsory public-school sex-education programs exposing Catholic children to possible moral corruption, psychological harm, and emotional damage. Such programs, moreover, contravene traditional Catholic principles in moral theology prohibiting indiscriminate, public, mass-standardized, classroom sex instruction and, especially so, when divorced from religious values. The programs gaining widespread acceptance in *both* public and parochial schools are over-clinical in their presentation, too detailed in content, and, in the words of Pius XII, exaggerate "beyond measure the sexual element in life" and give it "the meaning and value of an end in itself."[483]

These are more or less external, accidental problems associated with these programs — problems involving material being taught in the wrong time and place and by the wrong people. But of course the problem went deeper than that — to the material being taught itself, because the children were not, in these programs, being taught Christian principles for sexual behavior and a Christian understanding of sexual love, but radically anti-Christian principles, something the Likoudises went on to take note of:

> Such programs offend against the personal privacy and dignity of the child, and the personal freedom of parents to determine *when* to meet the highly individualized sexual needs of their children.

[483] James and Ruth Likoudis, "A Plea to Our Bishops," W, 4-10-69.

> ...We also wish to call to Your Excellencies' attention the scandal of certain so-called "leading Catholic authorities in the area of human sexuality" whose writings and activities...betray the bizarre resonances of the new morality and situation ethics. Some of these priests and laity have not scrupled to become affiliated with the naturalistically-oriented Sex Information and Education Council of the United States (SIECUS)....Rather than assisting Catholic parents, sex education in the classroom absorbs and usurps their duties. In our judgment, it is a pernicious abuse for Catholic schools with such programs — to assist Catholic parents, in effect, *to abdicate* their rights and responsibilities.[484]

Father Burns, in a May, 1969 column aptly titled "Experimentation With Immortal Souls," brought out this aspect of sex education by quoting a speech given not long before by Dr. Mary Calderone of SIECUS, one of the leading lights of the new sex education. Dr. Calderone had this to say:

> Sex is not something you turn off like a faucet. If you do, it is unhealthy....We need new values to determine when and how we should have sexual experiences. Nobody is standing on a platform giving answers. You are moving beyond your parents, but you can't just move economically or educationally, you must move sexually as well. You must learn how to use sex. This is it: first, to separate yourself from your parents; second, to establish a male and female role; third, to determine value systems; fourth, to establish your vocational role. Our sex expresses itself in everything we do....Sex is not just something you do in marriage, in bed, in

[484] Ibid.

> the dark, in one position....*Nobody from upon high determines this. You determine it.*[Italics added][485]

This is child abuse. At least Adam and Eve were adults when the serpent got to work on them, and had some chance of resisting. Children are helpless victims of this kind of propaganda. And the message, as the italicized lines above clearly tell us, is the serpent's message to our first parents: "You shall be as gods," not just knowing good and evil but determining for yourself what good and evil are. This is the destruction of human wholeness right at its foundation — man's relationship to his Creator. It tells man that the order of creation is not God's work, but his own. A group known as POPE (Parents for Orthodoxy in Parochial Education) called this "the spiritual, emotional rape of our children through various and devious methods of mind manipulation."[486]

Perhaps no one zeroed in quite so precisely on the first principles for Christian sex education, as well as on the destruction of human wholeness by un-Christian sex education, as did Dietrich von Hildebrand, so often cited in these pages. Von Hildebrand noted that, while modern pseudo-science (i.e., the "behavioral sciences") thinks that the higher must be understood in terms of the lower (reductionism), the Christian understanding is that the reverse is true — we understand the lower in terms of the higher. Thus we can understand human sexuality as a function of the whole human person, a spiritual, but incarnate, being. But if we try to understand the spiritual being as a function of sexuality, we create, as Freud did, a monstrous distortion of the true order of things. Von Hildebrand's attack on contemporary sex education in light of this principle is quite damning:

> To develop the right attitude and vision in the human person toward this sphere of sex, there exists only one possibility,

[485] Father Robert E. Burns, "Experimentation With Immortal Souls," W, 5-22-69.
[486] Bishop William L. Adrian, "Do Sex-Education Programs Corrupt Youth?" W, 4-17-69.

> namely, information about the mystery of sex must be disclosed in great reverence and in a strict due personal dialogue, of the father or the mother with their child. Absolutely excluded is the pseudo-scientific teaching about sex in a classroom — that is in a neutralizing and publicity-saturated atmosphere.
>
> ...We have seen that sex is in no way a mere biological instinct. We have seen its character of depth and intimacy. We have seen that it is destined to be the expression of true spousal love and the fulfillment of an ultimate union of the lovers in the sacred bond of marriage. We have also seen that the true nature and meaning of sex can be understood only in its function of serving an ultimate, mutual, irrevocable self-donation.[487]

The mystery of spousal love, in von Hildebrand's view, is the very essence of human sexuality, and is normative for our understanding of the merely biological aspect:

> "Sex education" which concentrates almost exclusively on bodily processes is, therefore, misinformation — a lie. It utterly fails to say anything about the true nature of sex. What is more, the classroom publicity of such education is absolutely incompatible with the disclosure of a sphere which, as we said before, is in some way the secret of every individual.[488]

A November, 1970 article under the byline "Romanus," called "School Sex Education Destroys Children," also did much to bring out the Christian first principles for evaluating sex education. Here again, we see, right at the center, the attack on that human wholeness which Catholic teaching tries to safeguard:

---

[487] Dietrich von Hildebrand, "Sex Education: The Basic Issues," W, 7-3-69.
[488] Ibid.

> In a front-page editorial in *L'Osservatore Romano* (dated November 14, 1970) the editor, Raimondo Manzini, assails the practice of teaching vivid details of the physiology of human reproduction to children under ten years of age. He finds that this kind of physiological "realism" destroys the characteristic idealism of the child, plunges him into morbid psychological conflicts which he might otherwise have avoided, stunts his growth toward the pure and noble understanding of human sexuality which only a fully mature person can have, and strips him ferociously of his natural simplicity at an age when his sexual drives have not yet created in him the problems presupposed by the class manuals.
>
> ...By destroying the moral fiber of an entire generation of children, the sex-educators know that they can frustrate the purpose of the Church and deal Christianity a devastating blow. The clear stand taken by *L'Osservatore Romano* will provide strength and encouragement to worried parents and educators, but its implications have yet to be tested. The vulnerability of children to the ravages of pansexualism does not end with the age of ten. Nor is the issue merely one of timing. As Manzini points out, the entire Christian ethos is at stake, which means also the Christian teaching regarding marriage, illicit acts, chastity, and the sacred inviolability of human life. And, finally, what action will be taken in the case of Catholic school systems which have already incorporated into their curricula from kindergarten upward the very methodology that *L'Osservatore Romano* has now so clearly condemned?[489]

By now the need for such action was becoming clear, as the new and radically anti-Christian sex education was more and more invading the Catholic, or formerly Catholic, schools. In March, 1971, James Likoudis did an extensive study, for *The Wanderer*, of the new *Becoming a Person*, a program put together specifically for Catholic

[489] Romanus, "School Sex Education Destroys Children," W, 11-26-70.

schools under the general editorship of a Catholic priest, Father Walter Imbiorski, of the Archdiocese of Chicago. Father Imbiorski was a member of the advisory board of the Family Life Division of the U.S. Catholic Conference, as well as a member of the board of directors of the unspeakable SIECUS. Likoudis's analysis is lengthy, but deserves a lengthy summation because the controversy over this program became a watershed event in the history of this issue, and because the debate placed in clear relief the truly anti-human essence of the sex-education movement.

Not the least of the anti-human elements in the *Becoming a Person Program* (BAPP) was, in Likoudis's view, its attack on the rights and responsibilities of parents:

> It is a grave matter that the New Jersey bishops appear to have been blissfully unaware of the serious problem of conscience they have unwittingly posed for those conscientious Catholic parents who (1) are in principle opposed to any classroom sex education; or (2) may find themselves opposed to a particular classroom program of sex education in their Catholic school or child's CCD course where content, materials, or instructors are discovered to be objectionable. How, moreover, the admitted primary role of parents in the sexual education of their children is safeguarded by formal classroom instruction given by others in full-blown K-12 or 1-8 grade programs (where parental control and influence over the classroom situation — to be realistic about it — is *nil*) is not explained.[490]

Likoudis's article goes on to focus on the appropriate relationship of religion to sexual values, noting that "religion is not superimposed by history upon sex; men from the beginning experienced sex as sacred; they could not understand it except in a religious setting."[491] Yet

[490] James Likoudis, "Fashioning Persons for a New Age? (A Critical Study of the 'Becoming A Person' Sex Education Program)," W, 3-25-71.
[491] Ibid.

BAPP consistently excludes religious concerns from any influence on sex education:

> What kind of Catholic sex education, therefore, is provided in Father Imbiorski's *Becoming A Person* program? Yes, indeed, what kind of integrated Catholic instruction in human sexuality is that contained in the eight volumes comprising the *children's* reading texts (526 pages in all) which nowhere mentions the word *Catholic*; nowhere uses the word *soul*; nowhere mentions the doctrine of *original sin* and the *fall of man* or the teaching of the Church on *concupiscence*; mentions the word *sin* only twice; recommends *prayer* once; studiously precludes any reference to the *fear of God*; deliberately avoids the expression *God's moral law*; refers to the *Ten Commandments* once; eschews completely any direct exposition of the *Sixth and Ninth* Commandments; presents a distorted positivistic definition of *conscience;* mentions the word *grace* but twice; makes but one explicit reference to a Christian *sacrament* that is clearly identified as such — namely Confirmation, and even then drastically diluting its meaning; ignores completely the holy *Sacrament of Penance*; nowhere mentions the powerful intercession of the *Blessed Virgin Mary, Mother of the Church,* ever ready to aid her sorely tempted children, or the example of the *saints* of God; and remains suspiciously vague concerning the *Last Things* (nowhere specifically mentioning Heaven, Hell, or Purgatory!)?
>
> Yes indeed! What kind of Catholic Christian formation is this that will be imbibed by the youthful readers of these texts? Whatever Father Imbiorski's *Becoming A Person* program may be, the integrity of Catholic doctrine, the unction of Catholic piety, and the love of the supernatural have no place in it.[492]

[492] Ibid.

By now this must be a familiar pattern to the reader: The treatment of inherently sacred things in a way that deprives them of their sacred character and reduces them to the level of the profane. That is how the modernist establishment dealt with the Mass, reducing the most sacred act in the universe to the level of a profane social gathering. People who are not afraid to desacralize the Mass are not likely to have qualms about desacralizing sexuality. Says Likoudis: "It is this appalling absence of sensitivity to the genuinely supernatural that is its [BAPP's] greatest weakness and renders it, in general, unfit for use by Catholics."[493] This sacred character is central to Christian teaching on sex, something Likoudis underscores by quoting a statement by Dietrich von Hildebrand to the effect that "his is not a puritanical or Manichean despisal of sex...but the Christian understands that sex belongs in a special manner to God, and that he may make such use of it only as explicitly sanctioned by Him. Only with God's express permission may he eat of the fruit of this tree."[494]

But the assertion that there can be things which require God's permission suggests, to the modern mind, the idea of divine law, something which is apparently anathema to the authors of BAPP:

> ...What is perplexing is the total failure to *explicitly* acknowledge the special role the *teaching authority of the Church* plays in the formation of a Christian conscience.
>
> ...However, in attempting to make morality a response not to law but to the needs of the person, another and even more serious deformation of Christian teaching is committed — namely, an unfortunate minimizing and blunting of the concepts of divine law and *sin* in the minds of the young.
>
> ...Catholic parents can only be amazed at the radical elimination of elements of orthodox religious catechesis in the effort to reorient Catholic children toward what is essentially a new morality based upon a "love-ethic" that is primarily empirical, existential, and anthropocentric in character.

---

[493] Ibid.

[494] Ibid.

> ...A veritable theology of ambiguity about "Love" and a distressing diminution of the sense of sin are the inevitable consequences of the philosophy of naturalistic personalism pervading the BAPP texts.[495]

Yet with all the claims that this kind of sex education is "humanistic," addresses the "whole person," and so on, it in fact diminishes the human person by depriving him of his spiritual essence:

> It is not an accident that nowhere does the child encounter in his texts the word *soul*!...What is unnecessarily obfuscated here is recognition that it is chiefly in his *soul* that the image of God is found in a man; and that the soul is naturally like God because it is a *spiritual substance* endowed with intellect and will....It is to be noted, therefore, that not all man's acts of "loving," "creating," "caring," and "serving" are necessarily *supernatural* acts done "in God's image." This lamentable confusion of the natural and supernatural orders will be seen to vitiate BAPP's entire religious perspective....The disastrous clouding in the mind of the child of his possession of an *immortal spiritual soul* is reminiscent of the treatment afforded *soul* in the notorious Dutch Catechism and other works by neomodernist theologians. The result is that despite repeated statements about man being a "unique person," "a special creation," "a very special creation," and the use of other traditional Christian language ("made in God's image," "God's great creation," "Only God is the source of all life," "God's plan," etc.), the essential *qualitative* difference between his nature and that of other animals remains strangely blurred. The child is not taught clearly that he has an immortal spirit which was directly created by God at the moment of conception....The authors and consultants are, in effect, communicating to their youthful readers the alleged benefits of a "new theology of the human person" as a psychological

[495] Ibid.

> whole which denigrates Catholic teaching that it is because of his immortal soul that man is a living intellectual (rational) being.[496]

To deny the reality of the soul and therefore the life of the spirit is to attack man's wholeness as an incarnate being, an incarnate spirit, whatever the alleged intentions of such a program may be. One of the bitter fruits of such an attack is a morbid obsession with sex to the detriment of all other aspects of human life:

> Another distressing feature in BAPP texts is the gross emphasis that Catholic children view men and women and themselves as "sexual persons." This indicates intrusion into the program of an erroneous pansexualist psychology that does not scruple to trumpet the effrontery that "sex is the determining factor in our human relations."...*Becoming A Person*'s transmogrification of the entire ethos of the supernatural and peculiar pansexualist treatment of the "person" is more likely to produce Christians who are spiritually anemic, worldly, and other-directed sentimentalists — the inevitable harvest of an emasculated and desacralized Catholicism.[497]

And there we have it. The sex educationist's alleged affirmation of the person in fact distorts true personhood, creating what Eric Voegelin called "spiritual eunuchs" instead of persons.

In 1972, the American Bishops produced the first draft of a proposed pastoral on sex education, entitled, "To Teach as Jesus Did." This document, which for the most part appeared to endorse atrocities like the BAPP program, quickly got responses from *Wanderer* types, among them, as usual, James Likoudis, who reacted to it in an article aptly titled, "Do the Pied Pipers of Sex Education Teach as Jesus Did?" Once again, the focus was on the attack on the wholeness of the person which these horrendous sex education programs embodied:

---

[496] Ibid.
[497] Ibid.

> It is precisely this profound Christian view of the primacy of the person and the legitimate autonomy of the family amidst the social structures of a community which is utterly lacking [in] our sex-education planners. It is assuredly a distorted collectivistic concept of "community" which dares to subordinate parental judgment concerning the "needs" of the child to the often arbitrary whims of "professional educators."[498]

John Mulloy, never one to hold back when the faith is threatened, sent an open letter to the bishops of the United States, trying to warn them against further endorsement of programs like BAPP (the bishops were then getting ready to consider a proposal by the Family Life Division of the U.S. Catholic Conference for an episcopal endorsement of classroom sex education). His remarks leave the reader in no doubt that these programs are in fact a particularly vicious form of child abuse:

> As one striking example of what could happen, we have the program in sex education set up for the New York Archdiocese in 1968-9, with the assistance of the Catholic Family Life Division of the USCC. An indication of the kind of books and films thought suitable and recommended as basic for the course in sex education, is the book *The Freedom of Sexual Love* by Joseph and Lois Bird. The book describes, in detail, erotic stimulation, primary and secondary sexual stimuli, vaginal and clitoral orgasms, sex play, "techniques" for prolonging ejaculation, as well as various positions for sexual intercourse. It is utterly explicit in describing oral genital activity....The list on which this book, and others like it appeared, was mailed out by the Catholic Family Life Division "to every grammar school convent in the United States," some 10,000 in all, according to the statement of Father James T. McHugh, head of the division.

---

[498] James Likoudis, "Do the Pied Pipers of Sex Education Teach as Jesus Did?" W, 11-9-72.

> ...If the bishops were to give approval to the kind of sex education which has already been carried on in different dioceses — often indeed under the name of religious education — how would they be able to prevent a further decline in the Catholic moral conscience related to such matters as masturbation, premarital intercourse, divorce, abortion, homosexuality, etc.?[499]

Clearly, preventing such a decline was the last thing on the minds of Father McHugh and company.

The political implications of sex education as a means of building the total state at the expense of the person were also not lost on *Wanderer* contributors during these years. Betty Hammer, in an article entitled "Sex Education: An Instrument of Revolution," pointed out that sex education was used in this way during the Marxist Mexican revolution:

> What happened in Mexico in the 1930s has been happening in the Catholic school system in our country for the past five or six years. The big difference here is that it is not the "Marxist hand" that is putting immoral sex education into our Catholic schools, but consecrated hands of bishops and priests, who have obviously been influenced by the Marxist-socialist doctrine.
>
> What a courageous contrast the Mexican bishops were in the 1930s to our American bishops in the 1970s! Many of our American bishops have for several years allowed sex education to be taught in their dioceses with their approval. In other dioceses all kinds of moral and doctrinal aberrations are being taught to our children under the guise of "religious education." Abundant proof has already been presented to the bishops, who refuse to recognize the "genuinely Marxist hand" in sex education as the Mexican bishops did in the

[499] John J. Mulloy, "Will the Bishops Clarify What They Mean by Sex Education?" W, 9-13-73.

> thirties. Likewise, our American Catholic Bishops refuse to dismiss our bureaucratic "Ministers of Prostitution" from office — namely, Monsignor James McHugh and Father Walter Imbiorski and their local counterparts.[500]

Not at all surprisingly, to *The Wanderer* and its readers, the actual result of these sex education programs was not the sexual utopia predicted by their advocates, but tremendous social and personal disorder. The decade of the 1970s saw great increases in all the measures of social disorder: teenage pregnancy, venereal disease, abortion, drug addiction, suicide, etc. Unfortunately, one of the characteristics of utopian ideologues is the inability to learn from experience. Many years ago, Eric Voegelin commented on this phenomenon: When the attempt to force the gnostic dream on reality produces disastrous real-world consequences, the gnostic ideologue blames these consequences, not on his ideology, but on the immorality of other people who fail to behave the way the ideology says they should behave. The answer, as far as they are concerned, is a still stronger dose of the ideology which caused the problems in the first place. That is what has happened in the case of our sex educators, as Donald A. Doyle pointed out in a January, 1980 article:

> Consequently, one would expect the school authorities to recognize that sexual behavior is not an area of their responsibility or competence and simply scrap classroom sex education altogether! As the president of New York University recently pointed out: "In thrusting the schools to the forefront of social change, we have directed their energies from their basic purpose — education." Yet the unquestioned assumption that classroom sex education can have worthwhile results persists. Indeed, the very department that presented the "alarming proportions" of the teenage sexual problems con-

[500] Betty Hammer, "Sex Education: An Instrument of Revolution," W, 11-15-73.

> cluded that what is necessary is a more explicit sex education curriculum.[501]

In December, 1981, *The Wanderer* published a key document in the sex education controversy, a position paper issued by the National Federation of Catholic Physicians' Guilds, entitled "Education in Wholesome Chastity." This document took as its point of departure the Second Vatican Council's statement (from the Declaration on Christian Education) that "as they grow older [children and young people] should receive a positive and prudent education in matters relating to sex." It then goes on to demonstrate how thoroughly negative and imprudent our current programs of sex education are. It starts by emphasizing the role of parents in a truly positive and prudent program:

> It is the position of the National Federation of Catholic Physicians' Guilds that sex resides as much in the affective as the cognitive domain; that adult sexuality is a personal response, not merely an intellectual function; that a child learns about sex primarily by responding affectively to his parents' affective behavior; and therefore that healthy sexuality cannot be taught in the classroom, it cannot be taught by strangers, it cannot be taught apart from the family. When parents fail in their responsibility to their children, it is they who must be educated, for, for better or for worse, it is they who will educate their children in these matters.[502]

Now here is a genuinely humanistic approach, one that is directed at the whole growing person living in a world and responding to the world. It is an approach that connects with the way real human beings learn about life and love, in sharp contrast to the established programs which seem to be directed to some kind of abstract subject or some kind of bundle of behaviors:

---

[501] Donald A. Doyle, "Classroom Sex Education: A Failure," W, 1-31-80.
[502] "Education in Wholesome Chastity," W, 12-10-81.

> From infancy the child normally learns about sex from his parents' actions, attitudes, and example. By the age of two he (or she) knows his own gender. He learns to identify with the parent of his own sex, and to anticipate his own growth into manhood or womanhood. He sees and internalizes how his parents treat each other, not only in the bedroom but in the living room and in the shopping center. As he grows he forms relationships with peers of his own sex and of the opposite. As he is educated he reads the great literature and learns the great themes of romantic love, and in his imagination he lives the emotional and moral conflicts of the great heroes. He learns the principles of science and biology. If his education is Catholic, he learns the natural and the moral law. If he attends a good Catholic high school or college today, he studies the powerful and profound weekly addresses of Pope John Paul II on the nuptial meaning of the body.
>
> Thus the child who grows up in a home with loving parents, who is taught by good Catholic teachers, and who interacts normally with his peers will be well-educated in sexuality without ever having been exposed to CSE [classroom sex education].
>
> Does such a scenario exist? Did it ever? Can it? These questions underlie current controversy. Those who promote CSE hold that such informal education in sexuality is so inadequate that it must be replaced by formal CSE. Those who oppose CSE hold that *only* the scenario described above is "positive and prudent" and that CSE is *inherently* negative and imprudent. The National Federation of Catholic Physicians' Guilds holds the latter position.[503]

This remarkable document, ignored by nearly the whole world, then goes so far as to show that CSE is in fact anti-human and anti-sexual:

[503] Ibid.

> Two contradictory views of human sexuality currently prevail — the traditional view that sex is inextricably linked to marriage and family, love and children, personal union and procreation; and the neo-puritanical view that sex is fun, casual, "natural" (actually divorced from nature), value-free, and oriented toward the pleasure of the individual....The sexual revolution is inherently *anti-sexual.* It is yet another permutation of Catharism, Albigensianism, Manichaeanism, Jansenism, and the other Hydra-heads of Gnosticism which the Church has battled for millennia.
>
> ...It may be true that teenage pregnancy, venereal disease, abortion, and promiscuity (as well as suicide, delinquency, drug use, etc.) are increasing dramatically. But to assume that ignorance is the cause of and CSE the solution to these problems is not only unfounded, it is contrary to the available evidence. In fact, CSE has generally been accompanied by an increase in sexual activity, with all the effects of that activity. Surveys of pregnant teenagers have repeatedly shown that contraceptive knowledge was not lacking, but that either consciously or unconsciously pregnancy was chosen.[504]

The sexual revolution is thus fundamentally a dream-world notion — unfortunately, not only for its proponents but for its countless victims, reality has a way of avenging itself on dream-world thinking:

> Although the sex educators neglect the connections between sex and passion and between sex and life, their victims, the "sexually active" teenagers, do not. Interviews with pregnant teenagers reveal that sexual activity inevitably leads to a longing for a deeper intimacy than occurs in casual liaisons and that pregnancy is an attempt to fulfill this longing (by eliciting love for the teenaged girl from the baby's father, from her own parents, or from the baby himself). Thus promiscuous teenagers inevitably discover the truths that the sex

---

[504] Ibid.

> educators never told them: Sex means love. Sex means babies. Unfortunately, this discovery often comes after their lives are wrecked.[505]

The federation's answer to this, an answer still well worth considering, is sex education, not for children, but for their parents:

> Sex education for parents should be designed to counter puritanism in the home by fostering the wholesome chastity of marriage. Teachers must understand and embrace the constant teaching of the Magisterium that genital sexuality is wholesome only in the context of permanent, monogamous, life-giving marriage. They must be fully versed in the many errors prevalent in society (even among Catholics) and they must know why these views are false. They must recognize that those parents who live according to the laws of nature and the laws of the Church will be able to educate their children positively and prudently in matters relating to sex.[506]

Sadly for our world, the sex education movement, like the distorted moral theology of which it was the offspring, pretty much won the short-term battle for worldly acceptance and implementation. In doing so, it wreaked terrible destruction on the young and helpless human beings who were its victims. The new and anti-Christian sex education radically separates sex from the very idea of the covenanted love of man and woman. Sex becomes merely a self-centered appetite to be satisfied and not a gift of self to another. As a result, what this kind of education produces is the lonely, autonomous individual. This is the ultimate in alienation. The autonomous individual is alienated even from his own body, which becomes to him only a thing, too — a thing to be used as a means to his autonomous pleasure. The end result is depersonalization which, if it lasts into eternity without being healed, means eternal loss.

Few have put it as eloquently as Randy Engel did:

---

[505] Ibid.

[506] Ibid.

> Is it any wonder that the state must wage war against the family? For the state requires not individuals who dream, and think, and pray, but rather what has come to be called "the mass man" — rootless, unaffirmed, a reactor — a mere reed blowing in the wind — a thing to be manipulated, to be used, to be disposed of, but never, never, to be loved, for the giant has no heart. And since the modern state has no heart, that which men previously have done out of love, must now be done out of fear, and hatred, and brute force.[507]

So clearly, contemporary sex education, "Catholic" or otherwise, is a profound attack on human dignity and on the human person. This thesis is central to the Vatican's 1995 document, *The Truth and Meaning of Human Sexuality*, still another chapter in the Church's counterattack against the modernists. If there is a central concept uniting the various sections of this document, it is "respect": 1) Respect for human wholeness and for the incarnate nature of human love, sexual and otherwise; 2) respect for the dignity and inviolability of the person, especially the child; 3) respect for the rights and duties of parents in the education of their children in human love; 4) respect for human life itself. Let us examine these one at a time.

As we have seen throughout this discussion of moral issues, the Church sees man in a radically non-dualistic way, not as a spirit somehow loosely connected to a body, but as an incarnate spirit, meant to be incarnate not merely in this life, but for eternity, in the resurrection of the dead. Being incarnate involves us of necessity in self-giving, which creates community. The *Truth and Meaning* document clearly reflects this in its treatment of the nature of sexual love:

> Love is a gift of God, nourished by and expressed in the encounter of man and woman. Love is thus a positive force directed toward their growth in maturity as persons. In the plan of life which represents each person's vocation, love is also a

[507] Randy Engel, "The Family Under Siege," W, 3-6-80.

> precious source for the self-giving which all men and women are called to make for their own self-realization and happiness. In fact, man is called to love as an incarnate spirit, that is, soul and body in the unity of the person. Human love hence embraces the body, and the body also expresses spiritual love. Therefore, sexuality is not something purely biological, rather it concerns the intimate nucleus of the person. The use of sexuality as physical giving has its own truth and reaches its full meaning when it expresses the personal giving of man and woman even unto death.[508]

All this being the case, chastity, as the right use of sexuality, must be understood, contrary to most popular notions on the subject, as something positive and affirming, not something negative, not merely a matter of not doing something, of "none of this and none of that," as an old expression has it:

> Educating children for chastity strives to achieve three objectives: (a) to maintain in the family *a positive atmosphere of love, virtue, and respect for the gifts of God*, in particular the gift of life; (b) to help children to understand the value of sexuality and chastity in stages, sustaining their growth through enlightening word, example, and prayer; (c) to help them understand and discover *their own vocation to marriage or to consecrated virginity for the sake of the Kingdom of Heaven* in harmony with and respecting their attitudes and inclinations and the gifts of the Spirit.[509]

All this requires self-control, hence the centrality of chastity:

> One cannot give what one does not possess. If the person is not master of self — through the virtues and, in a concrete way, through chastity — he or she lacks that self-possession

[508] *The Truth and Meaning of Human Sexuality (Guidelines for Education Within the Family)*, issued by the Pontifical Council for the Family (The Wanderer Press and Human Life International, 1996), n. 3.
[509] Ibid., n. 22.

> which makes self-giving possible. *Chastity is the spiritual power which frees love from selfishness and aggression.*[510]

From the respect for the nature of sexuality as a properly human capacity, it follows that sex education must be firmly grounded in respect for the dignity of the human person, especially the child. Hence, among other things, there must be respect for the innocence of the child, something usually not found in today's sex education programs:

> In some societies today, there are planned and determined attempts to impose *premature sex information* on children. But, at this stage of development, children are still not capable of fully understanding the value of the affective dimension of sexuality. They cannot understand and control sexual imagery within the proper context of moral principles and, for this reason, they cannot integrate premature sexual information with moral responsibility. Such information tends to shatter their emotional and educational development and to disturb the natural serenity of this period of life. Parents should politely but firmly exclude any attempts to violate children's innocence because such attempts compromise the spiritual, moral, and emotional development of growing persons who have a right to their innocence.[511]

Respect for modesty, a closely related concern, is also of crucial importance:

> **No one should ever be invited, let alone obliged, to act in any way that could objectively offend against modesty or which could subjectively offend against his or her own delicacy or sense of privacy.**
>
> This *principle of respect for the child* excludes all improper forms of involving children and young people. In this regard,

[510] Ibid., n. 16.
[511] Ibid., n. 83.

> among other things, this can include the following *methods that abuse sex education*: (a) every "dramatized" representation, mime, or "role playing" which depicts genital or erotic matters, (b) making drawings, charts, or models, etc., of this nature, (c) seeking personal information about sexual questions or asking that family information be divulged, (d) oral or written exams about genital or erotic questions.[512]

And, of course, "**No material of an erotic nature should be presented to children or young people of any age, individually or in a group.**"[513]

The denial that schools have the authority to engage in such abuses of the children in their charge is closely correlated with the Church's teaching that it is, first and foremost, the parents who have authority in the area of sex education. Hence respect for parental prerogatives in this area is central to the document:

> *It is recommended that parents be aware of their own educational role and defend and carry out this primary right and duty.* It follows that any educative activity, related to education for love and carried out by persons outside the family, must be subject to the parents' acceptance of it and must be seen not as a substitute but as a support for their work....Frequently, parents are not lacking in awareness and effort, but they are quite alone, defenseless, and often made to feel they are wrong.[514]

> It is recommended that parents attentively follow every form of sex education that is given to their children outside the home, *removing their children whenever this education does not correspond to their own principles.*[515]

---

[512] Ibid., n. 127.
[513] Ibid., n. 127.
[514] Ibid., n. 113.
[515] Ibid., n. 117.

> Since each child or young person must be able to live his or her own sexuality in conformity with Christian principles, and hence be able to exercise the virtue of chastity, *no educator — not even parents — can interfere with this right to chastity....*[516]

Finally, because sexuality, as self-giving, is inseparable from the gift of life itself which men and women, in a kind of partnership with God, are allowed to give, sex education must always respect the sanctity of human life, something else which is not exceedingly common in today's programs:

> In the first place, parents must reject *secularized and anti-natalist sex education*, which puts God at the margin of life and regards the birth of a child as a threat. This sex education is spread by large organizations and international associations that promote abortion, sterilization, and contraception. These organizations want to impose a false lifestyle against the truth of human sexuality. Working at national or state levels, these organizations try to arouse the fear of "the threat of overpopulation" among children and young people to promote the contraceptive mentality, that is, the "anti-life" mentality. They spread false ideas about the "reproductive health" and "sexual and reproductive rights" of young people. Furthermore, some anti-natalist organizations maintain those clinics which, violating the rights of parents, provide abortion and contraception for young people, thus promoting promiscuity and consequently an increase in teenage pregnancies.[517]
>
> ...Parents must also reject the promotion of "safe sex" or "safer sex," a dangerous and immoral policy based on the deluded theory that the condom can provide adequate pro-

[516] Ibid., n. 118.
[517] Ibid., n. 136.

> tection against AIDS. Parents must insist on continence outside marriage and fidelity in marriage as the only true and secure education for the prevention of this contagious disease.[518]

Wanderer reaction to the *Truth and Meaning* document was, as always, enthusiastic as well as heavily focused on its practical implications as a tool for correcting the abuses that had crept (or, more accurately, galloped) into Catholic schools in the name of sex education. Paul Likoudis quickly indicated that the document had come just in time, considering the extent of the atrocities involved.[519] Another article goes into more detail, focusing on the importance of the document's teaching on the role of parents:

> The long-awaited document on sex education promised to Catholic parents more than two years ago by the Pontifical Council for the Family and released just before Christmas tells parents in direct language that they must assert their right to control the sex education of their children.
>
> It also effectively invalidates every sex education program used in Catholic and public schools in the United States today and nullifies the U.S. bishops' "mandate" for Catholic sex education, *Human Sexuality: A Catholic Perspective for Education and Lifelong Learning*, which they approved at their annual fall meeting in 1990.[520]
>
> The only "proper place" for sex education, says the document, is the home, and parents have the right and duty to protect their children from sex education programs that vio-

---

[518] Ibid., n. 136.

[519] Paul Likoudis, "Vatican Sex-Ed Document Comes Just in Time," W, 1-11-96.

[520] Paul Likoudis, "Parents Must 'Reclaim the Task' of Children's Sex Education," W, 1-4-96.

> late the latency period, offend modesty, and promote hedonistic and antinatalist ideologies.
>
> Though the entire text of *The Truth and Meaning of Human Sexuality* employs a positive tone, it does condemn any sex education program which promotes "safe sex" or "safer sex," teaches children and adolescents about contraception, sterilization, and homosexuality, employs "values clarification" techniques, or utilizes classroom exercises wherein students make drawings, charts, or models on genital matters, divulge family information, or take tests with genital or erotic questions.[521]

Likoudis also appreciates the document's role in presenting a positive view of sexuality which focuses on human wholeness:

> It is essentially the example of parents who manifest to their children their respect for life and the mystery of procreation which will "spare the child or young person from the false idea that the two dimensions of the conjugal act, unitive and procreative, can be separated at will," and it is incumbent on Christian parents, states the document, to raise their children with an understanding of the "very serious consequences" that follow when sexual activity is dissociated from married love.[522]

Father Paul Marx, writing a few months later, also shows his appreciation for the document as a tool in fighting the battle over sex education, while presenting, in almost apocalyptic terms, the terrible predicament Christian parents find themselves in today. His comments sum up the whole situation involving sex education in the Church about as well as anyone could, and deserve to be quoted at some length:

---

[521] Ibid.
[522] Ibid.

Comprehensive biological classroom sex education was the invention of Planned Parenthood — the Church's and humanity's greatest enemy.[523]

Anyone who has followed modern school sex education throughout the world will know that it has been a miserable failure everywhere. Given the separation of church and state in most countries, God, morality, and religious values may not be mentioned in the classroom. And yet only religious, moral, and spiritual values instilled in the young from very early on will form loving, self-giving, self-controlled persons.[524]

The great hope in the United States is the burgeoning movement of home-schooling: Of 40 million grade and secondary school students, one and one-half million are being home-schooled by parents. They have lost all confidence in public, private, and even Catholic schools, knowing only too well what goes on there. The main reasons: violence and poor intellectual performance, but above all offensive sex ed. Therefore, it would seem imperative that we educate and form parents as obviously the most important teachers in the world.[525]

The virtuous example of parents is absolutely crucial as the pontifical council's *Truth and Meaning of Human Sexuality* and Vatican II insist. The best thing parents can do for their children is to truly love each other properly.[526]

Again, the first thing parents owe their children is to love each other properly. Any conflicts between parents tend in-

[523] Father Paul Marx, O.S.B., "Educating in Love and Sexuality," W, 5-9-96.
[524] Ibid.
[525] Ibid.
[526] Ibid.

> evitably to be written into the personalities of their children, child psychologists often remind us.[527]
>
> The truly prepared Catholic couple could be taught and formed to be fully realistic, which means to understand the pagan culture and how to resist it in building a home that is a "little Church" (*ecclesiola*).[528]
>
> May I suggest that the next big project or meeting for the Pontifical Council for the Family should be how to prepare the young for marriage, parenting, and family life in today's anti-love/anti-life culture, and how to re-educate anxious parents today to instill and form chastity in their developing young.[529]

We have indeed "supp'd full with horrors." Yet hope is never to be abandoned. If the people who devour children in the name of "humanistic" sex education have won the worldly battles thus far, they have done so without *The Wanderer*'s help. *The Wanderer* is only one little newspaper, yet in its own small way it has provided a space for prophetic witness to the truth, a place where the light can hine in the darkness. Who knows what great things may yet come of that?

---

[527] Ibid.
[528] Ibid.
[529] Ibid.

EPILOGUE

EXTREMISM OR PROPHETIC WITNESS? A FINAL REFLECTION

Blessed are you when men hate you, and when they exclude you and revile you, and cast out your name as evil, on account of the Son of man! Rejoice in that day, and leap for joy, for behold, your reward is great in heaven; for so their fathers did to the prophets.... Woe to you, when all men speak well of you, for so their fathers did to the false prophets.

— Luke 6:22-23, 26

But we have no reason to assume that saving our society from disaster is what lies in God's providential purposes. However attached we are to our society, we must remember, as C.S. Lewis has emphasized, that only human persons have immortal souls, not societies and civilizations. The basic test of the value of any outcome, therefore is not whether it tends to the saving of society from disaster, but whether it leads to the saving of immortal souls.

— John Mulloy

A prominent feature of public debate in the contemporary world seems to be the nearly universal success of the kind of argumentation, if it can be called that, which ignores both evidence and logic, which, in fact, ignores the arguments it is trying to refute, and takes refuge simply in categorizing the opponent in such a way that he and his argument can be dismissed. That is largely the way the liberal Catholic world has dealt with *The Wanderer* for the past generation or so, the era which I have tried to chronicle in these pages. Its technique has consisted largely of labeling *The Wanderer*, its commentators, and its readers as extremists, as "outside the mainstream," to use a familiar metaphor.

This kind of non-reasoning has been used quite effectively by the Catholic Library Association to keep *The Wanderer*'s contribution to public debate within American Catholicism to a great extent outside the public record. That association is the source of the Catholic Periodical Index, a publication of critical importance for leading researchers to the documents which enable them to know what is going on within Catholic scholarly and journalistic circles. Future historians, when they get around to trying to understand the issues that late twentieth-century American Catholics debated and, indeed, fought over, will turn to the Catholic Periodical Index to orient them and guide them to the relevant documents. The problem is that, though *The Wanderer* has, whether anyone likes it or not, played a major role in this debate, scholars will not find it indexed there. They will find the *National Catholic Reporter* there, with its violently anti-Roman, anti-papal diatribes; its advocacy of abortion, contraception, and homosexuality, and so on *ad nauseam*. They will find any number of publications of a similar hue. But they will not find *The Wanderer*. The picture they will get of late twentieth century American Catholicism will be a badly skewed one as a result.

The CLA has tried to justify its decision not to index *The Wanderer* by stating that it is an extremist publication, "outside the mainstream," one that specializes in name-calling, ideological sloganeering, and appeals to emotion, with little effort at rational argumentation. The material sampled in these pages will, I think, help to refute that argument by actually showing the reader the level of rational debate achieved by many *Wanderer* contributors. Certainly, *The Wanderer* does not claim to be nonpartisan, to be covering the issues from a neutral perspective. Yet the same can be said of the *National Catholic Reporter*, the principal difference being that the latter's partisanship is on the left, while *The Wanderer*'s is on the right. Certainly, the CLA is right in indexing the *Reporter* because, if it were excluded, researchers would be deprived of valuable information when they tried to understand what was happening in our era. But the CLA seems unable to understand that the same reasoning applies to *The Wanderer*. Somehow, the *Reporter*, however extreme many of us may consider its positions to be, is respectable in the eyes of the CLA. To use some recent jargon, the *Reporter* is "politically correct." But *The Wanderer* is "outside the mainstream."

It especially galls many of us when some commentator makes a favorable reference to an article in *The Wanderer*, but considers it necessary to qualify that reference by saying something like, "I don't usually put much stock in *The Wanderer*, but in this case it seems to have a valid point." In effect, if you happen to agree with *The Wanderer*, you agree with it in spite of its being *The Wanderer*. Not much of a compliment, certainly.

So what we "Wanderer types" hope this volume will accomplish is to create a public record, for future generations, of the public witness we have tried to bear against the horrendous errors of our time, so that that witness will not be forgotten, despite the efforts of some of our opponents to drop it down the memory hole.

Perhaps we can best conclude this discussion by a short reflection on the meaning of all this rhetoric about the "mainstream" and whether one happens to be in it or out of it. That may also cast a light on the total meaning of *The Wanderer*'s witness.

I would like to suggest that in a society as deeply divided as is ours, not to mention a Church as divided as is the Catholic Church in America today, it is rather meaningless and simplistic to talk about *a* mainstream, but that, in reality, we have, speaking paradoxically, *two mainstreams* — that is, two streams, two currents of thought and action, and that those participating in each see their particular current as *the* mainstream. The two currents of thought and action are grounded in two radically different and contradictory understandings of what reality is all about — i.e., the meaning of man's existence in relation to himself, to others, to the world, and, ultimately, to God. Again and again, through all of human history, we see these two ways, these two paths, running, but perhaps never as clearly distinguished, as clearly standing out in their reality and in their distinctness from each other, as in our century of crisis. The two streams can be compared across a multitude of categories which should, by now, be familiar to the reader:

1) There is the stream that takes us, if we are good swimmers, toward wholeness, toward human integrity, and then there is the stream that leads to disintegration and dehumanization.

2) There is the current called love, in all its fullness as selfless love of God and neighbor, and then there is the current which leads to the exaltation of the isolated, autonomous self.

3) There is the stream that leads to freedom in obedient response to divine love, and then there is the stream that leads to an exaltation of a pseudo-freedom that is in reality the deepest slavery.

4) There is the current which flows toward Christ, true God and true man, as the center of all existence, and then there is the one that flows toward man as the center. Paradoxically, though, when man is worshipped as the center, the humanism that results actually attacks man and destroys the human person, because man's true humanity and his true selfhood come from his place as a creature of God, not as an autonomous ego.

5) There is the current that flows toward genuine human community in Christ, and there is the one that flows into the total state.

We could go on indefinitely with dichotomies like these, but I am sure the reader gets the idea by now. Mankind as a whole is engaged in a war between good and evil, a war for which this idea of the two mainstreams is a metaphor. At the moment, those who are in the second current, the current that flows away from God, away from genuine freedom, away from community, seem to be in the ascendancy, especially in the Catholic Church in America. From their own standpoint, they are the mainstream, and the only mainstream. It is easy to lose sight of the other stream, yet certainly every orthodox Catholic will see that stream as *the* mainstream in relation to God's whole plan for mankind, for his redemption, sanctification, and salvation.

It has been the "*Wanderer* gang's" mission, for some years now, to bear witness to certain basic truths about man's existence and his relation to God, world, and neighbor, and thus to help to constitute the true mainstream. Have we actually succeeded in totally embodying these truths? No, of course not. All men are sinners and subject to error, and we are no exception. It is always easy to drift away from truth even when we are trying to bear witness to it. I can testify, for one, to how easy it is, when one writes, to get caught up in pride and vanity and become more interested in appearing clever than in speaking the truth. A sound argument can suddenly get turned into an oversimplification of a complex issue, or a completely unnecessary personal attack on an opponent.

Nevertheless, we keep trying, and we keep on praying for the success of our apostolate and asking for the prayers of our fellow Christians everywhere. And as long as we strive in that way to be faithful to our witness, we need never fear being truly "outside the mainstream."

Mother Teresa has been quoted as saying that God does not call us to be successful, He calls us to be faithful. We might paraphrase it thus: God does not call us to be inside the mainstream, He calls us to be faithful watchmen, and that means being inside God's mainstream, but not the world's. That is the only success we need concern ourselves about. We are hardly infallible, and if, now and again, we, like Don Quixote, get chewed up by a windmill as a result of tilting at imaginary dragons, that is not too great a price to pay for the privilege of such a mission to prophetic witness.

INDEX

—A—

abortifacient pills, 154
abortion, 14, 20, 21, 33, 36, 66, 83, 87, 91, 93, 94, 95, 104, 109, 110, 111, 112, 113, 114, 115, 116, 117, 118, 119, 120, 121, 122, 123, 124, 125, 126, 128, 129, 131, 134, 135, 136, 137, 138, 139, 140, 141, 142, 143, 144, 145, 146, 147, 148, 149, 150, 152, 153, 154, 155, 156, 157, 158, 159, 160, 161, 162, 163, 164, 165, 166, 167, 168, 169, 170, 171, 173, 177, 178, 180, 181, 182, 183, 185, 186, 317, 342, 353, 354, 357, 362, 373, 377, 393, 394, 397, 404, 412
Action for Life, 117
adoption, 178
Adrian, William L., Bishop, 224, 385
adultery, 342, 357, 365, 373
affirmative action, 28
Africa, 241
AIDS (Acquired Immune Deficiency Syndrome, 278, 279, 404
Albigensianism, 397
Alcoholics Anonymous, 356
Alinsky, Saul, 28, 32, 54
American Life Lobby, 170
American Revolution, 29
Americanism, 18, 19, 20
Amos, Book of, 189
Andrews, Joan, 166
Anglican Church, 229
Apostles, the, 59, 255, 274, 290, 291, 332
Arian heresy, 50
Aristotelianism, 273, 317
Aristotle, 61, 123
Arizona, 110, 111
Arlington, Virginia, 86
artificial insemination, 83, 84
Auschwitz, 164
authoritarianism, 29, 32, 50, 74, 119, 378
authority, 34, 36, 41, 53, 54, 56, 58, 75, 99, 100, 101, 103, 105, 109, 110, 116, 124, 139, 142, 145, 146, 148, 152, 159, 183, 184, 186, 196, 200, 225, 227, 232, 235, 237, 238, 239, 240, 241, 242, 243, 247, 250, 251, 254, 255, 256, 257, 259, 263, 264, 265, 283, 284, 286, 320, 323, 324, 328, 342, 363, 364, 367, 383, 395

—B—

Baltimore Catechism, 284, 323
Baltimore, Maryland, 231, 232, 234, 235, 236, 237, 238, 239, 357, 358
Baptism, 224, 304, 319
Baton Rouge, Louisiana, 97
Becoming a Person, 387
Becoming a Person Program (BAPP), 388, 389, 390, 391, 392
Benziger catechism, 302
Bernardin, Joseph Cardinal, 149
Beseda, Curt, 164
Bible, 272, 274, 275, 277, 280, 282, 287, 289, 290
Binz, Leo, Archbishop, 195, 196
biology, 95, 287, 396
birth control, 21, 66, 71, 73, 74, 77, 92, 95, 97, 106, 109, 179, 343, 362. *See* contraception
Bishops' Bicentennial Committee, 26, 51
Blackmun, Harry, Justice, 122, 123
blacks, 28, 131, 142, 352
Blanchard, James, Governor, 141, 144

blasphemy, 344, 345
Bohemia, 199
Bolsheviks, 17
Borders, William, Archbishop, 357
Boston, Massachusetts, 115, 126, 140, 175, 370
Bozell, L. Brent, 117
Brady, William O., Archbishop, 67
Bray, Michael, 164
Brennan, William J., Jr., Justice, 139
Brown, Raymond, Father, 281, 282, 283, 284, 285, 286, 287, 288, 289, 290, 291, 292, 293
Bruskewitz, Fabian, Bishop, 376
Buckley Amendment, 153, 154
Buckley, James, Senator, 153
Buckley, William F., 128
Buddhism, 272
Bultmann, Rudolf, 289, 299
bureaucracy, 30, 35, 36, 37, 38, 54, 55, 131, 132, 135, 136, 139, 144, 261, 319, 320, 331, 382, 394
Bures, Nick, 15, 22
Burke, Florence A., R.N., 69, 110
Burns, Governor, 114
Burns, Robert, Father, 355, 356, 384
Bush, George, President, 117

—C—

Calderone, Mary, 384
Califano Doctrine, 138, 139, 141
Califano, Joseph, 138, 139
California, 113
Call to Action, 25, 27, 30, 31, 32, 39, 43, 44, 46, 47, 49, 50, 51, 53, 54, 55, 56, 57, 58, 59, 60, 65
capital punishment, 27, 146, 287
capitalism, 54
Cartesianism, 295
Casserly, Bernard, 235
catechesis, 218, 269, 270, 294, 316, 319, 322, 324, 325, 330, 390
catechetics, 285, 299, 300, 304, 311, 315, 316, 317, 322, 328, 332
Catechism of the Catholic Church, 325, 327, 328, 329, 330, 331, 375
catechisms, 284, 301, 302, 303, 304, 305
Catharism, 397
Catholic Coalition for Gay Civil Rights, 352
Catholic Committee on Pluralism and Abortion, 147
Catholic Library Association (CLA), 412, 413
Catholic Periodical Index, 412
Catholic Theological Society of America (CTSA), 342, 343, 344, 345, 346, 347, 349, 365
Catholic Traditionalist Movement, 230, 231, 232, 233, 236, 239, 240, 250
Catholic University of America, 70, 71, 104, 330, 362
Catholicism, 16, 20, 21, 26, 30, 55, 141, 263, 300, 304, 305, 312, 376, 392, 412. *See* Church, Catholic
Catholics United for the Faith, 35, 36, 38, 39, 41
celibacy, 33, 34, 77, 84
chastity, 84, 178, 180, 338, 341, 347, 387, 398, 400, 401, 403, 407
Chavez, Gilbert E., Archbishop, 137
Chicago, Illinois, 14, 37, 44, 387
child abuse, 155, 393
Christ, divinity of, 311
Christ, Jesus, 19, 34, 52, 59, 60, 69, 76, 86, 96, 101, 105, 106, 117, 132, 138, 149, 159, 160, 161, 165, 166, 174, 176, 177, 186, 191, 192, 193, 210, 211, 212, 213, 214, 215, 216, 217, 218, 219, 221, 222, 223, 224, 225, 226, 237, 249, 250, 257, 258, 269, 270, 271, 272, 273, 274, 280, 281, 289, 290, 291, 292, 293,

297, 301, 302, 304, 305, 306, 309, 311, 315, 326, 329, 332, 335, 360, 372, 375, 378, 392, 414
Christianity, 31, 273, 274, 277, 280, 281, 299, 302, 304, 309, 313, 315, 387
Christmas, 178, 243, 280, 405
Christology, 272
Church, Catholic, 5, 6, 13, 15, 17, 18, 19, 20, 21, 25, 26, 27, 28, 29, 30, 31, 32, 33, 34, 35, 36, 38, 40, 41, 43, 44, 45, 47, 48, 50, 51, 53, 54, 55, 56, 57, 58, 59, 60, 61, 63, 65, 66, 67, 68, 69, 70, 71, 72, 73, 74, 75, 76, 77, 78, 79, 80, 81, 82, 83, 85, 86, 88, 90, 92, 94, 95, 96, 97, 98, 99, 101, 102, 103, 105, 109, 114, 115, 117, 118, 119, 120, 127, 129, 131, 132, 133, 135, 136, 137, 138, 139, 142, 143, 144, 145, 147, 148, 149, 151, 156, 157, 171, 174, 179, 180, 181, 182, 185, 186, 189, 191, 192, 193, 195, 196, 197, 198, 199, 200, 201, 202, 203, 205, 206, 208, 211, 213, 216, 217, 219, 222, 223, 224, 225, 226, 227, 229, 230, 231, 233, 234, 235, 237, 238, 239, 240, 241, 242, 244, 245, 246, 247, 248, 249, 250, 252, 253, 254, 255, 256, 258, 261, 262, 263, 264, 265, 266, 269, 270, 271, 272, 273, 274, 275, 277, 278, 279, 280, 281, 282, 283, 284, 286, 296, 297, 302, 303, 305, 311, 312, 313, 317, 319, 320, 324, 325, 327, 328, 330, 331, 332, 337, 338, 339, 340, 341, 343, 344, 347, 349, 351, 352, 355, 356, 357, 358, 359, 360, 361, 362, 363, 364, 365, 366, 367, 368, 369, 371, 372, 373, 374, 375, 376, 377, 378, 379, 381, 382, 383, 387, 388, 389, 390, 397, 399, 400, 402, 406, 407, 413, 414
Cicero, 182
Cicognani, Amleto, Archbishop, 239
civil disobedience, 63, 116, 120, 152, 156, 159, 160, 161, 166, 182, 184, 185
civil rights, 142, 163, 352, 353
civil war, 184
Clark, Colin, 68
Clark, Paul, 182
Clinton, Farley, 16, 19, 20
collectivism, 54
Collegeville, Minnesota, 20
Commandments, the, 52, 171, 365, 389
Communion of Saints, 172
Communism, 376
community, 18, 28, 34, 52, 55, 58, 59, 89, 90, 92, 95, 119, 150, 167, 172, 180, 192, 193, 197, 203, 207, 212, 221, 222, 223, 242, 253, 295, 306, 317, 327, 332, 337, 340, 343, 344, 345, 355, 364, 369, 380, 381, 392, 400, 414
Confirmation, Sacrament of, 117
Confucianism, 273
Congar, Yves, 363
Congregation for Catholic Education, 366
Congregation for Divine Worship, 208, 261
Congregation for the Doctrine of the Faith, 136, 246, 347
conjugal love, 79, 80, 82, 85
conscience, 27, 33, 66, 76, 105, 125, 138, 139, 142, 164, 181, 199, 311, 343, 344, 364, 371, 372, 377, 379, 388, 389, 390, 393
conscientious objection, 182. *See* civil disobedience
conservatism, 18, 116, 117, 133, 237, 281, 283, 284
Constitution on the Sacred Liturgy, 264

Constitution, U.S., 21, 121, 122, 123, 124, 129, 153, 154, 156, 196
contraception, 14, 20, 33, 65, 66, 68, 70, 72, 73, 74, 76, 79, 80, 83, 85, 86, 87, 88, 89, 90, 91, 92, 93, 94, 95, 97, 98, 99, 100, 101, 104, 105, 109, 139, 169, 178, 179, 182, 342, 343, 362, 365, 377, 404, 405, 412
Cook, Mary E., 134, 168, 169
Coriden, James A., Father, 39
Corum, James Sterling, 357, 358
Covington, Kentucky., 326
Cowden-Guido, Richard, 146, 161, 162, 171
Credo of the People of God, 77, 243, 294
CSE (classroom sex education), 397, 398
culture of death, 174, 175, 176, 177, 178, 180
culture of life, 174, 176
Culture Wars, 87
Cuomo, Mario, Governor, 146, 147
Curia, Roman, 36
Curran, Charles, Father, 47, 70, 71, 99, 101, 326, 362, 363, 364, 365, 366, 367

—D—

Daly, Gabriel, Father, 331
Dante Alighieri, 25, 27
Davies, A. Powell, Mrs., 66
Dearden, John Cardinal, 27, 35, 206
death, 16, 25, 80, 91, 105, 106, 109, 110, 115, 147, 166, 174, 175, 176, 177, 178, 180, 224, 244, 245, 251, 257, 273, 274, 276, 278, 280, 284, 304, 350, 360, 382, 400
Decalogue, 302
Declaration On Certain Questions Concerning Sexual Ethics, 339, 351, 358
democracy, 27, 30, 32, 35, 39, 40, 44, 45, 46, 47, 50, 74, 114, 155, 158, 183, 184, 185, 284, 299, 375
demythologization, 191, 274
DePauw, Gommar, Father, 231, 232, 233, 234, 235, 236, 237, 238, 239, 240, 241, 250, 251, 265
Descartes, René, 78, 87
Detroit, Michigan, 14, 25, 27, 30, 31, 35, 45, 53, 54, 55, 56, 57, 58, 59, 60, 65, 142, 326
development of doctrine, 102, 105, 328
Devil, the, 43, 155
Dignity, 356, 361
disarmament, 28
Division of Research and Development in Religious Education, NCCB, 307, 311
divorce, 14, 20, 28, 352, 393
Docherty, Jerome, Father, 209, 281, 285
Dogmatic Constitution on Divine Revelation, 290
Doino, William, Jr., 330, 331
Dominicae Cenae, 226
Down's syndrome, 171
Doyle, Donald A., 395
Dozier, Carroll T., Bishop, 135
Dred Scott decision, 128
Drinan, Robert, Father, 139
Droleskey, Thomas A., 374
drug addiction, 394
drugs, 72
Dulles, Avery, Father, 363
Dutch Catechism, 33, 391
Dutch Pastoral Council, 42
Dwyer, Robert, Archbishop, 204, 205, 206, 227

—E—

Ecclesia Dei, 247, 250, 251, 252, 265
Eckhardt, Eugene, 15
Econe, Switzerland, 242, 246
Ederer, Rupert J., 262, 263
Edinburgh University, 72
education, 28, 41, 133, 138, 165, 173, 174, 270, 302, 303, 304, 307, 308, 309, 311, 312, 318, 319, 320, 324, 339, 366, 379, 380, 381, 382, 384, 385, 386, 387, 388, 390, 392, 393, 394, 395, 396, 397, 398, 399, 400, 401, 402, 403, 404, 405, 406, 408
egalitarianism, 52
Eisenhower, Dwight D., President, 66
Eliot, T.S., 191
Emmitsburg, Maryland, 231
Engel, Randy, 399
England, 5, 199
Enlightenment, the, 26
enovid, 68
Ephesians, Epistle to the, 49
epistemology, 316, 318
Equal Rights Amendment, 28, 46
Eucharist, 28, 49, 137, 148, 193, 214, 216, 218, 219, 222, 223, 224, 226, 230, 269
Europe, 179, 317
euthanasia, 66, 95, 104, 154, 177, 181, 182, 186, 362
Evangelium Vitae, 174, 175, 179, 181, 182, 183, 185. *See* Gospel of Life
Everett, Aaron, 163
Everett, Lawrence P., Father, 73
evolution, 277
evolutionism, 51
existentialism, 269, 276, 277, 301, 317

—F—

family, 14, 16, 27, 28, 58, 66, 70, 85, 90, 91, 92, 93, 94, 97, 112, 116, 127, 139, 178, 179, 180, 297, 337, 345, 357, 380, 381, 382, 387, 392, 393, 396, 397, 399, 400, 401, 402, 403, 405, 407
Family Life Bureau of the National Catholic Welfare Conference, 112
Family Life Division of the U.S. Catholic Conference, 387
Faveri, Luigi, Bishop, 234, 239
Feeneyism, 265
Felici, Pericle Cardinal, 75
feminism, 32, 87, 88, 90, 121
Ferraro, Geraldine, 145, 146
Finkbine, Sherri, 110, 111, 112
First Vatican Council, 303
Flanagan, John W., Father, 242, 243
fornication, 342, 365, 373
Forrest, Michael D., Father, 224
Forty Hours devotion, 223
Fourteenth Amendment, 123, 124, 125
Foy, Vincent, Monsignor, 96
freedom, 14, 17, 50, 56, 116, 119, 175, 177, 313, 339, 346, 359, 364, 369, 370, 371, 372, 373, 374, 377, 379, 380, 381, 383, 414
French Revolution, 26, 29, 317
Freud, Sigmund, 337, 385
fundamental option, 319, 373

—G—

Gagneret, Rosaire, O.P., 101
Gagnon, Edouard Cardinal, 245
Galatians, Epistle to the, 345
Gallup polls, 36
Gantin, Bernardin, Cardinal, 246
gay rights, 27, 28, 352, 357
Geaney, Father, 235

Genesis, Book of, 86, 191
Georgetown Campus Ministry, 225
Georgetown University, 225
Georgia, 121
Germany, 16, 17, 83, 179, 199
Gibbons, James Cardinal, 20
Gill, Joseph T., 104, 105, 106, 140, 141, 144, 145, 169, 170, 200, 201
Gnosticism, 397
Goldsby, Matthew, 161, 164
Goldwater, Barry, Senator, 117
Gospel of Life, the, 174
Gospel, the, 36, 90, 174, 175, 176, 178, 180, 280, 281, 286, 287, 288, 291, 302, 355, 359, 365
Government, U.S. Federal, 124
Greek civilization, 210, 272
Greek language, 328
Greeley, Andrew, Father, 27
Gregorian chant, 196, 212, 213, 227, 258, 261, 262, 264, 265
Gumbleton, Thomas, Bishop, 326
Gut, O.S.B., Benno Cardinal, 208
Guthrie, Mary Anne, Sister, 135

—H—

Hagen, John, 168
Hallett, Paul, 206
Hammer, Betty, 394
handicapped, the, 27, 29, 110, 171
Happel, Stephen P., Father, 51
Haring, Bernard, Father, 363
Hartnett, John J., Father, 103
Hatch Amendment, 155, 170
Hauf, J.C., 157
Heaven, 31, 80, 178, 219, 248, 389, 401
Hebrews, Epistle to the, 60
Hell, 26, 257, 389
hermeneutics, 294
Herod, 115, 156
Herodotus, 304
Hickey, James Cardinal, 367
hierarchy, 33, 50, 54, 56, 139, 148, 149, 252, 367
Hindmarsh, Cathaleen, 198, 199
Hinduism, 272
Hitchcock, James, 262
Hitler, Adolf, 17, 67, 113, 171, 197, 201
Hogan Amendment, 153, 154
Hogan, Lawrence J., Rep., 153
Holland, 31, 33, 34, 199
Holy Ghost Fathers, 241
Holy Innocents, 115
Holy See, 21, 143, 144, 197, 210, 218, 229, 230, 232, 233, 235, 239, 243, 246, 247, 254, 259, 366
homosexuality, 27, 33, 52, 97, 131, 139, 326, 342, 343, 345, 346, 350, 351, 352, 353, 354, 355, 356, 357, 358, 359, 360, 361, 362, 365, 377, 393, 405, 412
Hughes, John, Bishop, 326
Human Life Amendment, 46, 154
Human Life in Our Day, 84, 91
human life, sanctity of, 21, 91, 112, 113, 115, 119, 132, 133, 134, 174, 175, 182, 185, 269, 403
Human Sexuality, 342, 343, 346, 347, 348, 365, 400, 404
Human Sexuality: A Catholic Perspective for Education and Lifelong Learning, 405
Humanae Vitae, 33, 63, 65, 73, 74, 75, 76, 77, 78, 79, 82, 83, 84, 85, 86, 87, 88, 89, 90, 91, 94, 95, 96, 98, 99, 100, 101, 102, 103, 104, 105, 106, 127, 134, 243, 348
humanism, 50, 68, 78, 82, 84, 86, 88, 176, 177, 328, 341, 374, 390, 396, 408, 414
Hurley, Francis T., Archbishop, 104

—I—

ICEL (International Commission on English in the liturgy), 204, 206, 207, 208, 209, 211, 256, 257, 260, 261
iconoclasm, 213, 214, 376
ideology, 17, 29, 31, 32, 45, 48, 51, 52, 69, 141, 227, 269, 271, 276, 289, 316, 317, 319, 372, 376, 394, 395, 405, 412
illegal aliens, 28
illegitimacy, 178
Imbiorski, Walter, Father, 387, 388, 389, 394
in vitro fertilization, 84
Incarnation, 21, 193, 219, 225, 254, 269, 270, 275, 280, 289, 291, 294, 311, 344, 371
India, 66
individualism, 18, 52, 318
infanticide, 95, 112, 171, 177
Instrument for the Evaluation of Religion Textbooks, 307, 308, 309, 310, 311, 312, 314, 315, 394
Interrante, Stanley, 31
intrauterine device (IUD), 154
Ireland, 331
Islam, 179, 282
Israel, 172, 310
Italy, 179, 236

—J—

Jansenism, 257, 397
Jeremiah, 17, 172
Jews, 67, 115, 116, 132, 326
John Paul II, Pope, 146, 174, 175, 182, 183, 184, 226, 244, 246, 247, 248, 326, 327, 369, 370, 371, 373, 375, 376, 377, 397
John XXIII, Pope, 128, 152, 183, 195, 196, 199, 200, 229, 282, 285
Jones, E. Michael, 87, 88
Journet, C. Cardinal, 90, 91
Joyce, Mary R., 94, 95, 155, 156
judicial review, 124
just war, 161

—K—

Kane, Theresa, R.S.M., 143, 325
Kendall, George A., ii, 5, 148, 149, 166, 172, 174, 211
Kierkegaard, Soren, 276
King, Martin Luther, Jr., Rev., 118, 301
Kingdom of God, 35
Klaproth, Hugo, 16
Knott, John C., Father, 112
Knox, James Cardinal, 262
Knox, James, Cardinal, 261
Kohlberg, Lawrence, 324
Kosnik, Anthony, Father, 342
Kurz, Blaise S., Bishop, 234

—L—

L'Osservatore Romano, 386, 387
Labato, Ned, 159, 160
labor unions, 28
laissez-faire capitalism, 17
laity, 30, 31, 35, 38, 40, 41, 42, 45, 104, 134, 209, 367, 384
Lambeth Conference, 92
Lane, Thomas, General, 92, 93, 167
Last Things, 389
latency period, 405
Latin, 195, 196, 197, 198, 199, 200, 201, 202, 203, 204, 207, 208, 210, 211, 213, 227, 229, 230, 231, 232, 238, 248, 252, 253, 256, 257, 258, 259, 261, 262, 263, 264, 265, 328
Latin Liturgy Association, 262
Latin Mass, 197, 198, 201, 202, 203, 252, 263

Latin Mass Society, 252
Lawrence, Michael, 117
Laymen's Commission on the English Liturgy, 208, 259, 260, 261
Lefebvre, Marcel, Archbishop, 240, 241, 242, 243, 244, 245, 246, 248, 250, 263, 265
Leo XIII, Pope, 18
Lercaro, Giacomo Cardinal, 206
Letter to Bishops of the Catholic Church on the Pastoral Care of Homosexual Persons, 358
Lewis, C.S., 173, 411
liberalism, 20, 21, 30, 88, 103, 104, 106, 114, 141, 146, 149, 184, 185, 195, 234, 240, 245, 247, 275, 284, 318, 331, 350, 361, 362, 367, 373, 411
liberation theology, 32, 277
liberty, 32, 156, 163, 164, 295, 369, 381
life, right to, 115, 123, 124, 128, 140, 141, 153, 155, 158, 166, 170, 171, 173, 181
life, sanctity of, 387
Likoudis, James, 322, 324, 378, 379, 381, 382, 387, 388, 389, 392
Likoudis, James and Ruth, 382, 383
Likoudis, Paul, 376, 404, 405
Lincoln, Abraham, 162
Lincoln, Nebraska, 376
Liturgical Commission of the Diocese of Pittsburgh, 211
Liturgical Consilium, 206
liturgical movement, 20, 21
liturgical reform, 20, 195, 197, 202, 227, 250
liturgy, 20, 21, 39, 193, 194, 195, 196, 197, 198, 199, 200, 201, 202, 203, 204, 205, 206, 207, 208, 209, 210, 211, 212, 213, 214, 215, 219, 220, 224, 226, 227, 229, 230, 231, 232, 233, 240, 241, 243, 247, 248, 249, 250, 252, 253, 254, 255, 256, 257, 259, 260, 261, 262, 264, 265, 266
Los Angeles, California, 44, 198
Louis XVI, King, 26
Lucier, James, 259
Luke, Gospel According to, 43, 106, 380, 411
Lunn, Sir Arnold, 252
lust, 89, 254, 344, 345, 350
Lustiger, Cardinal, 326
Luther, Martin, 240
Lutheran Church, 16

—M—

Magi, 156
Magisterium, 54, 57, 71, 73, 74, 77, 81, 102, 104, 105, 186, 233, 237, 241, 242, 253, 254, 255, 283, 284, 289, 290, 328, 332, 349, 362, 365, 366, 398
Maher, Archbishop, 148
Maher, Bishop, 137
Mamie, Pierre, Bishop, 242
Manichaeanism, 57, 80, 390, 397
Mansour, Agnes, R.S.M., 141, 142, 143, 144, 145
Manzini, Raimondo, 386, 387
March for Life, 170
Markley, Edward, Father, 166
Marra, William, 259, 311, 312
marriage, 14, 69, 81, 84, 85, 94, 95, 96, 97, 177, 178, 179, 180, 346, 347, 362, 384, 386, 387, 397, 398, 401, 404, 407
Marriage, Sacrament of, 359
Martin, Malachi, 325, 329
Marx, Paul, Father, 97, 169, 178, 406
Marxism, 32, 44, 394
Mary, Blessed Virgin, 231, 292, 389
Masons, 16

Mass, the, 48, 75, 145, 191, 192, 193, 194, 195, 196, 197, 198, 199, 200, 201, 202, 203, 204, 205, 206, 207, 208, 209, 210, 211, 212, 213, 214, 215, 216, 218, 221, 222, 223, 224, 225, 226, 229, 230, 231, 244, 245, 247, 252, 253, 256, 257, 258, 259, 261, 262, 263, 264, 265, 326, 389
masturbation, 326, 343, 345, 362, 365, 393
materialism, 21
Matt family, 20
Matt, Alphonse J., Jr., 16, 31, 37, 38, 39, 50, 51, 127, 134, 135, 136, 139, 140, 150, 209, 210, 243, 248, 259, 265, 266, 342, 375
Matt, Alphonse J., Sr., 15, 16, 21, 69, 70
Matt, Joseph, 16
Matt, Walter, 16, 233, 234, 236, 237
Matthew, Gospel According to, 287
Mauro, Robert, 134
Mauro, Robert L., 134, 140, 145, 147
May, John L., Archbishop, 266
Mayer, Cardinal, 265
McBrien, Richard, Father, 146, 325, 363
McCarthy, John F., Monsignor, 248, 249, 343, 344, 345, 346, 347
McCormack, Arthur, Father, 69
McCormick, Richard, 363
McCrossen, Vincent A., 199, 200
McGucken, Joseph T., Bishop, 69
McHugh, James T., Father, 393, 394
McInerny, James, Father, O.P., 259
McNulty, Father, 326
Medeiros, Humberto, Archbishop, 115, 126, 140
media, 36, 53, 106
Media*tor Dei*, 253
Medicaid, 141, 142, 143
medicine, 123, 167
Memphis, Tennessee, 135
Mensheviks, 17
mercy killing. *See* euthanasia
metaphysics, 289, 318
Methodist Church, 75
Michel, Dom Virgil, 20
Michigan, 14, 121, 141, 142, 143
Migliorino, Monica, 146
Milwaukee, Wisconsin, 14, 325
Minnesota Historical Society, 18
miracles, 281, 289, 299
Missale Romanum, 260
modern consciousness, 299, 304
modernism, 15, 20, 21, 31, 44, 143, 192, 224, 227, 235, 243, 244, 250, 251, 252, 265, 266, 274, 275, 276, 277, 278, 279, 281, 287, 293, 294, 297, 303, 316, 325, 339, 340, 344, 367, 371, 374, 381, 389, 391, 400
modesty, 402, 405
Molloy, M.B., Monsignor, 189
morality, 17, 52, 54, 66, 82, 85, 97, 127, 128, 138, 178, 184, 270, 271, 307, 310, 317, 324, 337, 338, 339, 342, 343, 348, 349, 350, 352, 354, 365, 367, 370, 372, 375, 379, 380, 382, 390, 406
Moran, Gabriel, Brother, 315
Morriss, Frank, 6, 30, 34, 37, 40, 41, 47, 51, 53, 63, 99, 100, 114, 133, 134, 137, 138, 140, 147, 148, 156, 157, 159, 160, 162, 163, 165, 218, 219, 225, 226, 259, 316, 317, 319, 367, 377
Moses, 310
Most, William G., Father, 225
Mt. St. Mary's Seminary, 231
Muggeridge, Malcolm, 72
Mulloy, John J., 9, 37, 38, 41, 58, 59, 105, 118, 127, 135, 137, 173, 259, 260, 261, 280, 281, 286, 289, 290, 291, 292, 293, 300, 301, 307, 309, 310, 311, 312, 313, 314, 320, 328,

352, 353, 354, 364, 365, 392, 393, 411
multilingual education, 28
multinational corporations, 28
Mundelein College, 37, 38, 40, 43
Murphy, John D., Archbishop, 82, 90
Myers, Edith, 281, 284, 285, 314, 315
Mysterium Fidei, 222, 223
mythology, 272, 280, 281, 288, 303, 317, 352

—N—

National Catechetical Directory, 316, 317, 318, 319, 320, 321, 323
National Catholic Reporter, 69, 361, 378, 412
National Conference of Catholic Bishops (NCCB), 35, 37, 42, 132, 133, 260, 307
National Conference of Catholic Bishops Committee for Pro-Life Affairs, 126
National Conference of Catholic Bishops Committee on Liturgy, 260
National Federation of Catholic Physicians' Guilds, 395, 396, 397
National Organization of Women (NOW), 137, 138
National Pastoral Council, 31, 35, 36, 37, 38, 39, 40, 41, 42, 43
National Right to Life Committee, 113
natural family planning, 179
natural law, 72, 122, 138, 157, 183, 186, 372
Nazi Party, 17
Nazism, 376
NCEA (National Catholic Educational Association), 281, 286
necessity, common law of, 158
necessity, defense of, 158, 159, 163
Netherlands, the. *See* Holland
Nevins, Albert J., Father, 342, 343
New Covenant, 225
New Jersey, 388
New Morality, 302, 383
New Order of the Mass, 202
New Roman Missal, 208
New Testament, 328
New Ways Ministry, 355, 356
New World Order, 180, 181
New York City, 75, 112, 146, 147, 233, 234, 237, 358, 393
New York Times, 234
New York University, 395
New York, State of, 233
Newman, John Henry Cardinal, 203
Newton, Robert R., S.J., 323, 324
Nicene Creed, 302
Nixon, Richard M., President, 91, 92, 116
nominalism, 122, 289
Noordwijkerhoot, 33
North American Martyrs, 58
North Dakota, 121
North-American Man-Boy Love Association (NAMBLA), 355, 356
Notitiae, 202
Notre Dame University, 146
Novus Ordo, 208, 241, 243, 254, 255, 256, 257, 258, 259, 260, 261, 262, 264
nuclear war, 28
Nugent, Robert, Father, 352, 353, 354, 355

—O—

O'Beirne, Nancy, 113
O'Boyle, Patrick Cardinal, 75
O'Connor, J. Paul, Monsignor, 37, 39, 40, 41
O'Connor, John Cardinal, 36, 358

O'Toole, Christopher J., Father, 104
Officiorum Omnium, 253
Orange County, California, 44
organ transplants, 33
orthodoxy, 15, 21, 33, 40, 43, 48, 49, 63, 71, 93, 115, 126, 208, 211, 237, 239, 240, 241, 247, 250, 251, 252, 269, 279, 281, 284, 292, 309, 311, 314, 315, 319, 325, 327, 331, 364, 374, 390, 415
Ottaviani, Alfredo Cardinal, 239
overpopulation, 92, 404

—P—

Pacem in Terris, 183
pacifism, 163
Pakistan, 76
parental rights, 93, 133, 381
Parish liturgical commissions, 227
Paul VI, Pope, 34, 70, 73, 74, 75, 89, 90, 106, 199, 200, 202, 207, 208, 216, 225, 236, 238, 241, 242, 258, 260, 264, 294, 302, 339, 351
Paul, St., 49, 103, 119, 342, 369
Paulist catechism, 302
peace, 28, 106, 132, 140, 159, 160, 196, 255
Pediatrics, American Academy of, 171
Penance, Sacrament of, 389
Pennsylvania, 135, 211
Pensacola, Florida, 161, 162, 164
People's Organization, 54, 55, 56
People of God, the, 46, 51, 77, 193, 215, 243, 286, 294
Persian Gulf War, 112
Persona Humana, 348
Peter, St., 165, 166
Philippines, 75
philosophy, 51, 122, 123, 171, 212, 272, 276, 288, 289, 295, 297, 317, 376, 390
Pill, the, 68, 69
Pilon, Mark, Father, 138
Pius V, Pope, 255, 256
Pius X, St., Pope, 200, 242, 245, 246, 251, 275
Pius XI, Pope, 18, 73, 253
Pius XII, Pope, 20, 73, 208, 253, 383
Planned Parenthood, 93, 170, 179, 406
Plato, 304
Platonism, 273
Playboy Magazine, 72
pluralism, 114, 134, 352, 354
Poland, 15, 76
Pontifical Council for the Family, 407
POPE (Parents for Orthodoxy in Parochial Education), 41, 339, 362, 385
Popek, Alphonse, Monsignor, 59
population control, 66, 91, 116, 119
pornography, 136, 168
pragmatism, 20, 119
premarital intercourse, 33, 362, 393
prince of this world, the, 35
privacy, right of, 123, 128
pro-choicers, 95
procreation, 69, 70, 79, 84, 94, 96, 97, 177, 271, 345, 348, 397, 405
progressivism, 33, 43, 44, 47, 49, 54, 57, 65, 74, 157, 192, 231, 287, 324, 382
promiscuity, 397, 404
propaganda, 53, 136, 182, 263, 353, 384
property rights, 18
prophecy, 16, 21, 35, 36, 38, 55, 58, 59, 72, 78, 85, 93, 94, 95, 106, 111, 113, 119, 125, 132, 133, 137, 139, 140, 172, 173, 174, 230, 361, 408, 415
prophets, 310
Pro-Pig Manifesto, 171

prostaglandins, 93
Protestantism, 14, 15, 19, 92, 139, 237, 240, 275, 300, 369, 376
psychology, 86, 287, 312, 316, 317, 318, 322, 392
Pulver, Charles, 281, 286, 287
Purgatory, 26, 389
Puritanism, 390

—Q—

Quinn, John, Archbishop, 105, 326
Quo Primum, 255, 259

—R—

racism, 27, 28, 58, 136, 142
Rahner, Karl, 363
Rambush, Robert, 39
rationalism, 295
Ratzinger, Joseph Cardinal, 84, 244, 245, 246, 249, 250, 358, 359, 361, 362, 366
Reagan, Ronald, President, 113
Real Presence, 222
Rehnquist, William, Justice, 124, 125
relativism, 104, 105, 285, 322, 349, 376
Renovatio, 102
Representatives, U.S. House of, 135
Resurrection, 6, 80, 289, 290, 299
revelation, 84, 210, 270, 274, 275, 277, 282, 289, 290, 296, 297, 300, 303, 310, 313, 317, 319, 345, 364, 371
revolution, 16, 18, 20, 21, 26, 29, 31, 32, 39, 45, 50, 53, 70, 121, 122, 150, 155, 194, 195, 199, 208, 209, 210, 214, 227, 228, 229, 230, 237, 251, 252, 265, 270, 338, 339, 394, 397, 398
Rhodesia (Zimbabwe), 76
Rice, Charles, 93, 94, 116, 146, 150, 153, 156, 157, 160, 162, 163, 164, 170, 171
Richmond, Virginia, 326
Riga, Peter, 97
right to life movement, 157, 170
Roberts, William, 259
Robinson, Carol Jackson, 281, 287, 288
Rochester, New York, 112
Rock, John, Dr., 68, 69
Roe v. Wade, 120, 121, 125, 126, 127, 128, 129, 133, 134, 138, 158, 161, 165, 171, 185
Roman Catechism, 257
Romans, Epistle to the, 350
romanticism, 53
Romanus, 386, 387
Rome, 5, 6, 19, 21, 34, 37, 70, 112, 142, 147, 196, 229, 231, 232, 233, 234, 237, 238, 239, 241, 243, 244, 245, 246, 247, 250, 358, 362, 363, 364, 366, 367
Roosevelt, E.K., 382
rosary, 160
Rousseau, Jean-Jacques, 52, 53
Russia, 179
Russian (Soviet) revolution, 29
Ryan, Juan, 113
Ryder, John H., S.J., 82, 83, 100

—S—

Sacramento, California, 326
Sacraments, 33, 77, 117, 200, 202, 305, 306
Sacred Congregation for Religious and Secular Institutes, 143
Sacred Congregation for the Liturgy, 227
Sacrosanctum Concilium, 253
Sadlier catechism, 302, 305
safe sex, 404, 405

Saginaw, Michigan, 14, 325
Santiago, Chile, 249
Satan, 250, 342
Scheidler, Joseph M., 149, 158
schism, 34, 235, 239, 243, 248, 250
Schlick, Franz, Sr., 15
Schmidberger, Franz, Father, 245
Schmitz, John C., Rep., 92
scholasticism, 317
Schuler, Richard J., Monsignor, 202, 203, 213, 214, 263, 264, 265
Scotland, 5, 72
Scripture, 6, 85, 191, 269, 272, 280, 282, 283, 287, 289, 306, 309, 328, 350, 351
seamless garment, 27, 136, 149, 150
Second Vatican Council, 5, 18, 22, 70, 193, 194, 195, 196, 197, 198, 199, 200, 201, 202, 208, 213, 225, 227, 234, 236, 238, 241, 242, 243, 245, 246, 248, 249, 256, 263, 264, 265, 266, 275, 282, 302, 303, 329, 347, 362, 395
secularism, 14, 15, 19, 20, 21, 128, 139, 292, 299, 300, 302, 308, 317, 381, 403
self-giving, 96, 221, 359, 400, 401, 403, 406
Sendak, John, 129
Seper, Franjo Cardinal, 347, 348
sex, 33, 70, 79, 80, 83, 85, 89, 94, 133, 180, 270, 337, 339, 341, 359, 379, 380, 381, 382, 384, 385, 386, 387, 388, 389, 390, 391, 392, 393, 394, 395, 396, 397, 398, 399, 401, 402, 403, 404, 405, 406, 407, 408
sex education, 134, 180, 380, 381, 382, 384, 385, 388, 392, 393, 394, 395, 399, 401, 403, 405, 406
Sex Information and Education Council of the United States (SIECUS), 384, 387
sexual revolution, 70, 270, 338, 339, 397, 398
sexuality, 79, 80, 84, 85, 87, 89, 97, 102, 119, 169, 177, 180, 271, 337, 340, 341, 345, 346, 347, 348, 354, 359, 365, 380, 383, 385, 386, 388, 389, 396, 397, 398, 400, 401, 403, 404, 405
Sheen, Fulton J., Archbishop, 67, 112, 113
Shehan, Lawrence Cardinal, 231, 232, 234, 238, 239
Simmons, Kathy, 161
Simmons, Thomas, 161
sin, 52, 89, 109, 111, 174, 178, 218, 270, 273, 278, 303, 313, 319, 340, 345, 357, 358, 375, 380, 388, 390
sin, actual, 301
sin, original, 301
Sinai, Mount, 310
Singer, Peter, 171
Sisters of Mercy, 143, 144
situation ethics, 31, 104, 384
Sixth Commandment, 104
slavery, 163, 165, 414
social engineering, 26, 53, 55, 119
social justice, 21, 54, 57, 116
social order, 21, 88, 91, 97, 118, 172, 352
socialism, 17, 54, 119
Society of St. Pius X, 242, 244, 245, 246, 251
sociology, 287
Socrates, 99, 172
solidarity, 28, 174, 175
Soviet Union, 17, 29, 46
Spanish Inquisition, 29
spiritual warfare, 49, 65, 119, 120, 169, 172, 174, 185
St. John's Abbey, 20
St. Paul, Minnesota, 5, 13, 14, 15, 19, 67, 195, 264
Statism, 18

Staub, Clemens, Father, 15
sterilization, 69, 83, 95, 156, 179, 362, 404, 405
subjectivism, 175, 276, 289, 294, 295, 305, 318, 322, 343, 348, 369, 374, 378
subjectivity, 175, 217, 297
subsidiarity, principle of, 18
suicide, 70, 92, 93, 154, 318, 394, 397
Sullivan, Joseph V., Bishop, 97, 98
Sullivan, Walter, Bishop, 326
Supreme Court, U.S., 121, 126, 128, 129, 147, 156, 157, 161, 168
Sweden, 111
Szoka, Edmund Cardinal, 142, 143, 144

—T—

teenage pregnancy, 394, 397
Teilhard de Chardin, Pierre, Pere, 277
Teskey, Frank, 45, 46, 48, 141, 143
Texas, 121
thalidomide, 110
The Mystery of Faith, 216
theology, 19, 31, 32, 70, 71, 123, 162, 192, 214, 218, 231, 249, 258, 269, 270, 273, 277, 282, 284, 285, 297, 299, 329, 332, 347, 362, 363, 366, 367, 369, 372, 383, 390, 391, 399
Thomas Aquinas, St., 282, 342
Thomism, 318
Tillich, Paul, 301
Tivoli-Rome, Diocese of, 232, 234, 236, 239
To Teach as Jesus Did, 392
totalitarianism, 17, 18, 26, 29, 32, 50, 51, 53, 56, 78, 89, 91, 115, 119, 132, 166, 184, 252, 269
Tracy, David, 363
Tradition, 186, 226, 248, 249, 286, 328
transfiguration, 216
transignification, 192, 216, 217, 218, 221
transsexualism, 343
transubstantiation, 192, 193, 214, 216, 217, 218, 219
Trent, Council of, 216, 236, 255, 256, 325
Tridentine rite, 202, 208, 241, 243, 244, 245, 247, 255, 263, 264
Trinity, 191, 204
Triumph, 16, 117
Trower, Philip, 274, 275, 276, 277, 278, 279, 295, 296
True Presence, 193, 217, 219
Truth and Meaning of Human Sexuality, The, 399, 400, 405, 407
Twyman, James E., 44, 45, 53, 54, 55, 56, 57, 58

—U—

U.S. Coalition for Life, 170
U.S. News & World Report, 354
Una Voce, 253
Unitarian Fellowship for Social Justice, 66
United Nations Universal Declaration of Human Rights, 56
United States, 5, 20, 25, 27, 30, 31, 33, 35, 41, 42, 54, 55, 57, 75, 92, 111, 112, 115, 121, 126, 129, 132, 135, 136, 139, 153, 179, 181, 196, 198, 199, 201, 202, 232, 234, 235, 238, 239, 251, 263, 316, 319, 323, 330, 354, 363, 364, 367, 382, 387, 392, 393, 405, 406
United States Catholic Conference (USCC), 27, 35, 37, 42, 126, 127, 132, 315, 393

United States Catholic Conference, Committee on Health Affairs, 126
University Microfilms, Inc., 18
Untener, Kenneth, Bishop, 325
USCC-NCCB, 37
utilitarianism, 21

—V—

Vagnozzi, Egidio, Archbishop, 234, 239
Vatican, 22, 43, 76, 97, 102, 194, 195, 196, 199, 200, 201, 202, 206, 234, 236, 237, 238, 241, 242, 244, 245, 246, 249, 252, 256, 257, 261, 263, 265, 279, 290, 302, 303, 319, 328, 338, 342, 347, 348, 356, 375, 395, 404, 407
Vaughan, Austin, Bishop, 36
venereal disease, 93, 178, 394, 397
Veritatis Splendor, 369, 370, 372, 374, 376, 377, 378, 379
Vietnam, War in, 116
Virgin Birth, 289
virginity, consecrated, 401
Voegelin, Eric, 271, 392, 395
von Hildebrand, Dietrich, 212, 213, 301, 302, 303, 385, 386, 390

—W—

Wales, 5
Wanderer, The, 5, 13, 15, 16, 17, 18, 20, 21, 22, 26, 30, 32, 33, 34, 35, 37, 39, 41, 42, 44, 45, 46, 47, 50, 54, 57, 66, 67, 69, 71, 72, 73, 74, 77, 78, 82, 91, 93, 94, 95, 97, 99, 102, 105, 109, 110, 111, 113, 115, 118, 119, 120, 121, 122, 125, 127, 133, 139, 140, 143, 144, 145, 148, 152, 153, 154, 156, 160, 165, 166, 178, 186, 187, 189, 193, 194, 195, 197, 200, 202, 207, 209, 211, 216, 226, 231, 232, 234, 235, 236, 237, 238, 239, 240, 241, 242, 243, 247, 254, 255, 256, 257, 258, 259, 262, 265, 266, 274, 281, 284, 292, 301, 307, 316, 325, 326, 327, 330, 332, 338, 343, 352, 355, 356, 361, 364, 366, 374, 381, 387, 392, 394, 395, 400, 404, 408, 411, 412, 413, 415
Washington, D.C., 35, 37, 117, 134, 164, 259, 363, 367
Weakland, Rembert, Archbishop, 325
Wearsch, William, Father, 69
Welsh, Thomas A., Bishop, 86, 87
Weyrich, Paul, 116, 117, 259, 260
White House National Goals Research Staff, 92
White, Byron, Justice, 124
Whitehead, K.D., 64, 85, 86, 305, 308, 330, 332
wicca, 325
Wiggins, Kay, 161, 164
Willerscheid, Adam, 15
Woman's Home Companion, 110
women, 27, 55, 69, 82, 87, 105, 110, 114, 118, 119, 131, 141, 144, 155, 251, 275, 325, 345, 346, 347, 350, 359, 377, 380, 391, 400, 403
Word and Worship, 301, 302
World War II, 18
Wrenn, Michael J., Monsignor, 330, 332
Wright, Jim, 44, 46, 47, 48, 60

—Y—

Year of Faith, 77
Youngchow, China, 234

—Z—

Zuhlsdorf, John T., Father, 327, 329